T0139758

Face Recognition Across the Imaging Spectrum

Thirimachos Bourlai
Editor

Face Recognition Across the Imaging Spectrum

 Springer

Editor
Thirimachos Bourlai
Multispectral Imagery Lab—MILab, LCSEE
West Virginia University
Morgantown, WV
USA

ISBN 978-3-319-80365-4   ISBN 978-3-319-28501-6   (eBook)
DOI 10.1007/978-3-319-28501-6

Printed on acid-free paper

This Springer imprint is published by SpringerNature
The registered company is Springer International Publishing AG Switzerland

Preface

Within the last two decades, we have noticed improvement in the performance of face recognition (FR) systems in controlled conditions, characterized by suitable lighting and favorable acquisition distances. However, over the years, the technology has steadily progressed to tackling increasingly more realistic conditions rather than adequately handling only well-controlled imagery. Most related research emphasizes the maintenance of high recognition performance, while coping with increased levels of image variability. Among the most insidious problems of visible-spectrum-based face recognition algorithms are (a) the variation in level and nature of illumination, (b) the fact that as the level of illumination decreases, the signal-to-noise ratio rises quickly, and thus, automatic processing and recognition become very difficult, and (c) dealing with degraded face images acquired at operational conditions, including nighttime and long stand-off distances.

In order to address these issues, recent research has moved into the use of infrared (IR) imagery, namely intensified near infrared (NIR), shortwave IR (SWIR), middle wave IR (MWIR), and long wave IR (LWIR). Hence, in recent years, we see an increase of face recognition applications, especially those related to security and identity verification in the digital world, where different spectral bands are used. Certain FR applications are focused on *same-spectral band face matching* (i.e., matching either visible against visible, or IR against IR face images), while other applications are focused on *cross-spectral band face* (i.e., matching IR face images against their visible counterparts). In fact, what we notice, especially over the last decade, is a significant progress in the area of face recognition across the imaging spectrum, owing to advances in imaging sensors and optics, and the fact that the cost of IR cameras has dropped considerably. For example, the cost of some good quality IR imaging sensors is now comparable to high-end, digital, single-lens reflex (DSLR) cameras (visible band). In addition, we see significant advances in computer vision techniques used for the preprocessing of multi-band face (plus ocular and/or iris) images, including techniques related to the modeling and analysis of such images. Therefore, the problem of designing and developing reliable face recognition systems across the imaging spectrum continues to offer a great challenge to computer vision and pattern recognition researchers.

There are two primary motivations that this book was based upon. The *first motivation* is the need for the development of efficient multispectral FR or FR-related algorithms and systems that can be reliably used in operational environments. The *second motivation* is the recent increased interest in research on face recognition-related technologies and the recent advances in computer vision, pattern recognition, and automated analysis, when using images of different biometric modalities, including face, periocular, and iris, from various parts of the imaging spectrum. The aforementioned motivations were identified when designing the original book structure and, as a result, helped in finding extraordinary researchers in the greater field of face recognition that could contribute with their book chapters.

The book is intended for biometrics researchers, including practitioners and students who either work or plan to become familiar with understanding and processing single-spectral, multispectral, or hyperspectral face images—when captured under controlled or uncontrolled environments, using a variety of imaging sensors, ranging from the state-of-the-art visible and infrared imaging sensors, to the usage of RGB-D and mobile phone image sensors.

The book provides various references for image processing, computer vision, biometrics, and security-focused researchers. The material provides information on current technology including discussion on research areas related to the spectral imaging of human skin, data collection activities, processing and analysis of multispectral and hyperspectral face and iris images, processing of mug shots from ID documents, mobile- and 3D-based face recognition, spoofing attacks, image alterations, score normalization techniques, and multispectral ocular biometrics.

More specifically, the book consists of 15 chapters, covering the aforementioned material, and discusses different components that can affect operational face recognition systems. Each chapter focuses on a specific topic, discussing background information, offering a literature review, presenting methodological approaches, experiments, and results, and, finally, concluding by pointing out challenges and future directions.

Chapter 1 provides an introduction to the interaction of energy in the electromagnetic spectrum with human tissue and other materials, the fundamentals of sensors and data collection, common analysis techniques, and the interpretation of results for decision making. The basic information provided in this chapter can be utilized for a wide range of applications where spectral imaging may be adopted, including face recognition.

Chapters 2 and 3 cover topics related to data collection of multispectral and hyperspectral face images. Chapter 2 details "best practice" collection methodologies developed to compile large-scale datasets of both visible and SWIR face images. All aspects of data collection are provided, from IRB preparation through data post-processing, along with instrumentation layouts for indoor and outdoor live capture setups. Details of past collections performed at West Virginia University to compile multispectral biometric datasets, such as age, gender, and ethnicity of the subject populations, are included. Insight is also given on the impact of collection parameters on the general quality of images collected, as well as on how these parameters impact design decisions at the level of algorithmic development.

Chapter 3 discusses that spectral imaging offers a means to overcome several major challenges specific to current FR systems. The authors review four publically available hyperspectral face databases (CMU, PolyU-HSFD, IRIS-M, and Stanford) toward providing information on the key points of each of the considered databases. In addition, a new hyperspectral face database is introduced (IRIS-HFD-2014) that can serve as a benchmark for statistically evaluating the performance of current and future hyperspectral FR algorithms.

Chapters 4–7 cover topics related to challenging face-based identification technologies when processing visible and different infrared face images. Chapter 4 discusses two thermal-to-visible FR algorithms, as well as the preprocessing and feature extraction techniques used to correlate the signatures in the feature subspace. The chapter presents recognition results on an extensive multimodal face dataset containing facial imagery acquired under different experimental conditions. Furthermore, it discusses key findings and implications for MWIR-to-visible and LWIR-to-visible FR. Finally, it presents a novel imaging technique for acquiring an unprecedented level of facial detail in thermal images, polarimetric LWIR, along with a framework for performing cross-spectral face recognition.

Chapter 6 introduces a methodology to explore the sensitivities of a facial recognition imaging system to blur, noise, and turbulence effects. Using a government-owned and an open-source facial recognition algorithm, system performance is evaluated under different optical blurs, sensor noises, and turbulence conditions. The ramifications of these results on the design of long-range facial recognition systems are also discussed.

Chapter 7 provides a thorough understanding of challenges in thermal face detection, along with an experimental evaluation of traditional approaches. Further, the authors adapt the AdaBoost face detector to yield improved performance on face detection in thermal images in both indoor and outdoor environments. They also propose a region of interest selection approach, designed specifically for aiding occluded or disguised thermal face detection. The results suggest that while thermal face detection in semi-controlled environments is relatively easy, occlusion and disguise are challenges that require further attention.

Chapter 8 provides an overview of spoofing attacks and spoofing countermeasures for FR systems, with a focus on visual spectrum systems in 2D and 3D, as well as near-infrared (NIR) and multispectral systems. The authors cover the existing types of spoofing attacks and report on their success to bypass several state-of-the-art FR systems. Experimental results show that spoofing attacks present a significant security risk for FR systems in any part of the spectrum. The risk is partially reduced when using multispectral systems. Finally, the authors provide a systematic overview of the existing anti-spoofing techniques, with an analysis of their advantages and limitations and prospective for future work.

Chapter 9 discuss that when face images are captured under desirable conditions, some intentional or unintentional face image alterations can significantly affect the recognition performance. In particular, in scenarios where the user template is created from printed photographs rather than from images acquired live during enrollment (e.g., identity documents), digital image alterations can severely affect the recognition results. In this chapter, the authors analyze both the effects of such alterations on face recognition algorithms and the human capabilities to deal with altered images.

Chapter 10 starts by discussing the factors impacting the quality of degraded face photographs from ID documents. These include mainly hairstyle, pose and expression variations, and lamination and security watermarks. Then, the authors focus on investigating a set of methodological approaches in order to be able to overcome most of the aforementioned limitations and achieve a high identification rate. They incorporate a combination of preprocessing and heterogeneous face matching techniques, where comparisons are made between the original (degraded) photograph, the restored photograph, and the high-quality photograph (mug shots). The proposed restoration approaches discussed in this chapter can be directly applied to operational scenarios that include border-crossing stations and various transit centers.

Chapter 11 deals with FR in mobile and other challenging environments, where both still images and video sequences are examined. The authors provide an experimental study of one commercial off-the-shelf and four recent open-source FR algorithms. Experiments are performed on several freely available challenging still image and video face databases, including one mobile database, always following the evaluation protocols that are attached to the databases. The authors supply an easily extensible open-source toolbox to rerun all the experiments, which includes the modeling techniques, the evaluation protocols, and the metrics used in the experiments, and provide a detailed description on how to regenerate the results.

Chapter 12 discusses existing RGB-D face recognition algorithms and presents a state-of-the-art algorithm based on extracting discriminatory features using entropy and saliency from RGB-D images. The authors also present an overview of available RGB-D face datasets along with the experimental results and analysis to understand the various facets of RGB-D face recognition.

Chapter 13 highlights both the advantages and disadvantages of 2D- and 3D-based face recognition algorithms. It also explores the advantages of blending 2D and 3D databased techniques, also proposing a novel approach for a fast and robust matching. Several experimental results, obtained from publicly available datasets, currently at the state of the art, demonstrate the effectiveness of the proposed approach.

Chapter 14 first introduces the reader to the concept of score normalization. Then, it discusses why methods of normalizing matching scores are an effective and efficient way of exploiting score distributions and when such methods are expected to work. The first section highlights the importance of normalizing matching scores and offers intuitive examples to demonstrate how variations between different biometric samples, modality components, and subjects degrade recognition performance. It also answers the question of why score normalization effectively utilizes score distributions. The next three sections offer a review of score normalization methods developed to address each type of variation. The chapter concludes with a discussion of why such methods have not gained popularity in the research community and answers the question of when and how one should use score normalization.

Chapter 15 discusses the use of multispectral imaging to perform bimodal ocular recognition, where the eye region of the face is used for recognizing individuals. In particular, it explores the possibility of utilizing the patterns evident in the sclera, along with the iris, in order to improve the robustness of iris recognition systems. The work discusses the assembly of a multispectral eye image collection to study the impact of intra-class variation on sclera recognition performance. Then, the authors discuss the design and development of an automatic sclera, iris, and pupil segmentation algorithm, before, finally, they demonstrate the improvement of iris recognition performance by fusing the iris and scleral patterns in non-frontal images of the eye.

Acknowledgments

There are a number of people that helped in making this book a reality. The list of the selected editorial board members of this book is provided below. The role of each member was to review and provide technical and structural suggestions for each of their assigned book chapter. There are also other researchers, including Multispectral Imagery Lab (MILab) students and researchers within and outside WVU that helped with the preparation of the book, by providing their valuable feedback in various ways. I would also like to thank Simon Rees, editor at Springer UK, for giving me the opportunity to work on this book, as well as for providing his valuable feedback, suggestions, and constant support that helped keeping me on schedule for the production of the book.

Editorial Board Members

- David W. Allen, Ph.D.,

  - *National Institute of Standards and Technology*, Sensor Science Division, 100 Bureau Drive/Mail Stop 8442, Gaithersburg, MD 20899-8442, USA, Tel.: (US) 301-975-3680

- Antwan Clark, Ph.D.,

  - Adjunct Associate Professor, *West Virginia University*

- Prudhvi Gurram, Ph.D.,

  - *U.S. Army Research Laboratory*, ATTN: RDRL-SES-E, 2800 Powder Mill Rd., Adelphi, MD 20783

- Shuowen (Sean) Hu, Ph.D.,

  - *U.S. Army Research Laboratory*, Electronics Engineer, ATTN: RDRL-SES-E, 2800 Powder Mill Rd., Adelphi, MD 20783, (301)394-2526

- Dalton Rosario, Ph.D.,

  - *US Army Research Laboratory*, Team Leader, Collection/Enhancement/ Visualization, Image Processing Branch, (W)301.394.4235, (C) 301.938.5628, dalton.s.rosario.civ@mail.mil

- Nathaniel Short, Ph.D.,

  - *U.S. Army Research Laboratory*, ATTN: RDRL-SES-E, 2800 Powder Mill Rd., Adelphi, MD 20783

Book Chapters Evaluation Process

Each book chapter was accepted after an extensive peer-reviewed process. First, the original abstracts submitted by the authors were reviewed. Then, each conditionally accepted chapter was assigned to 2–4 members of the editorial board, including the editor's independent review and meta-review. After the first rebuttal, the authors of each book chapter addressed all comments of the original review process and they submitted an updated draft. Next, each book chapter was reviewed and updated one more time before it was finally accepted.

October 2015   Thirimachos Bourlai

Contents

Chapter 1
An Overview of Spectral Imaging of Human Skin Toward Face Recognition

David W. Allen

Abstract Spectral imaging is a form of remote sensing that provides a means of collecting information from surroundings without physical contact. Differences in spectral reflectance over the electromagnetic spectrum allow for the detection, classification, or quantification of objects in a scene. The development of this field has largely benefited from Earth observing airborne and spaceborne programs. Information gained from spectral imaging has been recognized as making key contributions from the regional to the global scale. The burgeoning market of compact hyperspectral sensors has opened new opportunities, at smaller spatial scales, in a large number of applications such as medical, environmental, security, and industrial processes. The market is expected to continue to evolve and result in advancements in sensor size, performance, and cost. In order to employ spectral imaging for a specific task, it is critical to have a fundamental understanding of the phenomenology of the subject of interest, the imaging sensor, image processing, and interpretation of the results. Spectral imaging of human tissue has the strong foundation of a well-known combination of components, e.g., hemoglobin, melanin, and water that make skin distinct from most backgrounds. These components are heterogeneously distributed and vary across the skin of individuals and between individuals. The spatial component of spectral imaging provides a basis for making spectral distinctions of these differences. This chapter provides an introduction to the interaction of energy in the electromagnetic spectrum with human tissue and other materials, the fundamentals of sensors and data collection, common analysis techniques, and the interpretation of results for decision making. The basic information provided in this chapter can be utilized for a wide range of applications where spectral imaging may be adopted including face recognition.

D.W. Allen (✉)
National Institute of Standards and Technology, Gaithersburg, MD 20899-8442, USA
e-mail: dwallen@nist.gov

© Springer International Publishing Switzerland (outside the USA) 2016
T. Bourlai (ed.), *Face Recognition Across the Imaging Spectrum*,
DOI 10.1007/978-3-319-28501-6_1

1.1 Introduction

Spectral imaging has greatly advanced our ability to detect and identify objects on the ground from remote sensing platforms. The spectral information provided can be significantly greater than what the human visual system is capable of observing. The potential for spectral imaging to enhance facial recognition may manifest itself in a variety of ways that are complementary to the methods that have been used with standard color or monochrome cameras. For example, spectral imaging can be used to reliably detect human skin and segment the face from the background environment for further processing. It can be used to enhance spatial heterogeneities that are not clearly visible, such as patterns of vascularity unique to each individual. The spectral signature of an individual's face may also provide an additional spectral vector to be used in conjunction with the spatial vectors (including texture and topology) to improve recognition accuracy.

Remote sensing of the Earth has been performed by spectral imaging satellites orbiting the Earth for over 40 years [1]. Spectral imaging has provided a synoptic view of the Earth, allowing for the assessment of land-based vegetation, exposed soils and minerals, the oceans, and human activity. Over the decades, spectral imaging technology incorporated into sensors has advanced significantly and continues to provide vital information needed to understand the Earth's land, ocean, and atmospheric processes. In more recent years, the same principles used in the design of the spectral imagers and the processing of the imagery have migrated to compact and portable sensors that are allowing the potential of spectral imaging to be explored in a wide range of applications. Examples include medical imaging, forensics, agriculture, manufacturing, and defense. Much of the work has focused on exploring the potential of spectral imaging as a first step toward full integration into routine operations.

Automated facial recognition is considered a significant aid in the efforts to utilize technology to improve security [2]. Facial recognition software that uses two-dimensional (2D) images has advanced significantly. Researchers in the NIST Information Technology Laboratory (ITL) have developed standardized test methods that allow for the assessment of facial recognition algorithm performance [3, 4]. These methods provide a reliable way to evaluate the accuracy of different facial recognition algorithms against known data sets of images (one to many). The evaluations have primarily focused on posed images such as mugshots, visas, passport photographs, and drivers' licenses. The accuracy of the algorithms has increased as much as 30 % in recent years [4]. Unposed images such as those from webcams or live action shots are a significantly greater challenge using the same metrics.

While facial recognition technology has matured to be used as a reliable and routinely applied tool, there is much room for improvement. Some factors that are reducing performance are sensitivity to variable illumination geometries, changes in facial expression, and nighttime surveillance. Spectral imaging is one of several modalities (e.g., 3D imaging) that may enhance the performance of facial recognition systems. Spectral imaging can provide additional information both within the visible spectrum and outside of the visible spectrum, including the ultraviolet and infrared. This chapter is intended to introduce the topic of spectral imaging. It also provides background information relevant to facial recognition that will aid in providing context to the subject.

A significant aid to developing the potential application of spectral imaging for use in facial recognition is the establishment of spectral image databases of faces. While the collection of facial images using spectral imaging is relatively straight-forward, the best way to exploit this additional source of information is not. Spectral signature and image databases provide a means to evaluate new algorithms that include the spectral dimension. Several spectral face databases have been established [5–8]. These are reviewed in detail in the "Multispectral/Hyperspectral Face Databases" chapter of this book [9]. A caveat to the use of spectrally based facial databases is the nonstandardized methods used in the data collection. The performance specifications of the spectral imager used along with the methods employed in the collection may vary significantly from one to another. Many of these details are included in [9].

There is a relative paucity of studies that have explored the potential of spectral imaging as applied to face recognition. The studies that have been conducted provide significant insight into the phenomenology. Pan et al. [10] demonstrated a possible improvement in accuracy over conventional (non-spectral) methods. The spectral information is thought to provide an invariant signature that is not subject to facial expression or variations over weeks in time between measurements. What portion of the spectrum, or which bands in particular, is a subject of investigation. Di [11] found selecting optimized bands, as opposed to using the entire broad spectrum provided by a hyperspectral imager, yielded better results. Uzair [12] questions the ability to rely on the spectral signature of skin alone as a reliable biometric. In merging the spatial and spectral information for maximum benefit, there is a need to develop algorithms that use and combine the information. The spectral–spatial analysis of hyperspectral imagery is relatively new. One recent example of a spectral–spatial analysis for face recognition is provided by Uzair [13]. This study tested a spectral–spatial algorithm on several spectral databases and compared it to conventional face recognition methods. The results indicate there is a potential to significantly improve the current state of the art by including the spectral dimension in the analysis.

Imaging in regions of the spectrum outside the range of human vision has also yielded benefits that may enhance or even supplant imagers that operate in the visible spectral region. Rosario [14] conducted a field experiment using longwave infrared (LWIR) hyperspectral imaging (HSI). The work suggests the ability to reliably detect faces in an open environment at significant distances. Other studies have investigated the use of the midwave infrared (MWIR) and the LWIR for face recognition [15–18]. These spectral ranges were found to be not only capable of providing accurate face recognition but also improved performance.

One explanation is the avoidance of the apparent variability imposed by shade and shadow more common to the visible spectral range. They also provide the advantage of nighttime surveillance.

1.2 Fundamentals of Spectral Imaging

Spectral imaging is a generic term that refers to the use of imaging devices that collect light over several well-defined spectral bands—many of which are beyond the range of human vision. Terms that are synonymous or more specific include imaging spectroscopy, chemical imaging, multispectral imaging (MSI), and HSI. This chapter uses the term spectral imaging to include both multispectral and HSI. Multispectral imaging is generally considered acquisition of tens of spectral bands, whereas HSI is the acquisition of hundreds of narrow, contiguous spectral bands. Spectral imaging depends on light that is reflected off an object over some distance. It should be noted that light is a term that is commonly used for electromagnetic energy, though technically it is defined to mean the visible portion of the spectrum (having wavelengths ranging from 380–780 nm) [19]. Here, the term light is used in the general sense to also include regions outside of the visible spectral region. When light from a source, whether it be the Sun or a lamp, is incident on a surface, it can be transmitted, absorbed, reflected, or scattered (Fig. 1.1). Additionally, all materials above absolute zero emit energy at wavelengths proportional to the temperature.

These interactions are wavelength dependent and indicative of the optical properties of a given material. The collective series of reflectance values plotted versus wavelengths is called a spectrum. A spectrum specific to one substance is referred to as a spectral signature. Spectral signatures are analogous to fingerprints when depended upon for being uniquely attributed to a substance.

The reflected light observed by an imager is the net quantity that is accepted by the aperture of the imager over some finite geometry. The reflected light from the

Fig. 1.1 A diagram of the interaction of light with matter

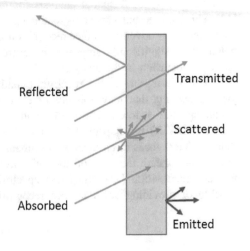

surface can be distributed over a range of angles from rough or scattering surfaces and is referred to as diffuse reflectance, or it can be reflected in parallel rays from a polished surface such as a mirror at an equal but opposite angle from the incident source, referred to as specular reflectance. The quantification of this distribution is referred to as a bidirectional reflectance distribution function (BRDF) [20]. Most real-world materials, such as human skin, have a combination of these properties and are in between these two extremes [21]. While polarization of reflected light is an important property, it is typically treated as a second-order effect and is an advanced topic in spectral imaging.

An important property of light is the energy of the photon. The energy of a photon is inversely proportional to wavelength. The relationship between the energy, E, and the wavelength, λ, is

$$E = \frac{hc}{\lambda}$$

E energy,
h Planck's constant,
c speed of light, and
λ wavelength.

The range of wavelengths of light is described as the electromagnetic spectrum. The wavelength of light is inversely proportional to the frequency and is described in Fig. 1.2.

For convenience, the electromagnetic spectrum is divided up into regions that relate to specific applications based on the phenomenology. Most all of spectral imaging occur from the UV (>250 nm) to the LWIR (<14 μm). Common length units used to denote the wavelength over this region are the nanometer (nm) and micrometer (μm). The distinction is sometimes made between the reflective region and the emissive region, where the reflective region depends on the Sun as the source and the emissive region self-emits electromagnetic energy as a radiator. While there is some overlap between these regions, the crossover is located at approximately 4 μm. Although spectral imaging methods can make use of both the reflective and emissive spectral regions, this chapter will focus on the reflective spectral region. However, many of the principles described in this chapter are applicable to the entire region (Fig. 1.3).

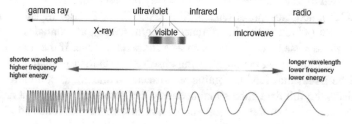

Fig. 1.2 The electromagnetic spectrum over a broad range (*Source* NASA)

Fig. 1.3 An illustration of the spectral peak and distribution for common sources of optical energy, the Sun, a candle, and the Earth (*Source* NASA)

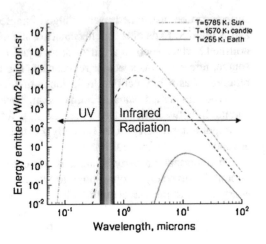

1.3 Spectral Imaging Sensors

Spectral imagers provide two spatial dimensions and one spectral dimension forming the basis for what is referred to as a data cube. There is a range of possible instruments designed to collect data cubes, many of which share design elements used in remote sensing from airborne and spaceborne platforms. Those systems commonly use either a point-scanning (also referred to as whisk broom) or a line-scanning (push broom) design. A whisk broom collects spectra at a single spatial element which is translated across the x dimension (also known as cross-track), while the sensor is moving in the forward, y direction (along-track direction). A push broom sensor collects spectra across the entire x dimension simultaneously as the sensor moves forward in the y dimension (Fig. 1.4). Spectral imagers typically utilize a prism or grating to disperse the light into separate spectral bands. In general, both of these designs require some movement of either the sensor or the object being imaged to acquire the second spatial dimension.

In the full image approach, i.e., wavelength scan in Fig. 1.5, both spatial dimensions are collected simultaneously. Each full image is collected as a function of wavelengths. The distinct difference with this third method eliminates the requirement of motion by the sensor relative to the object. A system of this nature is often referred to as a staring system, which may be based on a liquid crystal tunable filter (LCTF), acousto-optical tunable filter (AOTF), or Fourier transform imaging spectrometers (which utilize interference of light waves), as examples.

All of these systems collect the data as a function of time. If the time to acquire the images is longer than the object being observed is stationary, spatial and spectral registration issues may lead to significant artifacts. While not as common, a system that collects the full data cube simultaneously can provide a significant advantage. In this approach, all of the spectral and spatial information is collected at a single

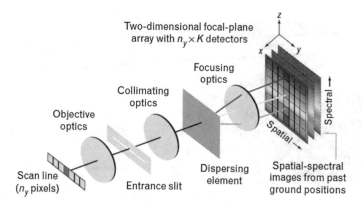

Fig. 1.4 This diagram shows a generic layout for a line-scanning (push broom) spectral imager [22]. It provides one common method of collecting spectral data cubes. All spectral imagers require the use of some methods of separating the light into individual spectral bands in a manner that the spectral reflectance can be registered for each spatial pixel in a scene. (Reprinted with permission of MIT Lincoln Laboratory, Lexington, Massachusetts)

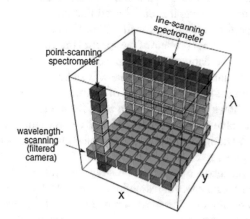

Fig. 1.5 This diagram represents a data cube and the processes associated with the three fundamental data collection methods [23]. They include point scanning, line scanning, and wavelength scanning. In contrast, a snapshot spectral imager provides a full data cube in one instant in time. (Reprinted with permission of SPIE, Bellingham, Washington)

point in time. These systems are referred to as snapshot hyperspectral imagers. This is a very desirable trait when considering actual use in environments where the scene is dynamic; e.g., human activity. Hagen et al. [23] have provided a review of this technology.

In general, the scanning imaging spectrometers, designed for forward motion as provided by an aircraft, provide high spectral and spatial quality but require special considerations when used in a stationary setting. Staring and snapshot imaging spectrometers provide the advantage of use from a stationary platform, however in

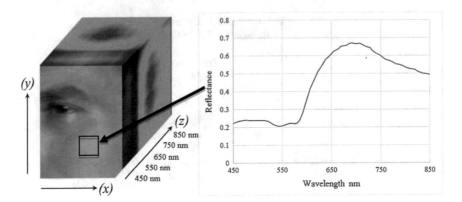

Fig. 1.6 An example of a spectral data cube subset as a region of interest from a larger data cube of a face. The face of the data cube represents the two spatial dimensions (*x*- and *y*-axes), while the sides represent the spectral reflectance (*z*-axis)

some cases at a cost in terms of spectral and spatial resolution and performance. As the designs continue to evolve, it is anticipated that new systems will provide both convenience and performance that is well within the needs of the end user.

The data cube is the output product of the spectral imager, while the spectrum is the fundamental datum. The data cube is composed of several to many images of two spatial dimensions (*x* and *y*), each at discrete wavelengths. Each pixel can be represented as a spectrum (or vector) indicative of the reflectance as a function of wavelength. Figure 1.6 shows a subset of a data cube from a face over the 400–850 nm spectral range. The blue represents low reflectance and red high reflectance, as a qualitative measure. The spectral plot on the right shows a mean spectrum (100 by 100 pixels) from the region represented by the box.

The basic specifications of spectral imaging beyond the data cube collection include the spectral range, spectral resolution, spatial resolution, radiometric resolution, and temporal resolution. The spectral range is one of the key parameters that is directly tied to the phenomenology of interest. The appropriate spectral range must be provided at a sufficient signal-to-noise ratio (with respect to the illumination source) to adequately cover the spectral distribution of interest. The key limiting factor is the type of detector used. The electromagnetic spectrum is often divided into regions relative to the broad spectral response of a given detector class for convenience. In general, the ultraviolet is defined as UV (250–400 nm), visible–near-infrared as VNIR (400–1100 nm), shortwave infrared as SWIR (1000–2500 nm), midwave Infrared as MWIR (3–5 μm) and longwave infrared as LWIR (7–14 μm). It is important to note that these definitions are not standardized and may vary between communities. It is always a best practice to explicitly state the wavelength when describing an imaging system in order to avoid ambiguity and misunderstanding.

The thermal infrared (TIR) may be any region where photons emitted by materials can be observed. This is a very broad range, however, most commonly it relates to wavelengths that are greater than 1 μm. At normal Earth surface temperatures, the wavelength ranges measured are in the MWIR and the LWIR. The specific wavelength selected for the TIR is based on Wien's approximation $\lambda_{max} = b/T$, where λ_{max} is the nominal peak wavelength emitted for a given temperature, b is the proportionality constant $b \approx 2900$ µm K, and T is the temperature in Kelvin [24]. As an example, if the apparent temperature of the surface of the Sun is nominally 5269 K, the peak wavelength would be 550 nm. This is where human vision has its peak sensitivity in the visible portion of the electromagnetic spectrum. In another example, the temperature of the human skin is in the range of 300 K and the peak emitted wavelength is about 10 µm. The trend is therefore the higher the temperature the shorter the peak observable wavelength.

The spectral resolution is the separation of light into distinct wavelengths which provides the ability to distinguish spectral features of a substance. The spectral resolution is limited by the spectral bandwidth (SBW) which is defined as the width of a spectral band at half the maximum peak. This is referred to as full width half maximum (FWHM). In some cases, this value may vary over the operating range of a spectral imager. Broader spectral bands may provide a greater signal; however, the SBW must be small enough to resolve the spectral features of interest. A common and sufficiently narrow spectral bandwidth for many applications is on the order of 3 nm.

The spatial resolution, the area represented by each pixel in the image, depends on the size of the pixels in the focal plane array in combination with the power of the optics. To some extent, this parameter can be modified by exchanging lenses on the imager. A greater number of pixels over a given area of the target of interest will also provide greater detail of the spectral variability over an area. The cost of higher spatial resolution may be a reduced signal, resulting in longer integration times. There is also a trade-off with respect to the spatial resolution and the field of view, where higher magnification may be gained at the cost of a limited field of view. Spatial resolution from roughly sub-millimeter to centimeter (over 1–100 m) may be available depending on the optics.

Radiometric resolution pertains to the number of grayscale values, as a result of an analog-to-digital conversion of the signal, for each pixel for each wavelength. The greater the radiometric resolution, the larger the number of levels that can be provided to represent the scale from dark to light. Ideally, a system can provide values over a wide enough dynamic range to collect all of the dark and light features without saturation. Spectral and spatial resolution typically are factors that require more attention than the radiometric resolution. Radiometric resolution, also referred to as bit depth, may range from 8 to 16, where an 8-bit system would provide 256 grayscale values and a 16-bit system would provide 65,536 grayscale values, as examples.

Temporal resolution is the length in time required to collect a full data cube of interest. This is dependent not only on the design of the system but also the overall setup since the time to acquire each image depends on sufficient illumination. If the temporal resolution is insufficient, the subject in the scene may be distorted spatially and spectrally. The frame rate is limited by the integration time of the imager. In the full frame collection scenario, 30 frames per second system would acquire 30 spectral frames per second. If the system had the capacity to collect over 120 spectral bands, it would require 4 s to collect one data cube, for instance. A snapshot spectral imager, by definition, would collect the entire data cube at each integration time.

1.4 Optical Properties of Human Skin

The spectral reflectance of the surface of human skin provides a wealth of information. Fully understanding the interaction of light and tissue is a challenge due to the heterogeneous structure of the various components that interact with light. The reflected light from skin varies significantly as a function of wavelength. Observed spectral reflectance is the result of a combination of absorption and scattering from the surface and within the tissue [25]. The variation over the spectral range is due to several dominant absorbers referred to as chromophores. The UV (250–400 nm) is primarily due to proteins and amino acids and the visible to NIR (400–1100 nm) is dominated by blood and melanin. Absorption at wavelengths longer than 900 nm is primarily due to water (Fig. 1.7).

Features over the surface of skin can vary significantly at spatial scales ranging from sub-millimeters to centimeters. Some of these features are due to variations in blood vesicles, distribution of melanin pigmentation, acne, wrinkles, and, erythema due to Sun exposure. Features including blood vessel patterns and pigmentation variation may be present over an extended portion of an individual's lifetime, while other prominent features such as acne, blushing, and sweating can be transient. Environmental factors of significance include cold, heat, or sunlight leading to pallor or erythema.

The spectral reflectance of human skin over the visible to NIR is distinct from most common materials found in the background environment. In comparison with vegetation, soils, fabrics, paper, plastics, and building materials, there is a significant degree of separability [26]. This is especially true when the spectral sampling interval is sufficient to resolve the most prominent features skin presents.

The spectral reflectance properties of human skin can vary significantly, both of an individual and between individuals. Obvious visual observations of skin differences may be attributed to melanin, vascularity, and surface texture. The degree of variability has been a subject of research by Cooksey et al. [27]. In that work, a

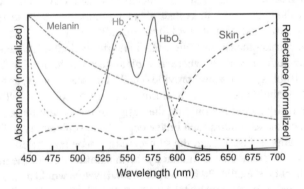

Fig. 1.7 The plot shows the dominant chromophores in skin (normalized absorbance) along with an example of a skin reflectance spectrum (normalized reflectance) (*Credit* C. Cooksey)

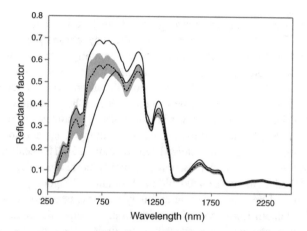

Fig. 1.8 This plot shows the range of spectral skin reflectance over the 250–2500 nm spectral range. The *dashed line* represents the mean, the *shaded area* is the variability over one standard deviation, and the *solid lines* are the minimum and maximum spectra [27]

measurement protocol was used to measure the inside of the forearm using an 8° directional hemispherical reflectance accessory used on a commonly available spectrophotometer. The intent of the experimental design was to collect skin reflectance spectra of a number of volunteers in a well-controlled environment using reference standards directly traceable to the national scale of reflectance. As a result, the variability attributed to measurement uncertainty is minimized and the resulting variability observed can be attributed to biological variability. That study indicated that the variability between subjects is much greater than the variability between measurements of the same subject. It also indicated the absorption bands attributed to hemoglobin in the visible spectral region are significantly muted, if not masked, for darker skin tones related to melanin content. In the shortwave infrared, there is a marked consistency between subjects in relation to the water absorption bands. This is likely due to the relatively constant proportion of water in tissue (Fig. 1.8).

Knowing the variability of skin reflectance across the population is an important factor in selecting a spectral imaging system and predicting the operational range. Although Cooksey et. al. have provided a sample of the population, the variability of the overall population is still not well established. This is especially true outside of the visible portion of the electromagnetic spectrum. Spectral regions from the UV and the NIR to the LWIR have not been studied in enough detail to represent the human population's variability. In some cases, the representation of the optical properties in the literature varies by orders of magnitude [28]. The source of this variability has not been explained. It is possible that the differences are due to differences in measurement instruments, measurement methods, or measurement error. Overall, this leaves significant room to expand the state of knowledge of light tissue interactions.

Optical medical imaging is an emerging field that utilizes spectral imaging as a key modality for observing human tissue. The key chromophore in tissue that provides significant promise in optical medical imaging is the absorption characteristic of blood. More specifically, hemoglobin, the oxygen carrier in blood, has distinct spectral features; oxy- and deoxy-hemoglobin provide distinct changes over the VNIR spectral region that can be used to estimate the concentration of each in the tissue [29]. The oxygenation level in tissue is a key indicator of many diseases. Cancer, as an example, may be associated with angiogenesis and increased metabolism resulting in changes in localized oxygenation [25]. The healing of wounds, including injuries, burns, and infections, is highly correlated with how well the tissue is supplied with oxygenated blood. Wounds with poor perfusion of oxygenated blood will become ischemic and may progress to necrosis. Surgical practices may also benefit from spectral imaging in procedures where the blood supply needs to be clamped during a procedure to limit excessive bleeding. Spectral imaging may play a key role in the future by providing a quantitative map of the oxygenation status of tissue to aid the clinician in making decisions related to intervention and treatment [30].

An example is provided of a porcine ischemic skin flap model. This example shows a wound, over a 5 cm by 15 cm area of the back. The restricted blood flow led to reduced oxygenation toward the center of the skin flap. The images shown are from a hyperspectral data cube collected on the 3rd day of monitoring. A color composite (Fig. 1.9a) is based on three spectral bands to approximate red, green, and blue. The false color composite (Fig. 1.9b) is the result of mapping the data cube to the signature of "healthy" oxygenated tissue. This provided a relative scale from blue (low) to red (high) relative oxygenation based on the reflectance

(a)   **(b)**

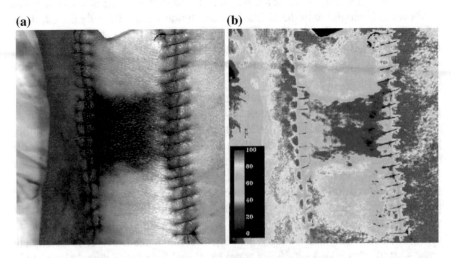

Fig. 1.9 **a** The image on the left is a color composite from a hyperspectral data cube of a porcine ischemic skin flap model. **b** The image on the right is a relative oxygen saturation map extracted from the hyperspectral data cube [30]

signature [30]. This application of spectral imaging can provide in-depth insight into the phenomenology that is of interest to developing spectrally based face recognition methodology.

1.5   Data Collection and Analysis

Currently, there is no standard algorithm or method used to extract information for facial recognition from the spectrally based imagery. The spectral information may be used to aid face recognition by narrowing the number of potential matches to those with similar spectral matches, by enhancing feature otherwise not visible, or by subsetting the face in preprocessing in order to remove the background (as illustrated in Fig. 1.10). This section describes the basic tools that are used routinely in spectral imaging across different disciplines and including facial recognition. Most HSI is performed as a research activity and as such is performed under prescribed and controlled conditions. Some of these conditions include the source of illumination, the angle between the illumination sources, the subject, and the spectral imager. Additionally, a white reference plaque with a known spectral reflectance in the scene is placed where the subject is expected to be positioned. With the white reference plaque in place, a reference data cube is collected. This provides the intensity and uniformity of the source. The collection of a dark data cube is also collected with the light blocked from entering the imager. The data cube files are often stored and processed separately in consideration of the fact that the file size is considerably larger than conventional images. In this case, there is an image for each wavelength resulting in possible 100s of images composed in one data cube. The data cube is typically preprocessed and then analyzed to exploit the desired content. It is worth mentioning this is a significantly different approach than a fully integrated operational system that would collect, analyze, and provide information in near real time. This level of operation can be achieved once the phenomenology is well established.

The preprocessing of the image requires the conversion of the raw data cube to reflectance. It is possible to utilize the spectral information from raw data cubes (relative signals). This level of information may be used to exploit the content in a given data set but will be of limited use if the data in the data cube are intended to be used as a source of comparison to other data sets collected under different conditions or to match the content to a database. The conversion to reflectance is achieved by taking a ratio of the data cube of the subject to the data cube of the white reference Eq. (1). The white reference also regarded as a calibration plaque is often composed of sintered polytetrafluoroethylene (PTFE). The dark data cube is subtracted from both. This ratio is then multiplied by the known reflectance values of the white reference plaque. Ideally, the white reference plaque values are traceable to a national metrology institute such as NIST [31]. This helps ensure repeatable results.

$$R(\lambda) = \frac{S(\lambda) - S_{\mathrm{d}}(\lambda)}{S_{\mathrm{s}}(\lambda) - S_{\mathrm{d}}(\lambda)} \cdot R_{\mathrm{s}}(\lambda), \tag{1}$$

where S is the data cube of the subject, S_{s} is the data cube of the standard, S_{d} is the dark signal, and R_{s} is spectral reflectance factor of the known reflectance standard.

It should be noted that the practice of using a calibration plaque is routine in research. This is practical in a controlled environment where the setup can be staged. In real-world operations, it may be challenging to position a calibration plaque at or near the same position as the person of interest. Beisley [32] developed and demonstrated a method that can eliminate the use of a calibration plaque. In that study, the illumination source was modeled in order to predict the expected skin signature. The results indicate that with a sufficient knowledge of the source illumination, the detection performance can remain high.

Once the data cube is converted to reflectance, its contents can be exploited. The subject of hyperspectral data exploitation is expansive. While there are routine tools that will be mentioned here, there is also a large body of knowledge that has resulted from decades of remote sensing research ranging from environmental to defense applications [33].

In comparing spectra, it is convenient to consider the set of reflectance values for each wavelength as a dimension in n-dimensional space. As an example, a reflectance spectrum composed of 100 discrete spectral bands would be considered as 100 dimensions, thus requiring multivariate analysis methods. The spectrum of all of the wavelengths can then be considered a vector in n-dimensional space. The most fundamental processing method is one that allows the matching of one spectrum to all of the spectra in the scene. A common method for measuring the distance between two vectors is the spectral angle mapper (SAM), Eq. (2) [34].

$$\theta_i = \cos^{-1}\left(\frac{S_r^{\mathrm{T}} S_i}{\|S_r\| \|S_i\|}\right) \tag{2}$$

S_r is the known reference spectrum of target of interest and S_i is each of the unknown spectra at each pixel location. The difference between the spectra, θ_i, is reported in radians. The spectrum with the smallest resulting angle is considered to be the closest match to the mean spectrum and is selected as the representative of the mean. This simple algorithm considers a spectrum of interest, either selected from the scene or from a database, as a vector. The spectrum of interest is then matched to all of the spectra in the data cube. The output is an angular distance value in radians that indicates how close a match the spectrum of interest is to all of the unknown spectra in the scene. A close match results in a value close to zero, while a poor match results in a value closer to one. In addition to its simplicity, it also has the desirable characteristic of being insensitive to levels of reflectance (i.e., light and dark). As an angular metric, it is an indicator of differences in spectral shape and not amplitude.

As an example, a grayscale image plane at 650 nm from a hyperspectral data cube of a face is shown in Fig. 1.10. A spectrum from the cheek (refer to Fig. 1.4) is used to develop a classification map of the scene. This example may serve as a preprocessing step in order to remove the background from the scene. All of the pixels in the data cube were evaluated against the reference spectrum to match values between 0 and 0.25 rad. Those matching pixels were then used to subtract the background and allow only the pixels that matched the skin reflectance spectrum to be displayed. Note the delineation between skin and non-skin on a pixel by pixel basis is not exact. Two factors that play a role are mixed pixels (skin and hair within the size of one pixel) and shadows where the signal is dominated by noise.

A significantly more effective method for detecting spectral similarity is the Mahalanobis distance (MD), Eq. (3). The MD uses the covariance matrix to take into account the variance in the distribution of the data cube. This is an important consideration since real-world reflectance spectra are represented by probability distributions as opposed to an exact deterministic values as discussed in the skin reflectance variability section. The MD Δ is calculated by using

$$\Delta^2 = (s - \mu)^{\mathrm{T}} \Gamma^{-1} (s - \mu), \tag{3}$$

where s is the reflectance spectrum of interest considered as a vector, μ is the mean vector of the data set, and Γ is the covariance matrix. This metric can be extended to be used as a target detector if a ratio is taken so that the MD of the unknown spectrum is divided by the MD of the background. This ratio is referred to as a matched filter and can be used to estimate the probability of detection and probability of a false alarm [35].

Another commonly used analysis tool for spectral imaging is principal component analysis (PCA) [36]. This too is useful in reducing the spectral dimensionality. With hyperspectral data, many of the closely spaced spectral bands are highly correlated and do not provide any additional information. This statistical method transforms a data set of possibly correlated variables into a set of linearly uncorrelated variables, or principal components, such that the first component has the largest possible variance and each succeeding (orthogonal) component has less

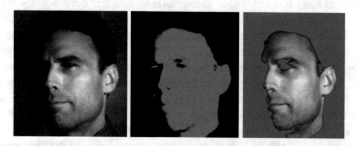

Fig. 1.10 The image on the *left* shows the 650-nm spectral image plane. The center image shows the pixels that matched the reference spectrum. The image on the *right* shows only the grayscale image pixels from the pixels classified as skin. Note the clothing, hair, and background are now removed (displayed as gray) leaving mostly pixels that match skin

variance than the previous. Typical hyperspectral data cubes can be reduced from 100 spectral bands to less than ten with the first several being the most significant. In practice, PCA can be used on the full data cube to separate different materials from the background (i.e., human skin from the background) or on a local scale by extracting a region of interest from the data cube (i.e., mapping the veins on the face) and then processing using the PCA transform. At this more restricted spatial scale, additional features may be observed that would otherwise be obscured by the dominating background. For example, features on a face such as blemishes, scars, and blood vessels may become visible with sufficient spatial resolution when the region is restricted to a region such as the cheek.

Statistical analysis methods, including the ones mentioned above, are available as software packages, both commercially and free, intended to be used in exploiting spectral imaging data. These tools can make it relatively easy to explore and display large data cubes using a variety of different analysis techniques.

1.6   Future Directions

The most compelling use of HSI is in research and exploration of new applications. Once the application is well known, a down selection to a select set of bands can be utilized for routine use with a multispectral imager. Cost of spectral imaging systems currently prohibits widespread use compared to conventional color imaging. There is currently an active area of research in developing the next generation of spectral imagers. The next-generation spectral imagers include a move toward user-friendly snapshot designs that include video-rate data cube collection capabilities.

Spectral analysis methods are intended for use in matching spectra for detection and classification. Most all of the spectral imaging methods are based on the sole use of the spectral content and disregard the spatial information. This approach is regarded as non-literal interpretation. New spectral–spatial analysis algorithms are beginning to be explored and implemented with anticipation of greater accuracy in hyperspectral classification. Facial recognition to date has been heavily dependent on spatial features alone. The addition of spectral information to spatial facial features is anticipated to aid in accuracy when combined with currently used strategies. Additionally, there are some opportunities to further exploit the spectral characteristics of skin based on the oxygenation of the blood in the observed tissue. Those methods are sufficiently served by the use of several carefully chosen spectral bands. Most work is assuming a static subject but there is significant variability as a function of time, heartbeat, respiration, stress, and activity level. This information may aid in not only facial recognition but also assessment of health status, i.e., live, dead, or impaired health [37]. It is likely that as knowledge of the phenomenology of spectral imaging of humans develops along with the next generation of spectral sensors, real-time monitoring of several factors may be possible, in addition to enhanced identification methods.

1.7   Discussion and Conclusion

This chapter covered the subject of spectral imaging with the intent on facilitating the use of spectral imaging in support of advancing current facial recognition methods. It provides researchers who are not familiar with spectral imaging with an overview of what is involved with the practice. It is not intended to be a comprehensive tutorial on the subject. For a more in-depth introduction, it is suggested the reader refers to the following references [22, 38]. It is also suggested that when considering a spectral imaging system on the market, one consider a demonstration for the particular application of interest. The nature of spectral imaging makes it useful for a wide range of applications. However, a spectral imaging system that is well suited for one application may not work equally well for another.

Spectral imaging of human skin is of particular interest since the spectral features are relatively unique and provide a rich source of information. The spectral distinctions between individuals and within the same individual provide a basis for feature extraction over what spatial information alone can provide. Many of the spectral features are not visible to the human eye even within the visible spectral region. Spectral regions outside of the visible region, namely infrared, may provide additional information and operational advantages.

The state of spectral imaging technology will likely continue to advance as a result of new sensor designs, collection, and processing methods, and a better understanding of the phenomenology of interest. Overall, spectral imaging provides a valuable tool in understanding of spectrally based facial features in addition to providing a potential path to enhanced practices.

References

1. Celebrating 40 years of Landsat. http://eijournal.com/print/articles/celebrating-40-years-years-of-landsat. Accessed 22 Sept 2015
2. Phillips, P.J.: In: Proceedings of IEEE Conference on Progress in Human ID, Advanced Video and Signal Based Surveillance (2003)
3. Grother, P.J., Quinn, G.W., Phillips, P.J.: Report on the Evaluation of 2D Still-Image Face Recognition Algorithms NIST Interagency/Internal Report (NISTIR)—7709, June 2010. http://www.nist.gov/customcf/get_pdf.cfm?pub_id=905968
4. Grother, P.J., Ngan, M.L.: Performance of Face Identification Algorithms NIST Interagency/Internal Report (NISTIR)—8009, May 2014. http://www.nist.gov/customcf/get_pdf.cfm?pub_id=915761
5. Chang, H.: Multispectral imaging for face recognition over varying illumination. Ph.D. dissertation, Department of Electrical Engineering and Computer Science, University of Tennessee, TN (2008) (IRIS-M database)
6. Di, W., Zhang, L., Zhang, D., Pan, Q.: Studies on hyperspectral face recognition in visible spectrum with feature band selection. In: IEEE Transactions on Systems, Man, Cybernetics A, Systems Humans, vol. 40, pp. 1354–1361 (2010) (PolyU database)

7. Denes, L., Metes, P., Liu, Y.: Hyperspectral face database. Technical Report CMU-RI-TR-02-25, Robotics Institute, Carnegie Mellon University, Pittsburgh, PA (2002) (CMU database)
8. Skauli, T., Farrell, J.: A collection of hyperspectral images for imaging systems research. In: Proceedings of SPIE 8660, Digital Photography IX (2013) (Stanford database)
9. Cho, W., Koschan, A., Abidi, M.A.: Multispectral/Hyperspectral Face Databases. In: Face Recognition Across the Electromagnetic Spectrum. Springer, Berlin (2016)
10. Pan, Z., Healey, G.E., Prasad, M., Tromberg, B.: Face recognition in hyperspectral images. In: IEEE Transactions on Pattern Analysis and Machine Intelligence, vol. 25, issue 12, pp. 1552–1560 (2003)
11. Di, W., Zhang, L., Zhang, D., Pan, Q.: Studies on hyperspectral face recognition in visible spectrum with feature band selection. In: IEEE Transactions on Systems, Man and Cybernetics, Part A: Systems and Humans, vol. 40, issue 6, pp. 1354–1361 (2010)
12. Uzair, M., Mahmood, A., Mian, A.: Hyperspectral face recognition with spatiospectral information fusion and PLS regression. In: IEEE Transactions on Image Processing, vol. 24, issue 3, pp. 1127–1137 (2015)
13. Uzair, M., Mahmood, A., Shafait, F., Nansen, C., Mian, A.: Is Spectral Reflectance of the Face a Reliable Biometric? Optics Express, vol. 23, issue 12, pp. 15160–15173, Jun 15 2015. doi:10.1364/OE.23.015160
14. Rosario, D.: Spectral LWIR imaging for remote face detection. In: IEEE International Geoscience and Remote Sensing Symposium (IGARSS), pp. 4419–4422 (2011)
15. Bourlai, T., Ross, A., Chen, C., Hornak, L.: A study on using mid-wave infrared images for face recognition. In: Proceedings of SPIE 8371, Sensing Technologies for Global Health, Military Medicine, Disaster Response, and Environmental Monitoring II; and Biometric Technology for Human Identification IX, 83711 K, 1 May 2012. doi:10.1117/12.918899
16. Choi, J., Hu, S., Young, S.S., Davis, L.S.: Thermal to visible face recognition. In: Proceedings of SPIE 8371, Sensing Technologies for Global Health, Military Medicine, Disaster Response, and Environmental Monitoring II; and Biometric Technology for Human Identification IX, 83711L, 1 May 2012. doi:10.1117/12.920330
17. Osia, N., Bourlai, T.: A spectral independent approach for physiological and geometric based face recognition in the visible, middle-wave and long-wave infrared bands. Image Vision Comput. J. Elsevier 32(11), 847–859 (2014)
18. Narang, N., Bourlai, T.: Face recognition in the SWIR band when using single sensor multi-wavelength imaging systems. Image Vision Comput. J. Elsevier 33, 26–43 (2015)
19. Cannon, T.W.: Light and radiation. In: Handbook of Applied Photometry American Institute of Physics (Chapter 1), p. 5, Woodbury, NY (1997)
20. Nicodemus, F., et al: Geometric considerations and nomenclature for reflectance, US Department of Commerce, NBS monograph 160 (1977)
21. Koch, B.M.: A Multispectral bidirectional reflectance distribution function study of human skin for improved dismount detection. Thesis, Air Force Institute of Technology (2011)
22. Shaw, G.A., Burke, H.K.: Spectral imaging for remote sensing. Lincoln Lab. J. 14(1), 3–28 (2003)
23. Hagen, N., Kudenov, M.W.: Review of snapshot spectral imaging technologies. Opt. Eng. 0001 52(9), 090901–090901 (2013)
24. CODATA Value: Wien wavelength displacement law constant. The NIST Reference on Constants, Units, and Uncertainty. US National Institute of Standards and Technology, June 2011. http://physics.nist.gov/cuu/Constants/
25. Lu, G., Fei, B., Medical hyperspectral imaging: a review. J. Biomed. Opt. 0001 19(1), 010901 (2014)
26. Cooksey, C.C., Neira, J.E., Allen, D.W.: The evaluation of hyperspectral imaging for the detection of person-borne threat objects over the 400 nm to 1700 nm spectral region. In: Proceedings of SPIE 8357, Detection and Sensing of Mines, Explosive Objects, and Obscured Targets XVII, 83570O, 1 May 2012. doi:10.1117/12.919432

27. Cooksey, C.C., Tsai, B.K., Allen, D.W.: Spectral reflectance variability of skin and attributing factors. In: Proceedings of SPIE 9461, Radar Sensor Technology XIX; and Active and Passive Signatures VI, 94611 M, 21 May 2015. doi:10.1117/12.2184485
28. Jacques, S.L.: Optical properties of biological tissues: a review. Phys. Med. Biol. **58**, R37 (2013)
29. Gnyawali, S.C., Elgharably, H., Melvin, J., Huang, K., Bergdall, V., Allen, D.W., Hwang, J., Litorja, M., Shirley, E., Sen, C.K., Xu, R.: Hyperspectral imaging of ischemic wounds. In: Proceedings of SPIE 8229, Optical Diagnostics and Sensing XII: Toward Point-of-Care Diagnostics; and Design and Performance Validation of Phantoms Used in Conjunction with Optical Measurement of Tissue IV, 822910, 1 Feb 2012. doi:10.1117/12.907107
30. Xu, R.X., Allen, D.W., Huang, J., Gnyawali, S., Melvin, J., Elgharably, H., Sen, C.K.: Developing digital tissue phantoms for hyperspectral imaging of ischemic wounds. Biomed. Opt. Express **3**(6), 1433–1445 (2012). doi:10.1364/BOE.3.001433
31. Barnes, P.Y., Early, E.A., Parr, A.C.: NIST Measurement Services: Spectral Reflectance. NIST Special Publication, pp. 250–48 (1998)
32. Beisley, A.P.: Spectral detection of human skin in VIS-SWIR hyperspectral imagery without radiometric calibration. Thesis, Air Force Institute of Technology (2012)
33. Velez-Reyes, M., Kruse, F.A.: Algorithms and Technologies for Multispectral, Hyperspectral, and Ultraspectral Imagery XXI Baltimore, Maryland, United States, 20 Apr 2015 (Note: this conference, including the preceding years, has produced over 1,000 papers on the subject of spectral imaging algorithms)
34. Kruse, F.A., Lefkoff, A.B., Boardman, J.B., Heidebrecht, K.B., Shapiro, A.T., Barloon, P.J., Goetz, A.F.H.: The spectral image processing system (SIPS)—interactive visualization and analysis of imaging spectrometer data. Remote Sens. Environ. **44**, 145–163 (1993)
35. Manolakis, D., Marden, D., Shaw, G.A.: Hyperspectral image processing for automatic target detection applications. Lincoln Lab. J. **14**(1), 79–116 (2003)
36. Richards, J.A., Richards, J.A.: Remote Sensing Digital Image Analysis, vol. 3. Springer, Berlin (1999)
37. Kaur, B., Hodgkin, V.A., Nelson, J.K., Ikonomidou, V.N., Hutchinson, J.A.: Hyperspectral waveband group optimization for time-resolved human sensing. In: Proceedings of SPIE 8750, Independent Component Analyses, Compressive Sampling, Wavelets, Neural Net, Biosystems, and Nanoengineering XI, 87500 J, 29 May 2013. doi:10.1117/12.2018334
38. Eismann, M.T.: Hyperspectral Remote Sensing SPIE Press, Apr 2012. ISBN 9780819487872

Chapter 2
Collection of Multispectral Biometric Data for Cross-spectral Identification Applications

J.M. Dawson, S.C. Leffel, C. Whitelam and T. Bourlai

Abstract The ultimate goal of cross-spectral biometric recognition applications involves matching probe images, captured in one spectral band, against a gallery of images captured in a different band or multiple bands (neither of which is the same band in which the probe images were captured). Both the probe and the gallery images may have been captured in either controlled or uncontrolled environments, i.e., with varying standoff distances, lighting conditions, poses. Development of effective cross-spectral matching algorithms involves, first, the process of collecting a cohort of research sample data under controlled conditions with fixed or varying parameters such as pose, lighting, obstructions, and illumination wavelengths. This chapter details "best practice" collection methodologies developed to compile large-scale datasets of both visible and SWIR face images, as well as gait images and videos. All aspects of data collection, from IRB preparation, through data post-processing, are provided, along with instrumentation layouts for indoor and outdoor live capture setups. Specifications of video and still-imaging cameras used in collections are listed. Controlled collection of 5-pose, ANSI/NIST mugshot images is described, along with multiple SWIR data collections performed both indoors (under controlled illumination) and outdoors. Details of past collections performed at West Virginia University (WVU) to compile multispectral biometric datasets, such as age, gender, and ethnicity of the subject populations, are included. Insight is given on the impact of collection parameters on the general quality of images collected, as well as on how these parameters impact design decisions at the algorithm level. Finally, where applicable, a brief description of how these databases have been used in multispectral biometrics research is included.

J.M. Dawson (✉) · S.C. Leffel · C. Whitelam · T. Bourlai
Lane Department of Computer Science and Electrical Engineering,
Statler College of Engineering and Mineral Resources,
West Virginia University, P.O. Box 6109, Morgantown, WV 26506, USA
e-mail: jeremy.dawson@mail.wvu.edu

T. Bourlai
e-mail: Thirimachos.Bourlai@mail.wvu.edu

© Springer International Publishing Switzerland 2016
T. Bourlai (ed.), *Face Recognition Across the Imaging Spectrum*,
DOI 10.1007/978-3-319-28501-6_2

2.1 Multispectral Face Imagery—Background

One of the key aspects to facial recognition (FR) technology is the proper development of algorithms, which are able to successfully and consistently identify subjects. Many challenges exist within this realm, ranging from image quality to subject pose angle. These challenges are impacted by not just the camera system, but also by the scenario in which the data are collected. These scenarios impact the strategy of the algorithms that need to be designed, to mitigate the scenario-specific challenges. For example, in defense or law enforcement surveillance applications, it is often necessary to covertly (but non-intrusively) or opportunistically collect facial biometric data. This data, in turn, must be used to match subjects against a gallery or watch list to identify an unaware or uncooperative subject. This operational scenario poses a set of challenges to FR systems in that a myriad of non-idealities must then be considered to achieve high-confidence match scores. Some of these challenges, as also discussed above, are face acquisition at variable or long distances, facial occlusions, poor lighting, and otherwise obscured faces.

Currently, the majority of facial recognition systems employ the use of visible images captured under controlled conditions as probes to match against galleries of visible data. This poses several challenges which, due to the physical limitations of the visible spectrum, in nighttime or non-uniform lighting scenarios, yield poorer quality images. Further work is required to successfully incorporate FR in challenging environments.

To overcome the issues associated with poor lighting, researchers have explored other, non-visible wavelengths as a means of capturing face images. In particular, the infrared (IR) spectrum has been investigated as a means of possibly extending the facial recognition technology. The IR spectrum can be divided into *two primary divisions*: *thermal* and *reflective*. The lower reflective bands resolve images with well-resolved facial features, closely resembling those captured at visible wavelengths. The lower bands can further be divided into NIR (near infrared) (750–1100 nm) and SWIR (short-wave infrared) (900–1900 nm) [1–3]. These bands have a particular advantage over traditional visible imaging as they do not suffer from illumination-based color shifting. Algorithms have trouble distinguishing the difference between an object change and the illumination of the object changing [4].

On the opposite end of the infrared spectrum exists what is referred to as thermal infrared. These bands are commonly classified as MWIR (mid-wave infrared) (3–5 μm) and LWIR (long-wave infrared) (7–14 μm) [5–7]. Research in the LWIR bands has incorporated polarimetric thermal imaging as a means of enhancing cross-spectral face recognition; this notably improved face detection performance by combining polarimetric and traditional thermal facial features [8]. Extended polarimetric thermal imaging research also allows for the geometric and textural facial detail recognition [9]. Progress has also been made with the employment of partial least-square-based face recognition and more specifically thermal to visible face matching [10]. While the resolved images do not yield the same level of detail, the associated wavelengths are able to show recognizable facial details. The advantage to this side of the spectrum is that it does not require an illumination source, as the detection is that of the emitted radiation from the subject rather than the reflected light.

When approaching the issue of matching visible galleries to infrared probe images, the shorter wavelengths promote a more natural transition from the visible gallery. Both the visible band and the shorter IR wavelengths have their advantages when applied to facial recognition, and thus, different applications have been developed. For instance, in 2009, a research group from the West Virginia High Technology Consortium Foundation (WVHTCF) developed an active-SWIR system, dubbed TINDERS, for detecting facial features at distances up to 400 m [11]. The group also demonstrated the ability to actively track human subjects at distances up to 3 km. Working on a part of the TINDERS face dataset, the authors in [1] worked on developing a heterogeneous FR matcher and demonstrated its capability and limitations at short as well as at long ranges. In 2010, the WVHTCF group was able to improve the TINDERS system to yield clearer, sharper images [12]. Since SWIR was chosen, an active illumination source was required. An advantage of that source is that it is considered eye safe for wavelengths greater than 1400 nm [11]. The SWIR spectrum also has the added benefit of being able to produce clear images in adverse weather conditions, such as heavy rain [13].

Different research groups have developed algorithmic approaches that allow matching of face images irrespective of their spectral view [1, 3]. The suggested approaches seem to preserve the facial structures and, thus, lending toward successful cross-spectral matches [3]. Similar approaches also lend promise toward the ultraviolet band [14], as well as the MWIR and LWIR bands making face detection, eye detection, and face recognition possible across the majority of the IR spectrum [6]. Lower IR (NIR) wavelengths can be eye safe and their biometric systems are mostly used in law enforcement applications [15]. However, NIR-based detectors suffer from issues of being detectable by silicon-based image sensors or in some case even the human eye [13].

As previously mentioned, the face images (probes) used in cross-spectral matching scenarios must be comparable to visible gallery photographs in some manner. This requires the development and implementation of cross-spectral face-matching algorithms. Allowing for accurate recognition and identification matching of non-visible probe images to visible galleries aides image matching from an ideal image (such as a photograph ID) to security footage, as recorded by an infrared camera in variable environmental conditions. In particular, SWIR has the added advantage of being able to operate in low-light scenarios, such as twilight or low illumination [11]. When natural or existing illumination is not sufficient, truly non-visible illumination sources are able to covertly illuminate a darkened area. SWIR band illumination can also be disguised from being detected by only illuminating selected wavelengths, e.g., 1550 nm, which will otherwise appear dark even in other SWIR wavelengths [5]. This capability enhances the covert nature of facial recognition in dark environments (where visible-based FR becomes very challenging) and has been shown to resolve better matching scores than visible data [16].

The SWIR spectrum also extends the viability of non-visible facial recognition by its wide applicability to both urban and rural environments. Urban environmental obstacles such as reflective and tinted glass become transparent [17]. Additionally, common urban particulates, such as pollution and smog, are eliminated when operating in the SWIR band [17]. In rural settings, particulates such as dust, fog, and haze can be removed from SWIR images [18]. This lends SWIR tactical imagers to be highly desirable for operating in extraordinarily obstructed visible environments. As discussed, the NIR band can also be used in tactical imagery systems with success [17, 19], the disadvantage being easy detection of active NIR illumination sources.

Other Challenges in the SWIR Band

Though the non-visible SWIR band has many advantages, there are many issues that negatively impact facial recognition. A notable issue is that, above 1450 nm, the moisture found in skin begins to absorb the infrared wavelengths. This causes the skin to appear black or dark [17]. In darkened settings, the issue becomes further complicated when eye-safe illumination is necessary. As mentioned above, eye-safe illumination is above 1400 nm; the resulting images, however, will result in darkened skin on subjects [11]. This poses a challenge to many facial recognition algorithms currently in place, commercial or in-house (academic). Similarly, membrane tissues, such as the eye, become darker as the wavelength increases, and thus, the efficiency of automated eye-detection methods can be negatively affected. This issue is driven by the fact that the pupil becomes obscured in these wavelengths. Certain oils produced by the skin reflect infrared light as well. This causes saturation effects in images with high-intensity sources, such as infrared-emitting lamps (e.g., tungsten bulbs) and direct sunlight. Many of these effects can, however, be mitigated through hardware filtering to specific SWIR bands.

Contributions

The advantages of multispectral imagery outweigh the current associated issues found therein. Through its involvement with the NSF-funded Center for Identification Technology Research (CITeR), a cooperative agreement as lead academic partner of the FBI CJIS Division Biometric Center of Excellence, and funding from other federal agencies, West Virginia University, has conducted numerous data collection projects to build repositories of multimodal biometric data that can be used to mitigate different challenges identified within the field of human identification. To overcome these issues, particularly those associated with infrared-focused or cross-spectral-based face imaging, several of these data collection activities have included wavelength-specific SWIR face image capture (highlighting specific bands across the SWIR spectrum) and the generation of multi-wavelength SWIR face image datasets. Together, with a database of visible face images (a visible gallery), algorithmic development tends toward cross-spectral face-matching systems. Table 2.1 presents a selection of available infrared databases featuring human subjects. The use of such datasets allows for the development of better and more universally viable face-matching algorithms.

This chapter will outline the methods and procedures used to collect and build the aforementioned WVU SWIR databases, as well as provide a summary of cross-spectral matching results for the respective datasets. Lastly, if a SWIR imager lacks the optical system needed to capture high-resolution face images at a distance,

Table 2.1 Databases containing infrared images of human features

Authors	Spectral band	Application	Environment conditions
Pan et al. [27]	Infrared in range 700–1000 nm	Hyperspectral face recognition using liquid crystal tunable filter (LCTF) wheel	Outdoor
Multispectral Imagery Lab (WVU) [1, 5, 6, 15, 28–30]	Infrared in range 900–1550 nm as well as Thermal IR	Multispectral eye and pupil detection, multispectral face recognition, and cross-spectral face-matching algorithms	Indoors and outdoors
Kang et al. [31]	Illumination source of 940 nm wavelength	Face recognition using principal component analysis (PCA) and linear discriminant analysis (LDA)	Indoor
Ngo et al. [32]	Infrared in range from 450 to 1550 nm	Multispectral iris acquisition system	Indoor
Steiner et al. [33]	Infrared in range from 900 to 1700 nm	Multispectral face verification using spectral signatures	Indoor
Pavlidis et al. [34]	Infrared in range from 1400 to 2400 nm	Automatic detection based on a fusion scheme	Indoor
Jacquez et al. [35]	Infrared in range from 700 to 2600 nm	Spectral reflectance from human skin	Indoor
Bertozzi et al. [36]	Infrared in range from 900 to 1700 nm	Pedestrian detection	Outdoor
Lemoff et al. [37]	Infrared in range from 900 to 1700 nm	Face matching using fusion scheme	Indoor/outdoor
Qianting et al. [38]	Infrared in range from 1000 to 1700 nm	Image mosaicing using global thresholding	Indoor

gait information may be used to perform identification. Thus, gait-based recognition will also be discussed as a means to supplement face image data acquired at long distances (i.e., more than 50 m).

2.2   Institutional Review Board (IRB) Preparation

Projects that involve human research, including biometric data collection, require an approved Institutional Review Board (IRB) protocol. An institutional review board is a committee of individuals that reviews project details relating to human subjects research to ensure that investigators comply with all federal, state, and institutional requirements and policies relating to the appropriate protections for human subjects. These protections include adequate provisions for minimizing subjects risk, documentation of subjects' consent forms, and, finally, protection of subjects' privacy and maintaining data confidentiality. For the research efforts described in this chapter, the IRB of the WVU Office of Research Integrity and Compliance provided reviews of all aspects of the data collection protocol, including participant recruitment, collection activities, remuneration, and biometric data privacy and storage. For the WVU IRB, the following two requirements are central to IRB approval:

1. *Training of personnel*: Any person affiliated with WVU (faculty, student, or staff) that is involved in the data collection or data processing is required to take a series of online courses to educate them on the ethics associated with human research related to social and behavioral studies (which WVU biometric collections fall under). At WVU, these courses are currently offered by the Collaborative Institutional Training Initiative at the University of Miami (ci-tiprogram.org). There are online tests associated with these courses that train personnel in proper human subject research ethics. All collection staff members must pass these tests in order for the proposed IRB protocol to be approved.

2. *Protocol Statement Description*: This form is submitted electronically to the WVU Institutional Review Board (IRB) by the Principal Investigator. The Protocol Statement form contains information about:

   - Research teams: Principal Investigator, affiliated and non-affiliated team members, primary study contact, etc.
   - Funding sources.
   - Research studies and activities location.
   - Exemption determination.
   - Design of the research, including the category of research, procedures, subjects, sample size, potential risks and discomforts, potential benefits, confidentiality, subjects' costs, payments to subjects, etc.
   - Consent procedures, which involves a *Consent and Information* form. This document informs the subject (research study participant) about the project and confirms the voluntarily participation of the subject in the project.
   - Advertisements—any email text, newspaper ads, or flyers used to recruit participants must be included along with the data collection protocol.

If a prototype device is not used, or if biological samples are not collected, biometric collection projects may be eligible for *Expedited Review* (ER). Within the expedited review process, the protocol may be reviewed by an individual, member of the IRB panel and that is not involved in full-board meetings. Please note that this process may vary from institution to institution. The ER process may allow the protocol to be approved within a period of one or two weeks rather than one month or more. After the submission of the IRB protocol to the appropriate office, an IRB panel reviews the submitted documents. One of the potential outcomes of the assessment is the request for further revisions, and/or the recommendation for the personnel to complete the appropriate course on human subject research (in case they did not). Next, required revisions are applied to the *Protocol Statement* form. Then, the form is resubmitted to the Office of Research Integrity and Compliance. Finally, the office approves the submitted IRB protocol under the conditions that human subject research is appropriate and conforms to federal regulations.

During the period for which the project is active, it is necessary that the project is annually reviewed, and thus, a *Continuing Protocol Review* (CR) needs to be completed. For a CR, statistical information pertaining to the study is gathered, including the number, gender, and race of the subjects enrolled in the study; the number of subjects from the special categories such as pregnant women and children, adverse events, number of subjects removed from the project, and grievances or complaints received about the study. All changes to the project, including added or removed researchers, new locations, new procedures or changes in procedures, new forms of advertisement, must be documented and submitted to the Office of Research Integrity and Compliance using as an amendment to the latest IRB protocol approved.

2.3 Standard Visible Mugshot Capture

In order to generate a baseline dataset of good-quality face images, a live subject-capture setup was used. It involves the necessary hardware (cameras, lenses, etc.) as well as a data collection protocol to be followed that uses the hardware under a specific scenario. In this work, the hardware typically employed for high-resolution ground truth capture of visible face images was a conventional DSLR camera, such as a Canon 5D Mark II or equivalent, with a telephoto zoom lens (such as a Canon EF 800 mm f/5.6L IS USM). This camera was used to capture 5 different poses: $-90°$, $-45°$, $0°$, $45°$, and $90°$. A schematic view of the indoor photograph collection is shown in Fig. 2.1.

Three-point lighting is used to meet the standards outlined in ANSI/NIST–ITL 1-2007 *Best Practice Recommendation for the Capture of Mugshots* [20]. The lighting is comprised of one 250-W fixture and dual 500-W fixtures. The positioning of these light sources, with respect to the participant, is slightly asymmetric. There is also sufficient distance between the backdrop (neutral gray) and the participant in order to avoid background shadows. In addition, plastic diffusers in front of the reflector-mounted light bulbs are utilized to avoid "hot spots" that may appear on face images. The following camera settings typically result in the best focal depth and image quality under the 3-point tungsten lighting, i.e., (i) White Balance: Tungsten, (ii) ISO: 1000, (iii) F/2.6: 1/10, and (iv) exposure set to 1/60.

Fig. 2.1 Photograph station
layout

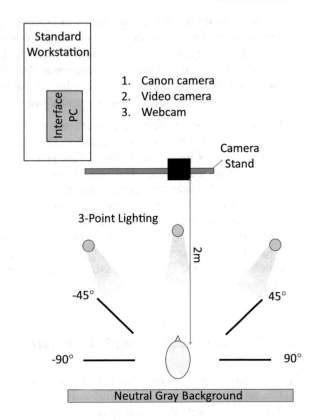

2.4 SWIR Face Data Collection Activities

SWIR face data collection activities were undertaken to create a challenging dataset comprised of obstructed views of participants' faces under varying lighting conditions. Obstruction in this case consisted of various types of tinted glass and sunglasses. In order to assess the extent to which these materials or conditions affected the capture, characterization of the semi-transparent materials was first conducted in order to down-sample the number of materials used in data collection efforts, as well as establish a collection scheme for an *indoor data collection* (*Phase I*). An *outdoor collection* was then performed (*Phase II*) in order to establish more effective recognition algorithms under uncontrolled lighting conditions. The *Phase I* and *Phase II SWIR face image capture activities* were performed at a standoff distance of two (2) meters.

West Virginia University (WVU) partnered with the WVHTCF to extend the original SWIR face image collection by performing a long-distance, nighttime SWIR face image collection. By utilizing a specialized SWIR hardware setup, designed for day- or nighttime face image acquisition at long standoff distances, the partnership resulted in an original face dataset that includes face images of 104 subjects captured at different standoff distances ranging from 100 to 350 m at night. At each distance, the following data were captured: neutral expression of participant looking directly at camera, participant rotating 360°, and neutral expression looking directly at camera through tinted glass. The following sections of this chapter will describe the SWIR data collections performed at WVU. First, characterization of tinted materials at different temperatures will be presented to illustrate the spectral transmission as a function of temperature. Next, indoor and outdoor data collection of face images will be discussed, highlighting the challenges of collecting SWIR face images through tinted materials in varying lighting conditions and standoff distances. Finally, a discussion of gait recognition based on SWIR video is provided as a complimentary means of recognition if facial features cannot be resolved in long-distance imagery.

2.4.1   Tinted Material Characterization

Prior to the initiation of cross-spectral face matching using images captured under challenging conditions (i.e., at night and/or through tinted materials), two studies were performed to understand how environmental factors, such as temperature and lighting, may impact the ability to see through tinted materials. The *first study* was aimed at understanding how changes in temperature may alter the spectral transmission properties of different materials. The *second study* explored how tint type/level coupled with internal and external lighting conditions affected the ability to image faces through glass. The material samples used in this study represent common architectural and automotive tinted glass with tint embedded in the material (all provided by Pittsburgh Plate Glass (PPG); Two (2) architectural samples include mirror coating), clear plate glass covered with tinted plastic film (Johnson Window Film), and various types of plastic lenses in eyewear (i.e., sunglasses) from several manufacturers. A detailed discussion of the results from this study is published in [21]. In summary, temperature change does not have a significant impact on the ability to see through tinted materials. Instead, different interior and exterior lighting conditions have the largest impact on the ability to acquire images though tinted materials. Contrast quality measures were applied to sample images taken under varying lighting conditions through materials of varying tint levels in order to rank materials according to transparency and image quality [21]. The tint transparency ranking was used to down-select the number of glass materials that were used in data collection efforts described in this chapter. Three samples were chosen representing low, medium, and dark tint.

2.4.2 SWIR Face Image Collections

Data collections were performed to provide operationally relevant data samples with which to develop eye and face detection techniques as well as SWIR face recognition algorithms that perform well under challenging conditions. Initial studies were performed on a dataset that was collected indoors under controlled lighting conditions (Phase I), with glass and sunglass types and lighting levels determined during the glass characterization experiments. After the completion of the Phase I data collection, a second collection (Phase II) was performed outdoors under varying daytime and nighttime lighting conditions to test the performance of and optimize recognition tools. This section summarizes the collection protocols and results of these two data collection efforts, with a brief description of other SWIR datasets that were developed in partnership with the WVHTCF.

2.4.2.1 Phase I—Indoor Collection Under Controlled Lighting Conditions

An InGaAs-based Goodrich SU640HSX-1.7RT SWIR camera was used for image acquisition based on previous work in this area [22, 23]. The solid-state InGaAs imaging array possesses high sensitivity in the 900–1700 nm spectrum and is capable of capturing images at 640 × 512 pixel resolution. The photograph booth and lighting setup shown in Fig. 2.2 was utilized to independently control interior and exterior light levels. The booth was designed with a removable front panel to which tinted materials with varying transparency would be affixed. The details of these materials are included in [21]. Due to interfering/obstructing reflections on the glass seen during initial testing using high exterior light levels at a short imaging

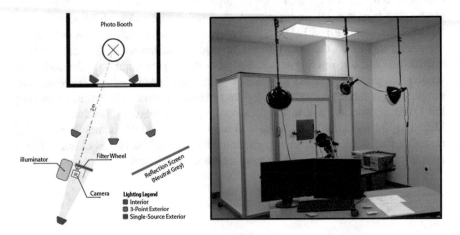

Fig. 2.2 Indoor data collection setup and lighting arrangement

distance (2 m), the camera setup was slightly angled ($\sim 12°$) to reduce the impact of reflections on images captured under these lighting conditions. In addition, a neutral gray background was placed in the reflection path to provide a constant background, further reducing the impact of image reflection.

An image collection protocol was designed to capture images for different materials under variable lighting conditions at wavelengths ranging from 1150 to 1550 nm. The wavelength filters were assembled in a wheel, which spun five (5) times in the process of collecting. Thus, we manage to acquire five (5) images per filter per participant.

Facial images were collected under the following scenarios, with all illuminance (lux) measurements taken at the interior booth seating location:

(A) External lighting eliminated, the only illumination source is the interior lighting at full intensity
(B) External lighting eliminated, the only illumination source is the interior lighting dimmed to ~ 60 lux
(C) External 3-point lighting only (~ 2 m distance; providing ~ 350 lux to booth interior), interior lighting eliminated
(D) Single external exterior light source only (~ 4 m distance, providing ~ 5 lux to booth interior)
(E) 1550 nm wavelength fiber couple laser operating at 500 mW; diffused to provide uniform face illumination (only applicable for 1550 nm SWIR filter)

Booth Panel ON:

1. *Clear w/0 % Film Tint* **Glass Panel**

(A) Full interior (~ 2600 lux), 0 lux exterior
(B) Minimum interior (~ 60 lux), 0 lux exterior
(C) 0 lux interior, 3-point exterior (~ 350 lux)
(D) Single external source (~ 5 lux)
(E) 500 mW 1550 nm active illumination

2. *Clear w/85 % Film Tint* **Glass Panel**

(A) Full interior (~ 2600 lux), 0 lux exterior
(B) Minimum interior (~ 60 lux), 0 lux exterior
(C) 0 lux interior, 3-point exterior (~ 350 lux)
(D) Single external source (~ 5 lux)
(E) 500 mW 1550 nm active illumination

3. *Solarcool (2) Graylite* **Glass Panel**

(A) Full interior (~ 2600 lux), 0 lux exterior
(B) Minimum interior (~ 60 lux), 0 lux exterior
(C) 0 lux interior, 3-point exterior (~ 350 lux)
(D) Single external source (~ 5 lux)
(E) 500 mW 1550 nm active illumination

Booth Panel OFF:

4. *Ground Truth (**No Glass Panel**)*

(A) Full interior (~ 2600 lux), 0 lux exterior
(B) 0 lux interior, 3-Point exterior (~ 350 lux)

5. *Oakley Flak Jacket **Sunglasses***

(A) 0 lux interior, 3-point exterior (~ 350 lux)
(B) Single external source (~ 5 lux)
(C) 500 mW 1550 nm active illumination

6. *Oakley Straight Jacket **Sunglasses***

(A) 0 lux interior, 3-point exterior (~ 350 lux)
(B) Single external source (~ 5 lux)
(C) 500 mW 1550 nm active illumination

7. *RB3449 59 **Sunglasses***

(A) 0 lux interior, 3-point exterior (~ 350 lux)
(B) Single external source (~ 5 lux)
(C) 500 mW 1550 nm active illumination

8. *RB3025 58 **Sunglasses***

(A) 0 lux interior, 3-point exterior (~ 350 lux)
(B) Single external source (~ 5 lux)
(C) 500 mW 1550 nm active illumination

Visible images were acquired for each case using a standard Canon DSLR camera (5D Mark II with kit lens). A custom software SWIR camera interface was created for the purpose of simplifying the data collection process of SWIR and visible photographs when various materials and lighting conditions were used. The complexity of constant adjustments of the Goodrich SWIR and Canon cameras (as well as other equipment/devices) necessitated the development of an easy-to-use interface for collection personnel. This allowed for a quicker collection process and had the added benefit of limiting errors and/or poor data capture.

Sample images for ground truth, tinted glass, and sunglasses are included in Tables 2.2, 2.3, and 2.4, along with optimal OPR and ENH values (user-defined

Table 2.2 Sample ground truth images from Phase I data collection

Visible	SWIR (OPR 5, ENH OFF)				
	1150	1250	1350	1450	1150

Table 2.3 Sample tinted glass images from Phase I data collection

Variable Lightning – Clear glass with 85% Tint					
	Full Internal, No External	**Minimal Interior, No Exterior**	**No Internal, Full External**	**Single-Source External**	**Active Illumination**
Visible					
OPR	6	8	7	9	9
ENH	OFF	OFF	ON	ON	OFF
1150 nm					
1250 nm					
1350 nm					
1450 nm					
1550 nm					

SWIR camera settings) for each condition (lighting and filter wavelength). Table 2.2 shows sample ground truth images collected in visible and 1150-1550 SWIR bands. These images were used to establish a base comparison of ideal (i.e., constant illumination, no facial obstruction) verses operational data (i.e., through tinted glass and with sunglasses, both with varying lighting conditions).

For the SWIR images, a notable darkening of the skin can be seen in wavelengths longer than 1350 nm. Also, the entire eye (sclera and pupil) becomes black, posing challenges to eye-finding algorithms. Table 2.3 provides sample images collected with the 85 % tint glass panel in place under varying lighting conditions. These images show how high levels of external lighting combined with low levels of internal lighting can lead to reflections that obscure facial features in SWIR imagery. Table 2.4 provides sample images of an individual-wearing Oakley Flak Jacket sunglass under varying lighting conditions. The SWIR imager allows the periocular region to be seen clearly, but the effects of blackening of the eye still

Table 2.4 Sample sunglasses images from Phase I data collection

Variable Lightning – Oakley Flak Jacket			
	No Internal, Full External	**Single-Source External**	**Active Illumination**
Visible			
OPR	6	9	7
ENH	OFF	OFF	OFF
1150 nm			
1250 nm			
1350 nm			
1450 nm			
1550 nm			

remain. It should be noted that none of the glasses chosen for this study possessed polarizing lenses. Polarization coatings can greatly reduce or even eliminate the ability to see through the tinted glass or polymer used to make sunglass lenses. This effect can be seen in both natural lighting and active illuminators, and is highly dependent on the polarization state of the light emitted by the source.

The OPR (Operational Setting) value listed in these tables is an integer value corresponding to settings associated with the camera hardware; specifically, a combination of optimally associated digital camera gain and integration time settings. While sensor gain and integration time of this particular camera can be altered individually, the camera manufacturer did not guarantee optimal imaging conditions at settings other than those associated with a fixed OPR value. The camera used in this collection has OPR values ranging from 0 to 11. The ENH (Enhancement) is a Boolean value and reflects image enhancement performed by the camera. The ENH setting ("OFF" or "ON") optimizes the 16-bit image to dynamically scale the image intensity. This allows oversaturated images or excessively dark images to appear more balanced, effectively normalizing pixel intensities within the image.

A total of 138 participants provided data between September 26, 2011, and December 4, 2011.

Figure 2.3 provides a breakdown of participant demographics by age, ethnicity, and gender, as well as a cumulative measurement of participation as a function of time.

Figure 2.3a indicates an average of ∼ 14 participants per week throughout the 10-week collection period, with highest participation during the week of 10/31. The week of 11/21 lacks participation due to West Virginia University being on Thanksgiving Break during that time. Figure 2.3b indicates that the majority of participants (67 %) were between 20 and 29 years of age, followed by 18–19, and 30–39 of age ranges. This is primarily due to student and staff participation in the data collection, conducted on the WVU campus. Only 6 % of participants were 50 or older. Figure 2.3c indicates that approximately half of the participants were Caucasian, followed by Asian Indian (18 %) and Asian (17 %) ethnicities. This demographic distribution is consistent with the student/staff population of WVU.

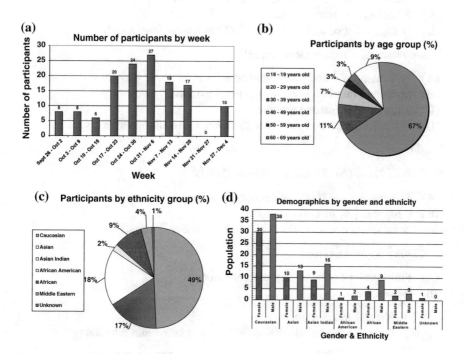

Fig. 2.3 Participant demographics for Phase I study

Figure 2.3d indicates that there was consistently higher male participation than female for all identified ethnic groups.

2.4.2.2 Phase II—Outdoor Collection Under Uncontrolled Lighting Conditions

Facial images were collected under the following scenarios, with all lux measurements taken at the interior booth seating location:

(A) External lighting was the ambient available light during collection, the only controlled illumination source is the interior lighting at full intensity
(B) Ambient external light sources, the only controlled illumination source is the interior lighting dimmed to ∼60 lux
(C) External ambient light only, all controlled light sources eliminated
(D) External ambient lighting, utilization of a 500 mW 1550 nm active illumination diffused laser light source was the only controlled light source.

Glass Panels:

1. *Clear w/0 % Film Tint* **Glass Panel**

   (A) Full interior (∼2600 lux), natural exterior
   (B) Minimum interior (∼60 lux), natural exterior
   (C) 0 lux interior, natural exterior
   (D) Natural exterior and 500 mW 1550 nm active illumination

2. *Solarcool (2) Graylite* **Glass Panel**

   (A) Full interior (∼2600 lux), natural exterior
   (B) Minimum interior (∼60 lux), natural exterior
   (C) 0 lux interior, natural exterior
   (D) Natural exterior and 500 mW 1550 nm active illumination

Sunglasses:

3. *Ground Truth* **(No Sunglasses/Glass Panel)**

   (A) Full interior (∼2600 lux), natural exterior
   (B) 0 lux interior, natural exterior
   (C) Natural exterior and 500 mW 1550 nm active illumination

4. *RB3025 58* **Sunglasses**

   (A) Full interior (∼2600 lux), natural exterior
   (B) 0 lux interior

       (i) Natural exterior only
       (ii) Natural exterior and 500 mW 1550 nm active illumination

An image of the outdoor data collection setup is shown in Fig. 2.4.

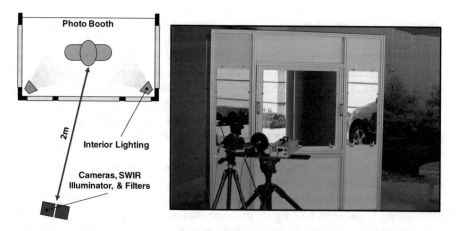

Fig. 2.4 Outdoor data collection setup

Sunglass images were taken outside of the booth with the participant facing toward and away from the sun to determine the effects of spurious reflections on eye-finding. A polarization filter was used in all cases (both sunglasses and glass panels) to reduce these reflections, but they were not completely eliminated. The collection location was varied and recorded from day to day (shade, full sun, etc.) to provide a variety of lighting conditions. Collections performed during the day with overcast sky or at night did not include "sunglasses toward sun," and added the active-SWIR illuminator to the "sunglasses away from sun" scenario. Table 2.5

Table 2.5 Sample daytime images for Phase II data collection

	Ray Ban Sunglasses		Tinted Glass Panel On		Tinted Glass Panel Off	
	Participant facing sun	Participant facing away From Sun	Interior booth lights On	Interior booth lights Off	Interior booth lights On	Interior booth lights Off
1150nm						
1350nm						
1550nm						
SWIR Illuminator						

shows sample images of data at different wavelengths using the three (3) band-pass filters.

Table 2.6 provides sample images indicating the imaging differences for differing sky/lighting conditions. This table is not meant to include examples of all scenarios considered, but serves to provide a qualitative indication of how uncontrolled conditions introduce a high degree of variability in image quality.

A total of 200 participants provided data between July 9, 2012, and September 14, 2012, with participation split evenly between day and night collection times (100 participants each).

Figure 2.5 provides a breakdown of participant demographics by age, ethnicity, and gender, as well as cumulative measured of participation as a function of time.

Figure 2.5a indicates an average of 19 participants per week throughout the 10-week collection period, with peak participation between July 23rd and August 3rd. Low participation rates during the periods from 7/9 through 7/13 and 8/6 through 8/17 were due to closure of the university for anational holiday and the beginning of the fall semester respectively. Figure 2.5b indicates the majority of participants (52 %) were between 20 and 29 years of age, followed by 30–39, and 50–59 age ranges. This is primarily due to student and staff participation in the data collection, conducted on the WVU campus. Minor age ranges were 18–19 (1 %) and 70–79 (2 %). Figure 2.5c indicates that slightly more than half of the participants were Caucasian, followed by African American (13 %), then Middle Eastern and Asian Indian (10 % each) ethnicities. This demographic distribution is consistent with the student/staff population of WVU. Figure 2.5d indicates Caucasian and Hispanic gender participation was nearly equal, while Middle Eastern, Asian, and African males participated more than females. The contrary is true for African Americans.

The images collected in both the indoor and the outdoor data collection efforts have been used to develop cross-spectral facial identification algorithms with automated face and eye detection and photometric normalization. A total 1020 face

Table 2.6 Variations in image quality with variable sky conditions (taken at 1550 nm)

	Glass On, Interior Lights Off, SWIR Illuminator On	Glass On, Interior Lights Off, No SWIR Illuminator	Ray Ban Sunglasses, Facing Away From Sun	Ray Ban Sunglasses, Facing Toward Sun	Ray Ban Sunglasses, No SWIR Illuminator	Ray Ban Sunglasses, SWIR Illuminator
Day						
Overcast						
Night (street lamp illumination)						

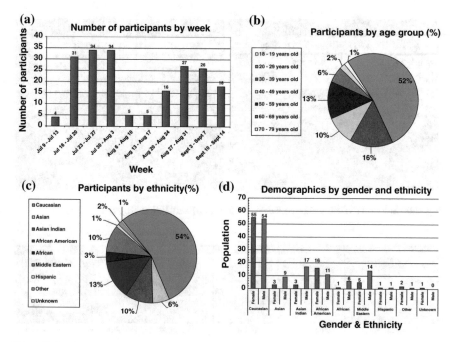

Fig. 2.5 Participant demographics for the Phase II study

images, including 980 SWIR face images (140 subjects × 7 scenarios) and 140 visible (ground truth) face images, were evaluated. Results indicate an eye-detection rate of greater than 96 % in the majority of the scenarios and a rank-1 identification rate of 94.26 %when using the ground truth data acquired in this collection [17].

2.4.3 Long-Range Face Image Collections

Our group collaborated with the WVHTCF to obtain long-range SWIR data collected both indoors and outdoors using the TINDERS camera system. An *indoor collection* was performed by WVHTCF personnel in their high-bay area, with images collected under active illumination at 50 and 106 m. A second, *outdoor collection* was performed with the assistance of WVU staff. This data collection took place at night on the WVU Evansdale campus, with images captured at 100, 200, and 350 m. Faces were unobscured/obscured by glass at each distance. Sample images for each of these datasets are shown in Figs. 2.6 and 2.7.

Fig. 2.6 Indoor TINDERS data collected at 50 m (*left*) and 100 m (*right*)

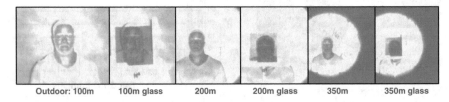

Outdoor: 100m   100m glass   200m   200m glass   350m   350m glass

Fig. 2.7 Outdoor TINDERS data collected from 100 to 350 m with and without glass

While not apparent in the indoor data, atmospheric effects, primarily thermal distortion caused by the warm asphalt surface, can be observed in the data captured at 350 m. It should also be noted that reflections from the illuminator are not an issue when imaging through tinted glass due to the separation distance between the imager and the participant.

Please note that the WVHTCF group has performed matching analysis of the long-range outdoor SWIR face data collected with their imager [12]. For the data collected indoors, custom academic algorithms [24, 25] were used to achieve matching results as high as 90 % rank 1 for 50 subjects' images captured at 50 m and 80 % for the 106 m distance. Matching experiments were performed on a subset of 42 images captured outdoors at night at 100 m (no glass obstruction), with 63 % matched to the correct gallery image at rank-1 and 90 % of the correct gallery image within rank-7 using a commercial (provided by MorphoTrust) face matcher plugin developed specifically for the TINDERS imager. It should also be noted that the average inter-pupillary distance for all long-distance images is approximately 60–70 pixels wide. This is a result of the zoom capabilities of the long-range SWIR camera used in this collection, which was designed to maintain inter-pupillary distance at all zoom levels.

2.5   SWIR Gait Collection

Although there are limitations associated with capturing faces at a distance, additional modalities may be available in long-distance SWIR imagery that could be exploited for identification purposes. One such modality is gait. To supplement SWIR face image collection, WVU performed an additional data collection focused on implementation of SWIR and depth-mapping camera technologies for the acquisition of video from walking individuals to determine the efficacy of soft biometric (body measurement) and gait-based recognition.

Two commercial cameras were used in this study: the Sensors Unlimited Goodrich SU640KTSX-1.7RT High Sensitivity InGaAs SWIR Camera (640 × 512 pixels) with a 50 mm f/1.4 SWIR lens used in face image collection and a Microsoft Kinect depth camera. The Goodrich camera was used to capture gait video at distances ranging from 20–50 m, and the Kinect camera was used to collect video from 1.5 to 4 m. Gait collection with the Goodrich camera was performed outside during daylight hours (natural sunlight illumination), with videos filtered at 1550 nm. Operational settings such as integration time were adjusted to achieve the best image quality based on daily environmental conditions (cloudy, sunny, etc.). The Kinect videos were captured inside under fluorescent illumination. The walking paths used to capture the indoor and outdoor gait cycles are illustrated in Figs. 2.8 and 2.9.

The trapezoidal path for the Kinect camera is required due to its limited field of view at short distances. A calibration pose is performed at an intermediate "center" distance (position "1"). The distances and walking paths chosen for the SWIR collection allowed six or more paces of walking to be collected in a variety of directions with respect to the camera field of view. Example images captured from the indoor and outdoor scenarios are shown in Fig. 2.10.

Fig. 2.8 Indoor Kinect collection layout. Walking paths: location 1 calibration pose, perimeter traversal beginning and ending at location 2, location 2–4 and back, location 3–5 and back

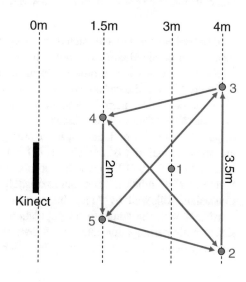

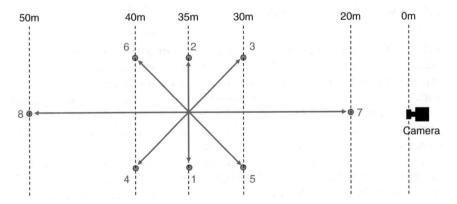

Fig. 2.9 Outdoor SWIR collection layout. Walking paths: location 1–2 and back, location 3–4 and back, location 5–6 and back, location 7–8 and back

Fig. 2.10 Kinect sample image (*left*) and SWIR sample image (*right*)

Data collection was completed on December 4, 2011, with gait and soft biometric data obtained from 157 individuals.

Figure 2.11 provides a breakdown of the participant demographics.

Figure 2.11a indicates an average of ∼14 participants per week throughout the 11-week collection period, with peak participation between October 24th and October 30th. Thanksgiving break and the corresponding university closure is responsible for the null participation during 11/21 through 11/27. Figure 2.11b indicates the majority of participants (71 %) were between 20 and 29 years of age, followed by 18–19 (12 %) which is consistent with student and faculty populations. Figure 2.11c indicates that approximately half (46 %) of participants were Caucasian, followed by Asian Indian (23 %). This demographic distribution is consistent with the student/staff population of WVU. Figure 2.11d shows a consistent male participation rate over female for all ethnicities with the exclusion of unknown/non-identified ethnicities (in which case was equal participation).

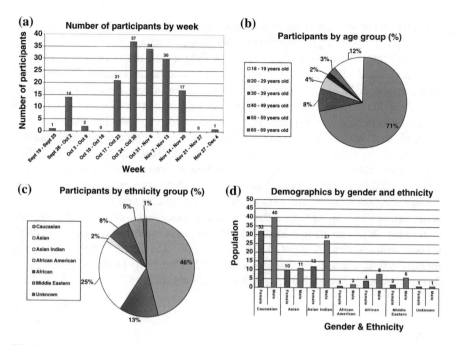

Fig. 2.11 Participant demographics for SWIR gait collection

This dataset was used to developed gait-based approaches to human identification. The results presented in [26] indicate 15–20 % rank 1 identification accuracy and 35–45 % rank 10 identification accuracy for algorithms based on gait energy image (GEI), gait curves, and Frieze pattern matching. Although the performance numbers of all three algorithms are significantly less than the numbers published for existing CASIA gait datasets, these results were obtained from gait data collected in an unconstrained outdoor environment (silhouette quality of WVU is ≈39 % and ≈64 % of the values for the CASIA B and C datasets), and should be viewed as foundational work in the area of SWIR gait recognition under uncontrolled conditions.

2.6   Summary and Conclusions

Face image capture in low-lighting conditions is made possible through SWIR-imaging hardware and novel cross-spectral face recognition algorithms. The development and refinement of cross-spectral face recognition systems is enabled by the collection of both visible and SWIR face images in controlled and operational or difficult conditions. This chapter has provided several examples of data collection efforts for multispectral SWIR face and gait capture, both indoors and outdoors and at varying standoff distances (2–350 m), along with initial results of matching experiments performed using the collected data.

Introducing non-idealities (e.g.: very low light levels, tinted materials, and long distances) into the data collection process *supplements* facial imagery data collected under ideal conditions, and *allows for* a larger range of operational scenarios to be considered in matching experiments. Gait recognition in the SWIR may also be used in cases where face image quality is not sufficient for confident identification.

While that datasets discussed in this chapter have been used in various academic publications to answer different research questions, there are still challenges that need to be mitigated, especially when related to image restoration efforts and cross-spectral face- and gait-matching activities. These challenges can be overcome through continued use of the existing datasets, supplemented by data acquired in additional collection activities that introduce non-ideal environmental factors. Continued collection of non-ideal face images, leveraged by advances in SWIR sensor technologies (e.g., GA1280JSX High Resolution High Sensitivity InGaAs SWIR Camera by Sensors Unlimited (Goodrich) [18]), is necessary to further mature this emerging area of biometrics research.

References

1. Kalka, N.D., Bourlai, T., Cukic, B., Hornak, L.: Cross-spectral face recognition in heterogeneous environments: a case study on matching visible to short-wave infrared imagery. In: International Joint Conference on Biometrics, 2011
2. Zhu, J.-Y., Zheng, W.-S., Lai, J.-H., Li, S.Z.: Matching NIR face to VIS face using transduction. IEEE Trans. Inf. Forensics Secur. 9(3), 1556–6013 (2014)
3. Klare, B., Jain, A.K.: Heterogeneous face recognition: matching NIR to visible light images. In: IEEE International Conference on Pattern Recognition, pp. 1513–1516 (2010)
4. Chang, H.: Multispectral imaging for face recognition over varying illumination. Ph.D. dissertation, Department of Electrical Engineering and Computer Science, University of Tennessee, TN (2008)
5. Bourlai, T., Chen, C., Ross, A., Hornak, L.: A study on using mid-wave infrared images for face recognition. SPIE Biometric Technol. Hum. Ident. 9, 83711K (2012)
6. Osia, N., Bourlai, T.: Holistic and partial face recognition in the MWIR band using manual and automatic detection of face-based features. In: IEEE Conference on Technologies for Homeland Security (HST), pp. 273–279 (2012)
7. Mendez, H., San Martin, C., Kittler, J., Plasencia, Y., Garcia-Reyes, E.: Face recognition with LWIR imagery using local binary patterns. In: Advances in Biometrics, pp. 327–336 (2009)
8. Short, N., Hu, S., Gurram, P., Gurton, K., Chan, A.: Improving cross-modal face recognition using polarimetric imaging. Opt. Lett. 40(6) (2015)
9. Gurton, K.P., Yuffa, A.J., Videen, G.W.: Enhanced facial recognition for thermal imagery using polarimetric imaging. Opt. Lett. 39(13), 3857–3859 (2014)
10. Hu, S., Choi, J., Chan, A.L., Schwartz, W.R.: Thermal-to-visible face recognition using partial least squares. J. Opt. Soc. Am. A 32(3), 431–442 (2015)
11. Martin, R.B., Sluch, M., Kafka, K.M., Ice, R., Lemoff, B.E.: Active-SWIR signatures for long-range night/day human detection and identification. In: SPIE, vol. 8734 (2013)

12. Lemoff, B.E., Martin, R.B., Sluch, M., Kafka, K.M., McCormick, W., Ice, R.: Long-range night/day human identification using active-SWIR imaging. In: SPIE: Infrared Technology and Applications, vol. 8704 (2013)
13. Nicolò, F., Schmid, N.A.: Long range cross-spectral face recognition: matching SWIR against visible light images. IEEE: Trans. Inf. Forensics Secur. 7(6), 1717–1726 (2012)
14. Narang, N., Bourlai, T.: Can we match ultraviolet face images against their visible counterparts? In: Algorithms and Technologies for Multispectral, Hyperspectral, and Ultra-spectral Imagery XXI, SPIE (Defense+Security), Baltimore, MD, April 2015
15. Bourlai, T., VonDollen, J., Mavridis, N., Kolanko, C.: Evaluating the efficiency of a nighttime, middle-range infrared sensor for applications in human detection and recognition. In: SPIE, Infrared Imaging Systems: Design, Analysis, Modeling, and Testing XXIII, Baltimore, USA, April 2012
16. Chang, H., Yao, Y., Koschan, A., Abidi, B., Abidi, M.: Spectral range selection for face recognition under various illuminations. In: Proceedings of IEEE International Conference on Image Processing, pp. 2756–2759 (2008)
17. Whitelam, C., Bourlai, T.: On designing SWIR to visible face matching algorithms. Intel Technol. J. 18(4), 98–118 (2014)
18. Goodrich (UTAS): Defense File, 06 April 2010 [Online]. http://www.defensefile.com/News_Detail_Lightweight_swir_sensor_for_target_detection_on_board_uav_equipment_7430.asp
19. Dowdall, J., Pavlidis, I., Bebis, G.: Face detection in the near-IR spectrum. Image Vis. Comput. 21, 565–578 (2003)
20. http://www.nist.gov/itl/ansi/upload/Approved-Std-20070427-2.pdf
21. Ice, J., Narang, N., Whitelam, C., Kalka, N., Hornak, L., Dawson, J., Bourlai, T.: SWIR imaging for facial image capture through tinted materials. In: Proceedings of SPIE, vol. 8353, p. 83530S (2012)
22. Hansen, M.P., Malchow, D.S.: Overview of SWIR detectors, cameras, and applications. Proc. SPIE 6939, 69390I–69390I-11 (2008)
23. John, J., Zimmermann, L., Merken, P., Borghs, G., Van Hoof, C.A., Nemeth, S.: Extended Backside-illuminated InGaAs on GaAs IR Detectors. Proc. SPIE 4820, 453–459 (2003)
24. Kalka, N.D., Bourlai, T., Cukic, B., Hornak, L.: Cross-spectral face recognition in heterogeneous environments: a case study of matching visible to short-wave infrared imagery. In: International Joint Conference on Biometrics (IEEE, IAPR), 2011
25. Zuo, J., Nicolo, F., Schmid, N.A., Boothapati, S.: Encoding, matching and score normalization for cross spectral face recognition: matching SWIR versus visible data. In: IEEE Conference on Biometrics Theory, Applications and Systems (BTAS 2012)
26. DeCann, B., Ross, A., Dawson, J.M.: Investigating gait recognition in the short-wave infrared (SWIR) spectrum: dataset and challenges. In: Proceedings of SPIE 8712, Biometric and Surveillance Technology for Human and Activity Identification, X, 87120J, May 31, 2013
27. Pan, Z., Healey, G.E., Prasad, M., Tromberg, B.J.: Hyperspectral face recognition under variable outdoor illumination. In: Proceedings of SPIE International Society of Optical Engineering (OE), Orlando, FL, USA, April
28. Whitelam, C., Bourlai, T.: Accurate eye localization in the short waved infrared spectrum through summation range filters. J. Comput. Vis. Image Underst. (CVIU) 139, 59–72 (2015)
29. Whitelam, C., Bourlai, T.: On designing an unconstrained tri-band pupil detection system for human identification. J. Mach. Vis. Appl. 1–19 (2015)
30. Narang, N., Bourlai, T.: Face recognition in the SWIR band when using single sensor multi-wavelength imaging systems. J Image Vis. Comput. 33, 26–43 (2015)
31. Kang, J., Borkar, A., Yeung, A., Nong, N., Smith, M., Hayes, M.: Short wavelength infrared face recognition for personalization. In: Proceedings of the IEEE International Conference on Image Processing (ICIP'06), pp. 2757–2760, October 2006, Atlanta, GA
32. Ngo, H.T., Ives, R.W., Matey, J.R., Dormo, J., Rhoads, M., Choi, D.: Design and implementation of a multispectral iris capture system. In: Signals, Systems, and Computers, 2009 Conference Record of the Forty-Third Asilomar Conference on, pp. 380–384, IEEE Piscataway, NJ (2009)

33. Steiner, H., Sporrer, S., Kolb, A., Jung, N.: Design of an active multispectral SWIR camera system for skin detection and face verification. J. Sens., Article ID 456368 (2015)
34. Pavlidis, I., Symosek, P.: The imaging issue in an automatic face/disguise detection system. In: Proceedings of IEEE Workshop Computer Vision Beyond the Visible Spectrum: Methods and Applications, pp. 15–24 (2000)
35. Jacquez, J.A., Huss, J., Mckeehan, W., Dimitroff, J.M., Kuppenheim, H.F.: Spectral reflectance of human skin in the region 0.7–2.6μm. J. Appl. Physiol. **8**(3), 297–299 (1955)
36. Bertozzi, M., Fedriga, R., Miron, A., Reverchon, J.-L.: Pedestrian detection in poor visibility conditions: would SWIR help? In: Petrosino, A. (ed.) Image Analysis and Processing—ICIAP 2013, vol. 8157 of Lecture Notes in Computer Science, pp. 229–238. Springer, Berlin (2013)
37. Lemoff, B.E., Martin, R.B., Sluch, M., Kafka, K.M., Dolby, A., Ice, R.: Automated, long-range, night/day, active-SWIR face recognition system. In: 40th Infrared Technology and Applications, vol. 9070 of Proceedings of SPIE, pp. 907031-1–907031-10, Baltimore, Md, USA, June 2014
38. Zhou, Q., Xu, Z., Liao, S., Wei, J.: Morphological modified global thresholding and 8 adjacent neighborhood labeling for SWIR image mosaic. In: International Conference on Optoelectronics and Image Processing (ICOIP), 2010, vol. 2, pp. 19, 23, 11–12 Nov 2010

Chapter 3
Hyperspectral Face Databases for Facial Recognition Research

Woon Cho, Andreas Koschan and Mongi A. Abidi

Abstract Spectral imaging (SI) enables us to collect various spectral information at specific wavelengths by dividing the spectrum into multiple bands. As such, SI offers a means to overcome several major challenges specific to current face recognition systems. However, the practical usage of hyperspectral face recognition (HFR) has, to date, been limited due to database restrictions in the public domain for comparatively evaluating HFR. In this chapter, we review four publically available hyperspectral face databases (HFDs): CMU, PolyU-HSFD, IRIS-M, and Stanford databases toward providing information on the key points of each of the considered databases. In addition, a new large HFD, called IRIS-HFD-2014, is introduced. IRIS-HFD-2014 can serve as a benchmark for statistically evaluating the performance of current and future HFR algorithms and will be made publicly available.

3.1 Introduction

To construct robust techniques for face recognition, numerous approaches to deal with the challenging factors specific to appearance variations have been proposed. However, there still exist serious challenges in uncontrolled conditions; e.g., unrestrained lighting, range of facial expressions, pose variations, and accessories. These challenges have motivated face recognition research, but as of yet, research has to reach a mature stage of contending with challenges that occur specific to the

W. Cho (✉) · A. Koschan · M.A. Abidi
Department of Electrical Engineering and Computer Science, University of Tennessee,
37996-2250 Knoxville, TN, USA
e-mail: wcho@utk.edu

A. Koschan
e-mail: akoschan@utk.edu

M.A. Abidi
e-mail: abidi@utk.edu

© Springer International Publishing Switzerland 2016
T. Bourlai (ed.), *Face Recognition Across the Imaging Spectrum*,
DOI 10.1007/978-3-319-28501-6_3

aforementioned highly unpredictable and uncertain circumstances [1]. Several of
the major challenges specific to current face recognition systems result from variations in illumination condition [2–12]. Since the radiance utilized by face recognition system is proportional to the product of surface albedo and incident
illumination, it is heavily dependent on illumination conditions. However, illumination conditions are not static, and as such, illumination variations are frequently
occurring. Such illumination variations continually change the appearance of facial
images and, accordingly, challenge the performance abilities of existing face
recognition systems to produce accurate results. One viable way to address this
complexity of face recognition is to incorporate spectral information gained from SI
modalities [2–9, 11–13].

SI enables us to collect a rich variety of spectral information at specific wavelengths by dividing the spectrum into multiple bands. The composite images
acquired in different sub-bands for each spatial location of interest carry spectral
reflectance information that is of particular relevance to illumination invariants [9,
14]. SI techniques incorporate conventional imaging and spectroscopic techniques
in order to attain both spatial and spectral information at the same time [14].
Compared with traditional broadband images captured by trichromatic (RGB) color
or monochromatic (grayscale) cameras, SI can be comprised of a large number of
wavelength-indexed channels or bands [9] as illustrated in Fig. 3.1. Each spectral
image is referred to as two-dimensional intensity data obtained over each of the
different spectral bands. Hence, if all the spectral images are stacked directionally
vertical or horizontal, spectral images model a three dimensional cube: two spatial
dimensions corresponding to the coordinates of pixel on the image lattice and one
spectral dimension corresponding to the wavelength [9].

The terms "multispectral" and "hyperspectral" imaging can be distinguished by
the number of spectral bands and how narrow/wide the bands are [14].

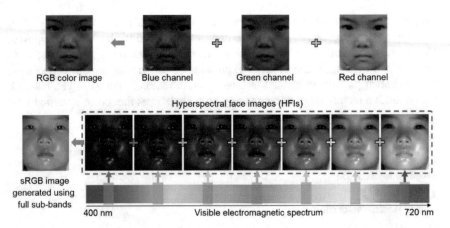

Fig. 3.1 Comparison between a traditional broadband facial image captured by a RGB color
camera and hyperspectral face images (HFIs) covering the visible spectral range from 420 to
700 nm

Multispectral sensors typically provide a few wide bands such as three channels (red, green, and blue) and infrared bands, while hyperspectral sensors measure energy in narrower and more numerous bands than multispectral sensors. Hyperspectral images can contain as many as 200 (or more) contiguous spectral bands. We refer the interested reader to [15–17] for more detail on multispectral face databases.

When SI is applied to face recognition systems, we believe that SI can reveal distinct patterns contained in human faces where such discriminative patterns cannot be captured by trichromatic or monochromatic cameras. Thus, by employing SI, the objects can be identified by the spectral properties of facial tissues measured over the visible spectrum and beyond [9, 12].

The development of HFDs has, to date, received minimal attention due to (1) the high cost of hyperspectral sensors compared to a trichromatic or monochromatic camera and (2) the considerable time and effort required for building HFD. Based on the foregoing reasons, there are few publicly available HFDs that comparatively evaluate face recognition algorithms. In Table 3.1, we list the acronyms used in this chapter, and Table 3.2 shows an overview of HFDs considered in this chapter.

Table 3.1 Summary of acronyms used in this chapter

Acronyms	Definitions
AOTF	Acousto-optic tunable filter
ETF	Electronically tunable filter
HFD	Hyperspectral face database
HFI	Hyperspectral face image
HFR	Hyperspectral face recognition
LCTF	Liquid crystal tunable filter
NIR	Near-infrared
SI	Spectral imaging
SNR	Signal-to-noise ratio
SPD	Spectral power distribution

Table 3.2 Overview of hyperspectral face databases in this chapter

Database	# of Subjects	Conditions	Spectral range (nm)	Link
CMU	54	Illumination direction and time delay	450–1100	[29]
IRIS-M	82	Illumination conditions and time delay	480–720	[21]
PolyU-HSFD	25	Pose and time delay	400–720	[22]
Stanford	45	Viewing distance	415–950	[30]
IRIS-HFD-2014	130	Accessory, pose, and time delay	420–700	[21]

We individually analyze four publically available HFDs: the CMU, IRIS-M, PolyU-HSFD, and the Stanford database toward providing reviews in subsequent sections. In Sect. 3.6, we introduce IRIS-HFD-2014, a new hyperspectral face database recently developed by the IRIS Laboratory at the University of Tennessee, which incorporates adjusted exposure time at each wavelength. Without adjusting appropriate exposure time at each wavelength, spectral information of SI systems cannot always be sufficiently captured due to lower transmittances of the SI sensors and lower intensities of synthetic and natural lights at specific wavelengths as mentioned in [12]. In Sect. 3.7, we guide the direction of future research involving the overview of the studied databases and draw conclusions.

3.2 CMU Database

The CMU database [13], collected at the Carnegie Mellon University, is comprised of hyperspectral images of 54 diverse faces covering the visible and near-infrared (NIR) ranges from 450 to 1100 nm in 10 nm steps (65 spectral bands). The hyperspectral imaging system is configured as shown in Fig. 3.2. Three light sources are placed at −45° (Fig. 3.2b), 0° (Fig. 3.2c), and +45° (Fig. 3.2d) according to the target (Fig. 3.2a). Each light source, individually and in tandem, can be configured to on/off status. The light status determines the illumination direction and, accordingly, results in differences specific to facial appearance. The hyperspectral face database (640 × 480 pixels) in frontal view was captured by acousto-optic tunable filters (AOTFs) under 600 W halogen lamps in a studio.

Fig. 3.2 Hyperspectral imaging system of the CMU database [13]: **a** target, **b–d** light sources placed at −45°, 0°, and +45° according (**a**), and **e** hyperspectral imaging sensor

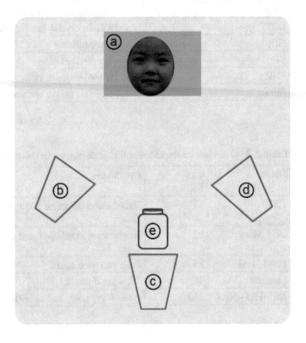

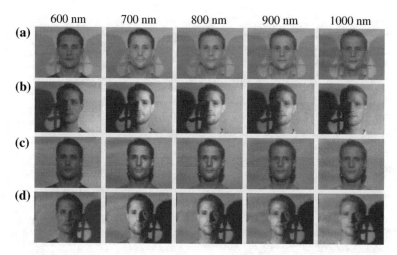

Fig. 3.3 CMU database: example of four different datasets gathered under four different illumination directions. The images taken from [29] are sampled in the range of 600–1000 nm in 100-nm intervals. **a** All light sources are turned on. **b** The left light source is turned on. **c** The center light source is turned on. **d** The right light source is turned on

AOTFs are electro-optical devices that include an optically transparent crystal bonded to a transducer that generates a high-frequency acoustic wave propagating the crystal. As the incoming light reaches the crystal, concurrently a radio-frequency acoustic wave propagates the crystal. During this process, the acoustic wave affects a variation in the refractive index, consequently performing as transmission diffraction. The selection of the specific wavelength can be controlled by adjusting the frequency of the acoustic wave [9]. The CMU database, utilizing a hyperspectral sensor, considered the effects of varying illumination directions on facial appearance. In addition, the facial data in the CMU database were taken during multiple sessions over a period of several weeks (approximately two months). As shown in Fig. 3.3, this database provides four different hyperspectral face datasets per each data subject; datasets were gained under varying illumination directions. Each of the hyperspectral face images can be aligned by using a 2D similarity transform (rotation, translation, and scale) [18] based on the eye coordinates distributed with the CMU database.

3.3 IRIS-M Database

Chang [3] created the IRIS-M database at the University of Tennessee which consists of 82 data subjects reflecting different ethnicities, ages, facial hair characteristics, and genders; hyperspectral facial data were gathered over 10 sessions. The IRIS-M database was developed in two different environments (see Fig. 3.4):

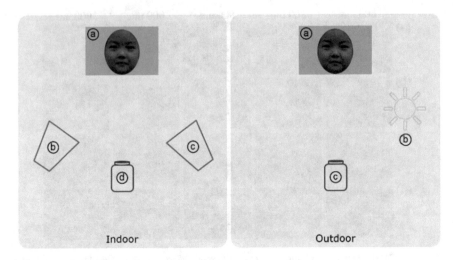

Fig. 3.4 Hyperspectral imaging system used to obtain the IRIS-M database. The *left figure* shows
a target, **b** and **c** light sources, and **d** hyperspectral imaging sensor. The *right figure* shows **a** target,
b natural illuminant (sun), and **c** hyperspectral imaging sensor

(1) indoor environment under either two halogen or two fluorescent lamps and
(2) outdoor environment under daylight. The spectral power distributions (SPDs) of
four different illuminants utilized in the IRIS-M database are shown in Fig. 3.5. The
IRIS-M database (640 × 480 pixels) in frontal view was collected by a
VariSpec VIS liquid crystal tunable filter (LCTF) in the visible spectral range from
480 to 720 nm in steps of 10 nm (25 bands) and by a Raytheon Palm-IR Pro
camera[1] for thermal infrared images.

As one of the electronically tunable filters (ETFs), LCTF is comprised of a set of
liquid crystal wave plates to tune a specific wavelength. LCTF offers a linear optical
path by polarizing a stack of wave plates and provides the ability to select any
wavelength in visible range or NIR range. Whereas LCTF is sensitive to polarization
and has intrinsic limitations specific to relaxation time of polarizing a stack of wave
plates for tuning a wavelength about 5–50 ms, LCTF is one of the most commonly
used ETFs for three main reasons [9]: (1) Light transmission is rapidly and readily
handled by electrical applications with a universal serial bus (USB) interface; (2) no
vibration occurs as adjusting a specific wavelength; and (3) LCTF supports a large
aperture and high image quality resulting from low spectral distortions. The RGB
images (2272 × 1704 pixels) in the IRIS-M database were captured by a Sony XC-75
camera.[2] In the development of the IRIS-M database, the effects of variations in
illuminant and time delay on the facial skin from hyperspectral and thermal imaging
were studied. Examples are shown in Fig. 3.6.

---

[1]http://www.palmir250.com/ir250pro.htm.
[2]http://www.subtechnique.com/sony/PDFs/xc-7573e.pdf.

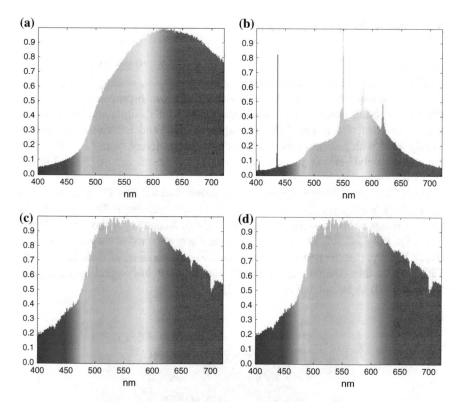

Fig. 3.5 The normalized SPDs in terms of four different light sources utilized in the IRIS-M database. The figures are taken from [9]. **a** Halogen. **b** Fluorescent 1. **c** Fluorescent 2. **d** Daylight

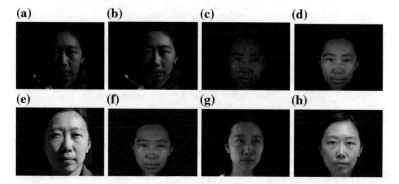

Fig. 3.6 HFIs in the IRIS-M database taken from [9]: **a** and **b** outdoor HFIs at 640 and 720 nm under daylight; **c** and **d** indoor HFIs at 640 and 720 nm under halogen lights; **e–h** gray images under daylight, halogen, fluorescent 1, and fluorescent 2, respectively, with regard to four different light sources employed in the IRIS-M database

3.4 PolyU-HSFD Database

The Hong Kong Polytechnic University Hyperspectral Face Database (PolyU-HSFD) [8] consists of 25 data subjects of Asian descent, ranging in age of years (21–38) and multiple genders (8 females and 17 males). It primarily considers the effects of varying poses on the facial appearance: frontal, right, and left view of a subject as illustrated in Fig. 3.7. The angles of right and left views are approximately ±45° with respect to the frontal subject, respectively. Sample sequences of the indoor PolyU-HSFD in three different poses are shown in Figs. 3.8, 3.9, and 3.10.

Each facial set (300 hyperspectral image cubes, 180 × 220 × 33 voxels) obtained by a CRI's VariSpec LCTF under a halogen light contains a 33-channel hyperspectral image in 10 nm steps from 400 to 720 nm. According to the data collection dates, the PolyU-HSFD provides four different sets obtained at roughly one month intervals. Note that the first six bands (400–450 nm) and the last three bands (690–720 nm) in this database are rejected due to very low signal-to-noise ratios (SNR < 6 db) as mentioned in [8, 11, 12].

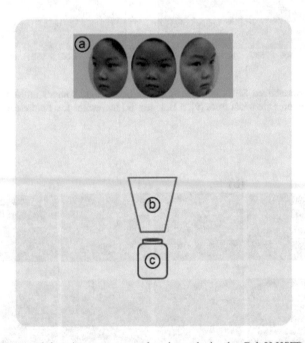

Fig. 3.7 Hyperspectral imaging system employed to obtain the PolyU-HSFD database [8]: (**a**) target in three different poses, (**b**) light source, and (**c**) hyperspectral imaging sensor

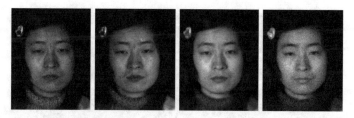

Fig. 3.8 HFI sequences of PolyU-HSFD frontal views where HFIs are sampled for every 50 nm step in the range from 500 to 650 nm. These sample images are taken from [22]

Fig. 3.9 HFI sequences of PolyU-HSFD right views where HFIs are sampled for every 50 nm step in the range from 500 to 650 nm. These sample images are taken from [22]

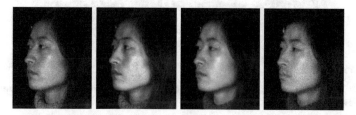

Fig. 3.10 HFI sequences of PolyU-HSFD left views where HFIs are sampled for every 50 nm step in the range from 500 to 650 nm. These sample images are taken from [22]

3.5   Stanford Database

The indoor Stanford database consists of 45 data subjects. It was established by Skauli and Farrell [19] and was acquired by a HySpex line-scan imaging spectrometers[3] under studio tungsten light. The HySpex camera is a pushbroom sensor developed at NEO. The primary advantage of the pushbroom sensor [14] is that it is able to collect all of the spectra relevant to each individual line, employing a line-by-line imaging collection approach. Nevertheless, the push broom sensor suffers from spectral distortion and is also heavily sensitive to a subject's movement, as shown in Fig. 3.11, as one line of the scene of interest is scanned at a time.

---

[3]http://www.neo.no/hyspex/.

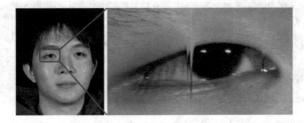

Fig. 3.11 Example of an artifact in Stanford database resulting from eye blinking during data acquisition. This sample image is taken from [30]

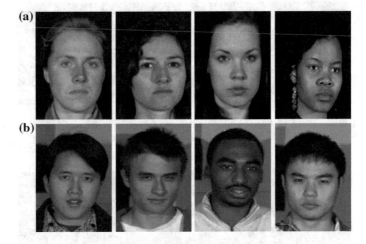

Fig. 3.12 Sample sRGB images in the Stanford database taken from [30]. **a** 1 m viewing distance. **b** 3 m viewing distance

The Stanford database in frontal view contains 148 bands spanning the visible and NIR range from 415 to 950 nm in steps of 4 nm. The Stanford database considered the effects of the variations in scale based on the viewing distance from a face to a detector (1–3 m) specific to hyperspectral face images. In Fig. 3.12, the samples of Stanford database in different viewing conditions are shown where they are displayed using sRGB values rendered under the CIE illuminant D65 [20]. The hyperspectral face data are denoted in an $n \times m \times w$ matrix: n corresponds to the number of rows in an image, m corresponds to the number of columns in an image, and w corresponds to the number of spectral bands (about 148 bands). Varying the number of rows and columns of an image for each subject is dependent on the scanning time. Moreover, the Stanford database provides software[4] to load and analyze hyperspectral face data in MATLAB.

---

[4]http://scien.stanford.edu/index.php/s_scenefrommultispectral-m/.

3.6   IRIS-HFD-2014

A new large HFD, IRIS-HFD-2014, was recently developed over multiple sessions in the IRIS Laboratory at the University of Tennessee. Similar to the PolyU-HSFD and the IRIS-M databases, an LCTF was employed to acquire the HFIs covering the visible spectral range from 420 to 700 nm in 10-nm intervals (29 narrow-bands). As shown in Fig. 3.13a, b, the IRIS-M database [21] and the PolyU-HSFD [22], both acquired with constant exposure time over the visible spectral range, introduce challenges to extract spectral properties from facial tissue used for facial discrimination at specific bands due to lower intensities and lower SNRs. Compared to the IRIS-M and the PolyU-HSFD, IRIS-HFD-2014 provides more spectral information captured by adjusting exposure time at each wavelength as shown in Fig. 3.13c. IRIS-HFD-2014 is designed to address several challenging problems in face recognition research, including, but not limited to, variations in time, pose (both frontal and profile views), and structural features (e.g., glasses). In addition, the database contains RGB color images of 116 data subjects. These images were captured by a traditional color camera with uncontrolled settings under varying illumination conditions; the resulting images were unfocused. IRIS-HFD-2014 consists of a total of 14,832 facial images of 130 data subjects; data subjects include 86 males and 44 females of several ethnic background and appearance. In short, IRIS-HFD-2014 includes (1) hyperspectral images of 130 individuals in three different neutral poses without glasses (frontal view, 45° left profile, and 45° right profile); (2) hyperspectral images of 51 individuals wearing glasses; and (3) RGB color images corresponding to the scenarios mentioned in (1) and (2).

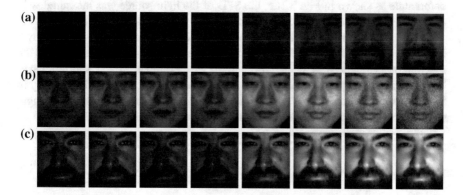

Fig. 3.13 Comparison of three HFDs using LCTFs: (**a**) the IRIS-M database [21], (**b**) the PolyU-HSFD [22], and (**c**) the IRIS-HFD-2014. The HFIs are covered by a range of 480–690 nm in 30-nm intervals. While (**a**) and (**b**) were acquired with constant exposure time over the visible spectral range, (**c**) was acquired with adjusted exposure times

3.6.1 Data Acquisition and Calibration

The practical usage of HFR has, to date, been limited due to the limited number of publically available databases for comparatively evaluating HFR algorithms. Thus, the purpose of the new database presented in this chapter is to meet the demands for a HFD that can serve as a benchmark for comprehensively and statistically evaluating the performance of current and future algorithms for HFR. From December 2013 to February 2014, IRIS-HFD-2014 was collected from 86 males (66 %) and 44 females (34 %), a total of 130 data subject participants representing several ethnic groups: 70 Caucasians (C), 40 Asians (A), 6 of African descent (AD), 6 of Middle Eastern descent (ME), 5 Asian Indians (AI), 2 Hispanics (H), and 1 Native American (NA). Figure 3.14 shows the summary of gender and ethnic diversities in IRIS-HFD-2014.

The configuration of the hyperspectral imaging systems is established, as shown in Fig. 3.15, where each of the hyperspectral imaging modules is displayed in Fig. 3.16. The HFD was acquired using an X-rite ColorChecker Classic[5] placed to the side of the individuals (Fig. 3.15) to allow the calibration and analysis of facial color. The VariSpec VIS LCTF[6] in Fig. 3.16a was mounted in front of a detector. Between the LCTF and the detector, a 25-mm fixed focal length lens was equipped, supporting a wide aperture of f/0.95. For the detector, a 1.3 megapixel monochrome 12 bit XIMEA xiQ usb3.0 camera[7] supporting a resolution of 1280 × 1024 pixels was employed. As a light source (Fig. 3.16b), a Lumia 5.1 Reef version[8] was used with 5 channel LEDs: (1) neutral white, (2) royal blue, (3) hyper violet, (4) deep red and turquoise, and (5) true violet and cool blue. Figure 3.17 shows the SPD of the light source for each channel where each channel can manually be controlled to on/off state as shown in Fig. 3.16c; the SPD of the light source was measured with an Ocean Optics Model USB2000 spectrometer[9] shown in Fig. 3.16d.

As the spectral transmittance of the LCTF decreases from long-to-short wavelengths, it is beneficial to properly adjust the camera exposure time according to the spectral transmittances at each wavelength. For example, at the shorter wavelengths, a longer exposure time is set in order to accumulate more radiant energy in the detector. Furthermore, to gain more radiant power in the short wavelength regions, the 4th channel of the light source is disabled (see Fig. 3.17).

---

[5]http://xritephoto.com/ph_product_overview.aspx?id=1192.

[6]http://www.spectralcameras.com/varispec.

[7]http://www.ximea.com/en/usb3-vision-camera/xiq.

[8]http://www.ledgroupbuy.com/lumia-5-1-100w-full-spectrum-5-channel-led/.

[9]http://oceanoptics.com/product/usb2000-custom/.

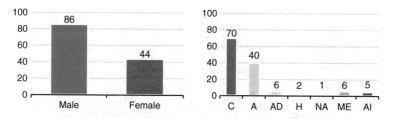

Fig. 3.14 Summary of gender and ethnic diversities in IRIS-HFD-2014

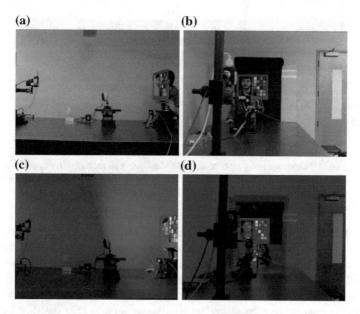

Fig. 3.15 (a) Lateral and (b) rear view of the data acquisition system when the light source is turned off; (c) lateral and (d) rear view when the light source is turned on

To determine a proper exposure time for each wavelength, the ColorChecker card was first replaced with an X-Rite ColorChecker Grayscale card[10] located to the right side, respectively, of the detector. Next, the brightest region was selected as a region of interest (ROI) within the white target of the Grayscale card where the size of the ROI was set to 100 × 100 pixels throughout the experiments. Then, the exposure time was increased until the average of the intensity values within the ROI reached about 86 % of the camera saturation value [23]. Figure 3.18a shows the SPD of the Lumia 5.1 Reef when the 4th channel was turned off. Figure 3.18b elucidates the adjusted exposure times at each wavelength during data acquisition.

---

[10]http://xritephoto.com/ph_product_overview.aspx?ID=1234.

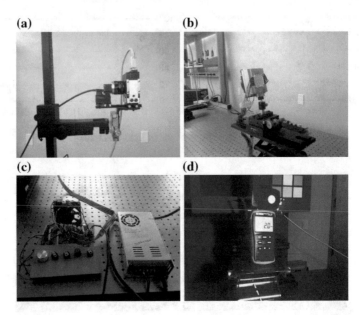

Fig. 3.16 The hyperspectral imaging modules. (**a**) VariSpec VIS mounted in front of XIMEA xiQ USB3.0 camera, (**b**) Lumia 5.1 Reef, (**c**) a controller for the light source, and (**d**) EasyView30 light meter and Ocean Optics USB2000

After proper exposure times were determined for each wavelength, dark current images were acquired using the same exposure time corresponding to the wavelengths by placing a cap on the front of the LCTF. To remove constant noises exhibited by CCD imagers depending on exposure duration, dark current images were subtracted from the radiance images. Then, the maximum intensity values of the radiance images were computed at each wavelength within the ROI located at the same position. The reflectance images were recovered by dividing the radiance images by the estimated maximum values at each wavelength [10]. Sample HFIs with the ColorChecker, after the process of recovering the reflectance images from the radiance images in each pose, are shown in Fig. 3.19. The images in the profile views were collected by asking the subjects to rotate their head ranging from $-45°$ to $+45°$. Figure 3.20 shows sample color images corresponding to different poses in the database.

In cases where HFIs are acquired with constant short exposure time, there is less concern about the inter-band misalignments as a subject's movement [11] is insignificant with shorter data acquisition time. Nevertheless, without properly

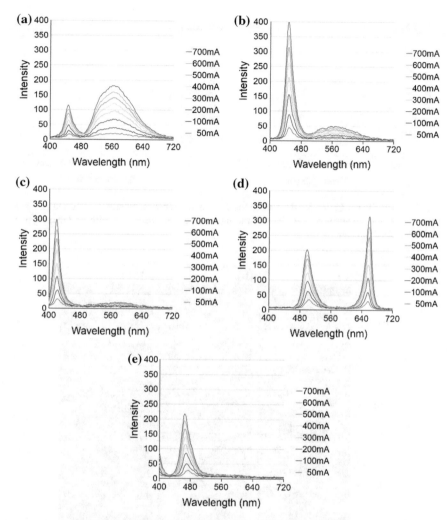

Fig. 3.17 The SPD of each channel of Lumia 5.1 Reef as increasing the current (mA) from 50 to 700 mA (best viewed in color)

adjusting the camera exposure time at each wavelength, the spectral information of SI systems suffers from two main limitations: (1) lower transmittances of the LCTF at the bands in the lower end of the visible spectral range as shown in Fig. 3.21 and (2) lower intensities of natural and synthetic lights at specific wavelengths. For example, as shown in Fig. 3.18a, the light source inherently has low intensities at 660–700 nm.

Toward addressing inter-band misalignments, a conventional approach based on eye coordinates [8, 11, 13] was used. The eye coordinate-based alignment approach is typically retained to align HFIs. For aligning HFIs, the canonical frame is set to

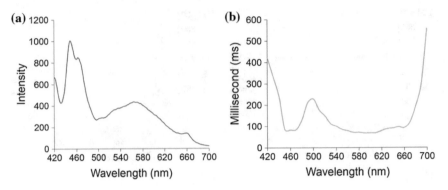

Fig. 3.18 (**a**) SPD of Lumia 5.1 Reef when the 4th channel is turned off and (**b**) adjusted exposure time during data acquisition. The SPD of the light source was measured with an Ocean Optics USB2000 spectrometer

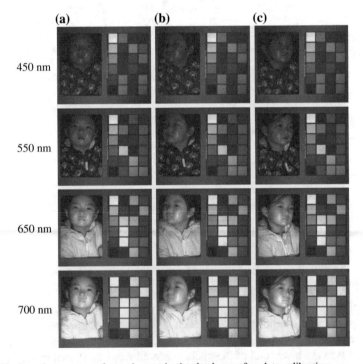

Fig. 3.19 Sample sequences for each pose in the database, after data calibration

be 140 × 160 pixels. The eye coordinates are manually selected to the middle of the eyes in each sub-band of IRIS-HFD-2014. The distance between the selected eye points is normalized to 80 pixels. Samples of aligned HFIs in three different poses are shown in Figs. 3.22, 3.23, and 3.24. Compared to the frontal view in Fig. 3.22,

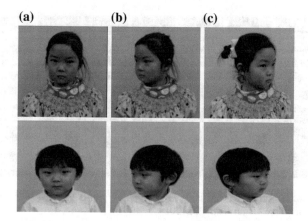

Fig. 3.20 Sample color images representing three poses in the database. **a** Frontal view. **b** Left profile. **c** Right profile

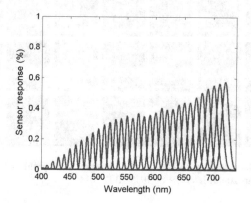

Fig. 3.21 Narrowband transmittances of a VariSpec VIS LCTF from 400 to 720 nm in 10-nm intervals

Fig. 3.22 Examples of the frontal aligned HFIs sampled in the range of 440–700 nm in 10-nm intervals on IRIS-HFD-2014

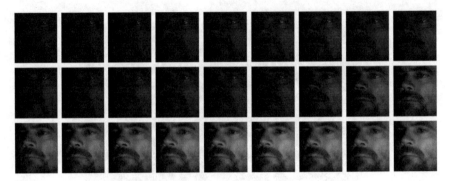

Fig. 3.23 Examples of the aligned HFIs in the 45° left profile sampled in the range of 440–700 nm in 10-nm intervals on IRIS-HFD-2014

Fig. 3.24 Examples of the aligned HFIs in the 45 degree right profile sampled in the range of 440 nm to 700 nm in 10-nm intervals on IRIS-HFD-2014

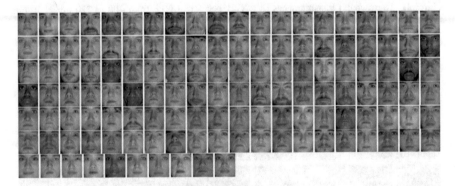

Fig. 3.25 Entire aligned datasets of IRIS-HFD-2014 in the frontal view where full sub-bands (420–700 nm in 10 nm steps) are displayed using the sRGB values rendered under a CIE illuminant D65 [10]

HFIs in both profile views shown in Figs. 3.23 and 3.24 cover a set of pose variations ranging from approximately $-45°$ to $+45°$ where pose variations introduce partial or entire occlusion of facial components including mouth, nose, or eyes. The aligned HFI pairs can be used for various evaluations of current or future face recognition algorithms to address several challenging problems in face recognition research including variations in pose (both frontal and profile views). Figure 3.25 shows all the aligned datasets in the frontal view of IRIS-HFD-2014 including several ethnic backgrounds and diverse physical appearance where full sub-bands are mapped to the sRGB values with respect to the CIE 1931 $2°$ standard observer and the CIE illuminant D65 [20].

3.7 Discussion and Conclusion

Whereas SI does address substantial challenges of face recognition systems, especially those caused by changes in lighting [2–7, 9, 10], broadly, three challenges specific to SI remain: (1) high dimensionality of spectral data; (2) inter-band misalignments when SI is applied to non-rigid objects; and (3) database restrictions in the public domain for comparatively evaluating HFR.

First, the high dimensionality of the spectral data causes limitations on physical experiments and detailed numerical analysis since spectral data include multiple sub-bands captured at each wavelength [24]. For this reason, there is a need for robust data compression techniques, specifically post-processing techniques, by means of extracting relevant basis functions from large quantities of high-dimensional spectral data. These techniques are crucial to analyze and represent a large set of spectral data and, finally, to model the processes.

Second, inter-band misalignments must be preferentially resolved to aid the subsequent processes, e.g., band selection, band fusion, and extraction of spectral features for face recognition within the compute vision community. To address inter-band misalignments in SI, conventional alignment approaches based on eye coordinates have typically been employed. However, it is difficult to consistently select the eye coordinates at the same positions by hand over a large hyperspectral face image set such as IRIS-HFD-2014. In the particular cases for the different profiles and structural feature (e.g., glasses), the conventional alignment approach should be limited due to the partial occlusion of one eye in the profile views and the problem of reflection on the glasses. Accordingly, it is necessary to develop automatic alignment approaches to deal with inter-band misalignments in HFIs.

Third, the development of HFDs has, to date, received less attention due to (1) the high cost of hyperspectral sensors compared to a trichromatic or monochromatic camera and (2) the considerable time and effort required for building HFDs. Therefore, there are few publicly available HFDs that can be used to comparatively evaluate face recognition algorithms. In this chapter, we provided a review in terms of five publicly available HFDs: CMU, IRIS-M, PolyU-HSFD, Stanford, and IRIS-HFD-2014. We note that there is one more publically available HFD, called UWA-HSFD, in preparation for being released into the public domain. UWA-HSFD consisting of 79 data subjects in the frontal view taken over 4 sessions [11, 12] was developed by the University of Western Australia.[11] Each hyperspectral image was captured by the VariSpec LCTF integrated with a photon focus camera. Each dataset of HFIs contains 33 bands covering the visible spectral range from 400 to 720 nm with 10 nm steps. As we adjusted the camera exposure time in during data acquisition, UWA-HSFD also considered the adaptation of the camera exposure time according to lower transmittances of the filter and lower illumination intensities in each band.

The robustness of the developed algorithms for HFR based on the studied databases can be verified through variations of a large number of factors: (1) face pose (PolyU-HSFD and IRIS-HFD-2014); (2) time delay (CMU, IRIS-M, PolyU-HSFD, and IRIS-HFD-2014); (3) illumination direction (CMU); (4) illumination condition (IRIS-M); (5) viewing distance (Stanford); and (6) accessory (IRIS-M and IRIS-HFD-2014). For the extraction of spectral properties of facial tissue in both the visible and the NIR ranges, CMU and Stanford databases can be used. In the case constrained to the visible range, spectral measurements of facial tissue can be achieved on IRIS-M, PolyU-HSFD, and IRIS-HFD-2014. We note that the IRIS-M database also contains 4228 pairs of visible and thermal IR face images of 30 subjects.

Although we mainly presented a study of publically available databases covering the visible and NIR spectrum in this chapter, there are three datasets in the visible and infrared spectrum particularly to evaluate cross-spectral face recognition performance (i.e., infrared-visible face recognition) [25–28]: (1) The UND Collection X1 developed by the University of Notre Dame (82 subjects in visible and LWIR imagery); (2) WSRI developed by the Wright State University (119 subjects in visible and MWIR imagery); and (3) NVESD developed by US Army Night Vision and Electronic Sensors Directorate (50 subjects in visible, MWIR, and LWIR imagery). We refer the interested reader to the paper [25] for more details.

Acknowledgement We would like to thank all the participants in IRIS-HFD-2014. This publication was made possible by NPRP grant #4-1165-2-453 from the Qatar National Research Fund (a member of Qatar Foundation). The statements made herein are solely the responsibility of the authors.

---

[11]http://www.csse.uwa.edu.au/~ajmal/.

References

1. Hua, G., Yang, M., Learned-Miller, E., Ma, Y., Turk, M., Kriegman, D., Huang, T.: Introduction to the special section on real-world face recognition. IEEE Trans. Pattern Anal. Mach. Intell. **33**, 1921–1924 (2011)
2. Bouchech, H., Foufou, S., Koschan, A., Abidi, M.: A kernelized sparsity-based approach for best spectral bands selection for face recognition. Multimedia Tools. Appl. (2014). doi:10. 1007/s11042-014-2350-2
3. Chang, H.: Multispectral imaging for face recognition over varying illumination. Ph.D. Dissertation, Department of Electrical Engineering Computer Science University of Tennessee TN (2008)
4. Chang, H., Koschan, A., Abidi, M., Kong, S., Won, C.: Multispectral visible and infrared imaging for face recognition. In: Proceedings of the IEEE Conference Computer Vision and Pattern Recognition Workshops (2008)
5. Chang, H., Yao, Y., Koschan, A., Abidi, B., Abidi M.: Spectral range selection for face recognition under various illuminations. In: Proceedings of the IEEE International Conference on Image Processing, pp. 2756–2759 (2008)
6. Chang, H., Yao, Y., Koschan, A., Abidi, B., Abidi, M.: Improving face recognition via narrowband spectral range selection using Jeffrey divergence. IEEE Trans. Inf. Forensics Secur **4**, 111–122 (2009)
7. Chang, H., Koschan, A., Abidi, B., Abidi, M.: Fusing continuous spectral images for face recognition under indoor and outdoor illuminants. Mach. Vis. Appl. **21**, 201–215 (2010)
8. Di, W., Zhang, L., Zhang, D., Pan, Q.: Studies on hyperspectral face recognition in visible spectrum with feature band selection. IEEE Trans. Syst. Man Cybern. A Syst. Humans **40**, 1354–1361 (2010)
9. Koschan, A., Yao, Y., Chang, H., Abidi, M.: Multispectral face imaging and analysis. In: Li, S., Jain, A. (eds.) *Handbook of Face Recognition*. Springer, London, pp. 401–428
10. Pan, Z., Healey, G., Prasad, M., Tromberg, B.: Face recognition in hyperspectral images. IEEE Trans. Pattern Anal. Mach. Intell. **25**, 1552–1560 (2003)
11. Uzair, M., Mahmood, A., Mian, A.: Hyperspectral face recognition using 3d-DCT and partial least squares. In: Proceedings of the British Machine Vision Conference (2013)
12. Uzair, M., Mahmood, A., Mian, A.: Hyperspectral face recognition with spatiospectral information fusion and PLS regression. IEEE Trans. Image Process. **24**, 1127–1137 (2015)
13. Denes, L., Metes, P., Liu, Y.: Hyperspectral face database. Technical Report CMU-RI-TR-02-25, Robot. Institute Carnegie Mellon University, Pittsburgh, PA (2002)
14. Robles-Kelly, A., Huynh, C.: Imaging Spectroscopy for Scene Analysis. Springer, London (2013)
15. Gross, R.: Face databases. In: Li, S., Jain, A. (eds.) Handbook of Face Recognition. Springer, London, pp. 301–327 (2004)
16. Kong, S., Heo, J., Boughorbel, F., Zheng, Y., Abidi, B.R., Koschan, A., Yi, M., Abidi, M.: Adaptive fusion of visual and thermal IR images for illumination-invariant face recognition. Int. J. Comput. Vis. **71**, 215–233 (2007)
17. CASIA HFB database. http://www.cbsr.ia.ac.cn/english/Databases.asp
18. Hasan, M., Pal, C.: Improving alignment of faces for recognition. In: Robotic and Sensors Environments, pp. 249–254 (2011)
19. Skauli, T.: Farrell, J.: A collection of hyperspectral images for imaging systems research. In: Proceedings of the SPIE 8660, Digital Photography IX (2013)
20. Stokes, M., Anderson, M., Chandrasekar, S., Motta, R.: Multimedia systems and equipment—colour measurement and management, part 2.1: colour management in multimedia systems—default RGB colour space—sRGB. In: International Electrotechnical Commission IEC 61966-2-1 (1998)
21. IRIS-M database. http://imaging.utk.edu
22. PolyU-HSFD database. http://www4.comp.polyu.edu.hk/ ∼ biometrics

23. Foster, D., Amano, K., Nascimento, S., Foster, M.: Frequency of metamerism in natural scenes. J. Opt. Soc. Am. A **23**, 2359–2372 (2006)
24. Cho, W., Sahyoun, S., Djouadi, S., Koschan, A., Abidi, M.: Reduced-order spectral data modeling based on local proper orthogonal decomposition. J. Opt. Soc. Am. A **32**, 733–740 (2015)
25. Hu, S., Choi, J., Chan, A., Schwartz, W.: Thermal-to-visible face recognition using partial least squares. J. Opt. Soc. Am. A **32**, 431–442 (2015)
26. Ice, J., Narang, N., Whitelam, C., Kalka, N., Hornak, L., Dawson, J., Bourlai, T.: SWIR imaging for facial image capture through tinted materials. In: Proceedings of the SPIE 8353 (2012)
27. Kalka, N., Bourlai, T., Cukic, B., Hornak, L.: Cross-spectral face recognition in heterogeneous environments: a case study on matching visible to short-wave infrared imagery. In: Proceedings of the International Joint Conference on Biometrics (2011)
28. Zhu, J., Zheng, W., Lai, J., Li, S.: Matching NIR face to VIS face using transduction. IEEE Trans. Inf. Forensics Secur. **9**, 1556–6013 (2014)
29. CMU database. http://www.consortium.ri.cmu.edu/hsagree/index.cgi
30. Stanford database. http://scien.stanford.edu/index.php/hyperspectral-image-data/

Chapter 4
MWIR-to-Visible and LWIR-to-Visible Face Recognition Using Partial Least Squares and Dictionary Learning

Shuowen Hu, Nathaniel J. Short, Prudhvi K. Gurram, Kristan P. Gurton and Christopher Reale

Abstract Cross-spectral face recognition, which seeks to match a face image acquired in one spectral band (e.g., infrared) to that of a face acquired in another band (e.g., visible), is a relatively new area of research in the biometrics community. Thermal-to-visible face recognition has been receiving increasing attention, due to its promising potential for low-light or nighttime surveillance and intelligence gathering applications. However, matching a thermal probe image to a visible face database is highly challenging. Thermal imaging is emission dominated, acquiring thermal radiation naturally emitted by facial tissue, while visible imaging is reflection dominated, acquiring light reflected from the surface of the face. The resulting difference between the thermal face signature and the visible face signature renders conventional algorithms designed for within-spectral matching (e.g., visible-to-visible) unsuitable for thermal-to-visible face recognition. In this chapter, two thermal-to-visible face recognition approaches are discussed: (1) a partial least squares (PLS)-based approach and (2) a dictionary learning SVM approach. Preprocessing and feature extraction techniques used to correlate the signatures in the feature subspace are also discussed. We present recognition results on an extensive multimodal face dataset containing facial imagery acquired under different experimental conditions. Furthermore, we discuss key findings and implications for MWIR-to-visible and LWIR-to-visible face recognition. Finally, a novel imaging technique for acquiring an unprecedented level of facial detail in thermal images, polarimetric LWIR, is presented along with a framework for performing cross-spectral face recognition.

S. Hu (✉) · N.J. Short · P.K. Gurram · K.P. Gurton · C. Reale
US Army Research Laboratory, Adelphi, MD, USA
e-mail: shuowen.hu.civ@mail.mil

© Springer International Publishing Switzerland (outside the USA) 2016
T. Bourlai (ed.), *Face Recognition Across the Imaging Spectrum*,
DOI 10.1007/978-3-319-28501-6_4

4.1 Introduction

Face recognition research has predominantly focused on the visible spectrum for within-spectral face recognition (i.e., matching faces acquired in the same spectral band), addressing challenges such as variations in illumination, pose, appearance, and resolution. Recently, there has been increasing interest in cross-spectral (also referred to as heterogeneous) face recognition, with the objective of matching a probe image acquired in one spectrum (e.g., infrared) to a gallery of face images acquired in another spectrum (e.g., visible). In this chapter, we focus on the emission-dominated thermal infrared bands, describing techniques to match thermal probe images to visible gallery datasets, and presenting performance evaluation results.

The thermal spectrum is dominated by emitted radiation and consists of two infrared sub-bands: mid-wave infrared (MWIR; 3–5 μm wavelength), and long-wave infrared (LWIR; 8–14 μm wavelength). In contrast, the visible spectrum consists of light with wavelength from 0.4 to 0.7 μm and is dominated by reflected radiation. Note that the near-infrared band (NIR; 0.74–1 μm wavelength) and short-wave infrared band (SWIR; 0.74–1 μm wavelength) are also reflection dominated. Figure 4.1 shows the visible, SWIR, MWIR, and LWIR face signatures of a subject. As can be observed, the emission-dominated MWIR and LWIR face signatures are similar to each other, but differ substantially from the reflection-dominated visible and SWIR face signatures. The fundamental difference in phenomenology leads to a highly challenging problem for thermal-to-visible face recognition. Successfully addressing this challenge will significantly improve

Fig. 4.1 Face signatures of a subject simultaneously acquired in the visible, SWIR, MWIR, and LWIR spectra. The spectral responses of the sensors are 0.9–1.7 μm for SWIR, 3–5 μm for MWIR, and 8–12 μm for LWIR

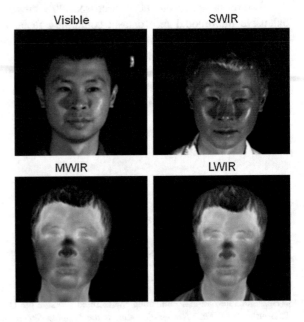

low-light or nighttime surveillance and intelligence gathering operations, when acquiring visible images is unfeasible. Developing this technology will ultimately provide the capability to surreptitiously acquire nighttime face imagery of a distant subject for identification with visible face images contained in government databases and watch lists.

In this chapter, we describe two different approaches developed to address thermal-to-visible face recognition. Both techniques involve preprocessing, followed by feature extraction, and then classification/recognition. The first approach consists of difference of Gaussian (DoG) preprocessing, histogram of oriented gradient (HOG) feature extraction, and PLS regression-based recognition. The second approach incorporates dictionary learning to learn and perform the mapping between thermal and visible feature spaces, prior to support vector machine (SVM)-based recognition. While the first approach seeks to implicitly learn the relationship between thermal and visible face signatures through PLS, the second approach explicitly maps the thermal features to the corresponding visible representation prior to recognition. We evaluate the performance of these techniques on a multispectral face database collected by US Army CERDEC-NVESD and US Army Research Laboratory. Finally, we introduce a novel face recognition technique based on polarimetric LWIR imaging, exploiting the polarization-state information of thermal radiation to acquire detailed facial features unavailable in conventional thermal imagery.

4.2   Background and Related Work

The first cross-spectral face recognition techniques focused on the reflection-dominated infrared band, specifically NIR-to-visible [1–3] and SWIR-to-visible [4–7]. Face recognition techniques in the emission-dominated thermal infrared spectrum preceded these studies, but initially focused on within-spectral (i.e., thermal-to-thermal) face recognition. Socolinsky and Selinger [8] compared the within-spectral performance of several face recognition algorithms in the visible spectrum and the LWIR band, finding that performance using LWIR face imagery was generally better than that using visible face imagery. However, the dataset employed in the study was collected under more challenging conditions for the visible spectrum than for the LWIR band [8]. Chen et al. [9], using principal component analysis (PCA) based face recognition, found that performance in the visible spectrum surpassed the performance in the thermal spectrum, especially when there was substantial time lapse between the acquisition of the gallery and probe images. When using both visible and LWIR imagery with fusion at the decision level, Chen et al. [9] demonstrated that the resulting face recognition performance was higher than achievable in either spectrum individually. For an extensive review of face recognition work in both the visible and infrared spectra, Kong et al. [10] provides a thorough examination of studies conducted prior to 2005. A physiology-based technique for within-spectral thermal face recognition was introduced by Buddharaju et al. [11], relying on more innate characteristics under the skin, which are expected to be less variable with respect to factors such as time lapse. Buddharaju et al. [11] used image morphology to localize the superficial blood vessel network and then extracted branching points, referred to as thermal minutiae, which are employed as features for a point-pattern-based face recognition approach. Though this method is effective for within-spectral matching, it cannot be readily applied to cross-spectral thermal-to-visible face recognition, due to the inability to image these blood vessels in the visible spectrum. More recently, Osia and Bourlai [12] proposed a physiological and geometric-based approach for within-spectral matching in the visible spectrum as well as the thermal (MWIR and LWIR) bands. Specifically, score-level fusion of a global matcher and a local matcher was proposed, both of which utilized extracted facial features such as veins, edges, wrinkles, and face perimeter outlines for within-spectral face recognition.

It is not until recently that cross-spectral thermal-to-visible face recognition has emerged as an area of interest in the face recognition community. Thermal-to-visible face recognition occupies a niche research area, with potential application for discreet surveillance and intelligence gathering operations in low-light or nighttime scenarios. In such scenarios, acquiring a visible face image is not feasible due to the lack of natural illumination and the need to avoid actively illuminating the scene. Therefore, acquiring the naturally emitted thermal radiation from human skin is ideal. The resulting thermal facial signature must then be matched to existing government databases and watch lists, which almost exclusively contain visible face images of individuals of interest. This necessitates the development of techniques capable of recognizing a thermal probe face image from a gallery containing only visible face images. Only a few recent studies have proposed algorithms to address this challenge.

Klare and Jain [13] proposed a nonlinear kernel prototype representation for features extracted from face images acquired in different spectra, followed by linear discriminant analysis (LDA) to enhance the discriminative capabilities of the prototype representation. They use the term heterogeneous to describe cross-spectral face recognition. Their heterogeneous face recognition framework was tested on sketch-to-photo, NIR-to-visible, and thermal-to-visible scenarios. For thermal-to-visible face recognition, Klare and Jain [13] trained on thermal–visible image pairs from 667 subjects and tested on 333 subjects, using a face database from the Pinellas County Sheriff's Office (PCSO). Furthermore, their gallery of 333 visible images from the test subjects was augmented with visible images from an additional 10,000 subjects, thus increasing the number of classes and creating a more challenging recognition problem. Klare and Jain [13] achieved a Rank-1 identification rate of 0.492 for face identification performance. For face authentication performance, their technique achieved a verification rate of 0.727 at a false alarm rate (FAR) of 0.001, and a verification rate 0.782 at FAR=0.01.

The study by Bourlai et al. [14] conducted a detailed assessment of different techniques for MWIR-to-visible face recognition, specifically evaluating the DoG and self-quotient image (SQI) preprocessing methods and six different feature

Table 4.1 List of studies in literatures on thermal-to-visible cross-spectral face recognition

Authors	Method	Database(s) used
Bourlai et al.	• DoG and SQI preprocessing • LBP, LTP, PHOG, SIFT, TPLBP, and FPLBP descriptors	50-subject WVU (MWIR)
Klare and Jain	Kernel prototype representation	1000-subject PCSO (MWIR)
Choi et al.	Partial least squares	82-Subject UND X1 (LWIR)
Hu et al.	Partial least squares + thermal cross-examples	• 82-subject UND X1 (LWIR) • 50-subject NVESD (MWIR and LWIR) • 200-subject WSRI (MWIR)

descriptors. Choi et al. [15] proposed a PLS regression-based matching framework for LWIR-to-visible face recognition, finding that DoG preprocessing and HOG feature extraction facilitated this cross-spectral matching. The extension of this PLS-based framework [16] is discussed in detail in Sects. 4.4 and 4.5 of this chapter. The list of thermal-to-visible face recognition studies reported in literature as well as the databases used for these studies are given in Table 4.1. The next section will describe these databases in more detail.

4.3   Multimodal Face Databases

Several multispectral databases containing both thermal and visible face images have been used in the previously described work to develop thermal-to-visible face recognition techniques and assess algorithm performance. The first extensive LWIR and visible face database was collected during 2002–2004 by the University of Notre Dame [9, 17], referred to as Collection X1. This database is publicly available and can be requested. It contains imagery of 82 subjects acquired under different lighting and facial expression conditions, with multiple images per subject acquired over time. However, the imager used at the time was a Merlin uncooled LWIR camera, which only has a resolution of 312 × 239 pixels. In contrast, the newer databases are acquired with higher-resolution thermal cameras. The dataset from the PCSO used by Klare and Jain [13] was acquired with a 640 × 480 pixel resolution FLIR Recon III ObserveIR camera. Bourlai et al. [14] used the FLIR SC8000 MWIR camera, which has a resolution of 1024 × 1024 pixels. Two multispectral face databases were used by Hu et al. [16]: a database from the Wright State Research Institute collected using a 640 × 512 pixel resolution FLIR SC6700 MWIR camera with a pixel pitch of 15 μm, and a database acquired by US Army CERDEC-NVESD. The work presented in the rest of this chapter primarily uses the NVESD database. The NVESD database was collected in 2012, containing simultaneously acquired face imagery in the visible, SWIR, MWIR, and LWIR

bands from a set of 50 subjects. The resolution for both the MWIR and LWIR
sensors was 640 × 480 pixels. The MWIR sensor had a pixel pitch of 12 μm, while
the LWIR sensor had a pixel pitch of 15 μm. All 50 subjects were imaged at three
different ranges: 1, 2, and 4 m. A subset of 25 subjects participated in the exercise
condition (fast walk) and were imaged at the three ranges before and after exercise.
For each acquisition, a video sequence of 15 s was collected at 30 frames per
second by all the imagers. To form the gallery set and probe set, a frame was
extracted at 1 s and another at 14 s from each acquisition.

4.4   Methodology

The thermal-to-visible face recognition algorithms discussed in this section are
composed of three distinct stages: (1) preprocessing, (2) feature extraction, and
(3) classification/matching. Preprocessing and feature extraction are addressed in
Sect. 4.1. Two different matching approaches are discussed in Sects. 4.2 and 4.3: a
PLS-based approach and a "dictionary learning + SVM"-based approach. Theory
and processing concepts for a novel face recognition imaging modality is presented
in Sect. 4.3.

4.4.1   Preprocessing and Feature Extraction

Prior to recognition, a face image must first be preprocessed, which consists of
several key steps: aligning the face to a set of canonical coordinates, cropping the
facial area, and filtering. Aligning the face to canonical coordinates is important so
that all face images are transformed to a common coordinate system. Typically,
several fiducial points (e.g., center of eyes, tip of nose, and center of mouth) are
marked in a raw face image. An affine transformation is computed and applied to
the raw face image so that these fiducial points are located at a common set of
spatial coordinates across all face images (irrespective of subject). This procedure
inherently normalizes all face images to a fixed resolution where the eye-to-eye
distance measured in pixels is the same. Following alignment, the facial region is
cropped to remove the background. The amount of cropping is subjective, but
generally varies from a loose crop (contains hair and outline of face) to a tight crop
only containing core facial region consisting of eyes, nose, and mouth [18]. The
aligned and cropped face images are typically then filtered to remove noise as well
as to reduce local variations that are detrimental to face recognition. In the visible
spectrum, illumination variations due to the position of natural or artificial lighting
sources represent a significant confound for accurate face recognition. Filtering
techniques such as SQI and DoG have been used to effectively reduce illumination
variations in visible face imagery. Since thermal imaging is emission dominated, it
is relatively unaffected by illumination conditions. However, due to face tissue

| Visible | MWIR | LWIR |

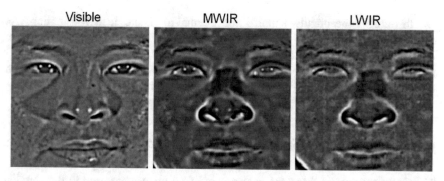

Fig. 4.2 Simultaneously acquired face images from the NVESD dataset in the visible, MWIR, and LWIR spectra after preprocessing

physiology, local variations in the form of heat patterns are present in the thermal face signature, resulting in a mottled facial appearance as can be observed in Fig. 4.1. For cross-spectral thermal-to-visible face recognition, the chosen filtering technique must be able to reduce illumination variations in the visible face image and heat pattern variations in the thermal spectrum. Choi et al. [15] compared SQI and DoG filtering for thermal-to-visible face recognition, finding that DoG filtering resulted in a substantially higher cross-spectral face identification rate. After filtering, an optional last step is to perform contrast enhancement/normalization to emphasize edges. Many contrast enhancement techniques have been developed over the years—histogram equalization-based methods such as CLAHE [19] can be used to enhance face images effectively. Note that contrast enhancement is typically not needed if the feature extraction technique (e.g., HOG) used in the next stage contains inherent normalization. Figure 4.2 shows the preprocessed face images, after alignment, tight cropping, DoG filtering, and contrast enhancement, corresponding to the respective raw intensity images shown previously in Fig. 4.1. DoG filtering reduces local illumination variations in the visible spectrum and heat pattern variations in the thermal spectrum.

The next stage after preprocessing is feature extraction, which seeks to extract relevant information that improves the discriminative capabilities of the subsequent classification/recognition stage. Choosing appropriate features is therefore critical for accurate and robust face recognition. Many different feature transforms have been developed for face recognition—local binary patterns (LBP), HOG, and Gabor features are three of the most well-known techniques. However, not all these features are suitable for cross-spectral thermal-to-visible face recognition. The LBP operator extracts texture-based facial details, which is substantially different between the thermal face signature and the visible face signature. The HOG features are edge orientation histograms formed using dense overlapping blocks [20], encoding key edge information. As can be observed in Fig. 4.2, key edges around the eyes, nose, and mouth are correlated between the thermal and visible face signatures—HOG features are therefore conceptually suitable for thermal-to-visible face recognition. As demonstrated quantitatively in the study of Choi et al. [15], HOG features do in fact outperform LBP and Gabor features for this cross-spectral scenario. Therefore, HOG features extracted from DOG filtered face images are used for the two classification approaches (PLS, dictionary learning SVM) described in Sects. 4.4.2 and 4.4.3.

4.4.2 Partial Least Squares-Based Approach

The features extracted from the preprocessed face images are used in the classification stage to recognize a thermal probe image from a gallery of visible subject images. In this section, a PLS regression method is discussed [15, 16, 21]. The PLS algorithm originated in the field of economics and was developed by Wold [22]. The PLS-based regression has been shown to be robust to multicollinearity [23], which frequently arises with high-dimensional features that are inherently correlated. Furthermore, PLS regression is also robust to sample imbalance [24], where the number of positive samples and the number of negative samples used to train a classifier are very different. Conceptually, PLS regression is highly suitable for face recognition, where the feature vectors are typically high-dimensional and the number of images per subject is substantially less than the number of subjects in the gallery.

The PLS regression algorithm seeks to find latent vectors t_i and u_i with maximal covariance by calculating a weight vector w_i according to Eq. 4.1.

$$\max \text{cov}(t_i, u_i)^2 = \max_{|w_i|=1} \text{cov}(Xw_i, y)^2 \quad i = 1, \ldots, p \qquad (4.1)$$

X is the matrix of descriptor variables, which in this work is a matrix whose rows are feature vectors of visible face images in the gallery. The vector y is the univariate response variable, a vector of class labels in this work (+1 for a positive sample, and −1 for a negative sample). A "one-vs-rest" approach is used here, generating a PLS model for each individual in the visible gallery. When building a PLS model for an individual in the gallery in the "one-vs-rest" framework, the visible images of that particular individual serve as positive samples and the visible images of the rest of the individuals in the gallery serve as negative samples. We also introduce thermal face images from a set of training subjects not in the gallery as negative samples, referred to as thermal cross-examples [16]. These thermal cross-examples enable the model building procedure to implicitly incorporate thermal information and improve the discriminative capabilities of the PLS classifiers.

After the PLS model building process is complete, face recognition is performed by measuring the response of the feature vector f extracted from a thermal probe face image to a given PLS model according to Eq. 4.2.

$$y_f = \bar{y} + [W(P^T W)^{-1} T^T y]f \tag{4.2}$$

In Eq. 4.2, W is the matrix of weight vectors, T is the matrix of latent vectors, and P is the matrix of loadings computed using T and the residual of X [16]. The scalar value y_f can be considered a similarity score (i.e., match score) between the thermal probe image and a subject in the gallery represented by a PLS model. For each gallery subject, or PLS model, a similarity score is obtained. For face identification, the person in the thermal probe image is recognized as the individual in the visible face gallery with the highest PLS similarly score.

4.4.3 Dictionary Learning + SVM-Based Approach

A dictionary learning-based approach using support vector classification is presented to explicitly learn the mapping between thermal and visible face signatures, whereas the PLS technique of Sect. 4.5 attempted to implicitly learn the relationship between visible and thermal face signatures for classification. The dictionary learning approach uses corresponding visible and thermal image training pairs to learn mappings for projecting samples into a common space prior to classification. In this section, we describe two variants of the dictionary learning approach: a K-SVD based coupled dictionary technique and a bi-level coupled dictionary technique.

Since the visible and thermal face images are quite different, HOG features that are extracted from visible images do not correspond well to the HOG features extracted from the thermal images. Hence, the test distribution is different compared to the training distributions used to learn the subsequent classifiers. To solve this issue, an explicit patch-by-patch mapping that transforms data samples from the thermal HOG feature space to the visible HOG feature space is built.

An algorithm based on paired dictionary learning is used to develop this mapping. Let $x^v \in R^d$ be the HOG feature vector from a patch of a visible face image and $x^t \in R^d$ be the HOG feature vector from the corresponding patch of the corresponding thermal face image. Then, two bases $D_v \in R^{d \times K}$ and $D_t \in R^{d \times K}$ are built to represent visible feature space and thermal feature space, respectively, such that same coefficients $\alpha \in R^k$ are obtained, when x^v and x^t are projected on to the bases D_v and D_t. Such bases are obtained by solving the following paired dictionary learning problem with sparse reconstruction coefficients, similar to [25],

$$\min_{D_v, D_t, \alpha} \sum_i \left(\left\| x_i^v - D_v \alpha_i \right\|_2^2 + \left\| x_i^t - D_t \alpha_i \right\|_2^2 \right) \tag{4.3}$$

such that $\|\alpha_i\|_1 \leq \epsilon \forall i, \|D_v(:,k)\|_2 \leq 1, \|D_t(:,k)\|_2 \leq 1 \forall k.$

After certain manipulations, this problem can be simplified into a standard dictionary learning and sparse coding problem and can be solved using K-SVD algorithm and orthogonal matching pursuit (OMP) algorithm [26]. One should note that even though thermal face imagery is used in learning the mapping from thermal HOG domain to visible HOG domain, the classification step does not use any thermal imagery in the training phase. Given a thermal probe image, HOG features are extracted from it patch-by-patch. Each of these HOG vectors is projected on to D_t to obtain the sparse projection coefficients α, which in turn can be used on bases D_v to obtain the corresponding HOG feature vector for that patch in the visible domain.

While the K-SVD-based algorithm captures some of the relationship between the imaging modalities, an alternative dictionary learning algorithm with bi-level constraints provides even better results. As in [27], we use the following dictionary learning formulation,

$$\min_{D_v, D_t, \alpha^v, \alpha^t} \sum_i \left(\left\| x_i^v - D_v \alpha_i^v \right\|_2^2 + \left\| x_i^t - D_t \alpha_i^t \right\|_2^2 + \gamma \left\| \alpha_i^v - \alpha_i^t \right\|_2^2 \right)$$

such that $\|D_v(:,k)\|_2 \le 1, \|D_t(:,k)\|_2 \le 1 \forall k.$

$$\alpha_i^v = \arg\min_z \left\| x_i^v - D_v z \right\|_2^2 + \lambda \|z\|_1 \forall i,$$

$$\alpha_i^t = \arg\min_z \left\| x_i^t - D_t z \right\|_2^2 + \lambda \|z\|_1 \forall i. \tag{4.4}$$

In this formulation, the sparse codes are explicitly tied to the solutions of the optimization problems that will be used to compute them in practice. This allows for a tighter coupling that can encode more common information captured by the thermal and visible imagers. The learned dictionaries are called bi-level coupled dictionaries (BCD) due to the optimization problem (sparse code calculation) as a constraint to another optimization problem (dictionary learning).

Following dictionary learning, which maps the thermal HOG features into the corresponding visible HOG representation, the well-known SVM is used for classification. SVMs are binary classifiers, which discriminate between two classes by building a hyperplane that maximizes the margin between the two classes [28–30]. Suppose that the samples in a two-class dataset can be represented as $\{x_i, y_i\}$ where $x_i \in R^d$ d-dimensional feature vector (concatenated HOG feature vector of each face image) of each data sample i and $y_i \in \{+1, -1\}$ represents the class to which the data sample belongs to. SVM tries to find an optimum separating hyperplane such that the separation/margin between the two classes is maximal. This can be expressed as a l_2 regularized constrained optimization problem shown in Eq. 4.5.

$$\min_{w,b} L(w) = \frac{1}{2} \|w\|^2 + C \sum_i \xi_i$$

subject to $y_i(\langle w, x_i \rangle + b) \ge 1, \quad \forall i = 1, 2, \ldots, N,$

$$\xi_i \ge 0, \quad \forall i = 1, 2, \ldots, N, \tag{4.5}$$

where N is the total number of training data samples, w is the normal vector of the separating hyperplane, b is the bias of the separating hyperplane from the origin, ξ_i are the slack variables introduced into the problem to allow for noisy samples or outliers during the training stage, and C is a hyperparameter that determines the trade-off between minimizing the training error and maximizing the margin [30]. The margin between the two classes is $2/\|w\|$, and minimizing the l_2 norm of the normal vector of the separating hyperplane maximizes the margin between the two classes.

Naturally occurring data distributions are typically highly nonlinear and multimodal, and cannot be separated using a hyperplane in the input space. To handle such distributions, the data are first transformed from the input space to a higher-dimensional (possibly infinite) feature space called the reproducing kernel Hilbert space (RKHS) using a nonlinear mapping Φ [31]. A linear separating hyperplane is built in this higher-dimensional RKHS, which in turn translates to a nonlinear separating hypersurface in the input space. Such a hypersurface theoretically provides better classification between the two classes in the input space. Consequently, the optimization problem can be expressed as

$$\min_{w,b} L(w) = \frac{1}{2} \|w^2\| + C \sum_i \xi_i$$

subject to $y_i(\langle w, \Phi(x_i)\rangle + b) \geq 1, \quad \forall i = 1, 2, \ldots, N,$
$$\xi_i \geq 0, \quad \forall i = 1, 2, \ldots, N,$$

(4.6)

where the separating hyperplane w is built in the RKHS. However, the nonlinear mapping function $\Phi(x)$ is not known explicitly [31]. A kernel trick is used to transform the data from the input space to the RKHS. According to this trick, the dot product of two points in the RKHS is known in the form of kernel function $(k(x_i, x_j) = \langle \Phi(x_i), \Phi(x_j)\rangle)$. In this work, a Gaussian radial basis function (RBF) kernel, with $k(x_i, x_j) = \exp\left(-\|x_i - x_j\|^2/2\sigma^2\right)$, σ being the bandwidth parameter, is used. A convex quadratic problem in its primal form can be constructed from Eq. 4.6 by applying Lagrange multipliers $\alpha_i, i = 1, 2, \ldots, N$. This problem can be solved either in its original primal form or dual form by applying the Karush–Kuhn–Tucker (KKT) conditions [31]. After obtaining the optimal Lagrange multipliers α_i^*, the decision on a test sample x_T is made by evaluating the following expression.

$$f(x_T) = \text{sgn}\left(\sum_i y_i \alpha_i^* k(x_i, x_T) + b\right)$$

(4.7)

Since the face recognition problem is a multiclass problem, we use "one-vs-rest" strategy [31], where the samples belonging to a single subject form one class and the samples belonging to the rest of the subjects are considered to be the second class. Therefore, for M subjects, we train M "one-vs-rest" SVM classifiers. The scores are compared, and the gallery subject corresponding to the classifier returning the maximum score is identified as the top match. This procedure is the same as for the PLS technique of Sect. 4.5.

4.4.4 Polarimetric Thermal Imaging for Face Recognition

In this section, a novel imaging modality for face recognition is presented that acquires the polarization-state information of radiation in the thermal spectrum. Similar to conventional thermal imaging, polarimetric thermal imaging in the MWIR or LWIR bands can be employed in low-light and nighttime scenarios to acquire thermal radiation naturally emitted by facial skin tissue. A significant advantage of polarimetric thermal imaging is that the data also contains polarization-state information of the radiation, which provides geometric and textural facial details that are not available in conventional thermal face imagery [32, 33].

First, we present the phenomenology and theory of polarimetric thermal imaging. In order to measure the polarization state of light that is either reflected or emitted from an object, one typically employs a Stokes method in which a series of simple optical measurements are conducted using linear and circular polarizers [34]. This method provides a measurement of the four Stokes parameters that completely define the polarization state of a photon. The four Stokes parameters, S_0, S_1, S_2, and S_3, are defined by,

$$S_0 = I(0^\circ) + I(90^\circ) \tag{4.8}$$

$$S_1 = I(0^\circ) - I(90^\circ) \tag{4.9}$$

$$S_2 = I(+45^\circ) + I(-45^\circ) \tag{4.10}$$

$$S_3 = I(R) + I(L), \tag{4.11}$$

where $I(0^\circ)$, $I(90^\circ)$, $I(+45^\circ)$, and $I(-45^\circ)$ represent the intensity of the incident light after passing through a linear polarizer that is orientated at 0, 90, +45, and −45°, respectively. 0° is defined to be aligned along the horizontal, and $I(R)$ and $I(L)$ represent the intensity of the light after passing through a right- or left-hand side polarization filter. These four Stokes parameters are extended to imaging methodologies by simply displaying each individual pixel value in a 2-D array as any one of the four Stokes parameters. It should be noted that the Stokes image S_0 represents the conventional, intensity-only, thermal image and does not possess any polarization information.

In addition to the four standard Stokes images S_0, S_1, S_2, and S_3, it is often useful to consider various linear combinations of Stokes images: degree-of-polarization (DoP), degree-of-linear-polarization (DoLP), and the degree-of-circular-polarization (DoCP) images. These product images are defined in Eqs. 4.12–4.14. Since they are all normalized with respect to the total intensity image, S_0, they represent the fraction of the light that possesses a particular polarization state, either total polarization (DoP), linearly polarized (DoLP), or circularly polarized (DoCP).

$$\text{DoP} = \sqrt{(S_1^2 + S_2^2 + S_3^2)}/S_0 \qquad (4.12)$$

$$\text{DoLP} = \sqrt{(S_1^2 + S_2^2)}/S_0 \qquad (4.13)$$

$$\text{DoCP} = S_3/S_0 \qquad (4.14)$$

It should be noted that for passive imaging in which there is no artificial illumination, there is little or no circularly polarized radiance in either the MWIR or LWIR regions; therefore, S_3 is taken to be zero for most applications.

In order to optimize polarimetric response for passive MWIR or LWIR imaging, it is important to understand the effects of ambient radiance in either band on the overall degree of polarization. Figure 4.3 shows the various sources of polarized radiance for a given scene in a typical passive imaging scenario. For polarimetric imaging in the thermal IR, there are two mechanisms for generating polarized radiance. The first, and most well understood, involves the generation of polarized light (usually linearly) that takes place when reflected from a surface of an object (i.e., Fresnel refection). In Fig. 4.3, ambient radiance is reflected from the surface of the thermal object that is being imaged by a polarimetric camera. This ambient radiance (light) can be either polarized or unpolarized; however, upon reflection, there is an induced preferential linear polarization state generated due to Fresnel

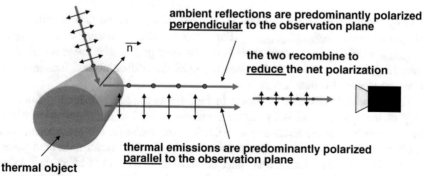

ambient (optical) background
unpolarized or partially polarized

ambient reflections are predominantly polarized
perpendicular to the observation plane

$\overline{n}$

the two recombine to
reduce the net polarization

thermal emissions are predominantly polarized
parallel to the observation plane

thermal object

Fig. 4.3 Schematic of the both reflection- and emission-induced polarization states for a typical passive imaging scenario. The two types of polarization (due to reflected and emitted radiation) are orthogonal and serve to produce a net reduction in the overall DoLP that is observed by the sensor. Therefore, it is advantageous to conduct thermal polarimetric imaging in environments in which the ambient radiance, within a given spectral response of the sensor, is minimized

reflection. This preferential linear polarization is aligned perpendicular to the observation plane, defined by the surface normal and the camera system's line of sight (LOS).

In addition to polarized radiance due to reflection, there is a component of polarized radiance that occurs when pure thermal emission (i.e., Plank radiation) generated by all nonzero temperature surfaces are observed at angles other than the surface normal [35]. To understand this phenomenon, it is important to recognize that the emissivity is not only a function of temperature and wavelength, $\varepsilon(T, \lambda)$ (ε compares an object's radiant energy at a given temperature, T, to an idealized blackbody at the same temperature), but is also a directional quantity, i.e., $\varepsilon(T, \lambda, \theta, \varphi)$, where θ is the angle between the surface normal, $\mathbf{n}$, and the camera's LOS, and φ is the azimuth angle taken about the normal. It is customary to deconstruct directional quantities and express them in terms of orthogonal components that are perpendicular and parallel to a given emission plane [36]. By doing so, the directional emissivity $\varepsilon(T, \lambda, \theta, \varphi)$ is represented in terms of two orthogonal components shown in Eq. 4.15.

$$\varepsilon(T, \lambda, \theta, \varphi) \rightarrow \varepsilon(T, \lambda, \theta) = \left(\varepsilon(\theta)_{\text{parallel}} + \varepsilon(\theta)_{\text{perpendicular}}\right)/2 \qquad (4.15)$$

By substituting Eqs. 4.8–4.10 into Eq. 4.13 and recognizing that the radiant intensity can be expressed in terms of the emissivity and the Plank function $B(T, \lambda)$, i.e., $I(T, \lambda, \theta) = \varepsilon(T, \lambda, \theta) * B(T, \lambda)$, the DoLP shown in Eq. 4.13 can now be expressed solely in terms of the orthogonal component that comprise the directional emissivity that are defined in Eq. 4.16,

$$\text{DoLP} = \frac{\varepsilon(\theta)_{\text{parallel}} - \varepsilon(\theta)_{\text{perpendicular}}}{\varepsilon(\theta)_{\text{parallel}} + \varepsilon(\theta)_{\text{perpendicular}}}. \qquad (4.16)$$

Only when the sensor's LOS is aligned along the surface normal does $\varepsilon(\theta)_{\text{parallel}} = \varepsilon(\theta)_{\text{perpendicular}}$. For all other observation angles, $\varepsilon(\theta)_{\text{parallel}} \neq \varepsilon(\theta)_{\text{perpendicular}}$, and there is an observed preferential linear polarization state. In general, as the angle between the LOS the surface normal increases, the observed DoLP also increases.

This polarized emittance is shown in Fig. 4.3 as the ray propagating from the body of the cylinder and is by nature polarized parallel to the observation plane. Since the polarized radiation due to reflection and emission are orthogonal, they combine at the sensor to produce a net *reduction* in the overall measured polarization. This is a key factor that must be taken into account if effective passive polarimetric imaging is to occur. An excellent review of all of these aspects can be found in [37].

In [38], we proposed an approach to polarimetric-based face recognition that exhibited significant improvements over conventional thermal imaging for cross-spectral face recognition. The polarimetric-based face recognition technique consisted of three stages: preprocessing, feature extraction, and recognition/

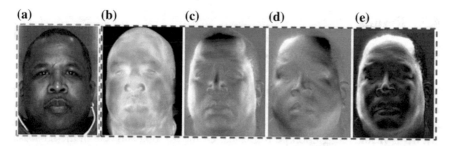

Fig. 4.4 Images of single subject as seen in **a** visible and **b** conventional thermal as represented by S_0. **c** S_1, **d** S_2 and **e** DoLP images illustrate the added information available using polarimetric imaging for face recognition

classification. To test the cross-spectral recognition algorithm, simultaneous visible spectrum and polarimetric thermal imagery was acquired. Polarimetric LWIR face imagery was collected by a division-of-time spinning achromatic retarder (SAR) system from Polaris Sensor Technologies [32]. The system consisted of a Stirling-cooled mercury cadmium telluride FPA, with pixel array dimensions of 640×480, and a spectral response range of 7.5–11.1 µm. A sequence of 32-bit images was recorded at 60-Hz frame rate, and a Fourier modulation method was applied to compute the Stokes images. In this section, we present an overview of the polarimetric-based face recognition framework used to perform cross-spectral face recognition and report results on a dataset of 40 subjects.

Figure 4.4 shows faces acquired with visible imaging, conventional thermal imaging, and polarimetric thermal imaging. From a visual observation, the polarimetric face images shown in Fig. 4.7c, d more closely resemble the visible face image than the conventional thermal face image. However, as results will show, the polarization information actually complements the conventional thermal information [38].

The recognition framework follows a similar methodology as discussed in previous sections for cross-spectral face recognition. For preprocessing, the DoG filter is applied on the visible gallery images as well as the Stokes images S_1 and S_2. HOG features are then extracted from each of the DoG filtered images. As seen in Fig. 4.6, the S_0 image provides highly correlated details around the ocular region (eyes and eyebrows) between the thermal and visible faces. In contrast, the S_1 and S_2 components provide a higher degree of correlation to the visible face signature around the nose and mouth regions. Since the Stokes images contain complementary details about the geometry and texture of the face, a feature-level fusion is performed to combine the HOG features from each Stokes image into a composite feature set [38].

4.5 Results

4.5.1 *Partial Least Squares Results*

To evaluate the performance of the PLS-based thermal-to-visible face recognition algorithm, the NVESD database was used. The NVESD database contains both MWIR and LWIR face images, enabling an assessment of MWIR-to-visible and LWIR-to-visible recognition performance. Of the 50 total subjects in the database, 48 subjects are used for performance evaluation—the remaining two subjects are used to provide thermal cross-examples. For PLS model building, a single visible image from each of the 48 subjects along with thermal cross-examples extracted from the remaining two subjects is used. This procedure is the same as in [16]. However, instead of the loose cropping style used in that study, a tight cropping style is used here, focusing on the core facial region consisting of the eyes, nose, and mouth as shown in Fig. 4.2. This tight cropping is more robust to small changes in face pose, which would have a large impact on the facial outline. Hair style, which may change from day to day, is also not present after tight cropping and therefore does not impact the recognition process. In addition, the impact of face resolution on recognition performance is examined here by using synthetic low-resolution imagery, generated by first convolving the high-resolution image with a Gaussian filter of bandwidth $d/4$ and then downsampling by the factor d. Figure 4.5 shows an example of an original thermal probe image at 174×174 pixels, as well as the synthetically generated counterparts through downsampling.

Face identification results are presented in Fig. 4.6, which shows the Rank-1 identification rate for MWIR-to-visible and LWIR-to-visible face. At the full image resolution of 174×174 pixels, the Rank-1 identification rate is 0.824 and 0.704, for MWIR-to-visible and LWIR-to-visible face recognition, respectively. These tight cropping results are lower when compared to the Rank-1 identification rates of

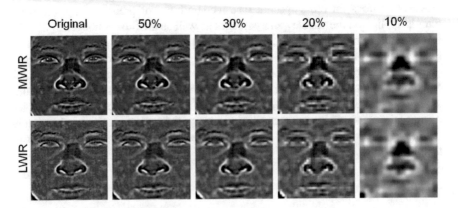

Fig. 4.5 Downsampled thermal imagery as a percentage of original image size of 174×174 pixels

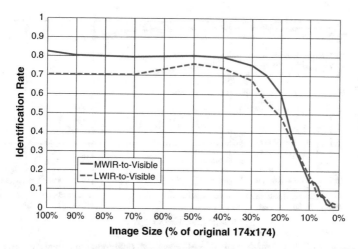

Fig. 4.6 Rank-1 identification rate versus resolution for PLS-based MWIR-to-visible and LWIR-to-visible face recognition

0.927 (MWIR-to-visible) and 0.813 (LWIR-to-visible) reported in [16], which used the loose cropping style. Face identification performance is consistent for resolutions ranging from 174 × 174 pixels down to 52 × 52 pixels (30 % of original image size), but drops sharply for lower resolution. This is expected as facial details are preserved down to 50 % (87 × 87 pixel resolution) of the original image size. For the downsampled images at 20 % and especially at 10 % in Fig. 4.4, significant facial details have been lost (based on a qualitative visual assessment), leading to a substantial reduction in thermal-to-visible face recognition performance. Note also that the MWIR-to-visible performance is consistently higher than LWIR-to-visible performance until the point where resolution decreases past 20 % of the original image size. The higher performance in the MWIR band can be expected, due to the higher spatial resolution of the shorter wavelength MWIR radiation.

4.5.2   Dictionary Learning + SVM Results

The thermal-to-visible face recognition performance of the dictionary learning SVM approach is shown in Fig. 4.7, plotting the Rank-1 identification rate as a function of the image resolution. As in Sect. 4.5, the original high-resolution image size is 174 × 174 pixels. The curves indicate that down to 40 % of the original image size, performance of both MWIR-to-visible and LWIR-to-visible face recognition remains similar using the dictionary learning SVM approach. As the image size decreases past 40 % of the original image size, performance slowly deteriorates for both thermal bands. This trend continues until the images are 20 % of the original size, after which it sharply declines. Furthermore, the results

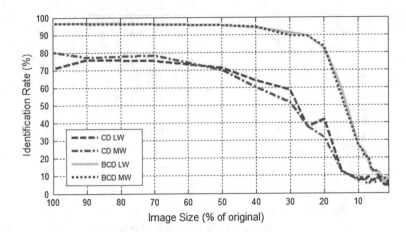

Fig. 4.7 Rank-1 identification as a function of image size (after downsampling) for cross-spectral face recognition using MWIR and LWIR probe images against visible gallery images using dictionary learning approach

show that the bi-level coupled dictionaries (BCD in Fig. 4.7) outperform the K-SVD-based coupled dictionaries (CD in Fig. 4.7) at all image sizes.

4.5.3 Polarimetric Thermal-Based Face Recognition Results

A dataset of 40 subjects was collected for experimentation, representing an extension of the 20-subject study by Short et al. [38]. Each subject was asked to remain still for eight seconds while visible and polarimetric thermal imagery was acquired at a distance of 2.5 m. Since the conventional LWIR radiometric data are represented by S_0, baseline comparisons were conducted with respect to S_0. Four samples of each subject were extracted from the visible and polarimetric LWIR video sequences using the same procedure as [38]. Figure 4.8 presents both face verification and face identification performance results when using S_0, S_1, S_2, DoLP, or the composite representation as the probe for cross-spectral face recognition. Figure 4.8a shows the ROC curves, which is a common indicator of performance in authentication scenarios. Figure 4.8b shows the CMC curves, which characterizes the face identification performance of the cross-spectral system. The composite feature representation, which is derived from a combination of the Stokes images, yields the highest performance in terms of the lowest FNMR at the examined FMR in Fig. 4.8a, compared to conventional thermal (S_0) or any individual Stokes components. Furthermore, the CMC curve shows that the composite feature representation yields the highest Rank-1 identification rate of 93.75 %, compared to conventional thermal, which has a Rank-1 identification rate of 75 %.

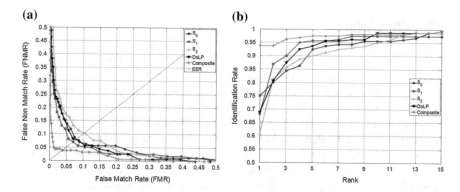

Fig. 4.8 **a** Receiver operating characteristic curve measuring face verification performance, and **b** cumulative match characteristics curves measuring face identification performance for cross-spectral matching of traditional LWIR (S_0), individual Stokes images (S_1 and S_2), **DoLP**, and proposed composite to a visible spectrum gallery/database

Table 4.2 List of key ROC and CMC data points from testing on the 40-subject dataset

Probe	EER (%)	FMR100 (%)	Rank-1 ID (%)	Rank-5 ID (%)
S_0	8.1	28.3	75.00	92.50
S_1	7.0	29.8	68.13	95.63
S_2	10.2	42.1	60.62	90.00
DoLP	7.8	33.7	68.75	93.75
Composite	*3.8*	*7.2*	*93.75*	*97.50*

Equal error rate (EER) represents the rate at which the false-positive and false-negative rates are equal

Table 4.2 lists values for several common face recognition performance metrics, taken from the ROC and CMC curves. The FMR100 is the FNMR where the FMR is fixed at 1 % and is a common measure for verification systems, as this scenario typically operates in a state where denying access to a genuine user is more acceptable than allowing access to a nongenuine user. Compared to the prior 20-subject study [38], the 40-subject results here also demonstrate that the performance using the composite features is higher than the performance using features only from the conventional (S_0) or only from the polarization-state images (S_1, S_2, DoLP) individually. However, the face identification rate and the face verification rate are slightly lower than in [38] as expected, due to the larger gallery size used here.

4.6   Discussion

Two different classification/matching techniques were presented, both using the HOG features extracted from the DoG filtered images as input for cross-spectral face recognition. The PLS-based technique implicitly incorporates thermal information into the model building process using thermal cross-examples, while the dictionary learning SVM approach attempts to explicitly find the mapping between the thermal and visible domains in the feature subspace before SVM classification. The K-SVD based coupled dictionary SVM technique resulted in similar performance as PLS at higher resolutions, but has lower performance than PLS at image sizes <50 % of original resolution. The face identification performance of the bi-level coupled dictionary SVM technique surpasses both that of the K-SVD based coupled dictionary SVM technique as well as the PLS technique, achieving >90 % Rank-1 identification rate at resolutions down to 52 × 52 pixels for both MWIR-to-visible and LWIR-to-visible face recognition. This demonstrates that the explicit use of thermal information is more beneficial than implicitly incorporating the thermal information during PLS model building.

Comparing the MWIR and LWIR bands for cross-spectral face recognition, PLS results show that MWIR-to-visible consistently outperforms LWIR-to-visible face recognition across a range of simulated thermal probe image resolutions. This is expected, as the shorter wavelength in the MWIR band has inherently higher spatial resolution than the LWIR band. Interestingly, for the dictionary learning SVM techniques, MWIR-to-visible and LWIR-to-visible face recognition performance were very similar. This may indicate that dictionary learning learns the MWIR-to-visible mapping and the LWIR-to-visible mapping equally well, even the LWIR face imagery is inherently smoother to some extent. Although the PLS and dictionary learning SVM approaches achieved robust performance across the higher and intermediate resolutions, once the face resolution of the downsampled thermal probe imagery decreased past 52 × 52 pixels, performance for both MWIR-to-visible and LWIR-to-visible face recognition deteriorated sharply.

A novel face recognition imaging modality, polarimetric thermal imaging, is also presented in this chapter. Polarimetric thermal imaging preserves the key benefit of conventional thermal imaging, illumination invariance, while providing additional geometric and textural facial details not available in conventional thermal face imagery. Therefore, as expected, complementing thermal facial features with polarimetric facial features resulted in a significant improvement in cross-spectral face recognition performance compared to conventional LWIR-to-visible face recognition.

4.7   Summary

In this chapter, cross-spectral thermal-to-visible face recognition was discussed, with results presented on the NVESD multimodal face database containing thermal imagery acquired in both the MWIR and LWIR bands. Performance of a PLS regression approach and a dictionary learning SVM approach were presented. A novel imaging modality for face recognition, polarimetric LWIR, was also presented in this chapter, showing that polarimetric information can provide complementary geometric and textural information to the conventional thermal face signature. The feature sets exploiting polarization-state information were shown to facilitate cross-spectral matching. Further advancements leading to operational use of thermal-to-visible face recognition are expected to enhance intelligence gathering and surveillance missions, especially during nighttime and low-light scenarios.

References

1. Yi, D., Liu, R., Chu, R.F., Lei, Z., Li, S.Z.: Face matching between near infrared and visible light images. Adv. Biomet. Lect. Notes Comput. Sci. **4642**, 523–530 (2007)
2. Klare, B., Jain, A.K.: Heterogeneous face recognition: matching NIR to visible light images. In: Proceedings of International Conference on Pattern Recognition, pp. 1513–1516 (2010)
3. Bourlai, T., Cukic, B.: Multi-spectral face recognition: identification of people in difficult environments. In: IEEE International Conference on Intelligence and Security Informatics (2012)
4. Bourlai, T., Kalka, N., Ros, A., Cukic, B., Hornak, L.: Cross-spectral face verification in the short wave infrared (SWIR) band. In: Proceedings of International Conference on Pattern Recognition, pp. 1343–1347 (2010)
5. Whitelam, C., Bourlai, T.: On designing SWIR to visible face matching algorithms. Intel Tech. J. **18**(4), 98 (2014)
6. Narang, N., Bourlai, T.: Face recognition in the SWIR band when using single sensor multi-wavelength imaging systems. Image Vis. Comput. **33**, 26–43 (2015)
7. Nicolo, F., Schmid, N.A.: Long range cross-spectral face recognition: matching SWIR against visible light images. IEEE Trans. Inf. For. Secur. **7**(6), 1717–1726 (2012)
8. Socolinsky, D.A., Selinger, A.: A comparative analysis of face recognition performance with visible and thermal infrared imagery. In: International Conference on Pattern Recognition, pp. IV, pp. 217–222 (2002)
9. Chen, X., Flynn, P.J., Bowyer, K.W.: IR and visible light face recognition. Comput. Vis. Image Underst. **99**(3), 332–358 (2005)
10. Kong, S.G., Heo, J., Abidi, B.R., Paik, J., Abidi, M.A.: Recent advances in visual and infrared face recognition—a review. Comput. Vis. Image Underst. **97**(1), 103–135 (2005)
11. Buddharaju, P., Pavlidis, I.T., Tsiamyrtzis, P., Bazakos, M.: Physiology-based face recognition in the thermal infrared spectrum. IEEE Trans. Pattern Anal. Mach. Intell. **29**, 613–626 (2007)
12. Osia, N., Bourlai, T.: A spectral independent approach for physiological and geometric based face recognition in the visible, middle-wave and long-wave infrared bands. Image Vis. Comput. **32**(11), 847–859 (2014)
13. Klare, B.F., Jain, A.K.: Heterogeneous face recognition using kernel prototype similarity. IEEE Trans. Pattern Anal. Mach. Int. **35**(6), 1410–1422 (2013)

14. Bourlai, T., Ross, A., Chen, C., Hornak, L.: A study on using mid-wave infrared images for face recognition. In: Proceedings of SPIE DSS, vol. 8371 (2012)
15. Choi, J., Hu, S., Young, S.S., Davis, L.S.: Thermal to visible face recognition. In: Proceedings of SPIE, vol. 8371, p. 83711L (2012a)
16. Hu, S., Choi, J., Chan, A.L., Schwartz, W.R.: Thermal-to-visible face recognition using partial least squares. J. Opt. Soc. Am. A **32**(3), 431–442 (2015)
17. Chen, X., Flynn, P.J., Bowyer, K.W.: Visible-light and Infrared Face Recognition. In: Proceedings ACM Workshop on Multimodal User Authentication, pp. 48–55 (2003)
18. Choi, J., Sharma, A., Jacobs, D.W., Davis, L.S.: Data insufficiency in sketch versus photo face recognition. In: Proceedings of Computer Vision and Pattern Recognition Workshops (2012b)
19. Zuiderveld, K.: Contrast limited adaptive histogram equalization. In: Graphic Gems IV, Academic Press Professional, pp. 474–485 (1994)
20. Dalal, N., Triggs, B.: Histogram of oriented gradients for human detection. In: Proceedings of IEEE Conference on Computer Vision and Pattern Recognition, pp. 886–893 (2005)
21. Schwartz, W.R., Guo, H., Choi, J., Davis, L.S.: Face identification using large feature sets. IEEE Trans. Image Process. **21**(4), 2245–2255 (2012)
22. Wold, H.: Estimation of principal components and related models by iterative least squares. In: Multivariate Analysis. Academic Press, Waltham (1966)
23. Helland, I.: Partial least squares regression. In: Encyclopedia of Statistical Sciences. Wiley, New York, pp. 5957–5962 (2006)
24. Barker, M., Rayens, W.: Partial least squares for discrimination. J. Chemometrics **17**, 166–173 (2003)
25. Yang, J., Wright, J., Huang, T., Ma, Y.: Image super-resolution via sparse representation. IEEE Trans. Image Process. **19**(11), 2861–2873 (2010)
26. Aharon, M., Elad, M., Bruckstein, A.: K-SVD: an algorithm for designing overcomplete dictionaries for sparse representation. IEEE Trans. Signal Process. **54**(11), 4311–4322 (2006)
27. Yang, J., et al.: Bilevel sparse coding for coupled feature spaces. In: IEEE Conference on Computer Vision and Pattern Recognition (CVPR). IEEE (2012)
28. Vapnik, V.N.: The Nature of Statistical Learning Theory, New York (2000)
29. Cortes, C., Vapnik, V.: Support vector networks. Mach. Learn. **20**, 273–297 (1995)
30. Burges, C.J.C.: A Tutorial on Support Vector Machines for Pattern Recognition. Data Min. Knowl. Disc. **2**, 121–167 (1998)
31. Scholkopf, B., Smola, A.J.: Learning with Kernels, Cambridge (2002)
32. Gurton, K., Yuffa, A., Videen, G.: Enhanced facial recognition for thermal imagery using polarimetric imaging. Opt. Lett. **39**(13), 3857–3859 (2014)
33. Yuffa, A., Gurton, K., Videen, G.: Three-dimensional (3D) facial recognition using passive LWIR polarimetric imaging. Appl. Opt. **53**(36), 8514–8521 (2014)
34. Hecht, E., Zajac, A.: Optics. Addison-Wesley Publishing, Reading (1979)
35. Siegel, R., Howell, J.: Thermal Radiation Heat Transfer. McGraw-Hill publishing, New York (1981)
36. Zissis, G.J.: Sources of Radiation. SPIE Optical Engineering Press, Bellingham (1993)
37. Tyo, S.J., Goldstein, D., Chenault, D., Shaw, J.: Review of passive imaging polarimetry for remote sensing applications. Appl. Opt. **45**(22), 5453–5469 (2006)
38. Short, N., Hu, S., Gurram, P., Gurton, K., Chan, A.L.: Improving cross-spectral face recognition using polarimetric imaging. Opt. Lett. **40**(6), 882–885 (2015)

Chapter 5
Local Operators and Measures for Heterogeneous Face Recognition

Zhicheng Cao, Natalia A. Schmid and Thirimachos Bourlai

Abstract This chapter provides a summary of local operators recently proposed for heterogeneous face recognition. It also analyzes performance of each individual operator and demonstrates performance of composite operators. Basic local operators include local binary patterns (LBP), generalized local binary patterns (GLBPs), Weber local descriptors (WLDs), Gabor filters, and histograms of oriented gradients (HOGs). They are directly applied to normalized face images. The composite operators include Gabor filters followed by LBP, Gabor filters followed by WLD, Gabor filters followed by GLBP, Gabor filters followed by LBP, GLBP and WLD, Gabor ordinal measures (GOM), and composite multi-lobe descriptors (CMLD). When applying a composite operator to face images, images are first normalized and processed with a bank of Gabor filters and then local operators or combinations of local operators are applied to the outputs of Gabor filters. After a face image is encoded using the local operators, the outputs of local operators are converted to a histogram representation and then concatenated, resulting in a very long feature vector. No effective dimensionality reduction method or feature selection method has been found to reduce the size of the feature vector. Each component in the feature vector appears to contribute a small amount of information needed to generate a high fidelity matching score. A matching score is generated by means of Kullback-Leibler distance between two feature vectors. The cross-matching performance of heterogeneous face images is demonstrated on two datasets composed of active infrared and visible light face images. Both short and long standoff distances are considered.

Z. Cao · N.A. Schmid (✉) · T. Bourlai
Lane Department of Computer Science and Electrical Engineering,
West Virginia University, Morgantown, WV 26506-6109, USA
e-mail: Natalia.Schmid@mail.wvu.edu

Z. Cao
e-mail: zcao1@mix.wvu.edu

T. Bourlai
e-mail: Thirimachos.Bourlai@mail.wvu.edu

© Springer International Publishing Switzerland 2016
T. Bourlai (ed.), *Face Recognition Across the Imaging Spectrum*,
DOI 10.1007/978-3-319-28501-6_5

5.1   Introduction

Face recognition has been an active area of research over the past few decades. Many major advancements have been reported in the literature. New applications have triggered new challenges, and new challenges have called for new research solutions. Surveillance at night or in harsh environments is one of the most recent applications of face recognition. Latest advancements in manufacturing of small and cheap imaging devices sensitive in active infrared range (near-and short-infrared) [21, 23] and the ability of these cameras to see through fog, rain, at night and operate at long ranges provided researchers with new type of imagery and posed new research problems [5–8, 10, 13, 28, 39, 40, 45]. As observed, active-IR energy is less affected by scattering and absorption by smoke or dust than visible light. Also, unlike visible spectrum imaging, active-IR imaging can be used to extract not only exterior but also useful subcutaneous anatomical information. This results in a very different appearance of face images in active-IR range compared to face images in visible spectrum. Acknowledging these differences, many related questions can be posed. What type of information should be extracted from active-IR images to successfully solve the problem of face recognition? How to match a face image in visible range to a face image in active-IR range? The latter falls in the scope of heterogeneous face recognition. Developing local operators for heterogeneous face recognition is the focus of this chapter. We will first provide a short overview of two general existing approaches to solve the problem of face recognition and later narrow it down to an overview of local operator-based approaches recently proposed and used in the field.

The literature identified two general categories of approaches to address the problem of face recognition: the holistic approach (also known as subspace analysis) and the local feature approach. The former represents the global photometric information of a human face using subspace projections. Examples include principal component analysis (PCA), independent component analysis (ICA), linear discriminant analysis (LDA), canonical correlation analysis (CCA), multilinear subspace learning (MSL), and their derivatives. Sirovich and Kirby [44] showed that PCA could be applied to a collection of face images to form a set of basis features which are known as eigenfaces. Later, Turk and Pentland [47, 48] expanded these results and presented the method of eigenfaces as well as a system for automated face recognition using eigenfaces. They showed a way of calculating the eigenvectors of a covariance matrix in a way that made it possible for computers at that time to perform eigen decomposition on a large number of face images. Jutten and Herault [27] introduced the general framework for ICA and then Comon [16] refined it. ICA can be seen as a generalization of PCA, in which ICA generates a set of basis vectors that possess maximal statistical independence, while PCA uses eigenvectors to determine basis vectors that capture maximal image variance. Motivated by the fact that much of the important information may be contained in the high-order relationship rather than that of the second-order, Bartlett at el. [3, 4] applied ICA to the problem of face recognition.

Fisher was the first to introduce the idea of LDA [20]. LDA determines a set of optimal discriminant basis vectors so that the ratio of the inter- and intra-class scatter matrices is maximized. It is primarily used to reduce the number of features to a more manageable number before classification. Each of the new dimensions is a linear combination of pixel values, which form a template. CCA was first introduced by Hotelling [25]. Given two random vectors $X = (X_1, \ldots, X_n)$ and $Y = (Y_1, \ldots, Y_m)$, and assuming a correlation among the variables, CCA finds the linear combinations of X_i and Y_j that result in the maximum correlation with each other. Melzera et al. [37] applied CCA to face recognition and proposed appearance models based on kernel canonical correlation analysis.

The second category of approaches use local operators instead and have advantages such as more robustness to illumination and occlusion, less strictly controlled conditions, and involvement of very small training sets. Examples of operators used in this category include Gabor filters, local binary patterns (LBPs), histogram of oriented gradients (HOGs), Weber local descriptor (WLD), and their generalizations and variants. Gabor filter is known to be a robust directional filter used for edge detection [36]. It has been found that simple cells in the visual cortex of mammalian brains can be modeled by Gabor functions [18, 34]. A set of Gabor filters parameterized by different frequencies and orientations are shown to perform well as an image feature extraction tool. Therefore, it has been widely used in image processing and pattern analysis applications [19, 26, 31, 33]. LBP is a particular case of the texture spectrum model proposed by Wang et al. [50]. It was first introduced by Ojala and Pietikinen [41, 42] for texture classification and found to be a powerful tool. LBP was thereafter applied to face recognition as well as object detection [1, 24]. Due to its discriminative power and computational simplicity as well as robustness to monotonic changes of image intensity caused by illumination variations, LBP has been expanded into several variant forms (see, e.g., [53, 54]). HOG analysis was introduced by Dalal et al. [17] and was initially used for the purpose of object detection. This operator is similar to other operators such as edge orientation histograms and scale-invariant feature transform, but differs in that it is computed on a dense grid of uniformly spaced cells and uses overlapping local contrast normalization for improved accuracy. Chen et al. [12] introduced the WLD operator inspired by Weber's law—an important psychological law quantifying the perception of change in a given stimulus [43].

Most of described methods have been developed for intra-spectral matching, to be more specific to match visible light images. Some operators were tuned to work with heterogeneous face images. For example, Chen et al. [14] conducted a face recognition study in thermal IR and visible spectral bands using PCA and Faceit G5. They showed that the performance of PCA in visible spectral band is higher compared to the performance of PCA in thermal IR spectral band and that these data fused at the matching score level resulted in a performance similar to the performance of the algorithm in visible band. Li et al. [32] proposed a method to compare face images within the NIR spectral band under different illumination scenarios. Their face matcher involved an LBP operator to achieve illumination invariance and was applied to near-infrared (NIR) images acquired at a short distance. In their recent works, Akhloufi and Bendada [2] experimented with images from database including visible, shortwave infrared (SWIR), mid-wave infrared (MWIR), and thermal infrared images. They adopted a classic local ternary pattern (LTP) and a new local adaptive ternary pattern (LATP) operator for feature extraction. The work of Klare and Jain [29] employed a method based on LBP and HOG operators, followed by a random sampling LDA algorithm to reduce the dimensionality of feature vectors. This encoding strategy is applied to NIR and color images for cross-spectral matching. The results are shown to outperform Cognitec's FaceVACS [15].

This chapter focuses on a discussion of local operators (algorithms from the second category) for heterogeneous face recognition. The methodology for feature extraction and heterogeneous matching adopted in this chapter does not require training data, which justifies its importance in practice. Once local operators are developed, they can be applied to any heterogeneous data (we particularly focus on matching visible images to active-IR images) and do not require any estimation or learning of parameters or retraining of the overall face recognition system.

We present and compare several feature extraction approaches applied to heterogeneous face images. Face images (in visible spectrum and active IR) may be first processed with a bank of Gabor filters parameterized by orientation and scale parameters followed by an application of a bank of local operators. The operators encode both the magnitude and phase of Gabor filtered (or non-filtered) face images. The application of an operator to a single image results in multiple magnitude and phase outputs. The outputs are mapped into a histogram representation, which constitutes a long feature vector. Feature vectors are cross-matched by applying a symmetric Kullback-Leibler distance. The combination of Gabor filters and local operators offers an advantage of both the selective nature of Gabor filters and the robustness of these operators.

In addition to known local operators such as LBP, generalized LBP (GLBP), WLD, HOG, and ordinal measures [11], we also present a recently developed operator named composite multi-lobe descriptor (CMLD) [9]. Inspired by the design of ordinal measures, this new operator combines Gabor filters, LBP, GLBP, and WLD and modifies them into multi-lobe functions with smoothed neighborhoods.

Performance of Gabor filters, LBP, GLBP, WLD, and HOG used both individually and in combinations and performance of CMLD are demonstrated on both the Pre-TINDERS and TINDERS datasets [51]. These datasets contain color face images, NIR and SWIR face images acquired at a distance of 1.5, 50, and 106 meters.

5.2 Heterogeneous Face Recognition

A typical system for heterogeneous face recognition can be described by three connected modules: a preprocessing module, a feature extraction module, and a matching module (see the block diagram in Fig. 5.1). In this work, the preprocessing

Fig. 5.1 A block diagram of a typical face recognition system

module implements an alignment, cropping and normalization of heterogeneous face images. The feature extraction module performs filtering, applies local operators, and maps the outputs of local operators into a histogram representation. The matching module applies a symmetric Kullback-Leibler distance to histogram representations of heterogeneous face images to generate a matching score. A functional description of each of the three modules is provided in the following subsections.

5.2.1 Preprocessing: Alignment, Cropping, and Normalization

In this work, the preprocessing module implements image alignment, cropping, and normalization. For alignment, positions of the eyes are used to transform the face to a canonical representation. Geometric transformations such as rotation, scaling, and translation are applied to each face image with the objective to project eyes to fixed positions. Figure 5.2 a, b, d illustrates the processing steps. In our work, the anchor

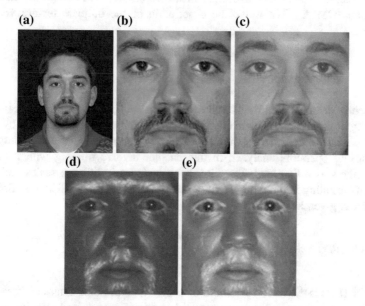

Fig. 5.2 Preprocessing of the face: **a** original color image, **b** aligned and cropped color face, **c** grayscale conversion of (**b**), **d** aligned and cropped SWIR face, and **e** log transformation of (**d**)

points—the fixed positions of the eyes—are manually selected. However, this process can be automated by means of a Haar-based detector trained on heterogeneous face images [49], as an example.

The aligned face images are further cropped to an area of size 120×112 (see Fig. 5.2b, d). After being cropped, images undergo an intensity normalization. Color images are converted to grayscale images using a simple linear combination of the original R, G, and B channels (see Fig. 5.2c). Active-IR images—SWIR and NIR images—are preprocessed using a simple nonlinear transformation given by $\log(1 + X)$, where X is the input image, as shown in Fig. 5.2e. The log transformation redistributes the original darker pixels over a much broader range and compresses the range of the original brighter pixels. The transformed image is brighter and has a better contrast than the original image, while the gray variation (trend) of the pixels is still preserved since the transformation is monotonic.

5.2.2 Feature Extraction

Feature extraction (implemented by the second module in the block diagram) is intended to extract an informative representation of heterogeneous face images with the objective of successful heterogeneous face recognition. In this chapter, we focus only on local operators. Below, we provide a brief mathematical description of Gabor filters, LBP, generalized LBP, WLD, HOG, as well as some variants or improvements such as Gabor ordinal measures (GOM) and composite multi-lobe descriptor (CMLD). We move the description of the ultimate feature vector to Sect. 5.2.3.

5.2.2.1 Gabor Filter

As recently demonstrated by Nicolo et al. [39, 40] and Chai et al. [11], a two-step encoding of face images, where encoding with local operators is preceded by Gabor filtering, leads to considerably improved recognition rates. Therefore, many combinations of operators analyzed in this chapter involve filtering with a bank of Gabor filters as a first step. The filter bank includes 2 different scales and 8 orientations resulting in a total of 16 filter responses. The mathematical description of the filter is given as follows:

$$G(z, \theta, s) = \frac{\| \mathscr{K}(\theta, s) \|}{\sigma^2} \exp \left[\frac{\| \mathscr{K}(\theta, s) \|^2 \|z\|^2}{2\sigma^2} \right] \left[e^{i \mathscr{K}(\theta, s) z} - e^{-\frac{\sigma^2}{2}} \right], \qquad (5.1)$$

where $\mathscr{K}(\theta, s)$ is the wave vector and σ^2 is the variance of the Gaussian kernel. The magnitude and phase of the wave vector determine the scale and orientation of the oscillatory term and $z = (x, y)$. The wave vector can be expressed as follows:

$$\mathscr{K}(\theta, s) = \mathscr{K}_s e^{i\phi_\theta}, \tag{5.2}$$

where $\mathscr{K}_s$ is known as a scale parameter and ϕ_θ is an orientation parameter. The adopted parameters for the complex vector in the experiments of this chapter are set to $\mathscr{K}_s = (\pi/2)^{s/2}$ with $s \in \mathbb{N}$ and $\phi_\theta = \theta\pi/8$ with $\theta = 1, 2, \ldots, 8$. The Gaussian kernel has the standard deviation $\sigma = \pi$.

A normalized and preprocessed face image $I(z)$ is convolved with a Gabor filter $G(z, \theta, s)$ at orientation ϕ_θ and scale $\mathscr{K}_s$ resulting in the filtered image $Y(z, \theta, s) = I(z) * G(z, \theta, s)$, where $*$ stands for convolution.

5.2.2.2 Weber Local Descriptor

WLD consists of two joint parts: a differential excitation operator and a gradient orientation descriptor. In this chapter, we adopt only the differential excitation operator to encode the magnitude filter response, resulting in a robust representation of face images.

The differences between the neighboring pixels of a central pixel are calculated and normalized by the pixel value itself. The summation of these normalized differences is further normalized by a monotonic function such as a tangent function. Finally, quantization is performed to output the WLD value.

The mathematical definition of WLD used in this chapter is given as follows:

$$\text{WLD}_{l,r,N}(x) = \mathcal{Q}_l \left\{ \tan^{-1} \left[\sum_{i=1}^{N} \left(\frac{x_i - x}{x} \right) \right] \right\}, \tag{5.3}$$

where x_i are the neighbors of x at radius r and N is the total number of neighbors (see Fig. 5.3). $\mathcal{Q}_l$ is a uniform quantizer with l quantization levels.

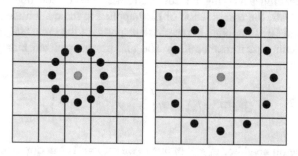

Fig. 5.3 Illustration of the neigboring pixels ($N = 12$) of a central pixel at different radii: the *left* corresponds r = 1; the *right* r = 2

5.2.2.3 Local Binary Pattern

An uniform LBP operator is described as follows:

$$\text{LBP}^{\mathcal{U}}_{r,N}(x) = \mathcal{U}\left\{\sum_{i=1}^{N} \mathscr{I}\{x_i - x\}2^i\right\}, \tag{5.4}$$

where x_i are the neighbors of the pixel x at radius r and N is the total number of neighbors. $\mathcal{U}$ is the uniform pattern mapping and $\mathscr{I}(\cdot)$ is the unit step function:

$$\mathscr{I}(x) = \begin{cases} 1, & x > 0 \\ 0, & x \leq 0 \end{cases} \tag{5.5}$$

Note that within this book chapter, we use only *uniform* sequences. A binary pattern is uniform, if it contains at most two bit-wise transitions from 0 to 1 or from 1 to 0, when the bit sequence is recorded circularly. For example, the sequence 011111111000 is a 12-bit uniform pattern, while the sequence 010001011111 is not uniform. The uniform mapping $\mathcal{U}(d)$ is defined as follows:

$$\mathcal{U}(d) = \begin{cases} d, & \text{if } d_B \text{ is uniform} \\ M, & \text{otherwise} \end{cases} \tag{5.6}$$

where d_B is the binary form of a number d and M is the total number of uniform patterns formed using N bits. We work with $N = 12$-bit sequences, which results in $M = 134$ uniform patterns.

5.2.2.4 Generalized Local Binary Pattern

A uniform GLBP operator is a generalization of the encoding method proposed in [22] by introducing a varying threshold t rather than a fixed one. Based on our empirical analysis, the combination of LBP applied to the magnitude response of a Gabor filter and GLBP applied to the phase response of the same Gabor filter boosts the cross-matching performance [39]. The uniform generalized binary operator is defined as follows:

$$\text{GLBP}^{\mathcal{U}}_{r,N,t}(x) = \mathcal{U}\left\{\sum_{i=1}^{N} \mathscr{T}_t\{x_i - x\}2^i\right\}, \tag{5.7}$$

where x_i is the ith neighbor of x at radius r (we set $r = 1, 2$ in our experiments) and N is the total number of neighbors. $\mathcal{U}(\cdot)$ is the uniform pattern mapping described in the previous subsection (see Sect. 5.2.2.3). $\mathscr{T}_t(\cdot)$ is a thresholding operator based on threshold t. It is defined as follows:

$$\mathcal{T}_t(x) = \begin{cases} 1, & |x| \leq t \\ 0, & |x| > t \end{cases} \tag{5.8}$$

The values for the thresholds in this chapter were evaluated experimentally and set to $t = \pi/2$.

5.2.2.5 Histogram of Oriented Gradients

Dalal and Triggs [17] were the first to introduce HOG in their work. The essential thought behind the HOG operator is that local object appearance and shape within an image can be described by the distribution of intensity gradients or edge directions.

An input image is computed using Gaussian smoothing followed by a derivative mask such as the very simple 1D mask $[-1, 0, 1]$. The directional derivatives can be expressed as follows:

$$G_x(x, y) = I(x+1, y) - I(x-1, y)$$
$$G_y(x, y) = I(x, y+1) - I(x, y-1), \tag{5.9}$$

where $I(x, y)$ is the input image. $G_x(x, y)$ and $G_y(x, y)$ denote the derivatives along x and y directions, respectively. Then, the magnitude and phase components of the gradient can be calculated as follows:

$$M(x, y) = \sqrt{G_x(x, y)^2 + G_y(x, y)^2}$$
$$\alpha(x, y) = \tan^{-1} \frac{G_x(x, y)}{G_y(x, y)}, \tag{5.10}$$

where $M(x, y)$ and $\alpha(x, y)$ are the magnitude and phase, respectively.

The next step is spatial and orientation binning. A weighted vote is calculated at each pixel for an edge orientation histogram channel based on the orientation of the gradient at that pixel, and the votes are accumulated into orientation bins over local small regions called cells (cells can be either rectangular or circular). The orientation bins are evenly spaced over $0° - 180°$ ("unsigned" gradient) or $0° - 360°$ ("signed" gradient). The vote is a function of the gradient magnitude at the pixel, very often the magnitude itself. The descriptor vector is thereafter normalized over non-overlapping blocks using the L_1 or L_2 norms, or their variants. An example of using L_2 normalization is given as follows:

$$\mathbf{v}^* = \mathbf{v}/\sqrt{\|\mathbf{v}\|_2^2 + \varepsilon^2}, \tag{5.11}$$

where $\mathbf{v}$ is the non-normalized descriptor vector and ε is a small constant.

5.2.2.6 Combination of Operators

A fusion of extracted features often leads to improved recognition performance. As shown in [38, 40], LBP and WLD applied to the magnitude of Gabor filtered images combined with GLBP applied to the phase of Gabor filtered images yielded a significant performance boost. Details of this fusion scheme can be found in [38, 40]. A block diagram of the fusion approach is displayed in Fig. 5.4.

5.2.2.7 Gabor Ordinal Measures

GOM is a recently developed local operator [11]. This operator combines Gabor filters (see Sect. 5.2.2.1) with ordinal measures, a measurement level which records the information about ordering of multiple quantities [46]. Following GOM, Chai et al. extracted a histogram representation and applied a dimensionality reduction by means of LDA to filtered and encoded face data.

The ordinal measure in [11] is modified using a smoothed neighborhood described by a Gaussian smoothing function. Therefore, the ordinal measure filter $f_{om}(\mathbf{z})$ can be expressed as follows:

$$
\begin{aligned}
f_{om}(\mathbf{z}) = C_p \sum_{i=1}^{N_p} & \frac{1}{\sqrt{2\pi}\sigma_{p,i}} \exp\left[\frac{-(\mathbf{z}-\mu_{p,i})^T(\mathbf{z}-\mu_{p,i})}{2\sigma_{p,i}^2}\right] \\
& - C_n \sum_{i=1}^{N_n} \frac{1}{\sqrt{2\pi}\sigma_{n,i}} \exp\left[\frac{-(\mathbf{z}-\mu_{n,i})^T(\mathbf{z}-\mu_{n,i})}{2\sigma_{n,i}^2}\right]
\end{aligned}
\tag{5.12}
$$

where $\mathbf{z} = (x, y)$ is the location of a pixel. $\mu_{p,i}$ and $\sigma_{p,i}$ denote the central position and the scale of the ith positive lobe of a 2D Gaussian function, while $\mu_{n,i}$ and $\sigma_{n,i}$ denote that of the ith negative lobe of the same Gaussian function. N_p and N_n are the numbers of positive and negative lobes, respectively, while constant coefficients C_p and C_n keep the balance between positive and negative lobes, i.e., $C_pN_p = C_nN_n$.

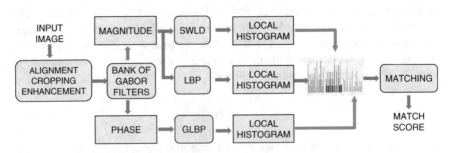

Fig. 5.4 A block diagram of the fusion scheme in [38]

5.2.2.8 Composite Multi-lobe Descriptor

In [9], a new operator named CMLD was proposed. CMLD combines Gabor filter, WLD, LBP, and GLBP and modifies them into multi-lobe functions with smoothed neighborhoods. The new operator encodes both magnitude and phase responses of Gabor filters. The combining of LBP and WLD utilizes both the orientation and intensity information of edges. The introduction of multi-lobe functions with smoothed neighborhoods further makes the proposed operator robust against noise and poor image quality. A block diagram of CMLD is provided in Fig. 5.5.

The multi-lobe version of LBP (referred to as MLLBP) is the same as the ordinal measure described in (5.12) (see Sec. 5.2.2.7). An illustration of such a MLLBP operator is provided in Fig. 5.6. The multi-lobe version of GLBP called MLGLBP is constructed in a similar way as MLLBP except for that the unit step function $\mathscr{I}(\cdot)$ in (5.5) is replaced by the thresholding function $\mathscr{T}_t(\cdot)$ in (5.8). The multi-lobe version of WLD (MLWLD) is a modification of the original WLD operator (see Sec. 2.2.2 for details) and is given by:

$$\text{MLWLD}_N(\mathbf{z}) = \mathscr{Q}_l \left\{ \tan^{-1} \left[\sum_{i=1}^{N} \frac{I(\mathbf{z}) * \hat{f}_{\text{MLWLD}}^{(i)}(\mathbf{z})}{I(\mathbf{z})} \right] \right\}, \tag{5.13}$$

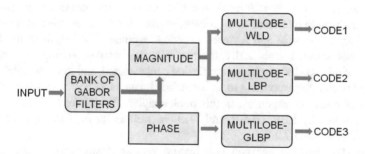

Fig. 5.5 A block diagram of composite multi-lobe descriptor

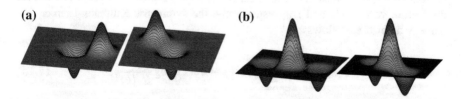

Fig. 5.6 Examples of kernels at different orientations used in multi-lobe operators: **a** a di-lobe function, **b** a trilobe function

where $I(\mathbf{z})$ is an input and $\mathbf{z} = (x, y)$ is the location of a pixel. $\hat{f}^{(i)}_{\mathrm{MLWLD}}(\mathbf{z})$ is the ith element of the set of $\Theta \times M$ kernel functions $\{f_{\mathrm{MLWLD}}(\mathbf{z}; \theta, L) : \theta = 1, 2, \ldots, \Theta;$ $L = 2, 3, \ldots, M\}$, where Θ is the total number of orientations and M is the maximum value of total lobe number. $f_{\mathrm{MLWLD}}(\mathbf{z}; \theta, L)$ is given by

$$f_{\mathrm{MLWLD}}(\mathbf{z}; \theta, L) = \sum_{l=1}^{L} \frac{C_l}{\sqrt{2\pi}\sigma_{l,\theta,L}} \exp\left[-\frac{(\mathbf{z} - \mu_{l,\theta,L})^T(\mathbf{z} - \mu_{l,\theta,L})}{2\sigma^2_{l,\theta,L}}\right], \qquad (5.14)$$

where $\mu_{l,\theta,L}$ and $\sigma_{l,\theta,L}$ are the center and the scale of the kernel function at orientation θ, and L is the total number of lobes. $\{C_l\}$ are the coefficients to keep a balance between the positive and negative lobes. A detailed description of MLLBP, MLGLBP, and MLWLD can be found in [9].

5.2.3 Histogram (Feature Vector) and Matching Metric

Each encoded response (the output of each local operator) is divided into 210 non-overlapping square blocks of size 8×8. Blocks are displayed in the form of histograms, and the number of bins is set to be equal to the level of the encoders mentioned in the previous section (e.g., 135 in our experiments). Then, a 135-bin histogram of each block is formed, and histograms of the blocks are concatenated and normalized to be treated as a probability mass function, resulting in a vector of length $135 \times 210 = 28{,}350$ for each encoded response. The length of the feature vector was selected empirically to maximize the cross-matching performance. Vectors of all encoded responses are further concatenated, and thus, the total size of a feature vector corresponding to an input face image is $28{,}350 \times P$, where P is the number of encoded responses. In this book chapter, $P = 96$ for the case of Gabor filters followed by LBP, GLBP, and WLD as well as for the case of CMLD (see Sects. 5.2.2.6 and 5.2.2.8).

When the distance between two feature vectors (histograms in our case) is evaluated, it is expressed as a sum of distances between all feature vector pairs. A sum of two Kullback-Leibler distances [30] is used as a distance metric to compare the feature vectors of heterogeneous images. For two images A and B with the feature vectors H_A and H_B, respectively, the symmetric Kullback-Leibler distance is defined as follows:

$$D_{KL}(A, B) = \sum_{k=1}^{K}(H_A(k) - H_B(k)) \log \frac{H_A(k)}{H_B(k)}, \qquad (5.15)$$

where K is the length of the feature vectors H_A or H_B.

5.3 Datasets

In our experiments, we use two datasets Pre-TINDERS (Tactical Imager for Night/Day Extended-Range Surveillance) and TINDERS collected by the Advanced Technologies Group, West Virginia High Tech Consortium (WVHTC) Foundation [35]. A summary of the datasets can be found in Table 5.1.

Pre-TINDERS is composed of 48 frontal face classes of total 576 images, at three wavelengths—visible, 980 nm NIR, and 1550 nm SWIR. Images are acquired at a short standoff distance of 1.5 m in a single session. Four images per class are available in each spectral band. A 980-nm light source is used to illuminate the face in the NIR spectral band, while a 1550-nm light source is used in the SWIR spectral band. The original resolutions of the acquired images (see Fig. 5.7) are 640 × 512

Table 5.1 Summary of the datasets

Dataset	Class	Total # images	Spectrum	Distance	Original resolution
Pre-TINDERS	48	576	Visible NIR SWIR	1.5 m	Visible: 1600 × 1200 NIR: 640 × 512 SWIR: 640 × 512
TINDERS	48	1255	Visible NIR SWIR	50 m 106 m	Visible: 640 × 480 NIR: 640 × 512 SWIR: 640 × 512

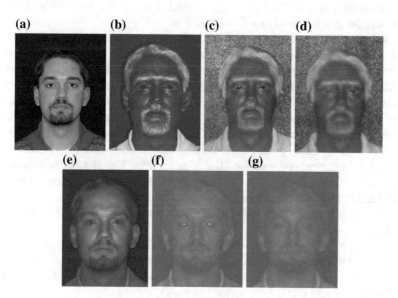

Fig. 5.7 Sample images: **a** visible, **b** SWIR at 1.5 m, **c** SWIR at 50 m, **d** SWIR at 106 m, **e** NIR at 1.5 m, **f** NIR at 50 m, and **g** NIR at 106 m

(png format) for both NIR and SWIR images and 1600×1200 (jpg format) for color images.

TINDERS is composed of 48 frontal face classes each represented by visible, NIR (980 nm) at two standoff distances (50 and 106 m), and SWIR at two standoff distances (50 and 106 m) images. At each distance and spectrum, four or five images per class are available. A total of 478 images with the resolution 640×512 (png format) are available in SWIR band. A total of 489 images with the resolution 640×512 (png format) are available in the NIR band. The visible (color) images with the resolution 480×640 (jpg format) are collected at a short distance and in two sessions (3 images per session), and all of them have neutral expression, resulting in a total of 288 images. Sample images from the Pre-TINDERS and TINDERS datasets are shown in Fig. 5.7.

It is important to note that although the original resolution of images in Pre-TINDERS and TINDERS is varying, we crop and normalize them to be the same size for each experiment described below. This is done to ensure a fair comparison.

5.4   Experiments and Results

In this section, we analyze the performance of various local operators used for encoding heterogeneous face images. In our experiments, galleries are composed of visible light face images, while NIR and SWIR face images are presented as probes. We match NIR and SWIR face images collected at 1.5, 50, and 106 m to visible light face images acquired at a distance 1.5 m.

For both SWIR and NIR spectra (at both short and long standoff distances), a total of 11 operators (including individual operators and their combinations) are implemented. We order and number them as follows: (1) LBP, (2) WLD, (3) GLBP, (4) HOG, (5) Gabor filter, (6) Gabor filter followed by LBP applied to the magnitude image (Gabor + LBP), (7) Gabor filter followed by WLD applied to the magnitude image (Gabor + WLD), (8) Gabor filter followed by GLBP applied to the phase image (Gabor + GLBP), (9) Gabor filter followed by LBP, GLBP, and WLD (Gabor + LBP + GLBP + WLD), (10) GOM, and (11) CMLD. The parameters in the experiments are chosen as follows. The number of orientations and radii for Gabor filters are set to 8 and 2, respectively. The number of radii for LBP, GLBP, and WLD is chosen as 2, and the number of neighbors around the central pixel is set to 12. The same parameters are used in operators to encode short- and long-range images.

The results of matching are displayed in the form of receiver operating characteristic (ROC) curves. We plot genuine accept rate (GAR) versus false accept rate (FAR). Summaries of equal error rates (EERs), d-prime values, and GARs at the FAR set to 0.1 and 0.001 are provided in tables.

5.4.1 Matching SWIR Probes Against Visible Gallery

Our first experiment involves matching SWIR face images to visible face images. The heterogeneous images are encoded using the eleven individual or composite operators as described earlier in this section. The performance of the individual encoders can be treated as benchmarks. The results of matching parameterized by different standoff distances are shown in Figs. 5.8, 5.9, and 5.10. In these experiments, visible light images form the gallery set. All SWIR images are used as probes.

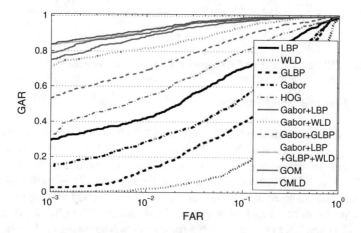

Fig. 5.8 ROC curves: matching SWIR probes at 1.5 m to visible gallery

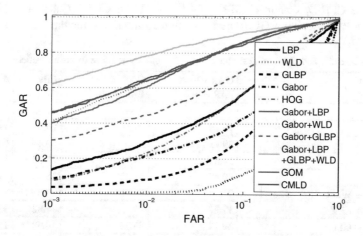

Fig. 5.9 ROC curves: matching SWIR probes at 50 m to visible gallery

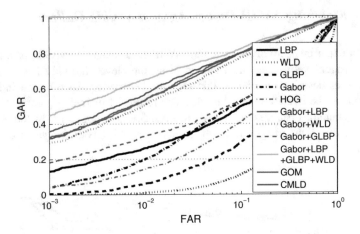

Fig. 5.10 ROC curves: matching SWIR probes at 106 m to visible gallery

5.4.1.1 Short Standoff Distance

For the case of the short standoff distance (pre-TINDERS dataset), the performance of single operators such as HOG, LBP, WLD, GLBP, and Gabor filters is inferior to the performance of the composite operators where Gabor filters are followed by LBP, WLD, and GLBP. It is also inferior to the performance of each CMLD and GOM, the composite multi-lobe operators. Within the group of single operators, HOG outperforms the other four operators closely followed by LBP and then Gabor filters. WLD appears to be less suitable for encoding heterogeneous face images in the framework of the cross-spectral matching.

Within the group of composite operators, the top five, following closely together, are CMLD, Gabor + LBP + GLBP + WLD, GOM, Gabor + LBP, and Gabor + WLD. Gabor + GLBP performs slightly inferior to the top three. Table 5.2

Table 5.2 EERs and GAR values: matching SWIR probes at 1.5 m to visible gallery

Method	GAR (%) at FAR = 10^{-1}	GAR (%) at FAR = 10^{-3}	EER (%)	d-prime
WLD	15.89	0.39	41.40	0.40
LBP	70.70	29.56	20.61	1.66
GLBP	39.71	2.60	33.46	0.98
Gabor	54.04	14.71	27.35	1.24
HOG	80.47	32.55	15.36	1.86
Gabor + WLD	94.14	71.88	7.68	2.74
Gabor + LBP	97.27	75	4.82	3.09
Gabor + GLBP	89.19	53.39	10.68	2.35
Gabor + WLD + LBP + GLBP	99.09	83.59	3.13	3.24
GOM	98.18	78.78	3.64	3.18
CMLD	**99.09**	**83.72**	**3.12**	**3.29**

presents a summary of EERs, d-prime values, and GAR values at FAR set to 0.1
and 0.001 values.

5.4.1.2 Long Standoff Distance

SWIR images at longer standoff distances (50 and 106 m in the case of TINDERS
dataset) experience some loss of quality due to air turbulence, insufficient illumination, and optical effects during data acquisition. This immediately reflects on the
values of matching scores. Figures 5.9 and 5.10 display the results of cross-spectral
comparison parameterized by 50 and 106 m standoff distances, respectively.
Gallery images are retained from the previous session. Note that in both figures,
Gabor + LBP, Gabor + WLD, CMLD, and GOM display a very similar performance. They are closely followed by Gabor + GLBP. The top performance in both
cases is demonstrated by Gabor + LBP + GLBP + WLD. Once again, composite
operators outperform single operators, which was anticipated. However, at longer
standoff distances, matching performance of all the operators and their combinations but Gabor + LBP + GLBP + WLD drops nearly two times for the case of 50 m
and 2.5 times for the case of 106 m. EERs, d-prime values, and GARs at FAR set to
0.1 and 0.001 are summarized in Tables 5.3 and 5.4.

5.4.2 Matching NIR Probes Against Visible Gallery

In the second experiment, NIR face images (probes) are matched to short-range
visible face images (gallery). The results of matching parameterized by the standoff
distances of 1.5, 50, and 106 m are shown in Figs. 5.11, 5.12, and 5.13,
respectively.

Table 5.3 EERs and GAR values: matching SWIR probes at 50 m to visible gallery

Method	GAR (%) at FAR = 10^{-1}	GAR (%) at FAR = 10^{-3}	EER (%)	d-prime
WLD	11.55	0.21	49.59	0.045
LBP	57.29	13.45	25.28	1.24
GLBP	31.86	3.71	37.07	0.65
Gabor	43.35	8.33	34.97	0.82
HOG	57.42	7.56	25.42	1.25
Gabor + WLD	85.57	40.90	12.74	2.19
Gabor + LBP	85.01	46.15	12.89	2.25
Gabor + GLBP	70.10	30.18	20.51	1.56
Gabor + WLD + LBP + GLBP	**91.88**	**62.11**	**8.90**	**2.57**
GOM	86.41	39.98	11.97	2.27
CMLD	86.76	45.73	12.03	2.31

Table 5.4 EERs and GAR values: matching SWIR probes at 106 m to visible gallery

Method	GAR (%) at FAR = 10^{-1}	GAR (%) at FAR = 10^{-3}	EER (%)	d-prime
WLD	11.39	0.10	48.69	0.0038
LBP	49.79	13.19	31.11	0.94
GLBP	29.31	0.49	36.49	0.57
Gabor	52.57	4.31	28.67	1.09
HOG	41.04	4.44	33.68	0.78
Gabor + WLD	77.57	29.31	16.96	1.83
Gabor + LBP	80.00	31.81	15.83	1.99
Gabor + GLBP	53.06	18.19	32.65	0.88
Gabor + WLD + LBP + GLBP	**82.50**	**44.79**	**14.17**	**2.00**
GOM	80.07	32.78	14.78	2.02
CMLD	80.28	35.97	15.76	2.04

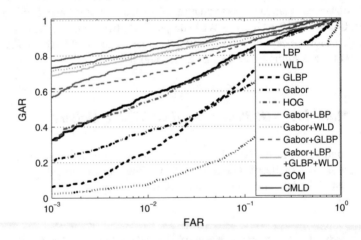

Fig. 5.11 The results of cross-matching short-range (1.5 m) NIR probes and visible gallery images

5.4.2.1 Short Standoff Distance

Among the group of single operators, LBP and HOG outperform the other operators, followed by GLBP and Gabor. Similar to the case of SWIR probe images, WLD operator performs poorly. All composite operators demonstrate a relatively high performance with ROC curves closely following one another. CMLD appears to outperform the other four composite operators. It is closely followed by GOM and then by Gabor + LBP + GLBP + WLD. Table 5.5 summarizes the values of EERs, d-primes, and GARs at FAR equal to 0.1 and 0.001.

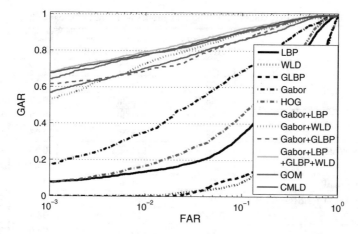

Fig. 5.12 The results of cross-matching long-range (50 m) NIR probes and visible gallery images

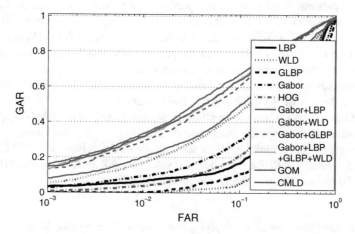

Fig. 5.13 The results of cross-matching short-range (106 m) NIR probes and visible gallery images

5.4.2.2 Long Standoff Distance

Long-range NIR probes display a cardinally different performance. As can be seen from Fig. 5.7, NIR images at 106 m have much lower contrast and overall quality compared to NIR images at 50 m. This difference in image quality immediately reflects on the matching performance of the two sets of probes (50 m probes and 106 m probes). This also reflects on the interplay among the 11 operators. Figures 5.12 and 5.13 display the cross-matching results for the two standoff distances (50 m and 106 m, respectively). Comparing the composite operators in terms of their performance, NIR at 50 m shows that Gabor + LBP + GLBP +WLD, CMLD,

Table 5.5 EERs and GAR values: matching NIR probes at 1.5 m to visible gallery

Method	GAR (%) at FAR = 10^{-1}	GAR (%) at FAR = 10^{-3}	EER (%)	d-prime
WLD	29.82	2.47	44.27	0.44
LBP	82.03	32.81	14.36	2.12
GLBP	66.54	6.38	20.57	1.467
Gabor	61.46	21.09	23.57	1.43
HOG	65.23	23.96	22.03	1.68
Gabor + WLD	89.19	71.098	10.54	2.38
Gabor + LBP	86.98	56.77	11.82	2.29
Gabor + GLBP	86.20	61.595	12.23	2.29
Gabor + WLD + LBP + GLBP	91.93	68.88	8.73	2.48
GOM	90.89	73.31	9.27	2.59
CMLD	**92.71**	**77.21**	**7.68**	**2.72**

and GOM perform equally well. Their performance is very close to the performance they demonstrate at 1.5 m. Note it is only slightly degraded. These three ROCs are closely followed by the ROCs of Gabor + GLBP and Gabor + WLD. At 106 m, NIR probes do not perform as well. In fact, the performance of NIR images encoded with composite operators drops at least three times compared to the performance of the same operators applied to NIR at 50 m. Figure 5.13 indicates that GOM followed by CMLD, Gabor + LBP + GLBP + WLD, and Gabor + GLBP, where GLBP is applied to phase images, seems to be more robust to degraded image quality in NIR spectrum compared to other composite operators. Among single operators, Gabor and HOG still outperform other single operators for both standoff distances. Tables 5.6 and 5.7 present a summary of EERs, d-primes, and GARs at FAR set to 0.1 and 0.001 for the case of 50 m and 106 m standoff distances, respectively.

Table 5.6 EERs and GAR values: matching NIR probes at 50 m to visible gallery

Method	GAR (%) at FAR = 10^{-1}	GAR (%) at FAR = 10^{-3}	EER (%)	d-prime
WLD	5.39	0.1	48.12	0.072
LBP	34.17	7.70	31.74	0.99
GLBP	11.06	0.1	49.01	0.12
Gabor	68.98	17.23	19.98	1.66
HOG	44.68	7.35	29.98	1.16
Gabor + WLD	89.85	53.011	10.07	2.40
Gabor + LBP	86.13	56.79	12.54	2.33
Gabor + GLBP	92.02	69.89	8.66	2.73
Gabor + WLD + LBP + GLBP	**92.23**	**68.21**	**8.71**	**2.66**
GOM	90.06	64.29	10.00	2.65
CMLD	90.76	67.51	9.52	2.65

Table 5.7 EERs and GAR values: matching NIR probes at 106 m to visible gallery

Method	GAR (%) at FAR = 10^{-1}	GAR (%) at FAR = 10^{-3}	EER (%)	d-prime
WLD	7.91	0.1	49.40	0.067
LBP	16.95	3.18	43.30	0.45
GLBP	10.52	0.1	50.21	0.038
Gabor	29.66	2.61	36.87	0.72
HOG	21.12	0.64	42.87	0.52
Gabor + WLD	45.97	5.23	30.48	1.05
Gabor + LBP	49.72	7.84	28.43	1.10
Gabor + GLBP	60.88	13.14	23.16	1.44
Gabor + WLD + LBP + GLBP	64.48	13.28	23.24	1.49
GOM	**67.30**	**15.53**	**21.65**	**1.58**
CMLD	64.12	14.62	22.55	1.51

5.5 Brief Analysis

1. Combining Gabor filter bank with other local operators results in considerably improved performance compared to the performance of individual local operators. This holds both for short and long standoff distances and for the both types of cross-spectral matching performed in this chapter.
2. As anticipated, quality of active IR probes affects matching performance. In this chapter, quality of probes is a function of a standoff distance. We use an adaptive sharpness measure [51] to calculate the image quality of the probes in both SWIR and NIR spectra at all the standoff distances (see Table 5.8 for the values). From the results, the matching performance of SWIR data degrades with standoff distance faster than the matching performance of NIR images. However, the overall sharpness measure values (and thus the matching performance) of SWIR images is higher compared to the sharpness measure values (and the matching performance) of NIR images.
3. Among the five individual operators, HOG outperforms other operators followed by LBP and Gabor for the case of 1.5-m standoff distance and SWIR probes. For the case of 50-m standoff distance and SWIR probes, LBP and HOG perform nearly equally well followed by Gabor. For the case of 106 m and SWIR probes, LBP, and Gabor, each outperforms HOG. This leads to a conclusion that LBP and Gabor are more robust to data acquisition noise compared to HOG.

Table 5.8 Sharpness measure of the probes in SWIR and NIR at different standoff distances

Statistics of sharpness measure	SWIR at 1.5 m	SWIR at 50 m	SWIR at 106 m	NIR at 1.5 m	NIR at 50 m	NIR at 106 m
Mean	0.5835	0.5112	0.4391	0.4390	0.3910	0.3741
Standard deviation	0.0707	0.0732	0.0730	0.0595	0.0461	0.0642

4. For the case of NIR probes and 1.5-m standoff distance, LBP and HOG perform equally well. Their ROC curves very closely following one another. For the case of NIR probes and both 50 m and 106 m standoff distances, Gabor filters substantially outperform HOG and LBP, which continue to show very similar performance. Thus, poor quality NIR images should be encoded with Gabor filters for robust cross-matching performance.

5. All composite operators, where Gabor filters are followed by the application of other local operators, perform equally well in nearly all cases of standoff distances and the two types of active-IR probes. Performance of the combination of Gabor + GLBP is slightly inferior to the other combinations in every case besides the case of NIR probes and 106-m standoff distance. This is the case where Gabor + GLBP applied to the phase of face images demonstrated superior performance compared to other operators. Thus, Gabor + GLBP appear to be very robust to severe image degradation for the case of NIR probes.

6. Multi-lobe operators, CMLD and GOM, and the composite operator Gabor + LBP + GLBP + WLD display the top performance in all three cases of standoff distance for both types of cross-spectral matching.

7. The improved performance of the composite operators comes at a cost of increased complexity. For a single operator, the feature vector (histogram) is formed from 2 outputs of the operator. For a composite operator, the feature vector is 16 times longer due to 16 outputs of Gabor filters each encoded with a local operator. The involvement of each additional local operator (applied to outputs of Gabor filters) doubles the length of the feature vector. Although the complexity of the feature vector grows, most of the operations can be implemented in parallel, which allows involvement of devices for parallel computing.

5.6 Summary

This chapter presented a short overview of recent advances in the field of heterogeneous face recognition, emphasizing the topic of local operators developed for matching active-IR face probes to a gallery composed of high-quality visible face images. A brief description of each individual and composite operator (11 in total) was provided. The list of individual operators included LBP, GLBP, WLD, HOG, and Gabor filters. Composite operators included Gabor + LBP, Gabor + GLBP, Gabor + WLD, Gabor + LBP + GLBP + WLD, GOM, and CMLD. We considered a very specific framework for cross-matching heterogeneous face images, assuming that each image is aligned, cropped, and enhanced at first. It was then filtered and encoded using local operators. The outputs of local operators were converted into a histogram representation and compared against histogram representations of images in the gallery by means of a symmetric Kullback-Leibler distance. This cross-matching approach does not require any training or learning, and it is shown to be robust when applied to a variety of heterogeneous datasets.

We presented the results of matching SWIR and NIR facial images to visible facial images. Both short (1.5 m) and long (50 and 106 m) standoff distances were considered. The results were documented in figures and tables. We presented ROC curves as well as GARs at two specific levels of FAR, EERs, and d-prime values. The combination of Gabor filters followed by other local operators substantially outperformed the original LBP and the other individual operators. As the standoff distance increased, the matching performance of all the operators dropped. This drop was attributed to a relatively low quality of imagery at long standoff distances (SWIR vs. visible and NIR vs. visible).

Acknowledgements The authors would like to thank Brian Lemoff of West Virginia High Technology Consortium Foundation for providing the Pre-TINDERS and TINDERS datasets employed in the described experiments in this book chapter.

References

1. Ahonen, T., Hadid, A., Pietikainen, M.: Face recognition with local binary patterns. In: Proceedings of European Conference on Comuputer Vision (ECCV), pp. 469–481 (2004)
2. Akhloufi, M., Bendada, A.H.: Multispectral infrared face recognition: a comparative study. In: Proceedings of Quantitative InfraRed Thermography (2010)
3. Bartlet, M.S., Sejnowski, T.J.: Independent components of face images: a representation for face recognition. In: Proceedings of 4th Annual Journal Symposium Neural Computation (1997)
4. Bartlett, M.S., Movellan, J.R., Sejnowski, T.J.: Face recognition by independent component analysis. IEEE Trans. Neural Netw. **13**(6), 14501464 (2002)
5. Bourlai, T., Kalka, N., Ross, A., Cukic, B., Hornak, L.: Cross-spectral face verification in the short wave infrared (SWIR) band. In: Proceedings of International Conference on Patterns Recognition, pp. 1343–1347 (2010)
6. Buddharaju, P., Pavlidis, I.T., Tsiamyrtzis, P., Bazakos, M.: Physiology-based face recognition in the thermal infrared spectrum. IEEE Trans. Pattern Anal. Machine Intell. **29** (4), 613–626 (2007)
7. Cao, Z., Schmid, N.A.: Recognition performance of cross-spectral periocular biometrics and partial face at short and long standoff distance. Open Trans. Info. Process. **1**(2), 20–32
8. Cao, Z., Schmid, N.A.: Matching heterogeneous periocular regions: short and long standoff distances. In: Proceedings of the IEEE International Conference on Image Processing, pp. 4967–4971 (2014)
9. Cao, Z., Schmid, N.A.: Composite multi-lobe descriptor for cross-spectral face recognition: matching active ir to visible light images. In: Proc. SPIE. **9476**, pp. 94,760T–94,760T–13 (2015)
10. Cao, Z., Schmid, N.A.: Fusion of operators for heterogeneous periocular recognition at varying ranges. Pattern Recogn. Lett. doi: 10.1016/j.patrec.2015.10.018. http://www.sciencedirect.com/science/article/pii/S0167865515003694. (2015)
11. Chai, Z., Sun, Z., Mendez-Vazquez, H., He, R., Tan, T.: Gabor ordinal measures for face recognition. IEEE Trans. Info. Forensics Secur. **9**(1), 14–26 (2014)
12. Chen, J., Shan, S., He, C., Zhao, G., Pietikeinen, M., Chen, X., Gao, W.: Wld: A robust local image descriptor. IEEE Trans. Pattern Anal. Mach. Int. **32**(9), 1705–1720 (2010)
13. Chen, X., Flynn, P., Bowyer, K.: PCA-based face recognition in infrared imagery: Baseline and comparative studies. In: Proceedings of IEEE International Workshop on Analysis and Modeling of Faces and Gestures, pp. 127–134 (2003)

14. Chen, X., Flynn, P.J., Bowyer, K.W.: IR and visible light face recognition. Comput. Vis. Image Understand. **99**(3), 332–358 (2005)

15. Cognitec: Facevacs software developer kit cognitec systems. (Online) http://www.cognitec-systems.de. Accessed 04 Jan 2015

16. Comon, P.: Independent component analysis, a new concept? Sig. Process. **36**(3), 287–314 (1994)

17. Dalal, N., Triggs, B.: Histograms of oriented gradients for human detection. In: Proceedings of IEEE Conference on Computer Vision and Pattern Recognition, pp. 886–893 (2005)

18. Daugman, J.G.: Uncertainty relation for resolution in space, spatial frequency, and orientation optimized by two-dimensional visual cortical filters. J. Opt. Soc. Am. A **2**(7), 11601169 (1985)

19. Daugman, J.G.: Complete discrete 2-d Gabor transforms by neural networks for image analysis and compression. IEEE Trans. Pattern Anal. Machine Intell. **36**(7), 1169–1179 (1988)

20. Fisher, R.A.: The use of multiple measurements in taxonomic problems. Ann. Eugenics **7**(2), 179–188 (1936)

21. Goodrich: Surveillance using SWIR night vision cameras. (online) http://www.sensorsinc.com/facilitysecurity.html. Accessed 01 Feb , 2015

22. Guo, Y., Xu, Z.: Local Gabor phase difference pattern for face recognition. In: Proceedings of International Conference on Pattern Recognition, pp. 1–4 (2008)

23. Hansen, M.P., Malchow, D.S.: Overview of SWIR detectors, cameras, and applications. In: Proceedings of SPIE: Thermosense XXX, pp. 69, 390I–69, 390I–11 (2008)

24. Heikkil, M., Pietikinen, M.: A texture-based method for modeling the background and detecting moving objects. IEEE Trans. Pattern Anal. Mach. Intell. **28**(4), 657–662 (2006)

25. Hotelling, H.: Relations between two sets of variates. Biometrika **28**(3), 321–377 (1936)

26. Jain, A.K., Ratha, N.K., Lakshmanan, S.: Object detection using Gabor filters. Pattern Recogn. **30**(2), 295309 (1997)

27. Jutten, C., Herault, J.: Blind separation of sources i. an adaptive algorithm based on neuromimetic architecture. Signal Process. **24**(1), 110 (1991)

28. Kirschner, J.: SWIR for target detection, recognition, and identification. (online) http://www.photonicsonline.com/doc.mvc/SWIR-For-Target-Detection-Recognition-And-0002 (2011). Accessed 04 Jan 2015

29. Klare, B., Jain, A.K.: Heterogeneous face recognition: matching NIR to visible light images. In: Proceedings of International Conference on Pattern Recognition, pp. 1513–1516 (2010)

30. Kullback, S., Leibler, R.A.: On information and sufficiency. Ann. Math. Stat. **22**(1), 79–86 (1951)

31. Lee, T.S.: Image representation using 2d Gabor wavelets. IEEE Trans. Pattern Anal. Mach. Intell. **18**(10), 959971 (1996)

32. Li, S.Z., Chu, R., Liao, S., Zhang, L.: Illumination invariant face recognition using near-infrared images. IEEE Trans. Pattern Anal. Mach. Intell. **29**(4), 627–639 (2007)

33. Lyons, M., Akamatsu, S., Kamachi, M., Gyoba, J.: Coding facial expressions with Gabor wavelets. In: Proceedings of IEEE International Conference on Automatic Face and Gesture Recognition, pp. 200–205 (1998)

34. Marelja, S.: Mathematical description of the responses of simple cortical cells. J. Opt. Soc. Am. **70**(11), 12971300 (1980)

35. Martin, R.B., Kafka, K.M., Lemoff, B.E.: Active-SWIR signatures for long-range night/day human detection and identification. In: Proceedings of the SPIE Symposium on DSS, pp. 209–218 (2013)

36. Mehrotra, R., Namuduri, K.R., Ranganathan, N.: Gabor filter-based edge detection. Pattern Recognition **25**(12), 14791494 (1992)

37. Melzera, T., Reitera, M., Bisch, H.: Appearance models based on kernel canonical correlation analysis. Pattern Recogn. **36**(9), 1961–1971 (2003)

38. Nicolo, F.: Homogeneous and heterogeneous face recognition: enhancing, encoding and matching for practical applications. Ph.D. thesis, West Virginia University (2012)

39. Nicolo, F., Schmid, N.A.: A method for robust multispectral face recognition. In: Proceedings of the International Conference on Image Analysis and Recognition, pp. 180–190 (2011)
40. Nicolo, F., Schmid, N.A.: Long range cross-spectral face recognition: Matching SWIR against visible light images. IEEE Trans. Inf. Forensics Secur. 7(6), 1717–1726 (2012)
41. Ojala, T., Pietikainen, M., Maenpaa, T.: Multiresolution gray-scale and rotation invariant texture classification with local binary patterns. IEEE Trans. Inf. Forensics Secur. 24(7), 971–987 (2002)
42. Ojala, T., Pietikinen, M., Harwood, D.: Performance evaluation of texture measures with classification based on Kullback discrimination of distributions. In: Proceedings of IAPR International Conference on Pattern Recognition, pp. 582–556 (1994)
43. Ross, H.E., Murray, D.J.: E. H. Weber on the Tactile Senses, 2nd edn. Erlbaum (UK) Taylor and Francis (1996)
44. Sirovich, L., Kirby, M.: Low-dimensional procedure for the characterization of human faces. J. Opt. Soc. Am. A 4(3), 519–524 (1987)
45. Socolinsky, D., Wolff, L., Neuheisel, J., Eveland, C.: Illumination invariant face recognition using thermal infrared imagery. In: Proceedings of the IEEE Conference on Computer Vision and Pattern Recognition, vol. 1, pp. 527–534 (2001)
46. Stevens, S.S.: On the theory of scales of measurement. Science 103(2684), 677–680 (1946)
47. Turk, M.A., Pentland, A.P.: Eigenfaces for recognition. J. Cogn. Neurosci. 13(1), 71–86 (1991)
48. Turk, M.A., Pentland, A.P.: Face recognition using eigenfaces. In: Proceedings of IEEE Conference on Computer Vision and Pattern Recognition, pp. 586–591 (1991)
49. Viola, P., Jones, M.: Rapid object detection using a boosted cascade of simple features. In: Proceedings of IEEE Conference on Computer Vision and Pattern Recognition, pp. 511–518 (2001)
50. Wang, L., He, D.C.: Texture classification using texture spectrum. IEEE Trans. Pattern Anal. Mach. Int. 23(8), 905–910 (1990)
51. WVHTCF: Tactical imager for night/day extended-range surveillance. (online) http://www.wvhtf.org/programs/advancedtech/ONR
52. Yao, Y., Abidi, B., Abidi, M.: Digital imaging with extreme zoom: System design and image restoration. In: Proceedings of the IEEE International Conference on Computer Vision Systems (2006)
53. Zhang, L., Chu, R., Xiang, S., Liao, S., Li, S.Z.: Face detection based on multi-block lbp representation. In: Advances in Biometrics, Lecture Notes in Computer Science, vol. 4642, pp. 11–18. Springer, Berlin, Heidelberg (2007)
54. Zhao, G., Pietikinen, M.: Dynamic texture recognition using local binary patterns with an application to facial expressions. IEEE Trans. Pattern Anal. Mach. Intell. 29(6), 915–928 (2007)

Chapter 6
Assessment of Facial Recognition System Performance in Realistic Operating Environments

Kevin R. Leonard

Abstract An end-to-end facial recognition system performance depends on a variety of factors. The optical system, environment, illumination, target, and recognition algorithm can all affect its accuracy. Typically, only the facial recognition algorithm has been considered when evaluating performance. The remaining environmental and system components have not been considered in the design of facial recognition imaging systems. However, in scenarios relevant to the military and homeland security, the effects of weather and range can severely degrade performance and it is necessary to understand the conditions where this happens. This work introduces a methodology to explore the sensitivities of a facial recognition imaging system to blur, noise, and turbulence effects. Using a government-owned and an open source facial recognition algorithm, system performance is evaluated under different optical blurs, sensor noises, and turbulence conditions. The ramifications of these results on the design of long-range facial recognition systems are also discussed.

6.1 Introduction

The current and future operating environments that the US Army faces are characterized by uncertainty and surprise [1]. Threats are coming from increasingly non-traditional sources and tactically relevant biometrics need to be applied at longer rages, at night, and in degraded environments. Most current commercial biometric systems are being designed for controlled situations and relatively short ranges. For many applications (e.g., access control, fixed entry points), these systems perform extremely well. However, military and homeland security applications put tougher demands on biometric systems. They need to be able to operate at longer ranges and perform well under degraded imaging conditions. Also, because

K.R. Leonard (✉)
U.S. Army RDECOM CERDEC Night Vision Electronic Sensors Directorate, RDER-NVM,
10221 Burbeck Rd, Fort Belvoir, VA 22060, USA
e-mail: kevin.r.leonard1.civ@mail.mil

© Springer International Publishing Switzerland (outside the USA) 2016   117
T. Bourlai (ed.), *Face Recognition Across the Imaging Spectrum*,
DOI 10.1007/978-3-319-28501-6_6

of the importance of these missions, it is critical to understand how sensitive an acquisition system performance is to various imaging conditions.

In this work, we will focus on exploring the effects of imaging system degradations on facial recognition performance. Facial recognition algorithm performance has increased dramatically over the last couple of decades as both industry and academia have invested heavily in this area. There are a variety of different types of facial recognition algorithms, including PCA-based eigenfaces [2, 3], LDA-based [4, 5], and Elastic Bunch Graphing [6] methods. A detailed survey of facial recognition techniques is outside of the scope of this work, but the reader is referred to Refs. [7–9] for a more detailed review of facial recognition algorithms.

One reason that facial recognition algorithm performance has increased so dramatically over the last decade is the increasing availability of diverse facial databases and rigorous systematic testing. Some of the most widely used facial databases are the Facial Recognition Technology (FERET) [10–12], Carnegie Melon University Pose Illumination and Expression (CMU PIE) and Multi-PIE [13, 14], Labelled Faces in the Wild (LFW) [15], AR Face [16], and Surveillance Cameras (SC) Face [17] databases. The FERET database was one of the first publically available databases and was originally used extensively by the National Institute for Standards and Technology (NIST) to perform independent assessments of facial recognition performance. The CMU PIE database includes images of subjects under different illuminations and expressions, whereas the Multi-PIE database extends the number of subjects and includes images for 15 viewpoints and 19 illumination conditions. LFW contains more than 13,000 faces collected from the Web to help researchers explore recognition of unconstrained facial imagery. The SC Face database is a set of still images taken from SC of varying image quality. Finally, the AR Face database contains color images from subjects and also includes facial occlusions such as sunglasses and scarves.

In addition to the growing number of available databases to test algorithms against, a lot of work has also been conducted on the systematic, independent evaluation of facial recognition algorithm performance [10–12, 18–23]. Most of the previous evaluations of facial recognition performance have focused on exploring the effects of pose [20], illumination [21], and age [24]. Phillips et al. have also looked at the effects of image compression [22]. These studies have done an excellent job in measuring and comparing current biometric algorithm performance on large datasets. These datasets were collected to try and capture different effects seen in traditional biometric applications such as uncontrolled illumination and subject pose. These tests have been designed to push the performance of algorithms and to show developers and researchers the areas needed for improvement. From the Facial Recognition Vendor Test in 2002 (FRVT2002) [19], it was pointed out that work was still needed in the recognition of faces in outdoor lighting conditions and under non-frontal poses. In the Multi-Biometric Evaluation Tests in 2010 [20], improvement on non-frontal poses was seen, and certain vendor algorithms performed extremely well at pose angles up to 20°.

This prior work has shown that the systematic testing of algorithms is critical to understanding how facial recognition algorithms will perform under different conditions. In [25], Phillips et al. point out that it is important to consider the conditions under which a biometric system will be utilized when evaluating potential candidate solutions. Therefore, a large factor for predicting biometric performance is understanding how it will be used and under what conditions it will be effective. To complement these prior studies, this work aims to extend how we evaluate algorithm performance to include optical system design considerations for more tactically relevant environments. Operational environments are different from traditional biometric application areas such as access control and fixed entry points. In surveillance applications, it is important to be able to use facial recognition algorithms at longer ranges and in non-ideal conditions. Under these circumstances, image blurring (due to defocus and/or motion), noise (in low-light conditions), and atmospheric turbulence effects can be common.

Much of the previous work in the facial recognition literature has been focused on overcoming the effects of pose and illumination on recognition performance. Overcoming the effects of blur, noise and turbulence have been less studied. Two methods for trying to overcome the effects of blur and sampling are image super-resolution [26–29] and deconvolution [30–32]. Wheeler et al. [27] show how an active appearance model (AAM) can be used to register faces for the purpose of increasing image resolution through a super-resolution technique. They demonstrate how the facial image resolution increases and leads to better facial recognition performance. Baker and Kanade [26] also demonstrate how super-resolution can be used to improve facial images that have been degraded due to downsampling. Alternatively, researchers have also explored deconvolution techniques for overcoming the effects of blur. In these methods, they attempt to determine the level and type of blur before applying a filter to the degraded image to improve its resolution before matching. Heflin et al. [30] estimate blur parameters to aid their deblurring algorithm and show improved recognition results for subsets of both the FERET and LFW databases. Each of these works points out that image blur degrades facial recognition performance and explores algorithmic means to overcome blur.

In low-light scenarios, noise can also cause significant degradations in image quality. Some work has previously been performed to explore how facial recognition algorithms can overcome the effects of different types of noise, such as Gaussian, Poisson, and salt-and-pepper noise. Both neural networks [33, 34] and support vector machines (SVMs) [35, 36] have been shown to improve facial recognition on noisy imagery. It is interesting to note that recent work in deep learning [37–39] has also shown that modern neural networks have the ability to perform comparably to humans in facial recognition tasks.

Finally, optical turbulence is known to affect imaging system performance under a variety of scenarios [40–42]. Its effects are most damaging in ground-to-ground, horizontal imaging conditions. Not much work has been done in this area to determine its effects on facial recognition performance. Hefflin et al. [30] discuss how their deblurring methodology could overcome some effects of turbulence, but they only address low turbulence conditions where space-varying distortions and blur caused by the atmosphere do not significantly affect image quality. Espinola et al. [42] have shown how turbulence can affect imaging system performance in operationally relevant scenarios. Leonard et al. [43] have also taken a preliminary look at how turbulence mitigation algorithms have the potential to improve facial recognition performance under turbulent conditions.

While prior work has explored algorithmic methods to overcome blur and noise degradations, they have not focused on how optical design and the environment can also affect the end-to-end facial recognition system performance. The rest of this work will outline a methodology to answer these types of questions. For example, "How do sensor noise and blur affect performance?" or "How tolerant are facial recognition algorithms to image degradations caused by atmospheric turbulence?" One approach to answering these types of questions is to try and determine the minimum image quality needed for facial recognition performance. Previous work has been performed to try and correlate image quality metrics (IQMs) to recognition performance [44–48]. In Abaza et al. [47], the authors explore a variety of IQMs and their sensitivity to changes in quality to propose their face quality index (FQI) as a benchmark for measuring facial image quality. Other quality benchmarks exist, including Hsu et al. [45], who developed a method to compare image quality against the ISO/IEC 19794-5 standards. These quality measures are often used to determine whether an image has the appropriate quality to be matched with the facial recognition algorithm. However, as Beveridge et al. point out in [49], two high-quality images may not always match, so while understanding image quality is important, it is not the only factor in a facial recognition system's performance.

The approach that we choose to use in this work is to simulate the optical imaging system degradations (e.g., blur, noise, and turbulence) on standard datasets to explore algorithm performance under different operationally relevant conditions. This allows one to conduct trade studies on optical system design, conduct sensitivity analyses, and explore how these trades would affect recognition performance.

6.2 Methodology

It is often very expensive and difficult to conduct extensive field trials to test biometric system performance. For this reason, many researchers use existing datasets to test their algorithms. However, these datasets are usually collected using a small set of controlled cameras, or in the case of datasets like Labelled Faces in the Wild [15], with a large variety of uncontrolled cameras. This makes it very difficult to use these datasets to explore how a system design, or adverse imaging conditions, could affect a recognition algorithm's performance.

In this work, we use a database of pristine facial images and simulate image degradations to measure system performance under different conditions. This enables us to take an existing dataset and generate imagery that would be representative of a tactical facial recognition imaging system. From this imagery, we can explore the effects of different system trades on a biometric system's overall performance by generating the imagery for the various conditions.

In the rest of this work, we show how this can be done for three different trade studies: blur, noise, and atmospheric turbulence. The facial images used in this study were taken from the publicly available FERET database [10–12]. The FERET database was sponsored by the DoD Counterdrug Development Program Office to support government-monitored testing and evaluation of facial recognition algorithms using standardized tests and procedures. The database consists of eight-bit grayscale images of human heads from 1196 subjects. The imagery has views ranging from frontal to left and right profiles and is freely available for researchers. In this work, unless otherwise noted, we will use the pristine "FA" frontal subset of the FERET data as the gallery (or target) images and the "FB" frontal subset as the probe set. The "FA" and "FB" images were captured during the same session, and the subjects were asked to change their facial expressions between images. In this study, the "FB" probe set will also be "degraded" by the different conditions described below before matching against the unmodified gallery set.

Two different facial recognition algorithms will be used to evaluate facial recognition performance for the various conditions. The first algorithm is government off-the-shelf (GOTS) facial recognition software. The GOTS algorithm is considered a black box system and it is unknown exactly how the internal matching is performed. However, if images meet a minimum image quality standard (e.g., a face and facial features can be detected), they can be enrolled by the GOTS algorithm for matching against a gallery.

The second algorithm used is a publicly available algorithm from the Colorado State University [50, 51] that uses principal component analysis (PCA) to match faces. Given a facial image and known eye coordinates, the CSU algorithm crops the face and performs histogram normalization on the input grayscale image. The PCA-based algorithm in this work was trained on the standard FERET training set. Once trained, image templates can be formed for both the probe and gallery sets. These templates represent where the images reside in the PCA-based space. The similarity of two images can then be calculated using standard distance measures. In this study, we calculate distances using the Mahalanobis cosine distance:

$$D_{\text{MahCosine}}(u, v) = -\cos(\theta_{mn}) = -\frac{m \cdot n}{|m||n|} \tag{6.1}$$

In order to assess facial recognition algorithm performance, we will be evaluating an access control verification scenario. In this scenario, subjects present their credentials to the system, and if the match score of the facial recognition software exceeds a certain threshold, they are granted access. Two types of results will be reported for the different imaging conditions, receiver operator characteristic (ROC) curves, and cumulative match characteristic (CMC) curves.

The ROC curve plots the genuine acceptance rate (GAR) for different false match rates (FMRs). The GAR is the rate at which genuine comparisons produce a similarity score above a certain decision threshold. For an access control scenario, users present their biometric credentials to the system and a similarity score is determined against their gallery entry. If the similarity score is above the decision threshold, then they are correctly granted access.

$$GAR(threshold) = \frac{\#of\ genuine\ comparisons\ with\ score\ above\ threshold}{Total\ \#\ of\ genuine\ comparisons} \qquad (6.2)$$

The FMR is the rate at which imposter comparisons produce a similarity score above a certain decision threshold. For the access control scenario mentioned above, this means that a subject would be incorrectly granted access to the system.

$$FMR(threshold) = \frac{\#\ of\ imposter\ comparisons\ above\ threshold}{Total\ \#\ of\ imposter\ comparisons} \qquad (6.3)$$

The CMC curves describe how well the facial recognition system does of including the genuine subject in the top number of matches. For instance, Rank 1 would report the percentage of matches where the genuine was the top match, while Rank 20 would report the percentage of genuine subjects correctly within the top 20 ranked matches. This allows one to consider the effectiveness of the facial recognition system in a scenario where an analyst is making a final determination and it is desirable to reduce the cognitive strain imposed upon them.

One final metric will be included in this work for the GOTS algorithm only. As mentioned above, the GOTS algorithm has an enrollment process for the probe images. During this enrollment step, the proprietary algorithm ensures that each probe image meets certain image quality standards (e.g., that there is a face in the image and its internal features can be detected) before matching it against the gallery database. Therefore, we report the GOTS algorithm enrollment rates as the percentage of probe images that pass the initial image quality assessment and thus can be matched against the gallery images. The CSU algorithm only needs to know the eye locations of the face within the image in order to conduct its matching. Since we are using the FERET database, we have this ground truth for all of the images, regardless of how degraded they become.

6.3 Effects of Image Blurring

The first condition that will be explored is the effect of image blurring on facial recognition performance. In general, image blurring can greatly affect a system performance for both human operators and automatic algorithms. Blur can be introduced into the optical system through a variety of factors. Defocus and camera/subject motions are two primary contributors to blur in real-life scenarios. First, we will use a simple additional Gaussian optics blur as an example of how such a resolution reduction could impact facial recognition performance. Figure 6.1 shows a series of facial images where the defocus-like blur was gradually increased. It can be seen that the sharp edges and features start to blend together and it gets harder to confidently recognize the face. The degradation in these images was

Fig. 6.1 Example of the effects of increasing Gaussian blur on facial images. The leftmost image is the pristine input image, followed by increasing blur kernel standard deviations (4 pixels, 5 pixels, 6 pixels, and 7 pixels)

simulated with a zero-mean Gaussian blur kernel. Increasing degrees of blur were simulated by changing the standard deviation of the kernel from the no blur condition, to a maximum standard deviation of 7 pixels. This is an important trade study because the quality of the imaging system's optics becomes more important as the camera-to-subject distance increases.

Figures 6.2, 6.3, 6.4, and 6.5 show the facial recognition results when run against the FERET "FB" probe set with the standard ferret gallery set, "FA." Figure 6.2a shows the ROC curve for the GOTS algorithm for the different cases. It can be seen that the system can handle some blurring and still get reliable results for the tested dataset. However, it can also be seen that performance begins to degrade significantly for a given FMR as the blur increases. For the 7-pixel blur, the GAR is only 77 % for a FMR of 0.1 %. The CSU PCA algorithm (Fig. 6.2b) shows similar performance degradation as blur increases, even though it shows overall worse performance. This is to be expected, as the GOTS algorithm is a much more sophisticated facial recognition algorithm than the standard PCA algorithm. In this case, we expected the two algorithms to perform significantly different, but the process demonstrates how this methodology could be used to compare different algorithms against the same degraded imaging conditions.

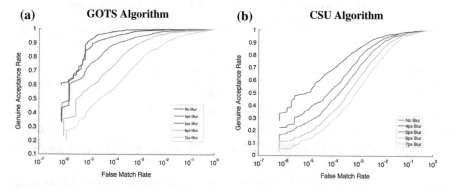

Fig. 6.2 Receiver operator curves for varying Gaussian blur levels. *Left* GOTS algorithm; *Right* CSU algorithm

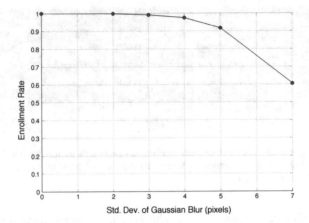

Fig. 6.3 Enrollment rate of the GOTS algorithm for increasing Gaussian blur levels. As the blur increases, a larger percentage of images do not pass the minimum quality needed for the GOTS algorithm to locate the faces for matching

As described above, it is important to note that for these tests, the GOTS algorithm requires a minimum image quality to actually enroll and match a probe face against the gallery, whereas the CSU algorithm does not because we have the ground truth of the FERET database eye locations. Therefore, it is critical that we also evaluate the GOTS algorithm enrollment performance as the blur level increases. Figure 6.3 shows how the probe set's enrollment rate drops significantly as the blur level increases. This means that at the peak blur level in this study, roughly 40 % of the subjects failed the minimum image quality tests internal to the GOTS algorithm and were unable to be matched against the gallery. Thus, these "un-enrolled" cases are not captured in the results.

Figure 6.4a, b, respectively, shows the GOTS and CSU algorithms' CMC curves. When a human is in the loop, it is sometimes more important to see how

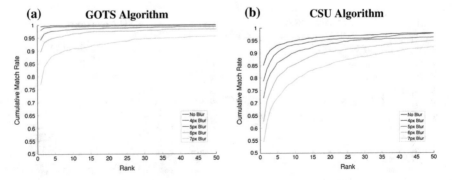

Fig. 6.4 CMC curve for the increasing defocus-like Gaussian blur cases. *Left* GOTS algorithm; *Right* CSU PCA algorithm

well the algorithms do in identifying the correct subject within the top number of matches. It can be seen from Fig. 6.4a, b that the algorithms reach a different peak cumulative match performance as the blur increases. Given a particular operational scenario, these graphs could help determine an acceptable level of image blur in order for the correct subject to be found within the top specified number of matches.

Finally, Fig. 6.5 shows a comparison of the algorithms for a fixed FMR. From this graph, it can be seen that the PCA algorithm has a faster drop-off in performance for the 4-, 5-, and 6-pixel Gaussian blur levels.

In addition to defocus-like blur, we can also simulate blur caused by camera or subject motion. Imaging systems have different integration times, and if a subject is moving while the imager is taking its picture, motion blur could degrade the quality of the imagery. Purely horizontal motion blur was added to the pristine imagery through a linear averaging filter:

$$f[i,j] = \sum_{k=1}^{n} h[k]g[i, j - k] \qquad (6.4)$$

where i and j are the vertical and horizontal pixel locations, respectively, f is the output image, g is the pristine input image, and h is a one-dimensional averaging filter with length n. For example, if you wanted to simulate a horizontal blur length of 5 pixels, $h = [0.2, 0.2, 0.2, 0.2, 0.2]$. This could easily be expanded to simulate motion blur of arbitrary angles by transforming h to a two-dimensional filter.

Figure 6.6 demonstrates the effects of varying levels of horizontal motion blur on an example facial image. It can be seen from these images, compared to Fig. 6.1, that the horizontal motion blur manifests itself differently and that some sharper features are retained compared to the Gaussian blur above. Given a notional 100-m long-range facial recognition system with a 1 m focal length, 8.5 μm pixel pitch, and 10 ms integration time, Table 6.1 lists example velocities for the different motion blur levels in Fig. 6.1. Note that the typical human walking speed is approximately 1.3 m/s.

Fig. 6.5 Comparison of algorithm performance under increasing Gaussian blur for a fixed false match rate of 0.1 %

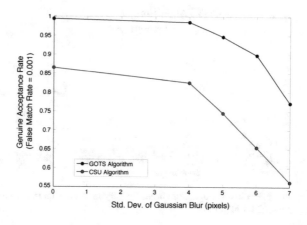

Fig. 6.6 Example of the effects of increasing horizontal motion blur on facial images. The leftmost image is the "pristine" input image, followed by increasing horizontal motion blurs (7 pixels, 14 pixels, 21 pixels, and 28 pixels)

Table 6.1 Corresponding target velocities for motion blur examples using a nominal 100-m long-range facial recognition system with 1 m focal length, 8.5 μm pixel pitch, and 10 ms integration time

Motion blur (pixels)	7	14	21	28
Target velocity (m/s)	0.60	1.19	1.78	2.38

Figure 6.7a, b, respectively, shows the ROC curves for the GOTS and CSU algorithms for the cases of increasing horizontal motion blur. Again, these results can be used to determine the sufficient operating envelope for these algorithms under these types of conditions. The GOTS algorithm had a GAR of 82 % at a FMR of 0.1 % for the 28-pixel horizontal blur case, while the CSU PCA algorithm had a GAR of 59 % (at a FMR of 0.1 %).

Figure 6.9 shows the enrollment rates for the GOTS algorithm for the linear motion blur cases, and Fig. 6.8 compares the performance of the two algorithms at a

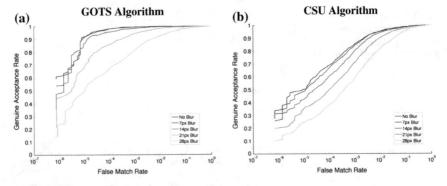

Fig. 6.7 Receiver operator curves for varying horizontal motion blur levels. *Left* GOTS algorithm; *Right* CSU algorithm

Fig. 6.8 Comparison of algorithm performance under increasing motion blur for a fixed false match rate of 0.1 %

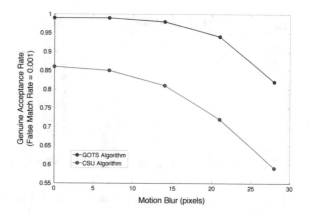

Fig. 6.9 Enrollment rate of the GOTS algorithm for increasing motion blur levels

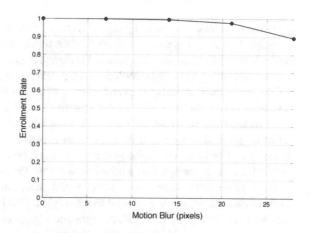

fixed FMR of 0.1 %. As with the defocus-like blur, the GOTS algorithm outperforms the CSU PCA algorithm for all the cases. However, unlike the Gaussian blur cases, the horizontal motion has a much smaller effect on enrollment rates.

Finally, Fig. 6.10a shows how the GOTS algorithm had a near-perfect CMR at Rank 20 for all but the worst blur case. The CSU algorithm also reached its maximum CMR for almost all the blur cases at Rank 20 as well (see Fig. 6.10b). These results suggest that, in general, facial recognition algorithms could be less susceptible to horizontal motion blur than Gaussian blur.

6.3.1 Effects of Noise

In addition to blur, noise can also significantly affect system performance. This is especially true when trying to operate in low-light conditions where systems are

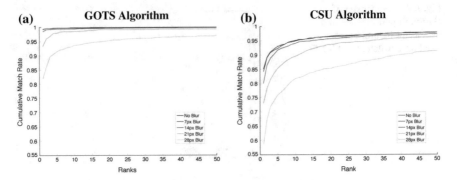

Fig. 6.10 CMC curve for increasing motion blur. *Left* GOTS algorithm; *Right* CSU PCA algorithm

light-starved. Noise can be a significant factor in both visible and infrared imagers. In visible imagery, it is most often seen when trying to operate at high frame rates and/or low-light conditions. For thermal imagery, uncooled systems can suffer from higher amounts of noise than cooled systems. Uncooled thermal imagers have size, weight, and power advantages over cooled systems, so it is important to understand how their performance is affected by system degradations. This work focuses on facial recognition performance on visible imagery, but it is important to note that the same methodology could be applied to imagery from any waveband. In the future, it will be important to be able to understand how these various degradations could affect facial recognition performance across the electromagnetic spectrum.

To explore how noise might affect facial recognition performance, different levels of Poisson noise were applied to the original FERET images. We adopted the method from Ref. [52] to simulate increased image noise for different levels of illuminance. Figure 6.11 shows example facial imagery for increasing amounts of noise (decreasing illuminance). From this imagery, it can be seen that the facial features remain sharp as noise increases, but it becomes increasingly difficult to

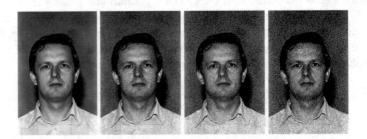

Fig. 6.11 Example of the effects of increasing Poisson noise (decreasing illuminance) on facial images. The upper leftmost image is the pristine input image followed by decreasing illuminance (0.09, 0.06, and 0.04 foot-candles, respectively; note: full moon is approx. 0.02 foot-candles). Images have been contrast-stretched to highlight the effects of the noise

separate the actual signal from the noise. The simulated illuminances were 0.09, 0.06, and 0.04 foot-candles, respectively. For reference, peak full moon illuminance is approximately 0.02 foot-candles [53].

Figure 6.12a, b shows the ROC curves for the GOTS and CSU algorithms, respectively. As in the other cases, the GOTS algorithm performs better for the baseline and low degradation cases. However, it can be seen that both algorithms degrade at approximately the same rate (Fig. 6.13). The same trends can be seen in Fig. 6.14a, b that show the CMR versus rank results. Finally, Fig. 6.15 presents the enrollment results for the GOTS algorithm. From these results, it can be seen that the noise does not prevent the GOTS algorithm from detecting the faces and recognizing the needed facial features, but it does introduce uncertainty into the matching results.

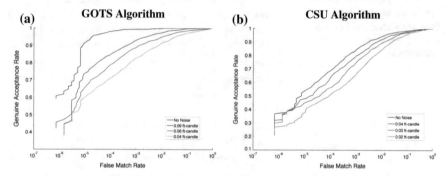

Fig. 6.12 Receiver operator curves for varying levels of Poisson noise (illuminance). *Left* GOTS algorithm; *Right* CSU algorithm

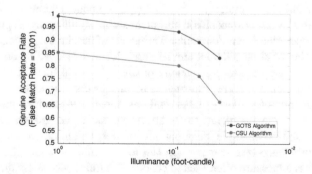

Fig. 6.13 Comparison of algorithm performance under increasing noise (decreasing illuminance) for a fixed false match rate of 0.1 %

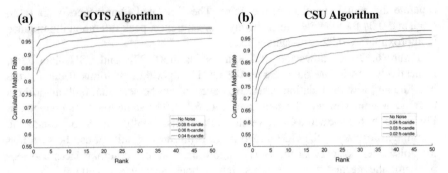

Fig. 6.14 CMC curve for increasing noise (decreasing illuminance). *Left* GOTS algorithm; *Right* CSU PCA algorithm

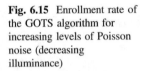

Fig. 6.15 Enrollment rate of the GOTS algorithm for increasing levels of Poisson noise (decreasing illuminance)

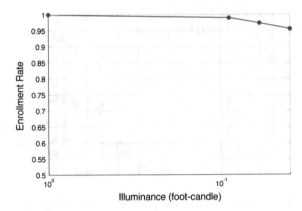

6.3.2 Effects of Atmospheric Turbulence

Atmospheric turbulence effects are the final type of image degradation that we will explore in this work. Atmospheric turbulence can significantly degrade optical imagery in operational environments. Turbulent eddies in the optical path arise from the mixing of air at different temperatures due to solar loading on the ground. These eddies cause random fluctuations of the index of refraction of light. This condition can cause severe blurring and image distortion, or dancing, for ground-to-ground surveillance tasks and, as mentioned above, has not been extensively studied with regard to its effects on facial recognition performance. Figure 6.16 shows example degradations on resolution target imagery under increasing turbulence levels. It is important to note that the atmospheric structure constant, C_n^2, is a measure often used to characterize turbulence strength. Roughly, a C_n^2 value of 1×10^{-14} m$^{-2/3}$ is considered low turbulence, 5×10^{-14} m$^{-2/3}$ is considered medium turbulence, and values greater than 1×10^{-13} m$^{-2/3}$ are considered high turbulence.

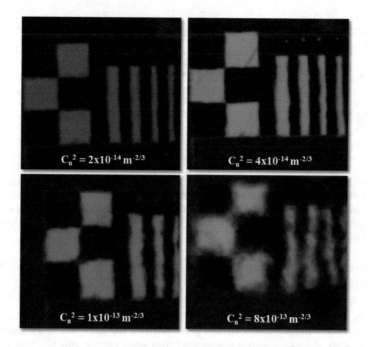

Fig. 6.16 Example of image degradation due to increasing levels of atmospheric turbulence. Resolution target was 1 km from the sensor; the target was 1.5 m high. Focal length of the optics was 800 mm, with most of the data taken at F/16. Pixel pitch of the sensor was 7.4 µm, and the average shutter speed was 0.5 ms [57]

Like the analysis conducted for the blurred and noisy imagery above, the turbulence degradations need to be simulated on the FERET database imagery. In order to simulate realistic turbulence degradations on facial imagery, we use a turbulence simulation algorithm outlined in Ref. [43]. This turbulence simulator is based on an algorithm from the Fraunhofer Research Institute for Optronics and Pattern Recognition (FGAN-FOM) [54]. It is an empirical model based on the analysis of imaging distortions in real image sequences recorded under different atmospheric conditions. The FGAN-FOM simulator was chosen for this work due to its processing speed and ability to recreate realistic image degradations. It has been shown in previous work that the image degradations created by the simulator correlate well with field data [54, 55]. Other methods to simulate turbulence exist, but are often more computationally expensive.

The simulator treats the space-varying image distortions and blurring caused by turbulence separately. Figure 6.17 pictorially describes how the distortions and blurs are generated and combined. For each image, a matrix of random numbers is generated with a given mean and variance that relate to the statistics of the turbulence condition being simulated for both the blur and distortion cases. A prescribed power spectral density is then applied spatially to ensure that the blur and distortion coefficients have the correct spatial correlations. After the coefficients

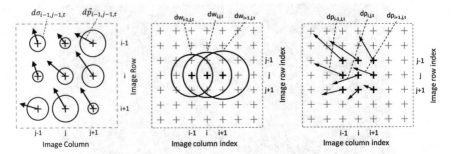

Fig. 6.17 Pictorial representation of the simulation method. The leftmost sketch shows a 3 × 3 pixel subimage where the pixel positions are marked by *black crosses*. The *black circles* represent the blur diameter (the standard deviation of the Gaussian), and the arrows represent pixel displacement. In a realistic simulation scenario, the blur and displacements can be larger than a single pixel [43]

are determined, the simulator first applies the blur for every pixel and then distorts the pixels accordingly.

Figure 6.18 demonstrates the effects of increasing turbulence applied to facial imagery. These images were simulated to represent a F/16 camera with a 1.9 m focal length at a range of 300 m. The pixel pitch of the camera was assumed to be 5.6 μm. Both the space-varying blur and distortion effects can be seen in these images. In the most severe cases, C_n^2 values of 2.5×10^{-13} m$^{-2/3}$ and 5.0×10^{-13} m$^{-2/3}$, the features within the face are significantly blurred out.

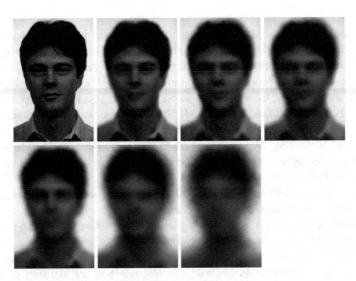

Fig. 6.18 Example of the effects of increasing atmospheric turbulence on facial images. The upper leftmost image is the "pristine" input image followed by increasing turbulence strength ($C_n^2 = 2.5 \times 10^{-14}$ m$^{-2/3}$, 5.0×10^{-14} m$^{-2/3}$, 7.5×10^{-14} m$^{-2/3}$, 1.0×10^{-13} m$^{-2/3}$, 2.5×10^{-13} m$^{-2/3}$, 5.0×10^{-13} m$^{-2/3}$, respectively)

Because of the processing time needed to generate the turbulence-degraded imagery, a 360 subject subset of the probe images was selected to match against the full 1196 subject gallery used above. Figure 6.19a, b shows the ROC curves for each of the algorithms as before, while Fig. 6.20 shows a comparison between the two algorithms for a fixed FMR of 0.1 %. As before, the GOTS algorithm outperforms the COTS algorithm for all of the cases. It can be seen that even though there are distortions in the images, the degradation is mainly caused by blurring that is most similar to the Gaussian blur explored earlier. Figure 6.21 shows the enrollment rates for the different turbulence cases. For the two highest turbulence cases, none of the probe images pass the minimum image quality for the GOTS algorithm. For the $C_n^2 = 1 \times 10^{-13}$ case, only approximately 45 % of the subjects are able to be enrolled for matching. This is the reason why the two highest turbulence cases do not appear on the GOTS algorithm results. In contrast, since the CSU algorithm uses the FERET eye locations as ground truth, it is able to generate results, despite their poor quality, for all the cases.

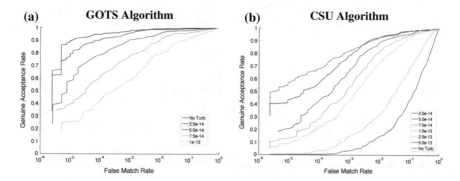

Fig. 6.19 Receiver operator curves for varying levels of atmospheric turbulence. *Left* GOTS algorithm; *Right* CSU algorithm

Fig. 6.20 Comparison of algorithm performance under increasing turbulence for a fixed false match rate of 0.1 %

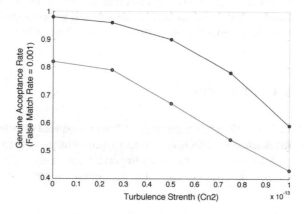

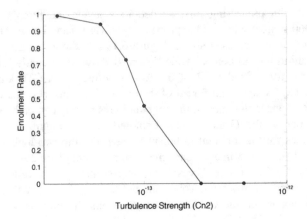

Fig. 6.21 Enrollment rate of the GOTS algorithm for increasing levels of turbulence

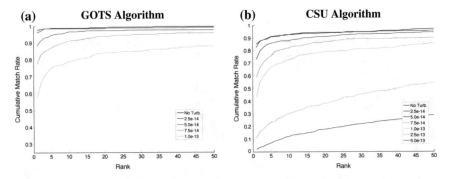

Fig. 6.22 CMC curve for increasing noise. *Left* GOTS algorithm; *Right* CSU PCA algorithm

Finally, Fig. 6.22a, b shows the CMC results for both algorithms, respectively. For the moderate turbulence cases ($C_n^2 \sim 10^{-14}$), the GOTS algorithm has a cumulative match rate of greater than 90 % at Rank 20. This is for a smaller dataset, but shows that the algorithm can perform under degraded conditions and provide value in a surveillance application with a human in the loop.

6.4   Summary

In this work, a methodology has been introduced to help system designers consider the deleterious effects of different types of image degradations on facial recognition performance. This becomes important for many military and homeland security environments where operating conditions cannot be controlled. The methodology also allows system designers to explore the sensitivity of their designs to these types of degradations.

Specifically, the effects of blur, noise, and atmospheric turbulence were explored. Each of these degradations caused different effects on the algorithms used in this study, and each algorithm had a different tolerance to the severity of the degradations. It was seen that motion blur is handled more easily by the algorithms than an overall Gaussian blur. The choice of the facial recognition algorithms used in this work was chosen solely on availability. The main focus was to demonstrate how accurate, controlled simulation could be combined with results from algorithm performance to serve as a guide for system design and analysis of sensitivity to environmental conditions. This methodology could be used to evaluate any facial recognition imaging system to understand under what conditions the system will provide adequate performance. The blur, noise, and turbulence simulations presented are also just examples and could be easily tailored to specific situations of interest. Finally, the presented technique is not limited to face acquisition and could be used by other biometric modalities and image-based acquisition systems in general.

The presented methodology allows users to answer complicated questions, such as "How tolerant is the facial recognition system (both camera design and algorithm) to image degradations caused by atmospheric turbulence?" Furthermore, work is being done at the US Army's RDECOM CERDEC Night Vision Electronic Sensors Directorate (NVESD) to automate this methodology using the Night Vision Imaging Performance Model (NV-IPM) and its image generation tool [56]. The image generation tool will allow users to conduct trade studies over dozens of system design parameters and obtain direct feedback regarding algorithm performance. Evaluating recognition algorithm performance against accurately simulated imagery provides a cost-effective approach to system design and specification.

Finally, while the results presented in this work focused on visible imagery, the process and tools presented could be used on imagery from any waveband. Furthermore, they are algorithm agnostic and provide a means to compare and contrast algorithms under different conditions. As we move into utilizing biometric recognition algorithms across the electromagnetic spectrum, this will become very important because the different systems will have different types of advantages and disadvantages in a tactically relevant environment.

References

1. U.S. Army Training and Doctrine Command: The U.S. Army Operating Concept: Win in a Complex World. (TRADOC Pamphlet 525-3-1), http://www.tradoc.army.mil/tpubs/pams/TP525-3-1.pdf. Last accessed 31 Mar 2015
2. Turk, M.A., Pentland, A.P.: Face recognition using eigenfaces. In: IEEE Computer Society Conference on Computer Vision and Pattern Recognition, pp. 586–591 (1991)
3. Turk, M., Pentland, A.P.: Eigenfaces for recognition. J. Cogn. Neurosci. 3(1), 71–86 (1991)

4. Belhumeur, P.N., Hespanha, J.P., Kriegman, D.J.: Eigenfaces vs. fisherfaces: recognition using class specific linear projection. IEEE Trans. Pattern Anal. Mach. Intell. **19**, 711–720 (1996)

5. Etemad, K., Chellappa, R.: Discriminant analysis for recognition of human face images. J. Opt. Soc. Am. A **14**, 1724–1733 (1997)

6. Wiskott, L., Fellous, J.-M., Krüger, N., Malsburg, C.V.D.: Face recognition by elastic bunch graph matching. IEEE Trans. Pattern Anal. Mach. Intell. **19**, 775–779 (1997)

7. Samal, A., Iyengar, P.A.: Automatic recognition and analysis of human faces and facial expressions: a survey. Pattern Recogn. **25**(1), 65–77 (1992)

8. Zhao, W., Chellappa, R., Phillips, P.J., Rosenfeld, A.: Face recognition: a literature survey. ACM Comput. Surv. **35**(4), 399–458 (2003)

9. Chellappa, R., Wilson, C.L., Sirohey, S.: Human and machine recognition of faces: a survey. Proc. IEEE **83**(5), 705–741 (1995)

10. Phillips, P.J., Wechsler, H., Huang, J., Rauss, P.J.: The FERET database and evaluation procedure for face-recognition algorithms. Image Vis. Comput. **16**(5), 295–306 (1998)

11. Phillips, P.J., Rauss, P.J., Der, S.Z.: FERET (facial recognition technology) recognition algorithm development and test results. ARL Technical Report 995 (1996)

12. Phillips, P.J., Moon, H., Rizvi, S.A., Rauss, P.J.: The FERET evaluation methodology for face-recognition algorithms. IEEE Trans. Pattern Anal. Mach. Intell. **22**(10), 1090–1104 (2000)

13. Sim, T., Baker, S., Bsat, M.: The CMU pose, illumination, and expression (PIE) database. In: Proceedings of the 5th IEEE International Conference on Automatic Face and Gesture Recognition, pp. 46–51 (2002)

14. Gross, R., Matthews, I., Cohn, J., Kanade, T., Baker, S.: Multi-PIE. Image Vis. Comput. **28** (5), 807–813 (2010)

15. Huang, G.B., Ramesh, M., Berg, T., Learned-Miller, E.: Labeled faces in the wild: a database for studying face recognition in unconstrained environments. Univ. Mass. Technical Report 07-49 (2007)

16. The AR Face Database: Ohio State Univ., http://www2.ece.ohiostate.edu/~aleix/ARdatabase. html. Last accessed 26 May 2015

17. Grgic, M., Delac, K., Grgic, S.: SCface—surveillance cameras face database. Multimedia Tools Appl. **51**(3), 863–879 (2009)

18. Phillips, P.J., Grother, P., Micheals, R., Blackburn, D.M., Tabassi, E., Bone, M.: Face recognition vendor test 2002. In: IEEE International Workshop on Analysis and Modeling of Faces and Gestures, p. 44 (2003)

19. Phillips, P.J., Scruggs, W.T., O'Toole, A.J., Flynn, P.J., Bowyer, K.W., Schott, C.L., Sharpe, M.: FRVT 2006 and ICE 2006 large-scale results. NIST Interagency Report 7408 (2007)

20. Grother, P.J., Quinn, G.W., Phillips, P.J.: Report on the evaluation of 2D still-image face recognition algorithms. NIST Interagency Report 7709 (2011)

21. Phillips, P.J., et al.: An introduction to the good, the bad, & the ugly face recognition challenge problem. NIST Interagency Report 7758 (2011)

22. Quinn, G.W., Grother, P.J.: Performance of face recognition algorithms on compressed images. NIST Interagency Report 7830 (2011)

23. Matas, J., Hamouz, M., Jonsson, K., Kittler, J., Li, Y., Kotropoulos, C., Tefas, A., Pitas, I., Tan, T., Yan, H., Smeraldi, E., Bigun, J., Capdevielle, N., Gerstner, W., Ben-yacoub, S., Abdeljaoued, Y., Mayoraz, E.: Comparison of face verification results on the XM2VTS database. In: Proceedings of the 15th ICPR, pp. 858–863 (2000)

24. Park, U., Tong, Y., Jain, A.K.: Age-invariant face recognition. IEEE Trans. Pattern Anal. Mach. Intell. **32**(5), 947–954 (2010)

25. Phillips, P.J., Martin, A., Wilson, C.L., Przybocki, M.: An introduction to evaluating biometric systems. Computer **33**(2), 56–63 (2000)

26. Baker, S., Kanade, T.: Limits on super-resolution and how to break them. IEEE Trans. Pattern Anal. Mach. Intell. **24**(9), 1167–1183 (2002)

27. Wheeler, F.W., Liu, X., Tu, P.H.: Multi-frame super-resolution for face recognition. In: First IEEE International Conference on Biometrics: Theory, Applications, and Systems, pp. 1–6 (2007)
28. Huang, H., He, H., Fan, X., Zhang, J.: Super-resolution of human face image using canonical correlation analysis. Pattern Recogn. **43**(7), 2532–2543 (2010)
29. Gunturk, B.K., Batur, A.U., Altunbasak, Y., Hayes, M.H., Mersereau, R.M.: Eigenface-domain super-resolution for face recognition. IEEE Trans. Image Process. **12**(5), 597–606 (2003)
30. Heflin, B., Parks, B., Scheirer, W., Boult, T.: Single image deblurring for a real-time face recognition system. In: 36th Annual Conference on IEEE Industrial Electronics Society, pp. 1185–1192 (2010)
31. Nishiyama, M., Takeshima, H., Shotton, J., Kozakaya, T., Yamaguchi, O.: Facial deblur inference to improve recognition of blurred faces. Computer Vision and Pattern Recognition, pp. 1115–1122 (2009)
32. Nishiyama, M., Hadid, A., Takeshima, H., Shotton, J., Kozakaya, T., Yamaguchi, O.: Facial deblur inference using subspace analysis for recognition of blurred faces. IEEE Trans. Pattern Anal. Mach. Intell. **33**(4), 838–845 (2011)
33. Reda, A., Aoued, B.: Artificial neural network-based face recognition. In: First International Symposium on Control, Communications and Signal Processing, pp. 439–442 (2004)
34. Uglov, J., Schetinin, V., Maple, C.: Comparing robustness of pairwise and multiclass neural-network systems for face recognition. arXiv:0704.3515 (2007)
35. Oravec, M., Lehocki, F., Mazanec, J., Pavlovicova, J., Eiben, P.: Face Recognition in Ideal and Noisy Conditions Using Support Vector Machines, PCA and LDA. INTECH Open Access Publisher, Rijeka (2010)
36. Bharadwaj, S., Bhatt, H., Vatsa, M., Singh, R., Noore, A.: Quality assessment based denoising to improve face recognition performance. In: IEEE Computer Society Conference on Computer Vision and Pattern Recognition Workshops (CVPRW), pp. 140–145 (2011)
37. Sun, Y., Liang, D., Wang, X., Tang, X.: DeepID3: face recognition with very deep neural networks," arXiv:1502.00873 (2015)
38. Taigman, Y., Yang, M., Ranzato, M., Wolf, L.: Deepface: closing the gap to human-level performance in face verification. In: IEEE Conference on Computer Vision and Pattern Recognition, pp. 1701–1708 (2014)
39. Zhou, E., Cao, Z., Yin, Q.: Naive-deep face recognition: touching the limit of lfw benchmark or not?. arXiv:1501.04690 (2015)
40. Fried, D.L.: Optical resolution through a randomly inhomogeneous medium for very long and very short exposures. J. Opt. Soc. Am. **56**(10), 1372–1379 (1966)
41. Andrews, L.C., Phillips, R.L.: Laser beam propagation through random media. SPIE Press, Bellingham (2005)
42. Espinola, R.L., Cha, J., Leonard, K.: Novel methodologies for the measurement of atmospheric turbulence effects. In: Proceeding of SPIE, **7662** (2010)
43. Leonard, K.R., Howe, J., Oxford, D.E.: Simulation of atmospheric turbulence effects and mitigation algorithms on stand-off automatic facial recognition. In: Proceedings SPIE, **8546** (2012)
44. Subasic, M., Loncaric, S., Petkovic, T., Bogunovic, H., Krivec, V.: Face image validation system. In: Proceedings of the 4th International Symposium on Image and Signal Processing and Analysis, pp. 30–33 (2005)
45. Hsu, R.-L.V., Shah, J., Martin, B.: Quality assessment of facial images. In: Biometric Consortium Conference, 2006 Biometrics Symposium, pp. 1–6 (2006)
46. Grother, P., Tabassi, E.: Performance of biometric quality measures. IEEE Trans. Pattern Anal. Mach. Intell. **29**(4), 531–543 (2007)
47. Abaza, A., Harrison, M.A., Bourlai, T.: Quality metrics for practical face recognition. In: 21st International Conference on Pattern Recognition, pp. 3103–3107 (2012)
48. Abaza, A., Harrison, M.A., Bourlai, T., Ross, A.: Design and evaluation of photometric image quality measures for effective face recognition. IET Biometrics **3**(4), 314–324 (2014)

49. Beveridge, J.R., Phillips, P.J., Givens, G.H., Draper, B.A., Teli, M.N., Bolme, D.S.: When high-quality face images match poorly. In: IEEE International Conference on Automatic Face Gesture Recognition and Workshops, pp. 572–578 (2011)
50. Bolme, D., Beveridge, R., Teixeira, M., Draper, B.: The CSU face identification evaluation system: its purpose, features and structure. In: International Conference on Vision Systems (2003)
51. Colorado State University: http://www.cs.colostate.edu/evalfacerec/index10.php, Last accessed 31 Mar 2015
52. Howell, C., Choi, H.-S., Reynolds, J.P.: Face acquisition camera design using the NV-IPM image generation tool. In: Proceedings of SPIE 9452 (2015)
53. Leibowitz, H.W., Ambient illuminance during twilight and from the moon. In: Proceedings on Night Vision Current Research and Future Directions, pp. 20–21 (1987)
54. Repasi, E., Weiss, R.: Computer simulation of image degradations by atmospheric turbulence for horizontal views. Proc. SPIE p. 8014 (2011)
55. Leoanrd, K.R., Espinola, R.L.: Validation of atmospheric turbulence simulations of extended scenes. In: Proc. SPIE 9071 (2014)
56. Teaney, B., Reynolds, J.: Next generation imager performance model. In: Proc. SPIE 7662 (2010)
57. Repasi, E.: Image catalogue of video sequences recorded by FGAN-FOM during the NATO RTG40 field trial, distributed to group members in Spring (2006)

Chapter 7
Understanding Thermal Face Detection: Challenges and Evaluation

Janhavi Agrawal, Aishwarya Pant, Tejas I. Dhamecha, Richa Singh
and Mayank Vatsa

Abstract In thermal face detection, researchers have generally assumed manual face detection or have designed algorithms that focus on indoor environment. However, facial properties are dependent on body temperature, surrounding environment, and any accessories or occlusion present on the face. For instance, the presence of scarfs, glasses, or any disguise accessories will alter the emitted heat pattern, thereby making it challenging to detect the face in thermal images. Similarly, daytime outdoor image acquisition has certain effects on the heat pattern compared to nighttime (or indoor controlled) image acquisition settings that affect automatic face detection performance. In this research, we provide a thorough understanding of challenges in thermal face detection along with an experimental evaluation of traditional approaches. Further, we adapt the AdaBoost face detector to yield improved performance on face detection in thermal images in both indoor and outdoor environments. We also propose a region of interest selection approach designed specifically for aiding occluded/disguised thermal face detection. Experiments are performed on the Notre Dame thermal face database as well as the IIITD databases that include variations such as disguise, age, and environmental

Janhavi Agrawal, Aishwarya Pant, Tejas I. Dhamecha: Equal contributions by the student authors.

J. Agrawal · A. Pant · T.I. Dhamecha · R. Singh · M. Vatsa (✉)
IIIT Delhi, New Delhi, India
e-mail: mayank@iiitd.ac.in

J. Agrawal
e-mail: janhavi11056@iiitd.ac.in

A. Pant
e-mail: aishwarya11011@iiitd.ac.in

T.I. Dhamecha
e-mail: tejasd@iiitd.ac.in

R. Singh
e-mail: rsingh@iiitd.ac.in

© Springer International Publishing Switzerland 2016
T. Bourlai (ed.), *Face Recognition Across the Imaging Spectrum*,
DOI 10.1007/978-3-319-28501-6_7

(day/night) factors. The results suggest that while thermal face detection in semi-controlled environments is relatively easy, occlusion and disguise are challenges that require further attention.

7.1 Introduction

Decades of research in face recognition has seen several research directions, mostly in the visible spectrum and many high-performing algorithms have been developed for this purpose. To instigate further research, several research programs such as Janus[1] have been initiated where the goal is to take face recognition to the next significant level. It is also well understood that in order to have a large-scale application, the technology has to encompass *face recognition both in and beyond visible spectrums*, i.e., developing capabilities to recognize face images/videos in visible, near infrared, and thermal spectrums. Compared to the visible spectrum, research in face recognition beyond visible spectrum is relatively less explored and has primarily focused on near infrared and thermal imagery [2, 3, 5, 6, 15, 19]. As shown in Fig. 7.1, face images in these three spectrums provide non-overlapping information and can be individually or in-combination used for identity management.

For recognizing face images captured in thermal images (spectrum range of 8–12 μm), the first step is the face detection followed by feature extraction and matching against gallery image(s). Similar to visible spectrum, thermal face detection can be modeled as a two-class problem (*face* and *non-face*). Trujillo et al. [25] proposed a thresholding-based approach for detecting faces in thermal images. Since the goal is to recognize expressions, face detection accuracy is not reported in that study. Selinger and Socolinsky [21] and Socolinsky and Selinger [23] applied boosted class-cover catch digraph (CCCD) [24] for face detection. They [23] observed that thermal face recognition performance degrades in outdoor environments. Since the overall goal was to identify the subject, the results of the intermediate face detection stage were not reported. In [23], the authors focused on face recognition and the results of detection were not reported. However, it is possible that in thermal spectrum the outdoor setting affects the detection stage too, particularly in thermal spectrum. Martinez et al. [18] utilized GentelBoost along with Haar-like features [26] and, the results showcase that, to an extent, boosting with Haar-like features can be utilized for face detection. However, evaluation in challenging environments remains an open research problem. Wang et al. [28] observed that Haar-like features with AdaBoost can be useful for detecting eyes, even in the presence of glasses. Zhang et al. [29] proposed a modified boosting approach in which visible images could also be utilized along with the images of other spectrum

---

[1]http://www.iarpa.gov/index.php/research-programs/janus.

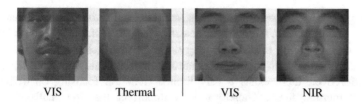

VIS   Thermal   VIS   NIR

Fig. 7.1 Sample face images captured in visible, thermal, and near-infrared (NIR) spectrum. NIR image has been taken from CASIA NIR-VIS 2.0 face database [14]

to train the cascade model. Table 7.1 briefly summarizes these algorithms on face detection in thermal images.

For designing an efficient face recognition algorithm, it is important that the face detection is accurate. It has been observed that imprecise eye localization and therefore imprecise face localization degrades the performance of the overall thermal face recognition pipeline [6]. Since the majority of researchers have used manually detected face images in the recognition pipeline, thermal face detection has not been well explored in the literature. Moreover, in order to learn an efficient face detector it is imperative to have access to a large amount of face and non-face images. The samples obtained in diverse conditions, such as indoor and outdoor

Table 7.1 Summary of related research for face detection in thermal images

Authors	Objective and technique	Dataset (#Images/#Subjects)
Trujillo et al. [25]	Face detection: thresholding. Facial regions: Harris detector with k-means clustering	IRIS dataset in OCTBVS [12] (4228/30)
Selinger and Socolinsky [21]	Face detection: boosted CCCD classifier [24]. Eye detection: Haar-like features with AdaBoost	Private (3732/207)
Socolinsky and Selinger [23]	Face detection: boosted CCCD classifier [24]. Eye detection: co-registration with the visible images	Private indoor-outdoor (3080/385)
Martinez et al. [18]	Face detection: patch intensities. Eye, nostril and mouth detection: Haar features with GentleBoost and self-similarity descriptor	Private (78/22)
Wang et al. [28]	Eye localization: Haar-like features with AdaBoost for 15 subregions around eyes and majority voting of results of multiple classifiers	NVIE [27] and Equinox dataset
Zhang et al. [29]	Face detection: R-TrBoost to train using visible and other spectrum images together	Private (7000 visible, 1400 spectrum 1, and 705 spectrum 2)
Bourlai and Jafri [1]	Blob analysis-based skin detection, template matching, and integral projection-based eye detection	West Virginia University visible-thermal database (2250/50)

environments, with session variations are necessary to learn a generalizable detector. In our opinion, thermal face detection and recognition research is impaired by the non-availability of a challenging database that includes face and non-face images captured in both indoor and outdoor environments with time lapse variations. Moreover, there exists a very limited literature focusing on detection of occluded thermal faces. Therefore, it is important that the challenge of face detection is addressed to achieve a fully automated and efficient thermal face recognition system. In view of existing limitations, this chapter attempts to bridge the gap in the following ways:

- A database, namely IIITD thermal face database, is prepared that consists of 614 face images pertaining to 65 subjects and 150 non-face images. Face images are captured in two sessions separated by two years time frame. Non-face images are captured in both indoor and outdoor settings. A small set, IIITD-People in Sun and Evening (IIITD-PSE), consisting 22 subjects is also prepared to study the variations due to outdoor day light (sun) and nighttime environments. The database and the ground truth annotations of face regions will be made publicly available for researchers to undertake research on thermal face detection via https://research.iiitd.edu.in/groups/iab/.
- Baseline experiments pertaining to face localization are performed on the IIITD thermal face, IIITD-PSE, and Notre Dame (ND) thermal face [6] databases with Haar- and LBP-cascaded AdaBoost to analyze the challenges associated with face detection in thermal images. Challenging scenarios such as cross-sensor thermal face detection and the effects of outdoor conditions (i.e., day or night) are also examined. A baseline evaluation of detecting faces under occlusion (using disguise accessories) is also performed on the IIITD In and Beyond Visible Spectrum Disguise (I^2BVSD) face database [8, 9]. A skin detection-based region of interest (ROI) selection is proposed, to improve the face detection performance. We also propose a novel face detection evaluation measure to evaluate the performance of face detection algorithms.

7.2 IIITD Thermal Face Database

As shown in Table 7.1, there are multiple thermal face databases available. However, all of them captured face data with the objective of face recognition in controlled environments and may not be suitable for understanding the state of the art of face detection algorithms in the thermal spectrum. Further, existing face detection algorithms have been optimized for the visible spectrum, and since both visible and thermal spectra have different characteristics, such optimized pre-trained models may not yield the best results. Therefore, we have collected the IIITD thermal face database with a focus on capturing the variations that may affect the appearance of facial regions in a thermal image, for instance, time lapse and environment. The IIITD database consists of 614 thermal face images pertaining to 65 individuals and 150 non-face images. All the images are captured using a thermal camera having micro-bolometer sensor operating in 8-14 μm spectrum range, also known as long-wave infrared spectrum. Face images are near frontal with neutral expressions and are captured in two sessions:

- Session I is captured in October/November 2011 and it consists of 82 images pertaining to 41 subjects.
- Session II is captured in January 2014 and it consists of 532 images from 65 subjects. There are 41 overlapping subjects in both the sessions.

A set of 150 non-face images is collected out of which equal number of images are captured indoor and outdoor. Since a face can appear very different during day and night in a thermal image, we collected a separate dataset named *IIITD-People in Sun and Evening (IIITD-PSE) database* to capture these variations. It consists of 120 images pertaining to 22 subjects acquired in outdoor settings during both day (around 2 p.m. and ~ 36 °C temperature) and night (around 10 p.m. and ~ 22 °C temperature). Both subsets, the IIITD-PSE-Day and IIITD-PSE-Night, contain 60 images pertaining to 15 subjects, with an overlap of 8 subjects.

All the images are of size 720×576 pixels. The details of both IIITD and IIITD-PSE datasets are summarized in Table 7.2. Figure 7.2 illustrates the variety of images contained in the IIITD and IIITD-PSE databases. For evaluating the performance of face detection algorithms, the ground truth has been manually annotated in terms of two eyes, nose, and mouth coordinates. To encourage the research on the problem of thermal face detection, the database and annotated ground truth will be made publicly available to researchers.

Table 7.2 Dataset details pertaining to sessions, subjects, and classes

Name	Class	Number of subjects and images
IIITD Thermal	Face	Session I: 41, 82
		Session II: 65 (41 + 24), 532
	Non-face	75 indoor and 75 outdoor
	Total = 65 subjects, 764 images	
IIITD-PSE	Face (outdoor)	Day: 15, 60
		Night: 15 (8 + 7), 60
	Total = 22 subjects, 120 face images	
ND	Face	Train: 159, 159
		Test: 82, 2292
	Total = 241 subjects, 2451 images	
I²BVSD	Face	Minor: 75, 307
		Major: 75, 231
	Total = 75 subjects, 538 images	

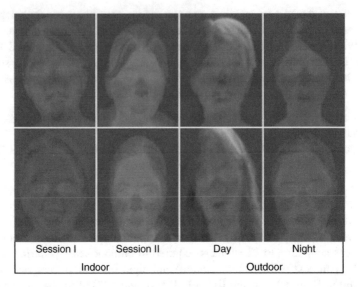

Session I	Session II	Day	Night
Indoor		Outdoor	

Fig. 7.2 Images illustrating the variations captured in the IIITD and IIITD-PSE thermal face database. Each row contains images of one subject under different environments

7.3 Databases, Algorithms, and Evaluation Measures

For understanding the performance of thermal face detection, Collection XI of the University of Notre Dame (ND) face dataset [6] and I^2BVSD database [8, 9] are used along with the IIITD and IIITD-PSE databases. The ND face database consists of 2292 infrared frontal face images of size 312 × 239 from 82 subjects. It also contains a separate training set of 159 face images. Figure 7.3 shows sample images of subjects from the ND database.

For studying the effect of occlusion using disguise accessories, we utilize the I^2BVSD face dataset [8, 9] which is the only publicly available dataset containing images with occlusion. The dataset consists of 681 face images pertaining to 75

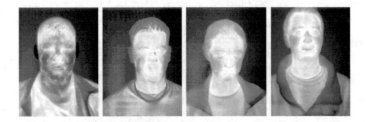

Fig. 7.3 Sample images from the ND thermal face database [6]

subjects in both visible and thermal spectra. The utilization of disguise accessories results in varying amount of face occlusion. Depending on the facial regions which are occluded, the dataset is divided into two parts, major disguises (231 images) and minor disguises (307 images). Sample images contained in the dataset are shown in Fig. 7.4. For this research, we utilize only the thermal spectrum images having disguise variations (538 images, 75 subjects).

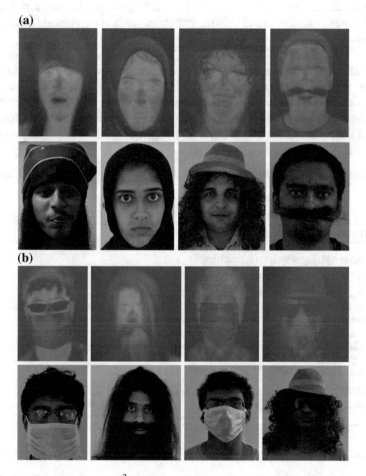

Fig. 7.4 Sample images from the I^2BVSD thermal face database [8, 9]. Face images from subsets pertaining to face occlusion due to **a** minor and **b** major usage of disguise accessories. While I^2BVSD database has images in both visible and thermal spectrum, we have used only thermal images in the experiments

7.3.1 Algorithms

The baseline performance has been established for two face detection algorithms:

1. *Haar-like features* [17, 26] *with cascaded AdaBoost classifier:* Haar-like features are computed from rectangular regions of the image. Every rectangle is divided into multiple non-overlapping sub-rectangles. Pixel intensities of each sub-rectangle are added and the differences of summed intensities of sub-rectangles are used as features. Sub-rectangles are created such that these differences provide coarse information about horizontal, vertical, and diagonal gradients.
2. *Local binary patterns (LBP) features* [16] *with cascaded AdaBoost classifier:* In LBP, the difference between every pixel and its neighbors is computed. The sign of differences is represented using a binary bit. The string of these binary bits for every pixel is converted to decimal. An LBP-coded image representation is obtained by replacing every pixel with its corresponding decimal values. The final feature is represented in terms of histograms obtained from local regions of the LBP-coded image representation.

Algorithm 1 briefly summarizes the cascade boosting face detection approach utilizing Haar/LBP.

Algorithm 1 Summary of cascaded Adaboost classifier.

- Initialize with equal weights for each training sample
- For each stage

  1. Normalize the weights such that sum of all the weights is one.
  2. Learn a weak classifier corresponding to every single feature. Compute the weighted error of each weak classifier. Also, assign the decision threshold such that false negatives are minimized.
  3. Choose the weak classifier with the minimum weighted error.
  4. Update the weights of correctly classified training samples by multiplying them with the ratio $\beta = \frac{accuracy}{error}$ of the current stage.

- Final strong classifier: A sub-window is classified as face if all the stages of the cascade classifies it as a face region.

7.3.2 Evaluation Measures

In the existing literature, performance and effectiveness of face detection algorithms is measured using metrics such as mean square error (MSE). However, these statistics only present the difference between the ground truth and automatically segmented landmark points. In our understanding, MSE is a more useful metric for landmark detection and it is not very informative if one wants to compare the regions of interest and analyze falsely detected and falsely rejected regions. The objective of a face detection algorithm is to be able to detect the complete region of interest so that it has maximum intersection with the ground truth. To evaluate the performance with respect to this intersection criterion, we propose the following two measures:

- *Ratio with ground truth* (*RG*): RG presents the ratio of intersection of the predicted region and ground truth with the area of ground truth segmentation.

$$RG = \frac{\text{Area}_{D \cap G}}{\text{Area}_G} \qquad (7.1)$$

- *Ratio with detection* (*RD*): RD presents the ratio of intersection of the predicted region and ground truth with the area of detected region.

$$RD = \frac{\text{Area}_{D \cap G}}{\text{Area}_D} \qquad (7.2)$$

Here, D and G represent the detected and ground truth face regions (rectangles), respectively. The visual interpretation of RG and RD together is shown in Fig. 7.5. High RD along with low RG indicates that while there is a good overlap between

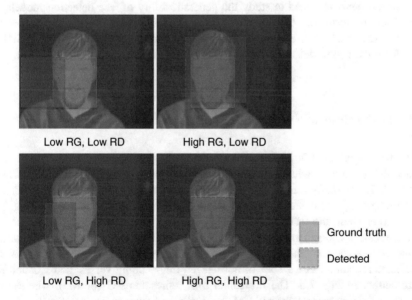

Low RG, Low RD   High RG, Low RD

Ground truth

Detected

Low RG, High RD   High RG, High RD

Fig. 7.5 RG and RD measures. High values of RG and RD together ensure a good face detection

the two, a smaller face rectangle is detected compared to the ground truth. Similarly, high RG along with low RD indicates that automatic face detection algorithm has detected a larger face rectangle compared to the ground truth. Their values lie in the range of [0, 1] and for ideal face detection, both should be very close to one. RG and RD can be more effectively used together to analyze the results. In this research, we observe that a threshold of 0.7 for both RG and RD can be used to consider successful face detection.

7.4   Results and Analysis

The performance of the algorithms has been evaluated in four different scenarios:

- *Testing with visible cascade*: The publicly available visible spectrum face detector model is utilized to detect faces in thermal spectrum images. This experiment establishes the baseline for performance evaluation.
- *Learning a model for thermal images*: We learn detectors using thermal face and non-face images. The images are preprocessed using histogram equalization followed by feature extraction using LBP or Haar.
- *Effect of environment and sensor*: The effect of environmental factors such as indoor/outdoor setting and day/nighttime is studied using the IIITD-PSE dataset. We evaluate the effect of sensor interoperability on face detection. This set of experiments is aimed to study the generalizability of face detection models.
- *Effect of occlusion*: In this set of experiments, we study the effectiveness of the learned thermal face detector on occluded faces. Along with LBP and Haar features, a skin detection-based ROI selection approach is also presented.

7.4.1   Testing with Cascade Trained on Visible Images

The first experiment is performed to evaluate the performance of pre-trained Haar cascades (available with OpenCV [4]) on thermal spectrum images. Since Haar cascade is originally trained for visible spectrum, this experiment also provides an understanding about face detection performance with cross-spectral training. For this experiment, the IIITD database (614 images) and the test partition of the ND dataset (2292 images) are utilized as test sets. In all the experiments, when multiple face rectangles are detected in an image, the largest one is considered as the detected rectangle. The graphs of normalized image count verses their RG and RD are shown in Fig. 7.6. The horizontal axis represents RG (or RD), whereas the vertical axis represents the ratio of the number of images having specific RG (or RD) to the total number of images. As it can be seen, very small proportion of face images resulted in high RG or RD values. This shows that pre-trained visible image cascade is not appropriate for face detection in thermal images. No face rectangle is

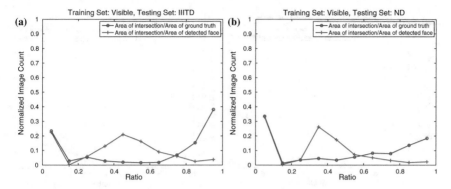

Fig. 7.6 Pre-trained Haar with face detection on the **a** IIITD dataset and **b** ND dataset. *Horizontal axis* represents the value of RG and RD. *Vertical axis* represents the normalized image count with corresponding RG and RD. Normalized image count is computed as
$$\frac{\#\,\text{images with corresponding RG or RD}}{\#\,\text{total images}}$$

Table 7.3 Summary of face detection results with pre-trained cascade and the cascade trained with thermal images on the IIITD and ND thermal face databases

Experiment	Training set	Test set	Normalized image count		Detection accuracy (RG > 0.7 and RD > 0.7)	Undetected Total
			RG > 0.7	RD > 0.7		
Visible's Cascade (Haar)	Pre-trained (OpenCV)	IIITD	0.60	0.12	0.05	98/614
		ND	0.40	0.07	0.01	723/2292
Thermal's Cascade (LBP)	IIITD	IIITD	0.84	0.70	0.62	0/307
	ND	ND	0.78	0.71	0.60	147/2292

detected in 15.9 % images of the IIITD dataset and 31.5 % images of the ND dataset. As shown in Table 7.3, for both IIITD and ND datasets, many images have low RG and RD, which further show poor face detection results.

7.4.2   Learning a Cascade Model for Thermal Faces

Since pre-trained cascade model does not exhibit effective performance, it is important to train the face detection model using thermal data. We utilize face and non-face images captured in thermal spectrum for this task. From the IIITD dataset, 307 randomly selected face images and all the 150 non-face images are used as the training set and testing is performed on the remaining (unseen) 307 images. For ND dataset, training is performed with a predefined set of 159 train images and testing with 2292 images. The LBP cascade model is trained and the results on the testing

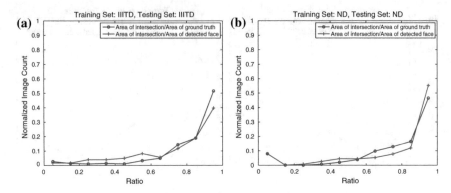

Fig. 7.7 Face detection using LBP cascade learned on the **a** IIITD dataset and **b** ND dataset

database are shown in Fig. 7.7. It can be observed that compared with pre-trained cascade, there is a substantial increase in the number of images with higher RG and RD when cascades trained on thermal images are used. At least one face rectangle is detected in each image of the IIITD dataset, whereas in 6.41 % images of the ND dataset no face rectangle is detected. Further, Table 7.3 also shows that training on thermal images helps in improving face detection results. However, there is a further scope of improvement, as faces are detected reasonably well in only about 60 % images.

7.4.2.1 Learning a Cascade Model from Combined Dataset

One possible way to further improve the face detection performance is to learn the model using data containing large variations. In order to achieve this, we train a model using both the datasets: 307 and 159 images from the IIITD and ND datasets, respectively, comprise the face samples of the training set for this experiment. The cascaded AdaBoost model is trained using LBP features. The results pertaining to this experiment are shown in Table 7.4 and Fig. 7.8a, b. Moreover, Table 7.4 shows that there is a significant improvement in the correct detections (RG > 0.7 and RD > 0.7 together), with 2 and 3 % improvement for IIITD and ND datasets, respectively. Also the number of undetected faces reduces significantly.

To further reduce the difference between images from the two databases, image histogram equalization is applied. It is our assertion that histogram equalization can help reduce the effect of the sensor- and/or environment-specific variations. Therefore, LBP features are obtained after preprocessing the images using histogram equalization. As shown in Table 7.4 and Fig. 7.8c, d, there is a slight improvement in performance when images are preprocessed using histogram equalization. The detection rate of 0.65 is obtained on both the sets.

On this combined training set, the effectiveness of Haar cascade is also evaluated with histogram equalization preprocessing. For this experiment, the cascaded

Table 7.4 Results of face detection when the model is trained with combined IIITD + ND databases and tested on IIITD and ND thermal face databases

Experiment	Test set	Normalized image count		Detection accuracy	Undetected Total
		RG > 0.7	RD > 0.7	(RG > 0.7 and RD > 0.7)	
No preprocessing and LBP features	IIITD	0.89	0.66	0.64	0/307
	ND	0.75	0.76	0.63	15/2292
Histogram equalization with LBP features	IIITD	0.88	0.70	0.65	0/307
	ND	0.77	0.79	0.65	14/2292
Histogram equalization with Haar-like features	IIITD	0.84	0.78	**0.70**	**2/307**
	ND	0.83	0.88	**0.77**	**18/2292**

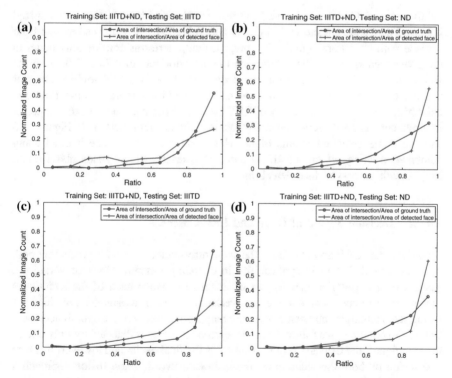

Fig. 7.8 Face detection using LBP cascade with training on combined ND and IIITD dataset and testing on the **a** IIITD dataset and **b** ND dataset. Corresponding result on **c** IIITD dataset and **d** ND dataset when the images are preprocessed using histogram equalization is obtained

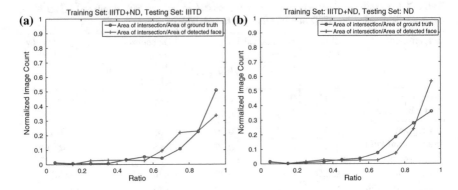

Fig. 7.9 Face detection using Haar cascade with training using histogram equalization preprocessed ND and IIITD dataset and testing on **a** IIITD dataset and **b** ND dataset

AdaBoost model is learned on the Haar features obtained from histogram-equalized images. The results are shown in Fig. 7.9 and Table 7.4. The results show that Haar cascade with histogram equalization preprocessing performs considerably better in the given scenario by further improving the detection rate to 0.70 and 0.77 on the IIITD and ND datasets, respectively. However, there is a trade-off in terms of training time and accuracy, with Haar cascade requiring more training time and exhibiting better results than that of LBP cascade. Note that there is still scope for improvement as the detection accuracy rate is in the range of 0.70–0.80. Figure 7.10 shows sample detection results of the Haar feature-based cascade learned using combined training set on the IIITD and ND datasets, which yields about 65 % images with successful face detection.

7.4.2.2 Decision Fusion of Haar and LBP Cascades

Since Haar and LBP do not encode the same information, one may expect that both of them should find their applicability in encoding different kinds of variations. Therefore, it is possible that the set of images for which each of the techniques works the best may not be completely overlapping. This is a plausible condition for fusing two techniques and can potentially help further improve the overall accuracy. In order to combine, we follow a simple approach: If face is detected by only one of the techniques, the detected region is taken as the final decision. However, if a face is detected by both the techniques, the following two decision fusion approaches can be applied.

- **Fusion Approach 1**: Out of the two candidate rectangles, select the smaller one. This approach assumes that the detection techniques are prone to overestimating the face rectangle size, thus selecting the smaller candidate rectangle should result in better detection.

(a)

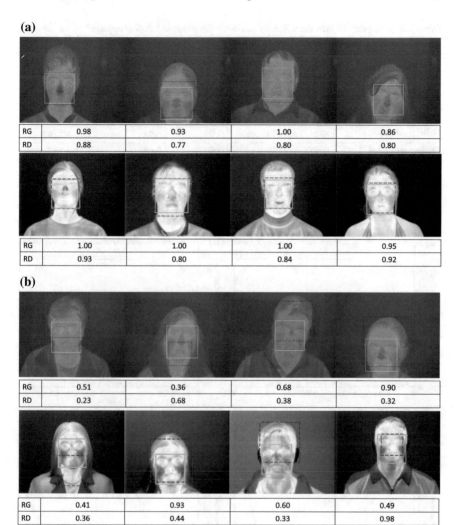

(b)

Fig. 7.10 Examples of **a** good (RG > 0.7 and RD > 0.7) and **b** poor detection results on the IIITD (*top row*) and ND (*bottom row*) datasets. *Green* (*solid lines*) and *red* (*dashed lines*) *rectangles* represent the ground truth and detected face region (using Haar feature-based cascade learned on combined training set), respectively

- **Fusion Approach 2**: Out of the two candidate rectangles, select the larger one. The second approach assumes that the detection techniques are prone to underestimating the size of face rectangle.

Both sets of experiments are performed along with histogram equalization and the results are shown in Table 7.5 and Fig. 7.11. As shown in Table 7.5, in both the

Table 7.5 Summary of face detection results with the proposed fusion approaches on the IIITD and ND thermal face databases

Algorithm	Test set	Normalized image count		Detection accuracy	Undetected Total
		RG > 0.7	RD > 0.7	(RG > 0.7 and RD > 0.7)	
Fusion approach 1 (LBP + Haar)	IIITD	0.84	0.85	**0.74**	**0/317**
	ND	0.75	0.93	**0.73**	**3/2292**
Fusion approach 2 (LBP + Haar)	IIITD	0.88	0.63	0.61	0/317
	ND	0.85	0.75	0.70	3/2292

The training set is created by combining the training sets of both IIITD and ND datasets

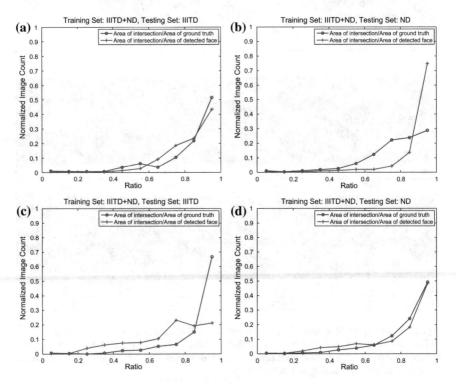

Fig. 7.11 Face detection using fusion approach 1 on the **a** IIITD and **b** ND datasets; and using fusion approach 2 on the **c** IIITD and **d** ND datasets

fusion approaches, at least one face rectangle is detected in all but three images. The results show that the first fusion approach exhibits better results for the IIITD dataset, and fusion has little effect on the ND dataset.

7.4.3   Effect of Sensor and Environment

Since thermal images are dependent on the heat emissivity of the object or surface, they may be affected by environmental aspects such as ambient temperature. These images are also dependent on the type of sensor used, and therefore, the interoperability of sensors can also affect the accuracy of the models learned from one camera. This section studies these two aspects of thermal face detection.

Effect of Day and Night Outdoor Environments We utilize the IIITD-PSE dataset to understand the challenges of thermal face detection in outdoor settings along with the effect of capture during day and night. Figure 7.2 shows sample images of the same person captured in day and night environments. Since fusion approaches yield better results on the IIITD and ND databases, this experiment is also performed with the fusion approaches only. The results of this experiment are reported in Fig. 7.12. It can be observed that the model learned from images captured in indoor settings (IIITD + ND) is not effective on images captured outdoors during daytime (IIITD-PSE-Day). However, as shown in Table 7.6, the results are relatively

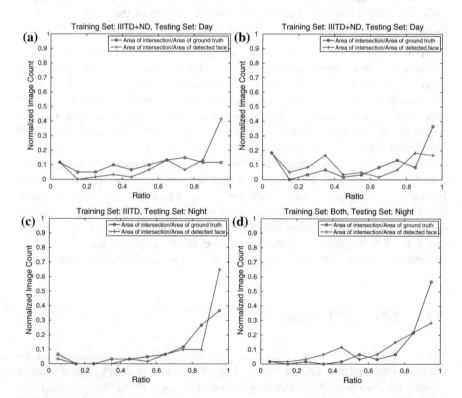

Fig. 7.12 Detection results on IIITD-PSE dataset. Face localization results on IIITD-PSE-Day set using **a** fusion approach-1 and **b** fusion approach-2. Similarly, results on IIITD-PSE-Night set using **c** fusion approach-1 and **d** fusion approach-2

Table 7.6 Summarizing the results of face detection with proposed fusion approaches on thermal images acquired in daytime and nighttime

Experiment	Training set	Test set	Normalized image count		Detection accuracy (RG and RD > 0.7)	Undetected Total
			RG > 0.7	RD > 0.7		
Fusion approach 1 (LBP + Haar)	IIITD + ND	IIITD-PSE-Day	0.38	0.61	0.31	0/60
		IIITD-PSE-Night	0.75	0.85	0.70	0/60
Fusion approach 2 (LBP + Haar)	IIITD + ND	IIITD-PSE-Day	0.58	0.41	0.38	0/60
		IIITD-PSE-Night	0.85	0.65	0.65	0/60
Cross-sensor (LBP)	IIITD	ND	0.51	0.65	0.42	211/2292
	ND	IIITD	0.87	0.53	0.47	0/614

The results of cross-sensor face detection experiments are also reported

better for outdoor nighttime images (IIITD-PSE-Night). During daytime, the temperature difference between the skin and the environment is smaller compared to nighttime, which might be affecting the overall contrast of the image. Therefore, daytime outdoor face detection in thermal spectrum needs further research.

Effect of Cross-sensor Training Previous experiments show that if the cascade is trained using the images from same database, it provides good results. However, it is important to have a model which can be utilized across multiple datasets captured using different thermal imaging sensors. As shown in Figs. 7.2 and 7.3, images captured using two different sensors might look quite different. Therefore, a logical step is to examine the challenges due to cross-sensor data (i.e., problem of sensor interoperability).

The cascades trained on individual datasets during the previous experiments are used for detecting faces pertaining to the other dataset. For example, the cascade trained using the ND database is used for detecting faces from the IIITD database and vice versa. The results in Fig. 7.13 show that the model learned from one dataset does not cross-validate well when tested on the other dataset. This may be due to the fact that different datasets include different properties such as capturing environment, set of subjects, imaging resolution, and sensor characteristics.

7.4.4 Effect of Occlusion

In order to study the effect of occlusion, we have performed experiments on the I^2BVSD face disguise dataset (thermal spectrum images only). The dataset is divided into two parts, (i) minor disguise and (ii) major disguise. The minor disguise subset consists of images of subjects wearing headgears, hair, and beard extensions which do not cover any of the vital features such as eyes, nose, and mouth. The major disguise subset consists of images of subjects wearing shades,

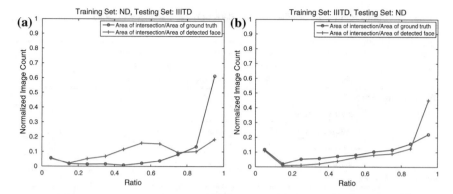

Fig. 7.13 Face detection using LBP cascade with **a** training on ND and testing on IIITD set and **b** training on IIITD and testing on ND dataset

mouth pieces, heavy beards, and/or any accessory which covers one of the vital features. The baseline evaluation is performed with cascaded AdaBoost models learned using combined training set (IIITD + ND). As shown in Table 7.7, detection accuracy for minor disguise subset is about 25 % for LBP and Haar-based cascaded AdaBoost detector. For major disguise subset, the LBP and Haar-based detectors yield 10 and 15 % detection accuracy, respectively. This shows that the cascaded AdaBoost-based approach is not very effective in the presence of occlusions. The corresponding results in terms of RG and RD are reported in Fig. 7.14. If we pose a constrained problem of face localization, i.e., *given that there is a face image, locate it*, we can utilize a skin detection-based approach for approximating facial regions with occlusion variations. Skin color-based region detection has been studied extensively in visible spectrum [11, 13, 20, 22]. However, to the best of our knowledge, skin color detection in thermal spectrum is still unexplored. Skin detection is comparatively easier in thermal spectrum because the heat patterns generated due to body temperature are typically distinct compared to background. Therefore, we present a skin detection-based ROI selection approach.

7.4.4.1 Skin Detection-Based ROI Selection

In order to reduce the number of falsely detected faces, we propose a skin detection-based ROI selection approach as a preprocessing stage to cascaded AdaBoost face detection. The steps involved in the proposed skin detection approach are shown in Fig. 7.15. Further details of skin detection are as follows:

- **Features**: For every pixel, a square neighborhood of $k \times k$ is chosen as the representation. Thus, for every pixel a k^2 dimensional feature vector is obtained; and an image of size $m \times n$ is represented using $mn \times k^2$ feature set. In this work, neighborhood of $k = 3$ is chosen. This feature representation helps encode every skin pixel with respect to its neighborhood.

Table 7.7 Summarizing the results of face detection on the faces occluded using disguised accessories

Experiment	Test set	Normalized image count		Detection accuracy (RG > 0.7 and RD > 0.7)	Undetected Total
		RG > 0.7	RD > 0.7		
Without skin detection					
LBP	Disguise minor	0.81	0.33	0.27	0/307
	Disguise major	0.57	0.25	0.10	1/231
Haar	Disguise minor	0.43	0.51	0.26	12/307
	Disguise major	0.31	0.57	0.15	7/231
Only skin detection					
Skin model	Disguise minor	1	0.00	0.00	n/a
	Disguise major	0.99	0.00	0.00	n/a
With skin detection					
LBP	Disguise minor	0.68	0.53	**0.42**	1/307
	Disguise major	0.20	0.47	**0.10**	5/231
Haar	Disguise minor	0.39	0.58	0.29	12/307
	Disguise major	0.21	0.65	0.13	0/231
Fusion approach 1 (LBP + Haar)	Disguise minor	0.41	0.64	0.33	0/307
	Disguise major	0.11	0.62	0.08	0/231
Fusion approach 2 (LBP + Haar)	Disguise minor	0.69	0.48	**0.38**	1/307
	Disguise major	0.31	0.52	**0.16**	0/231

- **Skin and Non-skin Modeling**: Using the ground truth face and non-face regions, corresponding skin and non-skin pixels are obtained. These distributions of skin and non-skin features are learned from the training data. The distributions essentially capture how the heat patterns of skin and non-skin pixels appear in the local neighborhood. Skin and non-skin distributions are modeled as:

$$f_s(\mathbf{x}) = \mathcal{N}(\mathbf{x}, \mu_s, \Sigma_s),$$
$$f_{ns}(\mathbf{x}) = \mathcal{N}(\mathbf{x}, \mu_{ns}, \Sigma_{ns})$$

where, f_s and f_{ns} denote the probability of $\mathbf{x}$ belonging to skin and non-skin regions, respectively. $\mathcal{N}(\cdot, \mu, \Sigma)$ denotes a normal distribution with mean μ and variance Σ. The training phase includes learning the mean and variance of skin and non-skin distributions.

- **Pixel classification**: A pixel with feature representation $\mathbf{x}$ is classified as skin, if $\log\left(\frac{f_s(\mathbf{x})}{f_{ns}(\mathbf{x})+\varepsilon}\right) > \varepsilon$ where ε is a very small positive real number.

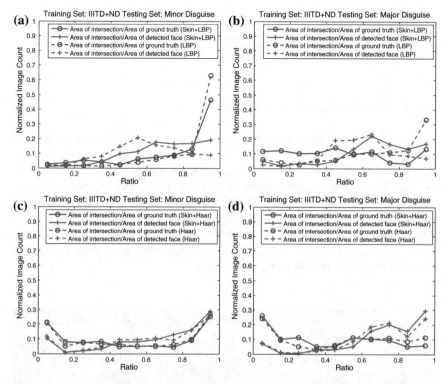

Fig. 7.14 Face detection using LBP cascade on **a** minor and **b** major disguise subsets, and using Haar cascade on **c** minor and **d** major disguise subsets. The results obtained using skin detection-based ROI selection are also reported

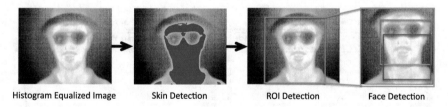

Histogram Equalized Image   Skin Detection   ROI Detection   Face Detection

Fig. 7.15 The face detection pipeline with skin detection-based ROI selection. The *blue*, *red*, and *green rectangles* represent the selected ROI, detected face region, and ground truth face region, respectively

- **ROI Selection**: At the end of the pixel classification stage, a binary mask is obtained for every image. Although almost all the facial regions are often obtained as skin regions, there may be some holes and/or there may be multiple connected components (due to occlusion). We propose to utilize the largest connected component of the binary mask, and the corresponding bounding box is utilized as the region of interest. Once the ROI is selected, a cascade classifier is utilized for finding the face location/bounding box.

7.4.4.2 Effectiveness of ROI Selection

Figures 7.16 and 7.17 show some examples of ROI selections and the effectiveness of the ROI selection approach, respectively. It can be observed that the proposed approach effectively rejects non-face regions of the image. As shown in Table 7.7 and Fig. 7.17, the skin modeling-based ROI selection alone, without any further face detector, yields RG of around 100 %. This shows that the ROI is almost always covering the face region. We further applied the AdaBoost cascade, learned in earlier experiments, on the ROI obtained using skin detection. As shown in Table 7.7, Fig. 7.14, and Fig. 7.18 ROI selection helps in improving detection accuracy, especially in case of minor disguise.

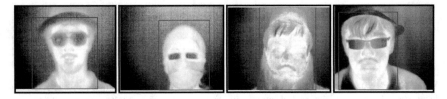

Fig. 7.16 Samples of skin detection-based ROI selection approach. The *red rectangle* represents the ROIs obtained

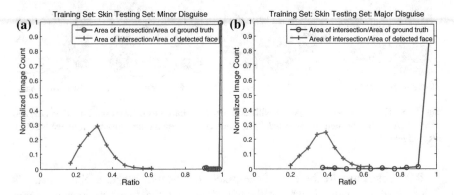

Fig. 7.17 Effectiveness of skin detection-based ROI selection is shown for **a** minor and **b** major disguise subsets. On both the sets, the RG values are comparatively very high for large number of images, suggesting that very little ground truth facial region is discarded in ROI selection

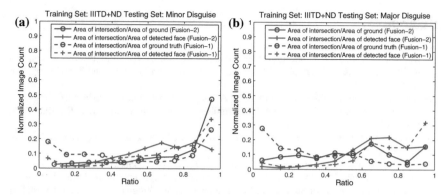

Fig. 7.18 Results of the proposed fusion approaches on **a** minor and **b** major disguise subsets

7.5 Conclusion and Future Research Directions

Thermal face detection has been a relatively unexplored area of research and there are multiple covariates that affect the performance of face detection algorithms. This chapter presents a study to understand the effect of thermal imagining-specific covariates on the performance of face detection in thermal images. There are three contributions of this chapter:

1. We prepared two thermal face databases, namely the IIITD thermal face database that contains 614 face images of 64 subjects and 150 non-face images, and IIITD-PSE database comprising 120 images captured during daytime and nighttime to study the effect of ambient temperature on thermal face detection.
2. We analyzed the performance of three algorithms: AdaBoost-based face detector with LBP features, AdaBoost face detector with Haar-like features, and fusion of the LBP and Haar-like features. The performance is analyzed not only on the IIITD thermal and PSE databases, but also on the Notre Dame and I^{2}BVSD face databases. The use of these two existing databases helps us to understand the impact of interoperability and occlusion on thermal face detection.
3. We propose two new metrics of face localization, RG and RD, which in combination provide the true performance of face detection.
   The results show that decision level fusion of Haar-like and LBP features is promising and preprocessing using histogram equalization also helps in improving the detection accuracy. This may point out that preprocessing is one of the key components in addressing environmental covariates in thermal face detection. Further, the results on cross-dataset experiments, indoor–outdoor and day–night variations, and occlusions using facial accessories reveal challenging nature of the problem.

Acknowledgements T.I. Dhamecha is partly supported through TCS Ph.D. research fellowship.

References

1. Bourlai, T., Jafri, Z.: Eye detection in the middle-wave infrared spectrum: towards recognition in the dark. In: IEEE International Workshop on Information Forensics and Security, pp. 1–6 (2011)
2. Bourlai, T., Ross, A., Chen, C., Hornak, L.: A study on using middle-wave infrared images for face recognition. In: SPIE, Biometric Technology for Human Identification IX, Baltimore, USA (2012)
3. Bourlai, T.: Mid-wave ir face recognition systems. SPIE Newsroom Magazine-Defense & Security (2013)
4. Bradski, G.: The OpenCV library. Dr. Dobb's J. Softw. Tools **25**(11), 120–126 (2000)
5. Chen, X., Flynn, P.J., Bowyer, K.W.: PCA-based face recognition in infrared imagery: baseline and comparative studies. In: IEEE International Workshop on Analysis and Modeling of Faces and Gestures, pp. 127–134 (2003)
6. Chen, X., Flynn, P.J., Bowyer, K.W.: IR and visible light face recognition. Comput. Vis. Image Underst. **99**(3), 332–358 (2005)
7. Cortes, C., Vapnik, V.: Support-vector networks. Mach. Learn. **20**(3), 273–297 (1995)
8. Dhamecha, T.I., Nigam, A., Singh, R., Vatsa, M.: Disguise detection and face recognition in visible and thermal spectrums. In: IEEE International Conference on Biometrics, pp. 1–8 (2013)
9. Dhamecha, T.I., Singh, R., Vatsa, M., Kumar, A.: Recognizing disguised faces: human and machine evaluation. PloS one **9**(7), e99212 (2014)
10. Haralick, R.M., Shanmugam, K., Dinstein, I.H.: Textural features for image classification. IEEE Trans. Syst. Man Cybern. **6**, 610–621 (1973)
11. Hsu, R.L., Abdel-Mottaleb, M., Jain, A.K.: Face detection in color images. IEEE Trans. Pattern Anal. Mach. Intell. **24**(5), 696–706 (2002)
12. IEEE OTCBVS WS Series Bench; DOE University Research Program in Robotics under grant DOE-DE-FG02-86NE37968; DOD/TACOM/NAC/ARC Program under grant R01-1344-18; FAA/NSSA grant R01-1344-48/49; Office of Naval Research under grant #N000143010022
13. Kovac, J., Peer, P., Solina, F.: Human skin color clustering for face detection, vol. 2. IEEE (2003)
14. Li, S.Z., Yi, D., Lei, Z., Liao, S.: The CASIA NIR-VIS 2.0 face database. In: IEEE Conference on Computer Vision and Pattern Recognition—Workshops, pp. 348–353 (2013)
15. Li, S.Z., Chu, R., Liao, S., Zhang, L.: Illumination invariant face recognition using near-infrared images. IEEE Trans. Pattern Anal. Mach. Intell. **29**(4), 627–639 (2007)
16. Liao, S., Zhu, X., Lei, Z., Zhang, L., Li, S.Z.: Learning multi-scale block local binary patterns for face recognition. In: Advances in Biometrics, pp. 828–837. Springer, Berlin (2007)
17. Lienhart, R., Maydt, J.: An extended set of Haar-like features for rapid object detection. In: IEEE International Conference on Image Processing, vol. 1, pp. I-900–I-903 (2002)
18. Martinez, B., Binefa, X., Pantic, M.: Facial component detection in thermal imagery. In: IEEE Conference on Computer Vision and Pattern Recognition—Workshops (2010)
19. Osia, N., Bourlai, T.: A spectral independent approach for physiological and geometric based face recognition in the visible, middle-wave and long-wave infrared bands. Image Vis. Comput. **32**(11), 847–859 (2014)
20. Phung, S.L., Bouzerdoum, A., Chai, D.: A novel skin color model in YCbCr color space and its application to human face detection. In: IEEE International Conference on Image Processing, vol. 1, pp. I–289 (2002)
21. Selinger, A., Socolinsky, D.A.: Face recognition in the dark. In: IEEE Conference on Computer Vision and Pattern Recognition-Workshops (2004)
22. Singh, S.K., Chauhan, D., Vatsa, M., Singh, R.: A robust skin color based face detection algorithm. Tamkang J. Sci. Eng. **6**(4), 227–234 (2003)
23. Socolinsky, D.A., Selinger, A.: Thermal face recognition in an operational scenario. In: IEEE Conference on Computer Vision and Pattern Recognition, vol. 2, pp. II-1012–II-1019 (2004)

24. Socolinsky, D.A., Neuheisel, J.D., Priebe, C.E., De Vinney, J., Marchette, D.: Fast face detection with a boosted CCCD classifier. Technical Report, Johns Hopkins University (2002)
25. Trujillo, L., Olague, G., Hammoud, R., Hernandez, B.: Automatic feature localization in thermal images for facial expression recognition. In: IEEE Conference on Computer Vision and Pattern Recognition—Workshops, pages 14 (2005)
26. Viola, P., Jones, M.J.: Robust real-time face detection. Int. J. Comput. Vision **57**(2), 137–154 (2004)
27. Wang, S., Liu, Z., Lv, S., Lv, Y., Wu, G., Peng, P., Chen, F., Wang, X.: A natural visible and infrared facial expression database for expression recognition and emotion inference. IEEE Trans. Multimedia **12**(7), 682–691 (2010)
28. Wang, S., Liu, Z., Shen, P., Ji, Q.: Eye localization from thermal infrared images. Pattern Recogn. **46**(10), 2613–2621 (2013)
29. Zhang, Z., Yi, D., Lei, Z., Li, S.Z.: Regularized transfer boosting for face detection across spectrum. IEEE Signal Process. Lett. **19**(3), 131–134 (2012)

Chapter 8
Face Recognition Systems Under Spoofing Attacks

Ivana Chingovska, Nesli Erdogmus, André Anjos
and Sébastien Marcel

Abstract In this chapter, we give an overview of spoofing attacks and spoofing countermeasures for face recognition systems, with a focus on visual spectrum systems (VIS) in 2D and 3D, as well as near-infrared (NIR) and multispectral systems. We cover the existing types of spoofing attacks and report on their success to bypass several state-of-the-art face recognition systems. The results on two different face spoofing databases in VIS and one newly developed face spoofing database in NIR show that spoofing attacks present a significant security risk for face recognition systems in any part of the spectrum. The risk is partially reduced when using multispectral systems. We also give a systematic overview of the existing anti-spoofing techniques, with an analysis of their advantages and limitations and prospective for future work.

8.1 Introduction

Thanks to the growing availability of inexpensive cameras, as well as the unobtrusiveness of capturing procedures, face has a guaranteed position as one of the most exploitable biometric modes. Its wide deployment is further reinforced by the

I. Chingovska · A. Anjos · S. Marcel (✉)
Idiap Research Institute, Martigny, Switzerland
e-mail: sebastien.marcel@idiap.ch

I. Chingovska
e-mail: ivana.chingovska@idiap.ch

A. Anjos
e-mail: andre.anjos@idiap.ch

N. Erdogmus
Department of Computer Engineering, IZTECH, İzmir, Turkey
e-mail: neslierdogmus@iyte.edu.tr

© Springer International Publishing Switzerland 2016
T. Bourlai (ed.), *Face Recognition Across the Imaging Spectrum*,
DOI 10.1007/978-3-319-28501-6_8

rapid advancement of face recognition systems, which nowadays provide reliable recognition even under challenging conditions. Historically, 2D face recognition in the visual spectrum (VIS) has got the most attention and has reached a stage where it provides a secure, robust, and trustworthy biometric authentication at different security checkpoints: ID control systems, protected Web services, and even mobile devices. On the other hand, face recognition in 3D, near-infrared (NIR), and thermal spectrum shows an increased popularity in the recent years [1, 2].

Unfortunately, face recognition systems can be an attractive target for spoofing attacks: attempts to illegally access the system by providing a copy of a legal user's face. Information globalization acts in favor of such system misuse: users' personal data, including face images and videos, are nowadays widely available and can be easily downloaded from the Internet. Printed photographs of a user face, digital photographs displayed on a device, video replays, and 3D masks have already proven to be a serious threat for face recognition systems in VIS. Spoofing attacks for NIR face recognition systems have not received as much attention, but recent spoofing attempts indicate on their vulnerability too [3]. Considering that the driving force of attackers is not how hard systems are to spoof, but how valuable are the resources they guard, it is not pessimistic to expect more and more sophisticated spoofing attacks in near future.

In this chapter, we will cover research attempts in spoofing and anti-spoofing for the face mode from two perspectives. Firstly, we will investigate to what extent the state-of-the-art face recognition systems are vulnerable to spoofing attacks. This is a vital step toward verifying the threat and justifying the need of anti-spoofing methods. In addition, this step may reveal whether a spoofing attack database is relevant to be used to develop and evaluate anti-spoofing methods. We perform this analysis on four state-of-the-art face recognition systems working in VIS and NIR. In VIS, we exploit two different publicly available face spoofing databases, one with 2D attacks, and one with 3D mask attacks. To perform the analysis in NIR, we develop and present the first publicly available face spoofing database containing VIS and NIR spoofing attacks. By fusing the scores of the systems working in VIS and NIR, we extend the analysis to multispectral systems as well.

Secondly, we give an overview of the recent advancements in countermeasures to spoofing attacks for face recognition systems. This includes systematic categorization of the anti-spoofing methods and investigation on the attacks they are effective against. While there is a plethora of anti-spoofing methods for VIS face recognition systems, the amount of methods for NIR and multispectral systems is significantly smaller.

Unfortunately, it is extremely difficult to comparatively evaluate the performance of the existing anti-spoofing methods, mainly due to two factors. Firstly, very few of the research papers release the source code and the exact parameters to reproduce the presented results. Secondly, many of them are evaluated on private databases or are targeting just one type of spoofing attacks. Therefore, while we most often omit performance numbers, we distinguish methods whose results are fully reproducible on publicly available databases.

This chapter is organized as follows. We cover 2D face recognition systems in VIS and NIR under 2D spoofing attacks in Sects. 8.2.1 and 8.2.2, respectively. In Sect. 3, we cover face recognition systems in VIS under 3D spoofing attacks. Conclusions and discussion follow in Sect. 4.

8.2   Face Recognition Systems Under 2D Spoofing Attacks

8.2.1   Visual Spectrum (VIS) Face Recognition Systems

Numerous spoofing attack trials to test the robustness of commercial devices [4, 5], as well as several face spoofing databases have proved that face recognition systems in VIS can be spoofed with many different types of attacks. The attacks differ by their complexity, their cost and the amount of effort and skills required for producing them. The effectiveness of the attacks is closely related with these properties.

The spoofing countermeasures developed to protect 2D face recognition systems in VIS are by now developed to a very good extent, for example, the 2nd competition of countermeasures to 2D face spoofing attacks [6], where two of the submitted algorithms achieved perfect spoofing detection rate. The objective of this section is to summarize the research efforts in this direction, in terms of available spoofing attack types and databases, as well as existing solutions. We focus on face verification systems, where the spoofing attacks make most sense.

8.2.1.1   Types of Attacks and Databases

Probably, the simplest type of face spoofing attack is the print attack, which consists of printing a photograph of a valid user's face on paper. A more sophisticated type of attack involves presenting a digital photograph on the screen of a mobile device. These two types of attacks retain the face appearance, but present only a static face shows no signs of vitality. More sophisticated versions of the printed attacks simulate vitality by perforating the eye region or moving, rotating, and warping the printed paper [7–9]. In addition, there are video replay spoofing attacks, where a face video of a valid user is presented on the screen of a mobile device. Examples of spoofing attacks based on drawing of a user's face or using makeup to masquerade as a valid user have been registered at the ICB 2013 spoofing challenge.[1] Attacks with 3D masks will be covered in Sect. 3.

Besides the way of reproducing the spoofed face, the spoofing attacks can differ in a number of other criteria. For example, they can be recorded in controlled or uncontrolled environments. Furthermore, a fixed or a hand support can be used for

---

[1]http://www.biometrics-center.ch/testing/ tabula-rasa-spoofing-challenge-2013.

holding the spoof medium [10, 11] defines the term scenic 2D spoofing attack referring to attacks where the background content of the presented spoofing attack image is visible alongside the spoofed face. Finally, for some attacks, the border of the spoofing medium may be fully visible. The available face spoofing databases cover different subsets of these types of attacks. Different types of spoofing attacks pose a different level of difficulty to detect and are usually addressed with different types of countermeasures.

The number of face spoofing databases which are publicly available is limited. Up to the present moment, the established countermeasures to 2D face spoofing attacks have been evaluated either on private databases, or on three publicly available face spoofing databases: NUAA Photograph Imposter Database [8], CASIA Face Anti-spoofing Database (CASIA-FASD) [9] and the Replay-Attack family of databases [10]. NUAA database consists of attacks with printed photographs. It contains still images of real accesses and attacks to 15 identities and is recorded in three sessions under three different illumination conditions. When capturing the attacks, the photographs of the users are translated, rotated or warped.

CASIA-FASD provides videos of real accesses and three types of attacks to 50 identities. The first type is performed with printed photographs warped in front of the camera. The second type is printed photographs with perforated eye regions, so that a person can blink behind the photograph. The third type is a video playback of the user. When recording the database, three imaging qualities are considered: low, normal, and high.

The Replay-Attack family of databases consists of Print-Attack [12] containing printed photographs, Photo-Attack [13] containing printed and digital photographs, and Replay-Attack [10], as a superset of the previous two databases to which video attacks have been added. There is a total of 50 identities, recorded in both controlled and uncontrolled conditions, with diverse acquisition equipment.

Not all of the spoofing databases have equally wide applicability for evaluating anti-spoofing systems. For example, a database which offers still images, like NUAA, cannot be used for evaluation of countermeasures which require video inputs, like the motion-based algorithm described in Sect. 2.1.3. In addition, some databases are lacking a protocol to precisely define training, development, and test set. Finally, as described in Sect. 2.1.2, spoofing databases should provide enrollment samples which can be used to train and evaluate a baseline face verification system [14]. Both NUAA and CASIA-FASD suffer from this last drawback, and hence, their effectiveness in bypassing face verification systems cannot be properly evaluated. This disadvantage is overcome by the databases of the Replay-Attack family.

8.2.1.2 Assessing the Vulnerability

When evaluating a face verification system, it is a common practice to report False Acceptance Rate (FAR) (or False Match Rate (FMR)) and False Rejection Rate

Fig. 8.1 Score distribution of
GMM-based face recognition
system for the samples in
Replay-Attack. Real accesses:
■, zero-effort impostors: ■,
and spoofing attacks: ■

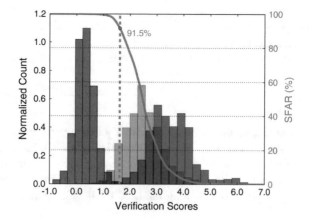

(FRR) (or False Non-Match Rate (FNMR)).[2] The error rate at the point where these
two values are equal is called Equal Error Rate (EER), while their average is called
Half Total Error Rate (HTER). If the systems are exposed to spoofing attacks, their
vulnerability is usually measured using Spoof False Acceptance Rate (SFAR) [14].
If the face verification system is tuned to work at particular operating point (decision threshold), SFAR gives the ratio of spoofing attacks whose score is higher
than that point and are thus accepted by the system.

In order to be used for evaluation of verification systems, spoofing attack
databases need to have properties that allow for their training [14]. In particular,
they need to contain enrollment samples used to enroll clients in the verification
systems. Out of the publicly available 2D face spoofing databases, only the
Replay-Attack family satisfies this property. Using Replay-Attack database, we
trained face verification system based on Gaussian mixture model (GMM), which
extracts discrete cosine transform (DCT) features from the input images [17].
Figure 8.1 shows the distribution of the scores for the real accesses, zero-effort
impostors and spoofing attacks from Replay-Attack for this system. The green line
depicts the point which is chosen as a decision threshold based on EER criteria
depending on FAR and FRR. The system shows a remarkable separability between
the score distributions of the real accesses and zero-effort impostors, resulting in an
almost perfect verification results (HTER = 0.14 %). However, the distributions of
the scores of the real accesses and spoofing attacks overlap by a large extent. As a
result, the system accepts 91.5 % of the spoofing attacks, which proves its high
vulnerability to spoofing.

We performed similar analysis for three additional state-of-the-art face verification systems, each of which is based on different features and modeling paradigm.
The first one uses local Gabor binary pattern histogram sequences (LGBPHS) [18],

---

[2]In their formal definition, FAR and FMR and FRR and FNRM are not synonymous [15].
However, they can be treated as such is some special cases, and we will do so, following the
practice adopted in [16].

Table 8.1 Verification error
rates and spoofing
vulnerability of baseline face
verification systems (in %)

System	FAR	FRR	SFAR
GMM	0.05	0.24	91.5
LGBPHS	1.47	2.13	88.5
GJet	0.28	0.24	95.0
ISV	0.00	0.17	92.6

the second one is based on Gabor jets comparison (GJet) [19], while the third one
uses inter-session variability modeling (ISV) [20]. The results are shown in
Table 8.1. All of the examined systems perform very well in the verification task.
However, with SFAR of 90 %, each one of them exhibits a high vulnerability to
spoofing, demonstrating the need for development of suitable countermeasures.

8.2.1.3   Spoofing CounterMeasures

The anti-spoofing methods for the face mode can be primarily categorized based on
the type of data that is used to detect the spoofing attacks. In this respect, they can
fall into two categories: hardware-based and software-based [21]. The
hardware-based solutions use additional hardware to detect the spoofing attacks,
which may be a thermal or near-infrared camera, 3D sensor, etc. The
software-based ones utilize solely the information which is captured by the camera
of the recognition system and try to directly exploit the characteristic of the input
images.

Some of the software-based methods require, either implicitly or explicitly, that
the user answers to some kind of interactive challenge. Yet, most of these methods
take the decision in a non-intrusive manner, without any requirement for an explicit
input from the user. They use different types of cues that may indicate the presence
of a live subject in front of the system: liveness, motion, visual appearance, contextual information, and 3D reconstruction information. Usually, the features
extracted for these purposes are handcrafted based on prior knowledge about the
task; however, there are algorithms which extract relevant features in a completely
data-driven fashion.

In the remainder of this section, we are going to cover the most prominent
representatives of face anti-spoofing methods and make a comparative analysis of
their performance and limitations. We will put an additional note to those which
depend on interaction with the user.

Before proceeding, it is important to notice that several researchers have made
attempts to increase the robustness of biometric recognition systems to spoofing
attacks by using multiple biometric modes [22]. The intuition behind these solutions is that an attacker may need more effort to spoof the system, because she
needs to spoof more modes. Within such multimodal framework, face has been
combined with fingerprint and iris [23–26], or with voice [27]. [23–26] have proven, however, that poorly designed combination rules for multimodal systems may

not be helpful. Combination rules designed specifically for the purpose of increased robustness have been designed in [25, 26].

Liveness Detection

The liveness detection anti-spoofing methods base their decision on the evidence of liveness present on the scene. Usually, eye-blinking, mouth movements, and in-voluntary subtle head movements are considered as evidence of liveness. One of the first attempts to employ eye-blinking for anti-spoofing is performed by [28], which uses conditional random fields (CRF) to model the state of the eye as open or closed and the correlation between its state and the observation. With a similar purpose, [29] uses active shape models to detect the eye contours and difference of images to detect the blinking activity. In [30], eye-blinking detection is combined with the analysis of the 3D properties of the subject.

A key, but limiting assumption of the liveness detection methods, is that the subject will experience the actions that suggest liveness within a given short time frame. For example, [28] assumes that eye blinks happen every 2–4 s, which may not be true always and for all the subjects. To be fully successful, these methods depend on user input like deliberate eyeblinks, which may give them a level of intrusiveness.

An attempt to overcome this limitation is done by methods which rely on more subtle changes in the face region, including color changes due to blood flow. To be able to detect these changes, [31] performs Eulerian motion magnification [32] as a preprocessing before applying a technique for analyzing the texture or the motion patterns.

Another drawback of the liveness methods is that, although they may be successful in the case of print and attacks (even when they are warped or rotated [28]), they may be easily deceived by spoofing attacks where liveness evidence is present, like video playback or 3D masks.

Motion Analysis

The motion-based methods try to find properties of the motion patterns of a person in front of the system, in order to distinguish them from motion patterns in the presence of a spoofing attack. A few of these methods base their approach on the assumption that a person's head, being a 3D object, moves differently than a 2D spoofing attack displayed on a planar media. For example, [33] uses optical flow method to track movements on different face parts. The authors assume that, in contrast to a face displayed on a 2D surface, a 3D face will generate higher amount of motion in central face parts closer to the camera (like the nose) then in the face parts which are further away from the camera (like the ears). Furthermore, a 3D face exhibits motion flows which are in opposite directions for central and peripheral face parts. On the other hand, [34] derives a heuristics for the optical flow field for four basic 2D surface motion types: translation, in-plane rotation, panning, and swing. On the contrary, a 3D face and facial expressions generate irregular optical flow field.

Another set of motion-based methods assumes a high correlation between the movements in the face region and the background in the case of a spoofing attack. Such a correlation is unlikely in the case of a real access. [12] bases the computation of the correlation on 10 quantities extracted from the face region and the background. For the same purpose, [13] relies on quantization of optical flow motion vectors, while [35] performs foreground–background consistency analysis.

Similarly to the liveness detection methods, the motion analysis approaches depend on the subtle involuntary movements of the user. In addition, sometimes they capture the motion introduced by an attacker who holds the attack media with his hands. If the presumed motion patterns are absent during the short acquisition process (e.g., a very still person who does not blink), the methods may fail. These methods are mostly targeting photograph spoofing attacks and will most likely fail in case of spoofing attacks by video playbacks or 3D masks. Furthermore, the methods based on motion correlation are particularly directed for scenic 2D spoofing attack, where the background of the spoofed image is visible.

Visual Appearance

The anti-spoofing methods analyzing the visual appearance stand behind a strong argumentation about the differences in the visual properties of real accesses and spoofing attacks, explained in a number of publications. Firstly, a real face and the human skin have their own optical qualities (absorption, reflection, scattering, refraction), which other materials that can be used as spoofing media (paper, photographic paper, or electronic display) do not possess [36]. Similar differences can appear as a result of the diffuse reflection due to a non-natural shape of the spoofing attacks [37]. Limited resolution of the device used for spoofing or the involuntary shaking of the spoofing media may cause a blurring in the case of spoofing attacks [37–39]. Artifacts appearing in the spoofing production process, like jitter and banding in the case of print attacks [35, 39] or flickering and Moire′ effect in the case of video attacks [40] are yet another sources of differences between the real accesses and spoofing attacks. Many of these visual properties are indistinguishable for the human eye, but often can be easily extracted using different image processing and computer vision algorithms.

The first approach leveraging on the argument that spoofing attacks are usually of lower resolution and thus contain less high-frequency components is proposed in [38]. The proposed feature vector is based on analysis of the 2D Fourier spectrum of the input image and its energy change over time. Instead of comparing the high-frequency content of the input, [8] and [9] base their discrimination on the high-middle band of the Fourier spectrum, which is extracted using difference of Gaussians (DoG) method.

Some publications assume that the differences between real accesses and attacks are most prominent within the reflectance component of the input image and estimate it in different ways: [8] uses the Lambertian reflectance model [41] and Variational retinex-based method, while [42] uses dichromatic reflection model. Then, [8] classifies the obtained features using sparse low rank bilinear discriminative model, while [42] compares the gradient histograms of the reflectance images.

A feature set inspired by a physics-based model for recaptured images, which reveals differences in the background contextual information, reflection, surface gradient, color, contrast, chromaticity, and blurriness, is created by [43]. Different sets of visual features related to texture, color, edges, and/or gradient are used by [44, 45]. [46] generalizes the appearance differences into quality differences and uses a feature vector composed of 25 different image quality measures.

Several publications make use of specific computer vision descriptors for texture analysis. Local binary pattern (LBP) [47] appears to be the most significantly exploited for the purpose of anti-spoofing, both in its single resolution [10] and multiresolution [37, 39, 48] variants. Histogram of oriented gradients (HOG) [37, 39, 44], gray-level co-occurrence matrix (GLCM) [44], Haar wavelets [35], and Gabor wavelets [39] are some of the other alternatives.

More recently, the analysis of the visual appearance has been enhanced into a temporal domain. In [40], the authors firstly extract the noise from each video frame and then summarize the relevant components of its 2D Fourier analysis into the so-called visual rhythm image. The properties of this image are then captured using GLCM. The method proposed in [49] utilizes LBP-TOP [50], where instead of LBP analysis on a single frame, dynamical LBP analysis on a frame and its neighboring frames is performed.

The methods described before present different rates of success, which cannot be easily compared because they are obtained on different types of attacks and usually on databases which are not released publicly. An interesting property of the majority of the visual appearance methods is that they can work even if only a single image is available at input. They are usually applied either on the face bounding box, face parts, or on the full input image. As one of their advantages, they are very user-friendly and non-intrusive and do not depend on the behavior of the user (unlike the liveness detection and motion analysis methods). Furthermore, an attack which can deceive them a priori has not been presented up to this moment. For example, they can be expected to successfully detect print, photograph, video, or even 3D mask attacks. Yet, their success may be put into question if the spoofing attacks are printed or displayed on high-resolution media, thus lacking some of the artifacts that these methods rely on. Their generalization properties when applied to different acquisition conditions or new types of attacks are also uncertain, since the visual appearance of the input images often depends on the light condition, acquisition devices, or display media.

Contextual Information

The context of the scene present as a background information in front of the recognition system is used as a cue to detect spoofing attacks. In [7], the authors notice that in the case of a spoofing attack, there will be a change in the contextual information of the background when the face appears. To detect such changes, the authors compare the regions around reference fiducial key points in the region around the face.

The approach presented in [51] is targeting attacks where the contextual information consists of the border of the spoofing medium. Hence, a prerequisite is that the spoofing medium is fully visible to the system. The method relies on HOG [52] to detect upper body and spoofing medium borders.

3D Information

The 3D property of a human face is a cue that unambiguously distinguishes real accesses from 2D spoofing attacks. This is used by several publications, which try to reconstruct or estimate the 3D information from the user's face. For example, [53] recovers and classifies the 3D structure of the face based on two or more images taken from different viewing angles. For similar purposes, [54] uses 3D projective invariants of a moving head. The disadvantage of these approaches is their intrusiveness: The user needs to be collaborative and moves his head to a different angle in the first case, or performs certain movements at random intervals in the second case. Avoiding such a constraint, [55] estimates the focus variabilities between two images taken consecutively and focused on different parts of the face. In the case of a 2D spoofing attacks, it is expected that focus variabilities will be absent.

It is important to note that the success of this set of methods is usually limited to 2D spoofing attacks and is likely to fail 3D mask attacks.

Challenge–Response Unlike the majority of motion analysis of liveness detection methods which rely on the involuntary movements of the user, challenge–response anti-spoofing methods explicitly ask the user to perform certain action to verify his liveness. Representatives of this type have been already mentioned [53, 54]. There are various types of challenges that a user can perform: taking a particular head pose [56] or following a moving point with a gaze [57] are some of them. Finding the static and dynamic relationship between face and voice information from a speaking face or modeling a speaker in 3D shape is an option for anti-spoofing in a multimodal audio-visual system [58]. It is important to note that the last approach can successfully detect not only visual, but even audio-visual spoofing attacks, such as video playbacks with recorded utterance or 3D synthetic talking heads.

The challenge–response methods are considered to be intrusive, non-friendly, and uncomfortable from the aspect of a user experience. In addition, they usually require that the authentication is performed during a prolonged time span. Finally, they are not transparent for the user. In this way, it is possible for a malicious user to guess the liveness cue and try to bypass it.

Feature Learning

Following a recent trend, the anti-spoofing community started experimenting with approaches where the anti-spoofing features are automatically learned directly from the data. This is in contrast to the previously discussed approaches, where the features are inspired by some particular characteristics that can be observed as common either for real accesses or for some types of spoofing attacks. It is argued, however, that the features engineered in this way are not suitable for different kinds of spoofing attacks [59, 60]. Both [60] and [59] are training a convolutional neural network (CNN) for the purpose. In [60], experiments with face images in 5 different resolutions are given, while in [59], the authors use an optimization procedure to select the best CNN to learn the features, out of a family of CNNs with different hyper-parameters.

Hardware-Based Methods

The hardware-based methods employ an additional piece of hardware along the camera used by the recognition system. These methods detect spoofing attacks using the cues captured by the additional hardware. For example, very often, these methods exploit the properties of the human body in different regions of the electromagnetic spectrum. In such a case, the additional hardware may refer to the sensor used to capture data at a particular wavelength, a light filter which is applied to the camera, or illuminator emitting light at a particular wavelength. Most often, the infrared (IR) region of the electromagnetic spectrum is used, from long wavelength (thermal IR) to NIR.

The idea originates from informal experiments presented in [61]. The paper presents examples of face images of individuals, taken in the long-wavelength infrared region of the spectrum (8−15 μm), also known as thermal infrared region. The images represent the thermal emissions naturally coming from the human body. Depending on the spoofing attack material, these thermal emissions can be significantly reduced if an individual holds the spoofing attack in front of the face.

Operating in the NIR spectrum [62] suggests that there is an apparent difference between the reflectance property of the human skin and other materials. [63] analyzes the reflectance properties of skin and artificial materials at two wavelengths: one in NIR and one in visual spectrum. The two obtained measurements form a feature vector for a multispectral-based spoofing detection. Trying to overcome the requirement for a particular distance from the sensor in [63, 64] finds the most suitable wavelengths and trains the system with data taken at multiple distances. In [65], the authors use multispectral filters to obtain an image which presents the different radiometric response of different parts of the face under a full-spectrum active light. The distinction between real accesses and spoofing attacks is made by analyzing the gradient of the image.

Going back to the visual spectrum, [66] measures the reflectance of the skin using a high-resolution, high-accuracy spectrograph. Using 8 different wavelengths in the visual spectrum, [67] creates a feature vector based on the RGB values of the obtained images.

It is important to notice that in the scenarios referred to in this section, the hardware-based methods using IR sensors are used to protect face recognition system in the visual spectrum. However, these methods are even more suitable to operate alongside face recognition systems in the IR spectrum. IR and multispectral face recognition systems will be covered in Sect. 2.2.

Another example of a hardware-based method is the recent approach [68] which uses, the newly developed light-field camera that records the direction and intensity of each light ray. This camera renders multiple focus images in a single shot. Using this technology, it is possible to distinguish between the multiple focus levels to distinguish between 2D spoofing attacks and real faces.

The need of an additional hardware renders the hardware-based method more expensive and less convenient from deployment perspective. This requirement implies that some of them cannot be used in certain applications, for example, mobile systems.

Fusion

The main motivation behind approaches proposing fusion of anti-spoofing methods is the fact that different types of spoofing attacks have different properties and it is difficult to address all of them only with a single feature type or method. In addition, [69] has made a proof of concept that the anti-spoofing systems are unable to generalize well on unseen spoofing attacks. The discussion in the previous sections, where we state which spoofing attacks are most likely to be detected by the various categories of methods, is an argument toward this direction. Hence, there is an emergence of a trend of fusing several different anti-spoofing methods to obtain a more general countermeasure effective against a multitude of attack types.

The first attempts of fusing have been performed by [45], where the authors develop a fusion scheme at a frame and video level and apply it to a set of visual appearance cues, and [44], where the fusion of visual appearance cues is done at feature level. The authors in [35] for the first time bring the intuition that the fusion can have a bigger impact if done with complementary countermeasures, i.e., those that address different types of cues at the spoofing attacks. In the particular case, although subject to some prerequisites of the videos, motion analysis method is fused with a visual appearance method.

To measure the level of independence of two anti-spoofing systems, and thus to get a measurement of the effectiveness of their fusion, [69] proposes employing a statistical analysis based on [70]. For the same purpose, [11] proposes to count the common error rates [11] further shows that fusing several simple anti-spoofing methods which do not involve complex inefficient classifiers may be favorable with respect to a single one which is memory and time requiring.

The trend of fusing multiple complementary anti-spoofing methods continued with [6]. While fusion at score level is the most dominant approach, future efforts should analyze what is the most effective fusion strategy, both in terms of error rates, and flexibility of incorporating a newly developed countermeasure into the fused system.

8.2.1.4 Discussion

2D spoofing attacks in VIS have attracted a lot of interest among researchers in the past years. This resulted in a large set of countermeasures belonging to different categories, with different efficiency and targeting different types of attacks. Besides this, the countermeasures differ in other important properties, such as their intrusiveness and the type of input they require. We believe that summarizing the available methods based on their properties is much more important than comparing their performance, because each one is tested and works on different conditions. For this purpose, we systematized them in Table 8.4, grouping them by category and listing their main properties. In this way, a user can decide which method to use based on the expected spoofing attacks, types of input the system provides, as well as ease of implementation and convenience of use.

From the results published in the literature so far, we can deduce two main conclusions which may serve to direct future research.

1. Many publications have already achieved close to zero or zero error rates in spoofing detection for the three main publicly available face spoofing databases. The community has recognized the limitations of the currently existing databases, ranging from small number of identities, to small set of spoofing attack types, to various types of biases. More challenging databases need to be created in future. Considering different materials to produce the spoofing attacks, using better quality equipment, creating more diverse illumination conditions and recording more clients are some of the ways to add to the adversity of the spoofing databases.

2. Several publications have shown that the proposed anti-spoofing methods do not generalize well on new spoofing attacks not seen during training time [60, 69]. However, good generalization capabilities should be a key feature for the anti-spoofing methods, as new types of spoofing attacks can never be anticipated. Therefore, future research effort should put an emphasis on methods which generalize well over multitude of different types of spoofing attacks.

8.2.2 NIR and Multispectral Face Recognition Systems

The face recognition systems which work in the infrared part of the spectrum have one major advantage over their counterparts in the visible spectrum: They are usually invariant to illumination changes in the environment. The thermal imaging face recognition systems capture the thermal emissions naturally coming from the human body [2] and use their pattern to recognize individuals. They are naturally resistant to any kind of 2D spoofing attacks, as the thermal signatures of 2 individuals are different [61]. Even more, such systems are resistant to surgically performed face alterations, because tissue redistribution, addition of artificial materials, and alteration of blood vessel flows that may happen during a surgery have a big impact on the thermal signature of a person [62]. Therefore, spoofing attacks for thermal imaging face recognition systems are out of the scope of this chapter.

On the other hand, the NIR face recognition systems need an active NIR light to illuminate the subject and capture the reflection of the face under that light. Examples of the robustness of these systems have been demonstrated in [71, 72]. Multispectral systems are created by fusing face recognition systems which work in different part of the spectrum, such as NIR and thermal, or NIR and VIS [2]. However, the robustness to spoofing attacks of these systems has been addressed very sparsely.

The objective of this section is to study several examples of face recognition systems working in NIR and to evaluate their vulnerability to a basic type of spoofing attacks. We present a new publicly available multispectral face spoofing database, containing face images in NIR and VIS spectrum. The systems are evaluated when working in VIS and NIR spectrum, as well as in multispectral scenario, by fusing the scores of the VIS and NIR systems.

8.2.2.1 Types of Attacks and Databases

The attempts to spoof face recognition system in NIR spectrum are by far less numerous than similar attempts in visual spectrum. The work in [62] presents a way to use NIR technology to detect spoofing attacks for visual spectrum face recognition systems. Some of them even present an empirical study on the success in detecting spoofing attacks. However, none of these studies creates and evaluates spoofing attacks designated to NIR and/or multispectral face recognition systems. That is, in fact, a basic preliminary step before developing a countermeasure.

To the best of our knowledge, only [3] has studied the effect of spoofing attacks on NIR and multispectral face recognition system. The authors develop a database with 100 clients, taking simultaneously visual spectrum and NIR images at each shot. Then, spoofing attacks are created from part of the recorded images in the two spectra, by printing them on a coarse paper. In this way, both visual and NIR spoofing attacks are created. A disadvantage of the study on [3] is that the database is not publicly available.

To alleviate this issue, we created a new publicly available database, called Multispectral-Spoof.[3] The total number of clients in the database is 21. The database is recorded using a uEye camera with CMOS monochrome sensor and a resolution of 1280×1024. The images in NIR were recorded using a NIR illuminator and a NIR cut filter of 800 nm attached to the camera. The images were taken in 7 different conditions: one in an uncontrolled hallway environment and 6 in office environment with natural light, ambient light, no light, illuminator spotlight from the left and from the right, and 2 illuminator spotlights. 5 images in visual spectra and 5 images in NIR were taken under each of these conditions.

Bearing in mind that the attacker may have an access to the best-quality real access samples of the clients, we selected the 3 best images from the visual and NIR samples of each client and printed them in black and white on a normal A4 paper, using a printer with 600 dpi. Then, using the same settings as before, we recorded the printed spoofing attacks in both visual and NIR spectrum in 3 different lighting conditions in an office environment: natural light, ambient light, and 2 illuminator spotlights. For an unbiased evaluation, the clients in the database are divided into 3 non-overlapping sets for training (9 clients), development (6 clients), and testing

---

[3]The link to download the database, together with manual face annotations, will be available as soon as this book chapter is accepted for publication.

Fig. 8.2 Real and spoofing attack samples from the database recorded in VIS. **a** Real access. **b** VIS attack. **c** NIR-attack

Fig. 8.3 Real and spoofing attack samples from the database recorded in NIR. **a** Real access. **b** VIS attack. **c** NIR-attack

(6 clients) purposes. Figs. 8.2 and 8.3 illustrate examples of real access and attack samples taken in VIS and NIR, respectively.

8.2.2.2   Assessing the Vulnerability

In this section, we study the effectiveness of VIS and NIR spoofing attacks in defeating VIS and NIR recognition systems. We would like to inspect whether it is possible to spoof VIS systems using NIR attacks and vice versa. First insight into this problem has been reported by [3]. The studied face recognition system [71] is based on Gabor wavelets. The authors conclude that while VIS system is vulnerable to VIS attacks and NIR system is vulnerable to NIR attacks, there are little chances that VIS attacks can bypass a NIR system and vice versa.

We perform similar analysis using the publicly available Multispectral-Spoof database. We analyze the same recognition systems described in Sect. 2.1.2: GMM, LGBPHS, GJet, and ISV, this time operating in two domains: VIS and NIR.[4]

The Multispectral-Spoof database contains a total of 1680 real access images (840 in VIS and 840 in NIR), as well as 3024 spoofing attack images (756 VIS and 756 NIR attacks for each of the two systems). To allow for training and evaluation

---

[4]The link to fully reproduce the results obtained here will be available as soon as this book chapter is accepted for publication.

of face recognition systems and following the example of Replay-Attack, 10 of the images of each client are reserved for enrollment purposes. During the evaluation, the vulnerability of each of the systems (VIS and NIR) when exposed to the two types of attacks (VIS and NIR) was assessed.

Independent VIS and NIR Systems

We firstly analyze the verification performance and the vulnerabilities of GMM-based system working in VIS mode. The score distributions for this system are given in Fig. 8.4, and the good separation between the distribution of the real accesses and spoofing attacks indicates that the system behaves relatively well in verification. However, Fig. 8.4a shows that the system is highly vulnerable to spoofing attacks recorded in VIS. More surprisingly, Fig. 8.4b shows that the system can be spoofed even with spoofing attacks taken in NIR spectrum, with probability of 30.56 %.

Figure 8.5 demonstrates similar analysis when the GMM-based system works in NIR mode. Again, the system shows relatively good verification performance. In this case, the system shows low vulnerability to VIS attacks, amounting to 13.96 %. The vulnerability to NIR attacks, however, goes as high as 71.8 %.

Table 8.2 presents the verification results and the vulnerabilities for the rest of the studied face recognition systems. All of them are moderately to highly vulnerable to spoofing attacks recorded in the spectrum that they operate in. For example, SFAR for VIS systems to VIS attacks ranges from 59.26 to 74.07 %. In NIR mode, the systems are even more vulnerable to NIR attacks: SFAR ranges from 71.76 to 88.89 %. As can be expected, the vulnerability to attacks recorded in the other spectrum than the one the systems work in is much lower. However, it still amounts to a considerable SFAR, especially in the case of VIS system: the SFAR for NIR attacks is between 27.78 to 38.89 %. Among the studied systems, GJet appears to be the most vulnerable, while ISV shows the greatest robustness to spoofing attacks, both in VIS and NIR mode.

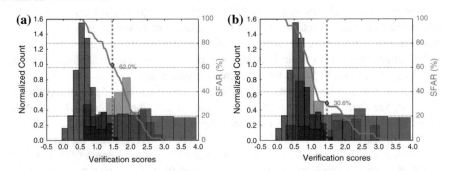

Fig. 8.4 Score distribution of GMM-based face recognition system for the samples in Multispectral-Spoof: VIS mode. Real accesses: ■; zero-effort impostors: ■; and spoofing attacks: ■. **a** VIS attack. **b** NIR-attack

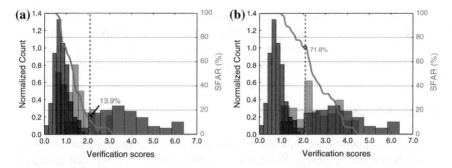

Fig. 8.5 Score distribution of GMM-based face recognition system for the samples in Multispectral-Spoof: NIR mode. Real accesses: ■; zero-effort impostors: ■; and spoofing attacks: ■. **a** VIS attack. **b** NIR-attack

Table 8.2 Verification error rates and spoofing vulnerability of baseline face verification systems (in %)

System	VIS system				NIR system			
	FAR	FRR	SFAR		FAR	FRR	SFAR	
			VIS attack	NIR attack			VIS attack	NIR attack
GMM	0.78	15	62.04	30.56	0	13.96	13.89	71.76
LGBPHS	13.11	3.33	69.44	54.17	4.13	11.17	25.93	74.07
GJet	9.89	6.11	74.07	38.89	3.35	6.15	27.78	88.89
ISV	1.44	16.67	59.26	27.78	0	12.29	14.81	72.22

Multispectral System

The analysis presented in [3] is extended to a multispectral system by fusing the scores of the attacks on the two systems. If simple SUM rule is used for the score fusion, the multispectral system appears to be vulnerable to any of the two types of spoofing attacks.

In our case, we investigate three different strategies to fuse the scores of VIS and NIR systems: SUM of scores, linear logistic regression (LLR), and polynomial logistic regression (PLR). The vulnerabilities of the GMM-based system working in multispectral mode are given in Table 8.3.

The results show that the vulnerability of the multispectral system is highly reduced, especially to VIS spoofing attacks. The vulnerability to NIR spoofing

Table 8.3 Verification error rates and spoofing vulnerability of multispectral GMM-based system (in %)

Fusion method	FAR	FRR	SFAR	
			VIS attack	NIR attack
SUM	0	11.17	11.11	33.02
LLR	0	14.53	9.26	25.12
PLR	0	10.06	9.72	53.95

attacks is reduced to a lesser extent. However, the obtained SFAR has moderately high level and suggests that VIS and NIR spoofing attacks present a considerable security threat even for multispectral systems. The results for the other face recognition systems (LGBPHS, GJet and ISV) bring to similar conclusions.

8.2.2.3 Discussion

Research on spoofing and anti-spoofing for NIR and multispectral face recognition system is still in its infancy. We contribute to the attempts to spoof such systems by creating a publicly available VIS and NIR face spoofing database that can be used in a multispectral setting as well. From our initial experiments, we see that it is possible to spoof VIS and NIR systems with both VIS and NIR spoofing attacks. We envision three main directions for future research.

1. Multispectral-Spoof database offers just the most basic spoofing attacks with printed photographs. More challenging spoofing attacks need to be created and evaluated, like 3D attacks, or image-level fusion of VIS and NIR images.
2. Multispectral systems appear to be more robust, but still not highly secure under NIR spoofing attacks. Examining different fusion strategies at different levels, fine-tuning the training of the systems, fine-tuning the operating frequencies of the NIR and VIS systems, and including spoofing attacks to train the fusion systems are some of the possible ways to improve the multispectral systems.
3. The set of spoofing countermeasures for these systems is very sparse. Several of the hardware-based anti-spoofing methods described in Sect. 2.1.3 could be readily employed for detecting spoofing attacks in NIR spectrum as well. Yet, they may still be classified as requiring additional hardware, because they operate at different wavelengths then the wavelengths used by Multispectral-Spoof database. In practice, only [3] has developed a fully software-based countermeasures for printed attacks to NIR and multispectral systems, but its efficiency to other databases and more challenging spoofing attacks is still to be tested.

8.3   Face Recognition Systems Under 3D Spoofing Attacks

It is repeatedly stated in the previous sections that an attacker can attempt to gain access through a 2D face recognition system (visual, near-infrared, or multispectral) simply by using printed photographs or recorded videos of valid users. It is also reported that most of these attack types devised until today can be successfully averted by using various anti-spoofing methods.

A substantial part of the work on spoofing detection capabilities for face is based on the flatness of the surface in front of the sensor during an attack. For instance, the motion analysis techniques detailed in Sect. 2.1.3 rely on the assumption of shape difference between an actual face and a spoofing attack instrument such as a paper or a tablet computer in order to distinguish motion patterns of a real person from an attacker. In a similar fashion, 3D shape information either extracted from multiple-view images or acquired using a 3D sensor (Sect. 2.1.3) can be exploited to positively detect 2D attacks. For instance, in [73], 3D data captured with a low-cost sensor is utilized to locate the face in an image as well as to test its authenticity.

These types of methods that rely on the assumption of a planar surface that displays a face image in front of the sensor are ineffective in case of 3D facial mask attacks [74]. Although the advancements in 3D acquisition and manufacturing technologies make this kind of attacks as untroublesome as their 2D counterparts, there have not been many studies published addressing this issue. In this section, an overview of the existing work is presented for several kinds of 3D attacks, face recognition systems, and spoofing countermeasures.

8.3.1 Types of Attacks and Databases

The earliest research works that target 3D attacks only aim to distinguish between facial skin and mask materials without analyzing the spoofing performances of the masks because they approach this problem as in an evasion or disguise scenario [61, 62]. The masks utilized for the experiments are not necessarily replicas of valid users.

Claiming that fake, by its definition, is indistinguishable for human eyes and visual spectrum cannot be sufficient to detect the attacks, a small group of studies follow the footsteps of early pioneers and propose multispectral analyses [63, 75] for mask and real face classification. The experiments in [63] are done on directly mask materials. In [75], some face-like masks are produced, but they do not mimic any real person. Unfortunately, no public database has been made available for further investigation.

Recently, another line of research in 3D spoofing has emerged for which the attacks are realized with 3D printed masks of valid users. Firstly, Kose et al. published a series of studies [76–79] on 3D mask attacks for which a non-public database of 16 users is utilized. In order to construct this database that is called Morpho database, a 3D face model of each client is captured by a 3D laser scanner. It consists of 207 real access and 199 mask attack samples as both 2D images and 3D scans (Fig. 8.6a).

Morpho database did certainly bring on a significant breakthrough and momentum in 3D spoofing attack research. Still, it was lacking a very crucial characteristic that is publicness. Taking this shortcoming into account, Erdogmus et al. collected the first public spoofing database with facial masks, called 3D Mask Attack Database (3DMAD) [80] and published a couple of spoofing and counter-measure analyses on several face recognition systems [80, 81]. The database contains 76500 real access and mask attack frames of 17 users, recorded using Microsoft Kinect.

(a)   (b)   (c)

Fig. 8.6 **a** Example shots from Morpho: The top row shows a real access from a user in *grayscale* texture (2D), depth map (2.5D), and 3D model format, while an attacker wearing the same users mask is displayed in the *bottom*. **b** Example papercraft mask from 3DMAD. **c** 17 Wearable resin masks from 3DMAD [81]

The masks used for Morpho database were printed using 3D laser scans of valid users. The acquisition process with such scanners requires cooperation since it is very sensitive movement and has range limitations. This makes the attack scenario less realistic. On the other hand, the masks for 3DMAD are manufactured using only 2D images of users via a private company which is specialized in facial reconstruction and in transforming 2D portraiture into 3D sculptures. Using this service, it is possible to construct a 3D face model from frontal and profile images of a person which can be easily obtained from a distance or found on the Internet. Once the 3D models are constructed, they can be turned into masks of various sizes and materials.

For 3DMAD, a life-size wearable mask and a papercraft mask are manufactured for each user (Fig. 8.6b, c). Papercraft masks can be just printed out and hand-crafted, so they are not recorded but made available within the database for the use of the biometrics community. Using Microsoft Kinect for Xbox 360, videos are recorded for real accesses and attacks with wearable hard resin masks. Since Kinect can capture both color and depth data, the database enables researchers to analyze the vulnerability of 3D face recognition systems to mask attacks and to devise countermeasures in 3D.

The two above-mentioned databases constitute the backbone of research on 3D spoofing attacks that investigate the ability of masks to spoof face recognition systems and the possible anti-spoofing techniques which will be detailed in the following subsections.

8.3.2 System Vulnerabilities

With both Morpho database and 3DMAD, vulnerabilities against spoofing with 3D masks have been analyzed extensively for 2D, 2.5D, and 3D face recognition systems.

In [79], a 2D system based on LBP and a 3D system based on thin plate spline (TPS) warping are analyzed for their robustness against mask attacks using the

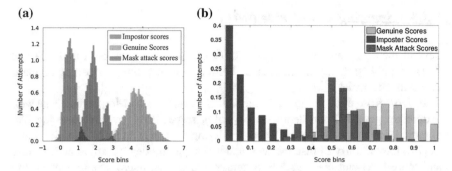

Fig. 8.7 Score distributions of genuine and impostor scores on the development set and mask attack scores on the test set of 3DMAD using **a** ISV [80]. **b** SRC [40], for 2D face verification

Morpho database. While both system performances decline remarkably as the attacks are introduced, 3D face recognition system which is completely based on 3D facial shape analysis is found to be affected more (EER increases from 1.8 to 25.1 %) than the 2D system (EER increases from 4.7 to 9.3 %). This is an expected outcome since the masks in Morpho database are highly precise in shape but have only grayscale texture. These findings are revised and extended in [77] with the addition of an LBP-based 2.5D face recognition system for which the EER increase from 7.27 % in normal mode to 14.26 % under spoofing attacks.

Similarly, 3DMAD is also assessed with regard to its spoofing ability on various face recognition systems. Firstly in [80], an inter-session variability (ISV)-based 2D face recognition algorithm is tried and 65.7 % of the mask attacks are found to be successful at EER threshold calculated on the development set of the database. The FAR at the same threshold would increase from 1.06 to 13.99 % if mask attacks are included in the probe partition together with the zero-effort impostors. The score distribution of the real access, zero-effort ,and mask attack impostors are given in Fig. 8.7a. The authors extend their study in [81] to include an ISV-based 2.5D and an Iterative Closest Point (ICP)-based 3D face recognition systems as well as all three baseline systems in [77]. Furthermore, spoofing performances are measured and reported separately for each mask. The experimental results reveal that the spoofing performances differ greatly not only between masks but also between modes and algorithms. Additionally, it is observed that the vulnerability to mask attacks is greater for more successful face verification algorithms that can generalize well to variations in facial appearance.

In a more recent work [82], 3DMAD masks are tested against another 2D face recognition algorithm which is based on the sparse representation classifier (SRC) and 84.12 % of the masks are found to be able to access the system at EER threshold (Fig. 8.7b).

All these findings expose that 3D mask attacks can be a real threat to all types of face recognition systems in 2D, 2.5D, or 3D and serious measures should be taken in order to detect and prevent them.

8.3.3 Spoofing CounterMeasures

Several methods have been proposed to detect 3D mask attacks in both 2D and 2.5D, mainly focusing on differences between micro-texture properties of mask materials and facial skin.

In [76], Kose et al. report 88.1 and 86.0 % accuracies on Morpho database with texture images (2D) and depth maps (2.5D), respectively, by concatenating histograms of different types of LBP and classifying them with an SVM classifier. Later in [79], they also try to fuse the two modes (image and depth map) at both feature and score level and reach 93.5 % accuracy. Other than micro-texture analysis via LBP, they also experiment with reflectance analysis to detect 3D mask attacks in [78] and report 94.47 % classification success. Finally, by fusing micro-texture and reflectance analyses in both 2D and 2.5D, an accuracy of 98.99 % is reached [83].

Spoofing countermeasure studies with 3DMAD also mainly revolves around LBP-based classification algorithms. In [80], the effectiveness of LBP-based features extracted from color and depth images to detect the mask attacks is analyzed. The results suggest that LBP features extracted from overlapping blocks give better results which achieve HTER of 0.95 and 1.27 % with images and depth maps separately. This study is elaborated further in [81] with best performance obtained by regular block-based LBP and a linear discriminant analysis (LDA) classifier at 0.12 ∓ 0.47 % and 3.91 ∓ 6.04 % HTER for 2D and 2.5D.

In addition to LBP, Raghavendra et al. propose to utilize binarized statistical image features (BSIF) to capture prominent micro-texture features [82] in 2D images both for the whole face (global) and the periocular (local) region. The LBP and BSIF features for each region are classified and the final scores are fused by weighted voting which results in an HTER of 4.78 %. Later in [84], the same protocol is also applied for 2.5D and the findings are incorporated via weighted score fusion. This addition is reported to push the HTER down to 0.03 %.

8.3.4 Discussion

Utilization of 3D masks for face spoofing has certainly become easier and cheaper. Many recent studies mentioned above have revealed the vulnerability of 2D, 2.5D, and 3D face recognition systems to such attacks. Additionally, many countermeasures have been proposed. However, as shown in [81], even though they are manufactured in similar ways, masks can behave very differently in various settings, making it very difficult to find one single solution that works for all.

Furthermore, in each of currently existing work, mask attack samples are utilized for training the anti-spoofing systems. This is not a realistic assumption for a biometric system since it cannot employ a different anti-spoofing module for each different mask. Worse still, it is always possible to encounter new and unseen types of masks.

Table 8.4 Categorization of anti-spoofing methods and overview of their main properties

Category	Method	Other category	Tested on public data	Source code	Intrusive	Type of input	Targeted attacks
Liveness detection	[28]	-	No	No	Somewhat	Video	Print
	[29]	-	No	No	Yes	Video	Print
	[30]	Motion analysis/fusion	No	No	Somewhat	Video	Print
	[31]	Visual appearance and motion analysis	Replay-Attack, CASIA-FASD	No	No	Video	All attacks
Motion analysis	[33]	-	No	No	No	Video	Print
	[34]	-	No	No	No	Video	Print/warped print
	[12]	-	Print-Attack	Yes	No	Video	Scenic print
	[13]	-	Photo-Attack	Yes	No	Video	Scenic print/photo
Visual	[38]	-	No	No	No	Video	Print
	[8]	-	NUAA	No	No	Image	Print
	[9]	-	CASIA-FASD	No	No	Image/video	Print/deformed print/video
	[42]	-	No	No	No	Image	Print
	[43]	-	No	No	No	Image	Print
	[45]	Fusion	Print-Attack	No	No	Image/video	Print
	[44]	-	NUAA, Print-Attack	No	No	Image	Print
	[46]	-	Replay-Attack	No	No	Image	Print/photo/video
	[48]	-	NUAA	No	No	Image	Print

(continued)

Table 8.4 (continued)

Category	Method	Other category	Tested on public data	Source code	Intrusive	Type of input	Targeted attacks
Appearance	[39]	Fusion	NUAA, Yale recaptured, Print-Attack	No	No	Image	Print
	[10]	-	Replay-Attack, NUAA, CASIA-FASD	Yes	No	Image	Print, photo, Video
	[37]	-	NUAA, Print-Attack, CASIA-FASD	Yes	No	Image	Print, Video
	[40]	-	No	No	No	Video	Print/Video
	[49]	-	Replay-Attack, CASIA-FASD	Yes	No	Video	Print, photo, Video
	[76]	-	-	No	No	Image	Mask
	[78]	-	Private database	No	No	Image	Mask
	[81]	-	3DMAD	Yes	No	Image	Mask
	[82]	Fusion	3DMAD	No	No	Image	Mask
Contextual	[7]	Liveness detection/fusion	No	No	Somewhat	Video	Scenic print/deformed print
Information	[51]	-	Yes	No	No	Image/video	Attacks with visible medium borders
3D information	[53]	Challenge response	No	No	Yes	Image sequence/video	2D attacks
	[54]	Challenge response	No	No	Yes	Video	2D attacks
	[55]	-	No	No	No	2 images	2D attacks
	[76]	-	-	No	No	Depth image	Mask
	[81]	-	3DMAD	Yes	No	Depth image	Mask
	[82]	Fusion	3DMAD	No	No	Depth image	Mask

(continued)

Table 8.4 (continued)

Category	Method	Other category	Tested on public data	Source code	Intrusive	Type of input	Targeted attacks
Challenge-Response	[56]	Motion analysis	No	No	Yes	-	-
	[57]	Motion analysis	No	No	Yes	Video	Print
Feature	[60]	-	Replay-Attack, CASIA-FASD	No	No	Image	All
Learning	[59]	-	Replay-Attack, 3DMAD	No	No	Image	All
Fusion	[11]	Motion analysis/visual appearance	Print-Attack	No	No	Video	Print
	[35]	-	Replay-Attack	Yes	No	Video	Scenic attacks

The anti-spoofing methods targeting 3D masks have been added to Table 8.4, together with the anti-spoofing methods for 2D attacks described in Sect. 8.2.1.3. Table 8.4 thus represents a comprehensive summarization of all the efforts in face spoofing detection in the visual spectrum that have been published so far.

8.4 Conclusions

Spoofing attacks are one of the most important reasons why face recognition may have a limited application in conditions where supervision is not possible. Face spoofing attacks have been proved to be effective for face recognition systems in visual spectrum in many occasions, including several face spoofing databases. So far, many countermeasures have been developed, and each of them tackles the problem from a different perspective. As a result, most of these countermeasures are effective just for a subset of the spoofing attack types. Having in mind the limitation of the currently available databases, as well as the possibility of new spoofing attacks appearing in future, more research efforts are needed to enhance the generalization capabilities of the countermeasures.

The work in spoofing face recognition systems in NIR is not as extensive. However, the newly developed Multispectral-Spoof database, which includes VIS and NIR attacks, demonstrates the vulnerability of both VIS and NIR systems to such attacks. Employing these systems in multispectral scenario significantly reduces the risks. Yet, development of suitable countermeasures is needed to provide acceptable security levels for multispectral face recognition systems.

The published research in anti-spoofing for face recognition rarely comes with data or source code that can be reproduced. This poses difficulties when comparing the performance of countermeasures. We would like emphasize the importance of publishing fully reproducible spoofing databases and countermeasures, as this will be of great benefit for building upon existing solutions and development to encourage the practice of new ones. In this chapter, we explicitly pointed out to solutions which are fully reproducible and we would like to encourage this practice for the future work.

References

1. Flynn, P.J., Faltemier, T., Bowyer, K.W.: 3D face recognition. In: Jain A.K., Flynn P., Ross A. A. (eds.) Handbook of Biometrics, pp. 293–313 (2008)
2. Socolinsky, D.A.: Multispectral face recognition. In: Jain A.K., Flynn P., Ross A.A. (eds.) Handbook of Biometrics, pp. 293–313 (2008)
3. Yi, D., Lei, Z., Zhang, Z., Li, S.: Face anti-spoofing: Multi-spectral approach. In: Marcel, S., Nixon, M.S., Li, S.Z. (eds.) Handbook of Biometric Anti-Spoofing, Advances in Computer Vision and Pattern Recognition, pp. 83–102. Springer, London (2014)
4. Duc, N.M., Minh, B.Q.: Your face is not your password. Black Hat Conference (2009)

5. Thalheim, L., Krissler, J., Ziegler, P.M.: Body check: Biometric access protection devices and their programs put to test. Heise Online (2002)
6. Chingovska, I., et al.: The 2nd competition on counter measures to 2D face spoofing attacks. In: International Conference of Biometrics (ICB) (2013)
7. Pan, G., Sun, L., Wu, Z., Wang, Y.: Monocular camera-based face liveness detection by combining eyeblink and scene context. Telecommun. Syst. **47**(3–4), 215–225 (2011)
8. Tan, X., et al.: Face liveness detection from a single image with sparse low rank bilinear discriminative model. ECCV **6**, 504–517 (2010)
9. Zhiwei, Z., et al.: A face antispoofing database with diverse attacks. In: Proceedings of the 5th IAPR International Conference on Biometrics (ICB'12), New Delhi, India (2012)
10. Chingovska, I., Anjos, A., Marcel, S.: On the effectiveness of local binary patterns in face anti-spoofing. In: Proceedings of the 11th International Conference of the Biometrics Special Interes Group (2012)
11. Komulainen, J., Anjos, A., Hadid, A., Pietikainen, M., Marcel, S.: Complementary counter-measures for detecting scenic face spoofing attacks (2013)
12. Anjos, A., Marcel, S.: Counter-measures to photo attacks in face recognition: a public database and a baseline. In: International Joint Conference on Biometrics 2011 (2011)
13. Anjos, A., Chakka, M.M., Marcel, S.: Motion-based counter-measures to photo attacks in face recognition. Inst. Eng. Technol. J. Biometrics (2013)
14. Chingovska, I., Anjos, A., Marcel, S.: Biometrics evaluation under spoofing attacks. IEEE Trans. Inf. Forensics Secur. **9**(12), 2264–2276 (2014)
15. Mansfield, A.J., Wayman, J.L.: Best practices in testing and reporting performance (2002)
16. Jain, A.K., Ross, A.: Handbook of Biometrics, chap. Introduction to Biometrics. Springer, Berlin (2008)
17. Cardinaux, F., Sanderson, C., Marcel, S.: Comparison of MLP and GMM classifiers for face verification on XM2VTS. In: Proceedings of the 4th International Conference on AVBPA. University of Surrey, Guildford, UK (2003)
18. Zhang, W., et al.: Local Gabor binary pattern histogram sequence (lgbphs): A novel non-statistical model for face representation and recognition. In: Proceedings of the Tenth IEEE International Conference on Computer Vision (ICCV'05) Volume 1—Volume 01, ICCV'05, pp. 786–791. IEEE Computer Society (2005)
19. Günther, M., Haufe, D., Wu¨rtz, R.P.: Face recognition with disparity corrected Gabor phase differences. In: Artificial Neural Networks and Machine Learning, *Lecture Notes in Computer Science*, vol. 7552, pp. 411–418. Springer Berlin (2012)
20. Wallace, R., McLaren, M., McCool, C., Marcel, S.: Inter-session variability modelling and joint factor analysis for face authentication. In: International Joint Conference on Biometrics (2011)
21. Schuckers, S.: Encyclopedia of Biometrics, chap. Liveness Detection: Fingerprint, pp. 924–931. Springer, Berlin (2009)
22. Ross, A., Nandakumar, K., Jain, A.K.: Handbook of Biometrics, chap. Introduction to multi-biometrics. Springer, Berlin (2008)
23. Akhtar, Z., Fumera, G., Marcialis, G.L., Roli, F.: Evaluation of serial and parallel multibiometric systems under spoofing attacks. In: 5th IEEE International Conference on Biometrics: Theory, Applications and Systems (2012)
24. Johnson, P.A., Tan, B., Schuckers, S.: Multimodal fusion vulnerability to non-zero (spoof) imposters. In: IEEE International Workshop on Information Forensics and Security (2010)
25. Rodrigues, R., Kamat, N., Govindaraju, V.: Evaluation of biometric spoofing in a multimodal system. In: Biometrics: Theory Applications and Systems (BTAS), 2010 Fourth IEEE International Conference on (2010)
26. Rodrigues, R.N., Ling, L.L., Govindaraju, V.: Robustness of multimodal biometric fusion methods against spoofing attacks. J. Vis. Lang. Comput. **20**(3), 169–179 (2009)
27. Chetty, G., Wagner, M.: Audio-visual multimodal fusion for biometric person authentication and liveness verification. In: Proceedings of the 2005 NICTA-HCSNet Multimodal User Interaction Workshop—Volume 57, pp. 17–24. Australian Computer Society, Inc. (2006)

28. Pan, G., Sun, L., Wu, Z., Lao, S.: Eyeblink-based anti-spoofing in face recognition from a generic webcamera. In: Computer Vision, 2007. ICCV 2007. IEEE 11th International Conference on, pp. 1–8 (2007)

29. Wang, L., Ding, X., Fang, C.: Face live detection method based on physiological motion analysis. Tsinghua Sci. Technol. **14**(6), 685–690 (2009)

30. Kollreider, K., Fronthaler, H., Bigun, J.: Verifying liveness by multiple experts in face biometrics. In: Computer Vision and Pattern Recognition Workshops, 2008. CVPRW'08. IEEE Computer Society Conference on, pp. 1–6 (2008)

31. Bharadwaj, S., Dhamecha, T., Vatsa, M., Singh, R.: Computationally efficient face spoofing detection with motion magnification. In: Computer Vision and Pattern Recognition Workshops (CVPRW), 2013 IEEE Conference on, pp. 105–110 (2013)

32. Wu, H.Y., Rubinstein, M., Shih, E., Guttag, J., Durand, F., Freeman, W.T.: Eulerian video magnification for revealing subtle changes in the world. ACM Trans. Graph. (Proceedings SIGGRAPH 2012) **31**(4) (2012)

33. Kollreider, K., Fronthaler, H., Bigun, J.: Non-intrusive liveness detection by face images. Image Vis. Comput. **27**(3), 233–244 (2009)

34. Bao, W., Li, H., Li, N., Jiang, W.: A liveness detection method for face recognition based on optical flow field. 2009 International Conference on Image Analysis and Signal Processing pp. 223–236 (2009)

35. Yan, J., Zhang, Z., Lei, Z., Yi, D., Li, S.Z.: Face liveness detection by exploring multiple scenic clues. In: 12th International Conference on Control, Automation, robotics and Vision (ICARCV 2012). China (2012)

36. Parziale, G., Dittman, J., Tistarelli, M.: Analysis and evaluation of alternatives and advanced solutions for system elements. BioSecure D 9.1.2 (2005)

37. Yang, J., Lei, Z., Liao, S., Li, S.: Face liveness detection with component dependent descriptor. In: Biometrics (ICB), 2013 International Conference on, pp. 1–6 (2013)

38. Li, J., et al.: Live face detection based on the analysis of Fourier spectra. Biometric Technology for Human Identification (2004)

39. Määttä, J., Hadid, A., Pietikäinen, M.: Face spoofing detection from single images using texture and local shape analysis. IET Biometrics **1**, 3–10 (2012)

40. Pinto, A.d.S., Pedrini, H., Schwartz, W.R., Rocha, A.: Video-based face spoofing detection through visual rhythm analysis. In: 25th Conference on Graphics, Patterns and Images (2012)

41. Oren, M., Nayar, S.K.: Generalization of the Lambertian model and implications for machine vision. International Journal of Computer Vision **14**(3), 227–251 (1995)

42. Bai, J., et al.: Is physics-based liveness detection truly possible with a single image? In: IEEE International Symposium on Circuits and Systems (ISCAS) (2010)

43. Gao, X., Ng, T.T., Bo, Q., Chang, S.F.: Single-view recaptured image detection based on physics-based features. In: IEEE International Conference on Multimedia & Expo (ICME) (2010)

44. Schwartz, W.R., Rocha, A., Pedrini, H.: Face Spoofing Detection through Partial Least Squares and Low-Level Descriptors. In: International Joint Conference on Biometrics (2011)

45. Tronci, R., et al.: Fusion of multiple clues for photo-attack detection in face recognition systems. In: IJCB, pp. 1–6 (2011)

46. Galbally, J., Marcel, S., Fierrez, J.: Image quality assessment for fake biometric detection: application to iris, fingerprint and face recognition. IEEE Trans. on Image Proc. **23**(2), 710–724 (2014)

47. Ojala, T., Pietikainen, M., Maenpaa, T.: Multiresolution gray-scale and rotation invariant texture classification with local binary patterns. IEEE Trans. on Pattern Anal. and Mach. Intell. **24**(7), 971–987 (2002)

48. Määttä, J., Hadid, A., Pietikäinen, M.: Face spoofing detection from single images using micro-texture analysis. In: International Joint Conference on Biometrics, pp. 1–7 (2011)

49. de Freitas Pereira, T., et al.: Face liveness detection using dynamic texture. EURASIP J Image and Video Proc. **2014**:2 (2014)

50. Zhao, G., Pietika¨inen, M.: Dynamic texture recognition using local binary patterns with an application to facial expressions. IEEE Trans. Pattern Anal. Mach. Intell. **29**(6), 915–928 (2007)
51. Komulainen, J., Hadid, A., Pietikainen, M.: Context based face anti-spoofing. In: Biometrics: Theory, Applications and Systems (BTAS), 2013 IEEE Sixth International Conference on, pp. 1–8 (2013)
52. Dalal, N., Triggs, B.: Histograms of oriented gradients for human detection. In: Computer Vision and Pattern Recognition, 2005. CVPR 2005. IEEE Computer Society Conference on, vol. 1, pp. 886–893 (2005)
53. Wang, T., Yang, J., Lei, Z., Liao, S., Li, S.Z.: Face liveness detection using 3D structure recovered from a single camera. In: Biometrics (ICB), 2013 International Conference on (2013)
54. De Marsico, M., Nappi, M., Riccio, D., Dugelay, J.: Moving face spoofing detection via 3D projective invariants. In: Biometrics (ICB), 2012 5th IAPR International Conference on (2012)
55. Kim, S., Yu, S., Kim, K., Ban, Y., Lee, S.: Face liveness detection using variable focusing. In: Biometrics (ICB), 2013 International Conference on (2013)
56. Frischholz, R., Werner, A.: Avoiding replay-attacks in a face recognition system using head-pose estimation. In: Analysis and Modeling of Faces and Gestures, 2003. AMFG 2003. IEEE International Workshop on (2003)
57. Ali, A., Deravi, F., Hoque, S.: Spoofing attempt detection using gaze colocation. In: Biometrics Special Interest Group (BIOSIG), 2013 International Conference of the. IEEE (2013)
58. Chetty, G., Wagner, M.: Multi-level liveness verification for face-voice biometric authentication. In: Biometrics Symposium 2006 (2006)
59. Menotti, D., Chiachia, G., Pinto, A., Schwartz, W., Pedrini, H., Falcao, A., Rocha, A.: Deep representations for iris, face, and fingerprint spoofing detection. Inf. Forensics and Sec., IEEE Trans. on **99**, 1 (2015)
60. Yang, J., Lei, Z., Li, S.Z.: Learn convolutional neural network for face anti-spoofing. CoRR **abs/1408.5601** (2014)
61. Prokoski, F.J.: Disguise detection and identification using infrared imagery. pp. 27–31 (1983)
62. Pavlidis, I., Symosek, P.: The imaging issue in an automatic face/disguise detection system. In: Computer Vision Beyond the Visible Spectrum: Methods and Applications, 2000. Proceedings. IEEE Workshop on, pp. 15–24 (2000)
63. Kim, Y., Na, J., Yoon, S., Yi, J.: Masked fake face detection using radiance measurements. J. Opt. Soc. Am A **26**(4), 760–766 (2009)
64. Zhang, Z., Yi, D., Lei, Z., Li, S.Z.: Face liveness detection by learning multispectral reflectance distributions. pp. 436–441 (2011)
65. Wang, Y., Hao, X., Hou, Y., Guo, C.: A new multispectral method for face liveness detection. In: Pattern Recognition (ACPR), 2013 2nd IAPR Asian Conference on, pp. 922–926 (2013)
66. Angelopoulou, E.: Understanding the color of human skin. pp. 243–251 (2001)
67. Vink, J., Gritti, T., Hu, Y., de Haan, G.: Robust skin detection using multi-spectral illumination. In: Automatic Face Gesture Recognition and Workshops (FG 2011), 2011 IEEE International Conference on, pp. 448–455 (2011)
68. Raghavendra, R., Raja, K., Busch, C.: Presentation attack detection for face recognition using light field camera. Image Proc., IEEE Trans. on **99**, 1 (2015)
69. de Freitas Pereira, T., Anjos, A., De Martino, J.M., Marcel, S.: Can face anti-spoofing countermeasures work in a real world scenario? In: International Conference on Biometrics (2013)
70. Kuncheva, L.I., Whitaker, C.J.: Measures of diversity in classifier ensembles and their relationship with the ensemble accuracy. Mach. Learn. **51**(2), 181–207 (2003)
71. Li, S.Z., Chu, R., Liao, S., Zhang, L.: Illumination invariant face recognition using near infrared images. IEEE Trans. Pattern Anal. Mach. Intell. **29**(4), 627–639 (2007)
72. Zou, X., Kittler, J., Messer, K.: Ambient illumination variation removal by active Near-IR imaging. In: Zhang D., Jain A.K. (eds.) Advances in Biometrics, Lecture Notes in Computer Science, vol. 3832, pp. 19–25 (2005)

73. Tsalakanidou, F., Dimitriadis, C., Malassiotis, S.: A secure and privacy friendly 2D+3D face authentication system robust under pose and illumination variation. In: Image Analysis for Multimedia Interactive Services, 2007. WIAMIS'07. Eighth International Workshop on, pp. 40–40 (2007)

74. Erdogmus, N., Marcel, S.: Spoofing 2D face recognition systems with 3d masks. In: International Conference of the Biometrics Special Interest Group (BIOSIG), pp. 1–8 (2013)

75. Zhang, Z., Yi, D., Lei, Z., Li, S.Z.: Face liveness detection by learning multispectral reflectance distributions. In: IEEE International Conference on Automatic Face & Gesture Recognition and Workshops (FG), pp. 436–441. IEEE (2011)

76. Kose, N., Dugelay, J.L.: Countermeasure for the protection of face recognition systems against mask attacks. In: International Conference and Workshops on Automatic Face and Gesture Recognition (FG), pp. 1–6. IEEE (2013)

77. Kose, N., Dugelay, J.L.: On the vulnerability of face recognition systems to spoofing mask attacks. In: IEEE International Conference on Acoustics, Speech and Signal Processing (ICASSP), pp. 2357–2361. IEEE (2013)

78. Kose, N., Dugelay, J.L.: Reflectance analysis based countermeasure technique to detect face mask attacks. In: International Conference on Digital Signal Processing (DSP), pp. 1–6. IEEE (2013)

79. Kose, N., Dugelay, J.L.: Shape and texture based countermeasure to protect face recognition systems against mask attacks. In: IEEE Conference on Computer Vision and Pattern Recognition Workshops (CVPRW), pp. 111–116. IEEE (2013)

80. Erdogmus, N., Marcel, S.: Spoofing in 2D face recognition with 3D masks and anti-spoofing with kinect. In: International Conference on Biometrics: Theory, Applications and Systems (BTAS), pp. 1–6. IEEE (2013)

81. Erdogmus, N., Marcel, S.: Spoofing face recognition with 3D masks. IEEE Trans. Inf. Forensics Secur. **9**(7), 1084–1097 (2014)

82. Raghavendra, R., Busch, C.: Novel presentation attack detection algorithm for face recognition system: Application to 3D face mask attack. In: International Conference on Image Processing (ICIP), pp. 323–327. IEEE (2014)

83. Kose, N., Dugelay, J.L.: Mask spoofing in face recognition and countermeasures. Image Vis. Comput. **32**(10), 779–789 (2014)

84. Raghavendra, R., Busch, C.: Robust 2d/3d face mask presentation attack detection scheme by exploring multiple features and comparison score level fusion. In: International Conference on Information Fusion (FUSION), pp. 1–7. IEEE (2014)

Chapter 9
On the Effects of Image Alterations
on Face Recognition Accuracy

Matteo Ferrara, Annalisa Franco and Davide Maltoni

Abstract Face recognition in controlled environments is nowadays considered rather reliable, and if face is acquired in proper conditions, a good accuracy level can be achieved by state-of-the-art systems. However, we show that, even under these desirable conditions, some intentional or unintentional face image alterations can significantly affect the recognition performance. In particular, in scenarios where the user template is created from printed photographs rather than from images acquired live during enrollment (e.g., identity documents), digital image alterations can severely affect the recognition results. In this chapter, we analyze both the effects of such alterations on face recognition algorithms and the human capabilities to deal with altered images.

9.1 Introduction

Face recognition is made very complex by the inherent variability characterizing face images, particularly in uncontrolled scenarios. However, also in controlled environments, some face recognition applications can be subject to pitfalls [1–3]. In particular, in scenarios where the user template is created from printed photographs rather than from images acquired live during enrollment (e.g., identity documents), particular care should be taken to avoid both unintentional and intentional image alteration. Some alterations are very likely to occur; for instance, geometric distortions could be produced by acquisition or printing devices, and even when not

M. Ferrara (✉) · A. Franco · D. Maltoni
Department of Computer Science and Engineering (DISI),
University of Bologna, Cesena, Italy
e-mail: matteo.ferrara@unibo.it

A. Franco
e-mail: annalisa.franco@unibo.it

D. Maltoni
e-mail: davide.maltoni@unibo.it

© Springer International Publishing Switzerland 2016   195
T. Bourlai (ed.), *Face Recognition Across the Imaging Spectrum*,
DOI 10.1007/978-3-319-28501-6_9

clearly visible, they can significantly alter the face geometry [2]. In some cases, the persons themselves could modify photographs to make them look more attractive; the availability of a large number of free online tools [4] makes this operation very easy. Besides these harmless intentions, some criminal intents could lead a subject to modify his image for example to avoid identity recognition or to assume someone else's identity [3]. Well-executed digital image alterations are difficult to detect by human experts and, as shown in the following, can easily fool automatic recognition systems. This makes the problem of face image alterations very difficult to deal with and requires the design of ad hoc solutions for alteration detection.

This chapter addresses this problem by presenting and discussing the effects of different kinds of alterations. In particular, the following possible causes of alterations are studied:

- Geometric distortion simulating the typical distortion produced by acquisition devices or image stretching that could result from an inaccurate acquisition/printing process;
- Digital beautification at different degrees, performed by free Web tools;
- Image morphing obtained by digitally mixing face images of two subjects.

Extensive experiments are carried out, also exploiting well-known commercial face recognition software, to evaluate to what extent the above-described alterations can compromise the recognition accuracy. Performance indicators such as equal error rate (EER) and DET curve are considered to better highlight the quantitative impact of image alterations.

Moreover, the study is enriched with experimentations aimed at evaluating the human capabilities [5] to detect the described image alterations. In particular, a set of volunteers has been enrolled and a statistical analysis of the human capability to detect image alterations is presented. The outcomes of both automatic recognition and human face recognition provide an overall insight on the feasibility of this threat.

The chapter is organized as follows: In Sect. 9.3, the alterations related to geometric distortions and digital beautification are reviewed and discussed; the effects of image morphing are proposed in Sect. 9.4, and finally, in Sect. 9.5, we draw some conclusions.

9.2 State of the Art

The problem of face image alteration and its impact on the accuracy of face recognition have been addressed by some works in the literature.

In the context of identity documents, some studies [6–8] deal with the problem of face recognition from degraded photographs (e.g., security-watermarked images) and propose ad hoc solutions to eliminate the noise present in these images in order to improve the image quality. The alterations addressed in these works characterize the printed photographs where a watermark is typically overlaid to the image for security reasons. In electronic identity documents, this problem is mitigated by the presence of the face image stored in the chip, but also in this case, the recognition accuracy may be affected by several factors.

Plastic surgery can significantly modify the face appearance with a relevant impact on the recognition accuracy. The problem is well discussed in [9] where an extensive experimentation is carried out to analyze the limitations of existing face recognition algorithms with respect to plastic surgery. Many works have been proposed to design face recognition techniques robust against this specific issue, and most of them highlight the importance of a local feature analysis which allows these algorithms to better deal with the typical variations introduced by plastic surgery. In [10], the combination of shape and local binary texture features has been proposed. In [11], the authors introduce a multimodal biometric approach based on principal component analysis and local binary pattern combined with periocular features. The authors of [12] adopt part-wise facial characterization, combined with a sparse representation approach. The proposed approach relies on training images from sequestered non-gallery subjects to fulfill the multiple image requirement of the sparse recognition method. In [13] and [14], the use of non-disjoint face granules at multiple levels of granularity is proposed. The feature extraction and selection process are carried out by a multi-objective genetic algorithm. A patch-based approach is also reported in [15] where the authors propose a new face recognition method based on the idea of dividing the face into patches, designing one component classifier for each patch, and finally fusing the rank-order list of each component classifier. Observing that the facial texture is significantly affected by plastic surgery, the authors of [16] adopt an edge-based Gabor feature representation, based on the hypothesis that the shape of prominent facial components remains unchanged after plastic surgery. Finally, in [1], the structural similarity (SSIM), providing a spatially varying quality map of the two images being compared, is used both to evaluate the location and degree of variations introduced by plastic surgery and to calculate a similarity score between two images.

Focusing on digital image alterations, which is the main topic of this chapter, as of today, very few solutions have been proposed in the literature. An interesting contribution is provided in [17] where a general approach designed to detect changes in a signal is proposed. The method is based on the observation that images from digital cameras contain traces of resampling as a result of using a color filter array with demosaicing algorithms. Demosaicing produces periodic correlations in the image signal which are affected by digital image alterations such as image morphing. Another technique for image distortion analysis is proposed in [18] where different features are combined and exploited for spoof detection.

Moreover, several works in the literature consider face morphing to design effective and robust face recognition algorithms. Approaches described in [19–21] adopt 2D or 3D face morphing to generate a frontal pose that can then be compared to the gallery images for identification. Another interesting approach is proposed in [22] where the authors suggest to use face morphing to artificially generate training images which are very close to the decision boundaries in the face space. In particular, to improve the recognition accuracy, for each subject in the gallery, two large sets of borderline images, projecting just inside and outside the decision boundaries, are generated, and a dedicated classifier is trained to discriminate them. One of the few works explicitly addressing face recognition in the presence of digitally altered images is [23] where a SIFT-based approach is presented to deal with image distortions.

The scarcity of literature related to this issue confirms that the problem is still open and worth of attention from the research community.

9.3 Geometric Distortions and Digital Beautification

This section describes some digital image alterations that could be unintentionally introduced due to the acquisition or printing devices (geometric distortions) or intentionally produced by the users with the innocent intent of looking more attractive (digital beautification).

9.3.1 Geometric Distortions

Image acquisition devices typically introduce the so-called barrel distortion (see Fig. 9.1a), while a careless printing process could produce image stretching, named

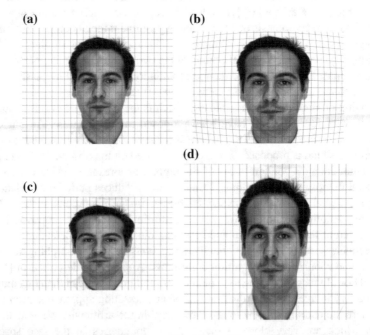

Fig. 9.1 Examples of geometric alteration: original image (**a**), altered images with barrel distortion (**b**), vertical contraction (**c**), and altered image with vertical extension (**d**). In all the images, a *squared grid* is superimposed on the image to better highlight the effects of geometric alterations

here "vertical contraction" and "vertical extension" that could affect the recognition performance.

For each kind of alteration, a set of distorted images was generated by applying the related transform at different levels of strength p (a large value of p denotes a more significant alteration).

9.3.1.1   Barrel Distortion

Barrel distortion [24] is one of the most common types of lens distortions and represents the typical defect that could be introduced by a low-quality acquisition device. In this transformation, a barrel distortion with a strength p is applied to the original image while preserving the image size. The approach described in [25] has been adopted to implement this transformation. The value of p is increased from 10 to 20 % with a step of 2 %, i.e., $p \in \{0.10, 0.12, 0.14, 0.16, 0.18, 0.20\}$. An altered image obtained applying the barrel distortion with $p = 0.20$ is shown in Fig. 9.1b.

9.3.1.2   Vertical Contraction

In this alteration, we vertically compress the image while keeping the width fixed. In particular, we reduce the original height by a multiplying factor of $(1 - p)$. The values of p are the same as those used to generate the barrel distortion. Figure 9.1c shows an altered image after vertical contraction with $p = 0.20$.

9.3.1.3   Vertical Extension

In vertical extension, the height is increased by a multiplying factor of $(1 + p)$ while keeping the width invariable. Here too, we increase the strength of extension from 10 to 20 % in a step of 2 %. An altered image after vertical extension with $p = 0.20$ is shown in Fig. 9.1d. This alteration (and the previous one), which is essentially a modification of the face aspect ratio, could be unintentionally introduced when processing the image with a photo-editor tool or could be the result of a bad printing.

9.3.2   Digital Beautification

To obtain this alteration, we use LiftMagic [4] an instant cosmetic surgery and anti-aging makeover tool that produces realistic image beautification. The tool presents a very simple Web interface that allows the user to load an image and to simulate different plastic surgery treatments at different levels. It makes available 17 treatments: 16 local treatments (e.g., injectable for forehead, eyelid fold enhancement, and

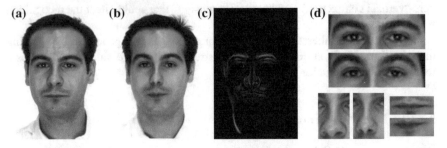

Fig. 9.2 An example of digital beautification. Original image (**a**), digitally beautified image (**b**), pixel-by-pixel difference between original and digitally beautified image (**c**), and a zoom on the main face regions affected by the beautification process (**d**)

lip augmentation) and one treatment integrating all the local ones. For each treatment, a specific selection bar allows the user to personalize the strength of the modification.

In this alteration, we consider only the integrated treatment and three different strengths obtained by positioning the selection bar at three equidistant positions. The three levels are referred to as 'low,' 'medium,' and 'high' ($p \in$ {low, medium, high}). Figure 9.2 presents the altered image after this alteration with $p = $ high.

9.3.3 Experimental Results

The effects of the above-described alterations on face recognition accuracy have been evaluated with a set of experiments conducted with three different state-of-the-art face recognition approaches: two commercial software [Neurotechnology VeriLook SDK 2.1 [26] (VL) and Luxand Face SDK 4.0 [27] (LU)] and a SIFT-based matching algorithm [28, 29] (SI). The performance measured for the three systems on the unaltered database described below is good (see Fig. 9.3), so they constitute a good test bed to evaluate the effects of alterations: In particular, the measured EER is 0.003 % (VL), 1.693 % (LU), and 2.217 % (SI).

9.3.3.1 Database

The choice of a proper face database is here an important issue. In fact, particularly in the context of electronic documents, face images are expected to be high quality; hence, variations caused by illumination, expressions, poses, etc., should be kept out. The selected database is AR face database [30]; this database consists of 4000 frontal images taken under different conditions in two sessions, separated by two weeks. The images relevant to our study are well controlled and high-quality images (with neutral expressions and good illumination), so the poses 1 and 14 are

Fig. 9.3 DET curves of the three reference systems on the unaltered database

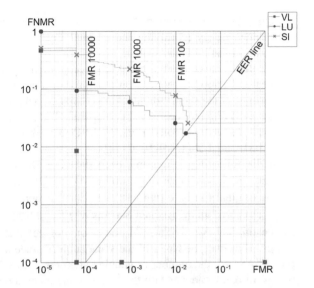

selected for the tests. We denote them as No. 1 and No. 14, respectively (see Fig. 9.4 for an example).

In our test, we assume that the images No. 14 are used during enrollment (i.e., are stored in the e-documents), while the images No. 1 are used as probe (i.e., at the point of verification). The alterations are thus applied to images No. 14 to simulate the inclusion in the document of an altered image.

9.3.3.2   Face Recognition Results

To evaluate the effects of the various alterations on face recognition accuracy, a systematic experimentation has been carried out. Starting from the original

Fig. 9.4 Two unaltered images of the same subject in the AR database (pose 1 on the *left*, pose 14 on the *right*)

database, for each alteration, face images with different alteration strengths have been generated by modifying the original images with different transformations described in the previous section.

The performance evaluation of face recognition algorithms is based on a set of genuine and impostor recognition attempts. In a genuine recognition attempt, two face images of the same individual are compared, while in an impostor attempt, two images from different persons are compared. The following performance indicators are used: *False Non-Match Rate* (FNMR) at a *False Match Rate* (FMR) of 1 % (FMR100) and 1 ‰ (FMR1000) [31].

In the following definitions, each database DB consists of two sets of face images: DB_e (acquired during enrollment) and DB_v (acquired during verification).

The original database (without alterations) is denoted as $DB^O = \{DB_e^O, DB_v^O\}$. DB_e^O is made of all the original No. 14s of 120 subjects, while DB_v^O is composed of all the original No. 1s (of 134 subjects). For genuine attempts, each No. 14 is compared against the No. 1 of the same subject; since only 118 subjects have both poses 1 and 14, the number of genuine attempts is 118. For impostor attempts, the No. 14 of one subject and all the No. 1 of the other subjects are compared. Hence, the total number of impostor attempts is 15,962.

As to the altered databases, for a given alteration a, let $DB_a^p = \{(DB_e)_a^p, DB_v^O\}$ be a database that simulates enrollment face images reporting alteration a with a strength of p. For genuine attempts, the original No. 1 and the altered No. 14 from the same subject are compared. Impostor attempts are the same as in the original database DB^O.

The results of the barrel distortion are reported in Fig. 9.5. It can be observed that both FMR100 and FMR1000 change slightly and irregularly as the degree of barrel distortion increases for LU and SI, while there is no significant performance change for VL. Overall, this alteration has no noticeable effects on the recognition accuracy.

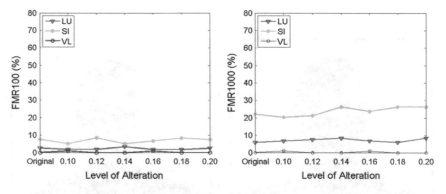

Fig. 9.5 Performance comparison before and after barrel distortion: FMR100 (*left*) and FMR1000 (*right*)

Figures 9.6 and 9.7 illustrate the results of the vertical contraction and extension, respectively. For both FMR100 and FMR1000, as the strength of the alterations increases, the accuracy of LU significantly decreases. SI shows a less noticeable performance drop than LU, while there is no significant performance change for VL.

The results of the digital beautification are reported in Fig. 9.8. For both FMR100 and FMR1000, this alteration produces a performance drop for all the three system (even if LU shows a less noticeable reduction of the recognition accuracy).

Overall, the experimental results show that the barrel alteration does not significantly affect the recognition accuracy. This is probably due to the fact that in the central part of the image containing the face, the barrel distortion produces simply a sort of scaling effect, which is well handled by the algorithms tested.

Aspect ratio alteration is critical for some approaches (for instance, the vertical contraction at the maximum strength causes a performance drop of FMR1000 of

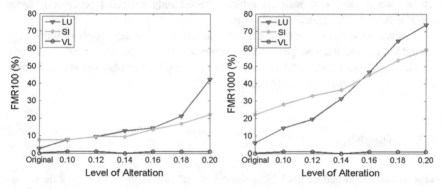

Fig. 9.6 Performance comparison before and after vertical contraction: FMR100 (*left*) and FMR1000 (*right*)

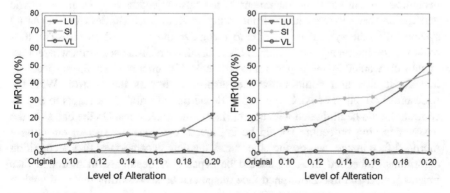

Fig. 9.7 Performance comparison before and after vertical extension: FMR100 (*left*) and FMR1000 (*right*)

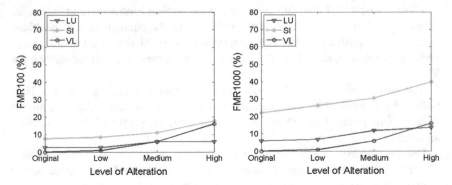

Fig. 9.8 Performance comparison before and after digital beautification: FMR100 (*left*) and FMR1000 (*right*)

about 11 times for LU), while it is just slightly disturbing other systems. In particular, we believe that face recognition based only on local features is quite insensitive to global geometric changes.

Finally, alterations such as digital beautification, when applied with high strength, produce marked performance drop to all the systems tested, as clearly visible in Fig. 9.8: The FMR becomes significantly higher than the original value when a strong alteration is applied.

9.4   Morphing

This section is aimed at analyzing the effects of image morphing on face recognition accuracy. The results in the previous section show that state-of-the-art face recognition algorithms are able to overcome limited alterations but are sensitive to more drastic modifications. In particular, some geometric alterations and digital beautification can cause an increment of the false rejection rate: In an automatic verification scenario (e.g., in an airport using an Automated Border Control (ABC) system [32]), the system is not able to recognize the owner of an eMRTD, thus requiring the intervention of a human operator; in a watch-list scenario, where a list of subjects wanted by the police has to be checked in order to block the suspects, an intentional alteration could allow the suspect to bypass the control. With the widespread adoption of ABC systems [33], the risk of criminal attempts to bypass controls should be mitigated with appropriate countermeasures. On the one side, the passport issuing procedure should be improved to reduce the risk of enrolling a morphed face image, and on the other hand, the new generation of face recognition algorithms embedded in ABC should be capable of dealing with morphed face images (i.e., avoid that a morphed face image can be successfully matched against two persons).

In this section, the robustness of automated face recognition system against morphing alterations has been evaluated. This operation could be for instance at the basis of a criminal attack to an ABC system. In this scenario, at the time of verification at an ABC, a face image (acquired live) of the person presenting the travel document is matched against the face image stored in the eMRTD. If a morphed image included in an eMRTD can be successfully matched with the face of two or more subjects, then different persons can share the same document. In an ABC system scenario, this would allow a criminal to exploit the passport of an accomplice with no criminal records to overcome the security controls. In more details, the subject with no criminal records could apply for an eMRTD by presenting the morphed face photograph; if the image is not noticeably different from the applicant face, the police officer could accept the photograph and release the document (see Fig. 9.9). It is worth noting that in this case the document is perfectly regular; the attack does not consist of altering the document content but in deceiving the officer at the moment of document issuing. The document released will thus pass all the integrity checks (optical and electronic) performed at the gates.

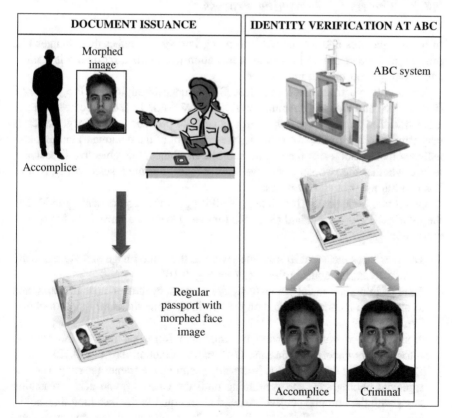

Fig. 9.9 A possible attack realized by means of a morphed photograph. The image is visually very similar to the applicant, but contains facial features of a different subject

In this section, we evaluate: (i) the feasibility of creating deceiving morphed face images, (ii) the ability of humans to detect morphed images, and (iii) the robustness of commercial recognition systems in the presence of morphing.

The attack was designed as follows:

1. Two images of different subjects have been selected: We chose two persons with some physical similarity but whose face images did not falsely match using the suggested threshold (for both SDKs); non-matching images were used because in case of matching, no morphing operations are required.
2. The two images were morphed into a new image as described in the following section.

The morphed image was used (i) to evaluate the ability of humans to detect morphing alterations and (ii) to estimate the accuracy of automatic face recognition in the presence of morphing.

9.4.1 The Image Morphing Process

In motion pictures and animations, morphing is a special effect that changes one image into another through a seamless transition [34]. Often, morphing is used to depict one person turning into another.

To morph two face images, the free GNU Image Manipulation Program v2.8 (GIMP) [35] and the GIMP Animation Package v2.6 (GAP) [36] have been used in this work. The aim of morphing is, in this case, to produce a face image which is very similar to one of the two subjects (the applicant of the document) but that also includes facial features of the second subject. Of course, this objective is easier to realize whether the two subjects have similar faces, but the results will show that this condition is not strictly necessary.

Given two high-quality face images (fulfilling all the requirements provided in the ISO/IEC 19794-5 standard [37]), the following steps are carried out to produce morphing:

1. The two faces are input as separate layers in the same image and are manually aligned by superimposing the eyes (see Fig. 9.10).
2. A set of important facial points (e.g., eye corners, eyebrows, nose tip, chin, and forehead) are manually marked on the two faces using the GAP morph tool (see Fig. 9.11).
3. A sequence of frames showing the transition from one face to the other is automatically generated using the GAP morph function (see Fig. 9.12).
4. The selection of the final frame is done by scanning the frames (starting from the applicant photograph) and continuing until the current frame gets a matching score with the criminal subject greater than or equal to the matching thresholds. For frame selection, the similarity with the applicant of the document was

Fig. 9.10 The first step for morphing—aligning the two images according to the eyes position

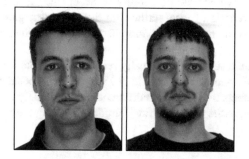

Fig. 9.11 The facial points labeled for the two images before morphing; such points will allow to obtain a better alignment between the two faces and a smoother morphing

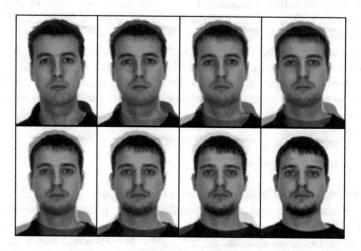

Fig. 9.12 Frames obtained by the morphing procedure, gradually shading from subject 1 (applicant) to subject 2 (criminal)

Fig. 9.13 The frame selected for matching before and after manual photograph retouch

privileged to maximize the probability of acceptance in the enrollment stage, under the hypothesis of face verification at unattended gates. Of course, it is possible to use an intermediate morphed image for other scenarios such as attended gates.

5. Finally, the frame selected is manually retouched to make it more acceptable as a genuine ICAO photograph (see Fig. 9.13). To this purpose, ghost shadows and other small defects must be manually removed and finally a sharpening filter is applied to remove the slight blurring introduced during the morphing operation.

9.4.2 Experimental Results

Several experiments have been carried out to evaluate the possibility of success of a morphing attack. In particular, in order to succeed, two conditions should be verified: (i) the morphed image should fool a human expert (e.g., the police officer issuing a passport) and (ii) the morphed image should be successfully matched with two different subjects using an automatic face recognition software. In this section, we describe the experiments carried out in relation to these two aspects. We first evaluate the ability of humans to detect morphed images, and then, we estimate the accuracy of automatic face recognition in the presence of morphing.

9.4.2.1 Morphing Database

The experiments have been carried out on the AR face database [30], chosen because it contains several images compliant to the quality standards in use for eMRTD. The database consists of 4000 frontal images taken under different conditions in two sessions separated by two weeks. In particular, poses 1 and 14 are selected for the morphing experiments since they present neutral expression and good illumination.

The morphing database has been assembled by mixing the images of two subjects, as described in the previous section. Overall, the database contains 10 pairs of male subjects (see Figs. 9.14 and 9.15) and 9 pairs of female subjects (see Figs. 9.16 and 9.17). Moreover, two extra experiments have been conducted mixing i) one man and one woman (see Fig. 9.18) and (ii) three men (see Fig. 9.19).

A visual inspection of the morphing results clearly shows that in most cases, the image alteration produced by morphing is difficult to detect and that it is possible and relatively easy to obtain a morphed image very similar to one of the two subjects involved.

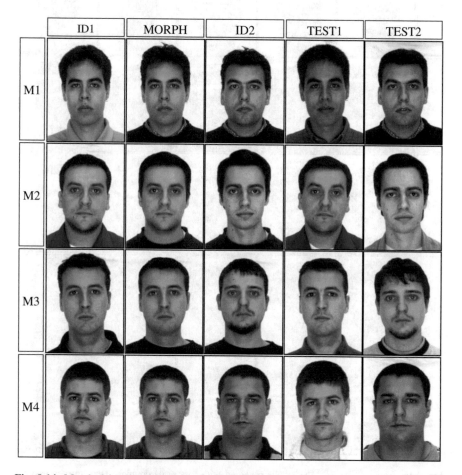

Fig. 9.14 Morphed images: the results obtained with six male couples. Two images used for morphing (columns ID1 and ID2), the resulting morphed face image (column MORPH), and the two images used for the matching test (columns TEST1 and TEST2) are reported for each row

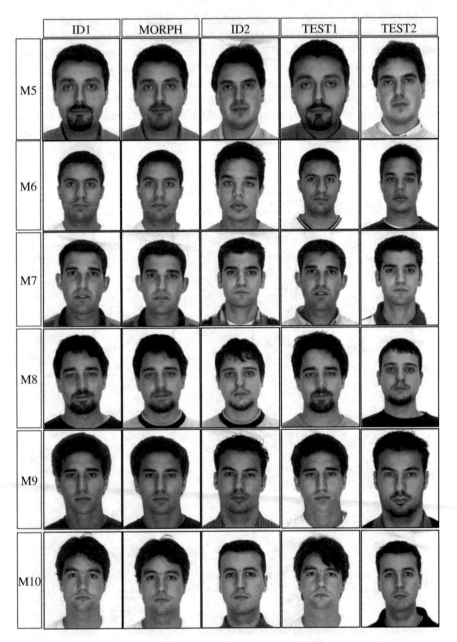

Fig. 9.15 Morphed images: the results obtained with four male couples. Two images used for morphing (columns ID1 and ID2), the resulting morphed face image (column MORPH), and the two images used for the matching test (columns TEST1 and TEST2) are reported for each row

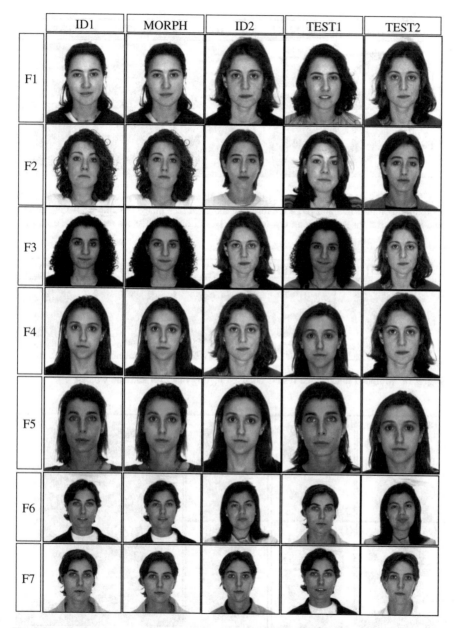

	ID1	MORPH	ID2	TEST1	TEST2
F1					
F2					
F3					
F4					
F5					
F6					
F7					

Fig. 9.16 Morphed images: the results obtained with seven female couples. Two images used for morphing (columns ID1 and ID2), the resulting morphed face image (column MORPH), and the two images used for the matching test (columns TEST1 and TEST2) are reported for each row

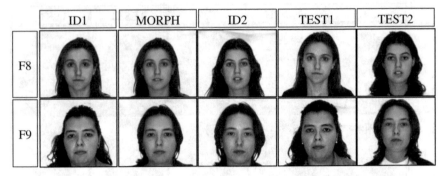

Fig. 9.17 Morphed images: the results obtained with two female couples. Two images used for morphing (columns ID1 and ID2), the resulting morphed face image (column MORPH), and the two images used for the matching test (columns TEST1 and TEST2) are reported for each row

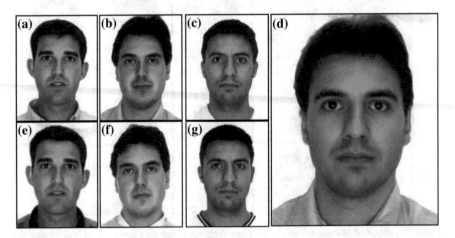

Fig. 9.18 Morphed images: the results obtained mixing one man and one woman

Fig. 9.19 Morphed image generated using three men photographs: the three images used for morphing (**a, b,** and **c**), the resulting morphed face image (**d**), and the three images used for the matching test (**e, f,** and **g**). In this example, the subject in (**c, g**) is the applicant. The matching scores between test images (**e, f, g**) and the morphed one (**d**) are 51, 72, and 565 using VeriLook SDK and 0.99965, 0.99904, and 1.00000 using Luxand SDK

9.4.2.2 Human Detection Capability

In order to evaluate the human capabilities to detect altered face images, two experiments were carried out by submitting a questionnaire to two groups of volunteers. The former group consisted of experts working in the field (44 border guards), and the latter covered a wider audience (543 persons, among which about 104 students and professors of the University of Bologna and about 439 researchers working in the field of biometric systems). The questionnaire includes a set of image pairs; some pairs represent the same subject in two different acquisitions, and others contain an image of a subject and a morphed image (from the morphing database) obtained by mixing the same subject with a different person. For each pair, the volunteers have to decide whether the two images belong to the same subject or to different (but very similar) subjects.

The results of the questionnaire for the border guard group and the non-expert subject group are reported in Figs. 9.20 and 9.21, respectively. The percentage values in the graph have been calculated considering that some subjects provided partial answers: In particular, 40 out of 44 border guards and 405 out of 543 non-experts filled the entire questionnaire. The percentage is thus calculated for each question on the basis of the number of answers received.

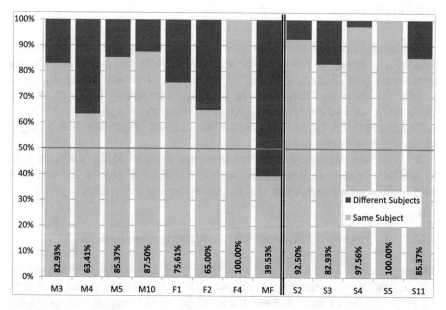

Fig. 9.20 Results obtained in the test with the human experts. The double *black line* represents the boundary between the pairs containing morphed images (*left*) and the pairs with original images (*right*)

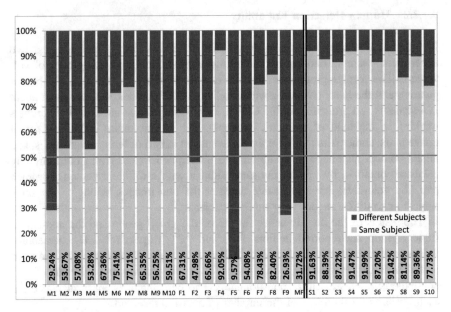

Fig. 9.21 Results obtained in the test with non-expert subjects. The *double black line* represents the boundary between the pairs containing morphed images (*left*) and the pairs with original images (*right*)

The results obtained show that in most cases, the morphed images are not detected (i.e., more than half of the subjects considered the two images as belonging to the same person), even if overall the percentage of persons voting for "same subject" is lower than that observed for pairs representing the same subject. However, if we exclude some isolated cases where the morphing effect is quite evident (i.e., M1, F5, F9, and MF), most of the morphed images have been accepted as genuine by a human expert.

It is also rather surprising to see that, as already stated in [5], the results obtained by the experts are not better than those obtained by a general audience, not specifically working in this area and not trained to face verification.

9.4.2.3 Experiments with Automatic Face Recognition Systems

The experiments have been conducted using two commercial face recognition software tools: Neurotechnology VeriLook SDK 5.5 [26] and Luxand Face SDK 4.0 [27]. In order to simulate a realistic attack to an ABC system, the operational thresholds of the face recognition software have been fixed according to the guidelines [32] provided by FRONTEX (the European Agency for the Management of Operational Cooperation at the External Borders of the Member States of the European Union) [38]. In particular, for ABC systems operating in verification mode, the face verification algorithm has to ensure a *False Acceptance Rate* (FAR)

Table 9.1 Provided and computed thresholds to achieve different values of FAR for both SDKs

SDK	FAR							
	1 %		0.1 %		0.01 %		0 %	
	Thr_P	Thr_C	Thr_P	Thr_C	Thr_P	Thr_C	Thr_P	Thr_C
VeriLook	24	28	36	39	48	49	100	57
Luxand	0.9900	0.8515	0.9990	0.9658	0.9999	0.9937	1.0000	0.9940

equal to 0.1 % and a *False Rejection Rate* (FRR) lower than 5 %. In the experiments, two different thresholds have been used for each SDK:

- Thr_P: score threshold value provided by the SDK to obtain a given level of FAR.
- Thr_C: score threshold computed internally on the basis of about 20,000 impostor comparisons, with the aim of achieving a prefixed FAR.

Table 9.1 reports provided and computed thresholds for both SDKs and different values of FAR.

The verification results obtained by the two SDKs for the different morphed images using both thresholds are summarized in Table 9.2. Most of the attacks were successful since for both SDKs, the matching score between the morphed face image and each of the test images (see Table 9.2) is higher than the thresholds. Moreover, the results obtained in the test with human experts confirm that the attack is perfectly feasible since the morphed image is very similar to one of the two subjects (ID1) and also human experts issuing the passport are easily fooled.

9.4.3   FMC Benchmark Area on FVC-onGoing

The results obtained with commercial software in the presence of image morphing clearly highlight that this topic is very challenging and that even top performing algorithms are unable to effectively deal with it. To foster the research on this issue and independently assess the robustness of face recognition algorithms against morphing alteration, a new benchmark area called *Face Morphing Challenge* (FMC) has been recently added to the FVC-onGoing framework.

FVC-onGoing [39, 40] is a Web-based automated evaluation system for biometric recognition algorithms. Tests are carried out on a set of sequestered datasets, and results are reported online by using well-known performance indicators and metrics. The aim is to track the advances in automatic recognition technologies, through continuously updated independent testing and reporting of performances on given benchmarks. FVC-onGoing benchmarks are grouped into benchmark areas according to the (sub)problem addressed and the evaluation protocol adopted.

Table 9.2 Verification results of the test and morphed images reported in Figs. 9.14, 9.15, 9.16, 9.17, and 9.18 obtained by the two SDKs using both thresholds

	VeriLook SDK 5.5				Luxand SDK 4.0			
	Thr_P		Thr_C		Thr_P		Thr_C	
	T1 - M	T2 - M	T1 - M	T2 - M	T1 - M	T2 – M	T1 - M	T2 – M
M1	✓	✓	✓	✓	✓	✓	✓	✓
M2	✓	✓	✓	✓	✓	✓	✓	✓
M3	✓	✓	✓	✓	✓	✓	✓	✓
M4	✓	✓	✓	✓	✓	✗	✓	✓
M5	✓	✓	✓	✓	✓	✓	✓	✓
M6	✓	✗	✓	✗	✓	✓	✓	✓
M7	✓	✓	✓	✓	✓	✓	✓	✓
M8	✓	✓	✓	✓	✓	✓	✓	✓
M9	✓	✓	✓	✓	✓	✓	✓	✓
M10	✓	✓	✓	✓	✓	✓	✓	✓
F1	✓	✓	✓	✓	✓	✓	✓	✓
F2	✓	✓	✓	✓	✓	✓	✓	✓
F3	✓	✓	✓	✓	✓	✓	✓	✓
F4	✓	✓	✓	✓	✓	✗	✓	✓
F5	✓	✓	✓	✓	✗	✓	✓	✓
F6	✓	✓	✓	✓	✓	✓	✓	✓
F7	✓	✓	✓	✓	✓	✓	✓	✓
F8	✓	✓	✓	✓	✓	✓	✓	✓
F9	✓	✓	✓	✓	✓	✓	✓	✓
MF	✓	✓	✓	✓	✓	✓	✓	✓

For more details on the new FMC benchmark area, please refer to the FVC-onGoing Web site [40]. Only the main information about the benchmark and a set of preliminary results obtained are reported in the following subsections.

9.4.3.1 Face Database

A new ad hoc dataset containing high-resolution face images with neutral expressions and good illumination has been created using public databases. It contains 731 images of 280 subjects, gathered from different sources:

- 236 images of 118 subjects from the AR database [30];
- 415 images of 162 subjects from the Color FERET database [41, 42];
- 80 morphed face images artificially generated.

9.4.3.2   Testing Protocol

To compute performance indicators, the following comparisons are performed:

- *526 Genuine attempts*—face images of the same subject are compared to compute the *FRR*.
- *19944 Impostor attempts*—face images of different subjects are compared to compute the *FAR*.
- *160 Morph attempts*—morphed face images are compared against face images of the subjects used for morphing to compute the *Morph Acceptance Rate* (MAR) as the ratio of the number of morphed images erroneously accepted by the system divided by the total number of morph attempts.

Starting from genuine, impostor, and morph scores, the following performance indicators have been computed:

- EER—equal error rate [31]
- FAR_{100}—the lowest FRR for FAR ≤ 1 % [31]
- FAR_{1000}—the lowest FRR for FAR ≤ 0.1 % [31]
- FAR_{10000}—the lowest FRR for FAR ≤ 0.01 % [31]
- $Zero_{FAR}$—the lowest FRR for FAR $= 0$ % [31]
- DET curve [31]
- $MAR@FAR_{100}$—the lowest MAR for FAR ≤ 1 %
- $MAR@FAR_{1000}$—the lowest MAR for FAR ≤ 0.1 %
- $MAR@FAR_{10000}$—the lowest MAR for FAR ≤ 0.01 %
- $MAR@Zero_{FAR}$—the lowest MAR for FAR $= 0$ %
- Graph of the trade-off between MAR and FAR.

9.4.3.3   Experiments

Three commercial SDKs (Neurotechnology VeriLook SDK 5.5 [26], Luxand Face SDK 4.0 [27], and EyeFace SDK 3.11.0 [43]) have been evaluated on the new benchmark.

Figure 9.22 reports the DET graph on the FMC benchmark. The graph shows that among the three SDKs, VeriLook is the only one that fulfills the operative requirements suggested for ABC systems since at a FAR of 0.1 % (10^{-3} in the x-axis of the graph) the FRR is below 5 %; for the other two SDKs, the FRR measured is significantly higher (see also Figs. 9.23, 9.24, and 9.25). This behavior will have positive effects on the ability of the SDK to detect morphed images (as detailed in the following graphs), but in practice, it would create serious problems in terms of efficiency of the verification process since it would make necessary human intervention in a large number of cases, thus mitigating the advantages provided by ABC systems.

Fig. 9.22 DET graph of the three SDKs on the FMC benchmark

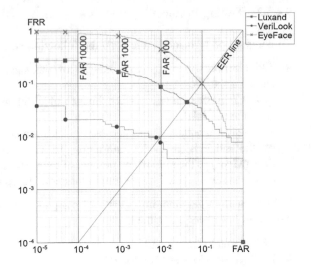

Figures 9.23 and 9.24 show FRR and MAR values computed for Thr_C and Thr_P at different levels of FAR (see Table 9.1) for Luxand and VeriLook SDKs, respectively. As to EyeFace, no suggested thresholds are provided with the SDK, so the graph has only been reported for Thr_C in Fig. 9.25. As expected, the graphs confirm that VeriLook presents the highest values of MAR. The other two SDKs present a lower MAR but at the cost of a higher FRR; in particular, EyeFace where at FAR_{1000},

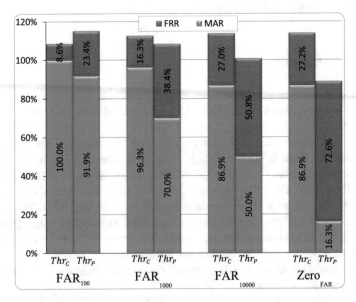

Fig. 9.23 FRR and MAR values computed for Thr_C and Thr_P at different levels of FAR for Luxand SDK

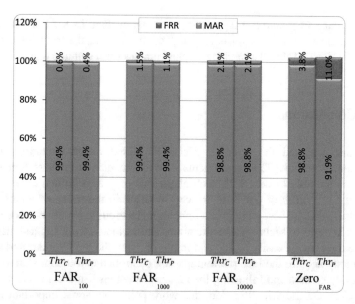

Fig. 9.24 FRR and MAR values computed for Thr_C and Thr_P at different levels of FAR for VeriLook SDK

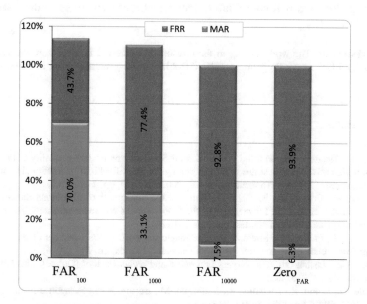

Fig. 9.25 FRR and MAR values computed for Thr_C at different levels of FAR for EyeFace SDK. The computed thresholds are 0.3544, 04836, 0.6282, and 0.6472 for FAR_{100}, FAR_{1000}, FAR_{10000}, and $Zero_{FAR}$, respectively

the percentage of genuine images rejected is more than 75 %. For Luxand and VeriLook, the MAR at FAR_{1000} is very high confirming that the software analyzed is not able to successfully distinguish morphed images from genuine ones.

9.5 Conclusions

This work analyzed the possible effects of digital image alterations on face recognition accuracy. The experiments carried out clearly suggest that existing algorithms are able to deal with such alterations only to a limited extent. In particular, the outcomes of our tests are very relevant in the scope of identity documents issuing where accepting printed photographs brought by citizens pose serious concerns in terms of security. The alterations shown in this work suggest that even a human expert can be easily fooled and in our opinion, the best workaround solution is to directly acquire the face photograph at a controlled enrollment station using a high-quality camera and following the recommendations listed in [37] (Informative Annex C.2). On the scientific side, this work points out some important research directions for researchers developing face recognition algorithms. We also believe that making available (through FVC-onGoing) to the community, a common benchmark to evaluate the robustness of face recognition algorithms to image morphing alteration will contribute to identify effective solutions to deal with this threat.

Acknowledgment The work leading to these results has received funding from the European Community's Framework Programme (FP7/2007-2013) under grant agreement n° 284862.

References

1. Sun, Y., Tistarelli, M., Maltoni, D.: Structural Similarity based image quality map for face recognition across plastic surgery. In: Proceedings of the IEEE Sixth International Conference on Biometrics: Theory, Applications and Systems (BTAS), pp. 1–8 (2013)
2. Ferrara, M., Franco, A., Maltoni, D., Sun, Y.: On the impact of alterations on face photo recognition accuracy. In: Proceedings of the International Conference on Image Analysis and Processing (ICIAP2013), Naples, pp. 743–751 (2013)
3. Ferrara, M., Franco, A., Maltoni, D.: The magic passport. In: Proceedings of the IEEE Int. Joint Conference on Biometrics (IJCB), Clearwater, Florida, pp. 1–7 (2014)
4. LiftMagic—Instant cosmetic surgery and anti-aging makeover tool [Online]. http://makeovr.com/liftmagic (2015, Jan)
5. White, D., Kemp, R.I., Jenkins, R., Matheson, M., Burton, A.M.: Passport officers' errors in face matching. PLos ONE 9(8) (2014)
6. Clark, A., Bourlai, T.: Methodological insights on passport image enhancement. In: SPIE Newsroom: Defense & Security (2013)
7. Bourlai, T., Ross, A., Jain, A.K.: Restoring degraded face images for matching faxed or scanned photos. IEEE Trans. Inf. Forensics Secur. 6(2), 371–384 (2011)

8. Bourlai, T., Ross, A., Jain, A.K.: On matching digital face images against passport photos. In: IEEE International Conference on Biometrics, Identity and Security (2009)
9. Singh, R., et al.: Plastic surgery: a new dimension to face recognition. IEEE Trans. Inf. Forensics Secur. **5**(3), 441–448 (2010)
10. Lakshmiprabha, N.S., Majumder, S.: Face recognition system invariant to plastic surgery. In: Proceedings of International Conference on Intelligent Systems Design and Applications, pp. 258–263 (2012)
11. Mun, M., Deorankar, A.: Implementation of plastic surgery face recognition using multimodal biometric features. Int. J. Comput. Sci. Inform. Technol. **5**(3), 3711–3715 (2014)
12. Aggarwal, G., Biswas, S., Flynn, P.J., Bowyer, K.W.: A sparse representation approach to face matching across plastic surgery. In: Proceedings of IEEE workshop on the Applications of Computer Vision, pp. 113–119 (2012)
13. Bhatt, H.S., Bharadwaj, S., Singh, R., Vtsa, M., Noore, A.: Evolutionary granular approach for recognizing faces altered due to plastic surgery. In: Proceedings of IEEE Conference on Automatic Face and Gesture Recognition, pp. 720–725 (2011)
14. Bhatt, H.S., Bharadwaj, S., Singh, R., Vatsa, M.: Recognizing surgically altered face images using multiobjective evolutionary algorithm. IEEE Trans. Inf. Forensics Secur. **8**(1), 89–100 (2013)
15. Liu, X., Shan, S., Chen, X.: Face recognition after plastic surgery: a comprehensive study. In: Proceedings of Asian Conference on Computer Vision, pp. 565–576 (2012)
16. Chude-Olisah, C.C., Sulong, G., Chude-Okonkwo, U.A.K., Hashim, S.Z.M.: Face recognition via edge-based Gabor feature representation for plastic surgery-altered images. EURASIP J. Adv. Sig. Process. (2014)
17. Ghatol, N.P., Paigude, R., Shirke, A.: Image morphing detection by locating tampered pixels with demosaicing algorithms. Int. J. Comput. Appl. **66**(8), 23–26 (2013)
18. Wen, D., Han, H., Jain, A.K.: Face spoof detection with image distortion analysis. IEEE Trans. Inf. Forensics Secur. **10**(4), 746–761 (2015)
19. Zhen, H., Lee, G., Lee, S.Y.: Integrating two-dimensional morphing and pose estimation for face recognition. J. Inf. Sci. Eng. **30**, 257–272 (2014)
20. Padilha, A., Silva, J., Sebastiao, R.: Improving face recognition by video spatial morphing. In: Delac, K., Grgic, M. (eds.) Face Recognition (2007)
21. Zou, X., Kittler, J., Tena, J.: A morphing system for effective human face recognition. In: Proceedings of International Conference on Visual Information Engineering, pp. 215–220 (2008)
22. Kamgar-Parsi, B., Lawson, W., Kamgar-Parsi, B.: Toward development of a face recognition system for watchlist surveillance. IEEE Trans. Pattern Anal. Mach. Intell. **33**(10), 1925–1937 (2011)
23. Chennamma, H.R., Rangarajan, L., Veerabhadrappa: Face identification from manipulated facial images using SIFT. In: Proceedings of 3rd International Conference on Emerging Trends in Engineering and Technology (ICETET), pp. 192–195 (2010)
24. Slama, C.: Manual of Photogrammetry, 4th edn. American Society of Photogrammetry, Falls Church, VA (1980)
25. Vass, G., Perlaki, T.: Applying and removing lens distortion in post production. In: Proceedings of 2nd Hungarian Conference on Computer Graphics and Geometry (2003)
26. Neurotechnology Inc.: Neurotechnology web site [Online]. http://www.neurotechnology.com/ (2015, Jan)
27. Luxand Inc.: Luxand web site [Online]. http://luxand.com (2015, Jan)
28. Lowe, D.G.: Distinctive image features from scale-invariant keypoints. Int. J. Comput. Vision **60**(2), 91–110 (2004)
29. Bicego, M., Grosso, A., Tistarelli, M.: On the use of SIFT features for face authentication. In: Proceedings of Conference on Computer Vision and Pattern Recognition Workshop, p. 35 (2006)
30. Martinez, A.M., Benavente, R.: The AR face database. Computer Vision Center, CVC Technical Report (1998)

31. Maltoni, D., Maio, D., Jain, A.K., Prabhakar, S.: Handbook of Fingerprint Recognition, 2nd edn. Springer, New York, NJ, USA (2009)
32. FRONTEX: Research and Development Unit. Best Practice Technical Guidelines for Automated Border Control (ABC) Systems,—v2.0 (2012)
33. IATA: Airport with automated border control systems [Online]. http://www.iata.org/whatwedo/stb/maps/Pages/passenger-facilitation.aspx (2015, Jan)
34. Wikipedia: Morphing [Online]. http://en.wikipedia.org/wiki/Morphing (2015, Jan)
35. GIMP: GNU image manipulation program web site [Online]. http://www.gimp.org/ (2015, Jan)
36. GIMP: GIMP animation package [Online]. http://registry.gimp.org/node/18398 (2015, Jan)
37. ISO/IEC 19794-5, Information technology—biometric data interchange formats—part 5: face image data (2011)
38. FRONTEX: FRONTEX Web Site [Online]. http://frontex.europa.eu/ (2014, July)
39. Dorizzi, B., et al.: Fingerprint and on-line signature verification competitions at ICB 2009. In: Proceedings 3rd IAPR/IEEE International Conference on Biometrics (ICB09), Alghero (2009)
40. BioLab: FVC-onGoing web site [Online]. http://biolab.csr.unibo.it/fvcongoing (2015, Jan)
41. Phillips, P.J., Wechsler, H., Huang, J., Rauss, P.J.: The FERET database and evaluation procedure for face-recognition algorithms. Image Vision Comput. 16(5), 295–306 (1998)
42. Phillips, P.J., Moon, H., Rizvi, S.A., Rauss, P.J.: The FERET evaluation methodology for face-recognition algorithms. IEEE Trans. Pattern Anal. Mach. Intell. 22(10), 1090–1104 (2000)
43. Eyedea Recognition Ltd.: Eyedea Recognition Web Site [Online]. http://www.eyedea.cz/ (2015, March)

Chapter 10
Document to Live Facial Identification

A.D. Clark, C. Whitelam and T. Bourlai

Abstract The National Institute for Standards and Technology (NIST) highlights that facial recognition (FR) has improved significantly for ideal cases such, where face photographs are full frontal, of good quality, and pose and illumination variations are not significant. However, there are automated face recognition scenarios that involve comparing degraded facial photographs of subjects against their high-resolution counterparts. Such non-ideal scenarios can be encountered in situations where the need is to be able to identify legacy face photographs acquired by a government agency, including examples such as matching of scanned, but degraded, face images present in drivers licenses, refugee documents, and visas against their live photographs for the purpose of establishing or verifying a subject's identity. The factors impacting the quality of such degraded face photographs include hairstyle, pose and expression variations, lamination and security watermarks, and other artifacts such as camera motion, camera resolution, and compression. In this work, we focus on investigating a set of methodological approaches in order to be able to overcome most of the aforementioned limitations and achieve high identification rate. Thus, we incorporate a combination of pre-processing and heterogeneous face-matching techniques, where comparisons are made between the original (degraded) photograph, the restored photograph, and the high-quality photograph (the mug shot of the live subject). For the purpose of this study, we, first, introduce the restorative building blocks that include threshold-based (TB) denoising, total variational (TV) wavelet inpainting, and exemplar-based inpainting. Next, we empirically assess improvement in image quality, when the aforementioned inpainting methods are applied separately and independently,

A.D. Clark (✉) · C. Whitelam · T. Bourlai
Lane Department of Computer Science and Electrical Engineering,
Statler College of Engineering and Mineral Resources, West Virginia University,
P.O. Box 6109, Morgantown, WV 26506, USA
e-mail: adclark@mail.com

C. Whitelam
e-mail: cwhitela@gmail.com

T. Bourlai
e-mail: ThBourlai@mail.wvu.edu

© Springer International Publishing Switzerland 2016   223
T. Bourlai (ed.), *Face Recognition Across the Imaging Spectrum*,
DOI 10.1007/978-3-319-28501-6_10

coupled with TB denoising. Finally, we compare the face-matching performance achieved when using the original degraded, restored, and live photographs and a set of academic and commercial face matchers, including the local binary patterns (LBP) and local ternary patterns (LTP) texture-based operators, combined with different distance metric techniques, as well as a state-of-the-art commercial face matcher. Our results show that the combination of TB denoising, coupled with either of the two inpainting methods selected for the purpose of this study, illustrates significant improvement in rank-1 identification accuracy. It is expected that the proposed restoration approaches discussed in this work can be directly applied to operational scenarios that include border-crossing stations and various transit centers.

10.1 Introduction

Facial recognition (FR) has a variety of uses in commercial and government applications that include searching for potential terrorists and criminals, performing security measures for automated teller machines (ATMs), and preventing people from obtaining false identification. According to a recent report from the National Institute of Standards and Technology (NIST), FR has improved significantly for ideal cases such as visa and mug shot photographs [1]. However, much remains to be explored for non-ideal conditions [2]. Research has shown that the process of matching degraded facial photographs of a subjects ID documents against their high-resolution counterparts (live subjects), also known as *document to live facial identification*, also fits into this category. The challenges associated with document to live facial identification can be grouped into the following three major categories [3, 4]:

1. *Person-related factors*—Factors that are based on the variation of the individual's facial appearance. Examples in this category include variations in pose, expression, and hairstyle. Aging also fits into this category because there is also a time lapse (that is often significant, i.e., up to a few years) between the comparison of the documented facial image and its higher resolution counterpart [5, 6].
2. *Document-related factors*—Factors that are based on the variation of the type of document. Examples in this category include security watermarks embedded in facial images, variations in image quality and tonality across the face, and color cast of the photographs.
3. *Device-related factors*—Factors that are due to various limitations of the device. Examples in this category include limited device resolution, artifacts due to lighting, the type of image file format or compression used, and operator variability.

Document to live facial identification poses a practical problem for security officers, because the person's identity document information can be potentially tampered, modified or stolen, and even duplicated into another document that can be used for illegal or unauthorized purposes. Therefore, even if a state-of-the-art-automated FR system is used, such a challenging scenario as document to live face matching may not allow for the identification system to achieve the same level of performance that can be achieved in ideal conditions. As a result, the officer may decide to no longer rely on the FR system and try to manually match the query face image against a set of face images in a database (e.g., watch-list) by making visual comparisons. Such a process is probe to errors but more importantly probe to significant delays. Hence, work is needed to design and develop a preprocessing methodology that is capable of restoring the degraded photographs from identity documents prior to comparing them against live (gallery) face images. In this regard, we first investigate several image restoration schemes in combination with academic and commercial face matchers. Then, through an empirical evaluation study, we determine the conditions that result in the highest identification rates. For the purpose of this study, we are using the West Virginia University (WVU) Identity Document Database, which is composed of 130 subjects coming from various countries.

In this section, we first provide a brief introduction on passport standardization. Next, related work in this area is highlighted, where previous restoration strategies are introduced. Finally, our motivations and contributions for the work presented in this chapter are also introduced.

10.1.1   Passport Standardization

Passport standardization was developed in 1980 under the guidance of the International Civil Aviation Organization (ICAO), to provide universal travel guidelines. This was because in the late twentieth century, when photography became widespread, it became popular to attach photographs to identity documents. However, disparities were made, as each country attempted to develop its own standard [7]. Recent ICAO standards include those for machine-readable documents, where some of the information, written in strings of alphanumeric characters, is printed in a manner suitable for optical character recognition [8, 9]. This allows security officers, such as border control and other law enforcement agents, the ability to process these passports efficiently, mitigating the need for manual data entries.

Figure 10.1 demonstrates that identification documents have changed dramatically over the years. It is also important to acknowledge that recent developments have been made to meet society's contemporary needs. A set of recent ICAO standards has been incorporated for *biometric passports* or *e-passports*. For these e-passports, critical information pertaining to the traveler is printed on the data page

(1884)   (1968)   (1987)   (2009)

Fig. 10.1 A collection of passports ranging from 1884 to 2009. All are real passports and are available in the public domain [7]

of the passport as well as stored in a radio-frequency identification (RFID) chip [7]. Additionally, face, fingerprint, and/or iris templates of the legitimate owner are embedded as an additional layer of protection. However, not all passports are bio-metric friendly and there is a possibility that the information stored in the RFID chip could be compromised [3]. For these instances, FR technology can be used as an alternative approach in order to confirm the traveler's identity. The limitations of FR, in this context, are primarily due to document- and device-related factors[1]—par-ticularly in the case of recent documents. In recent identification (ID) documents, security watermarks are observed across the face. Also, in some cases, a strong magenta cast can be observed on the photograph of the ID document. In both paradigms, the image quality can be severely impacted and the facial tonality can be diminished. Therefore, care must be taken to overcome these limitations of degraded photographs to improve image quality before face matchers are applied.

10.1.2 Related Work

Document facial identification was first explored by Starovoitov et al. [10, 11] who presented an automated system for matching face images, present in documents, against camera images. In that study, the authors constrained their work to the earlier versions of passports (circa 1990) that were issued from a single country. The facial images used were reasonably clear and not "contaminated" by any security markings. Hence, the system's ability to automatically identify the face photograph was not severely compromised. Later, Ramanathan and Chellappa [12] focused their attention in this area by addressing the issue of age disparity prior to identification. Hence, they introduced a Bayesian classifier that approximates age

---

[1]Person-related factors are affected here due to the time lapse between the document and ideal images used in comparison.

estimation by estimating the differences between pairs of facial images. Next, Bourlai et al. [3] addressed the problem of facial matching over a variety of international passports. In their work, the authors introduced the following process:

1. *Face Detection*—Used to localize the spatial content of the face and determine its boundary. To accomplish this step, the algorithm proposed by Viola and Jones [13] was employed.
2. *Channel Selection*—Used to perform the appropriate color space normalization. Typically, document images are color images composed of the red, green, blue (RGB) channels and color space normalization is applied to prepare for further processing.
3. *Normalization*—Photometric and geometric normalization schemes, respectively, are needed, first, to compensate for illumination variation and next, for slight perturbations in the frontal pose. Geometric normalization is composed of two major steps: eye detection and affine transformation, where the eye detection is needed to create a global perspective in reference to all faces of the subjects within the database at hand. Photometric normalization is performed by employing histogram equalization and contrast adjustment. Histogram equalization is a nonlinear image enhancement method that transforms image brightness, which can (under certain conditions) improve verification performance [14].
4. *Wavelet Denoising*—Wavelet-based image denoising is needed to remove the additive noise present in documented facial images [15]. This supplemental noise is caused by variations in security markings as well as paper defects. For this step, the translation invariant wavelet transform (TI-WT) [16] was used to average out the translation dependence of the wavelet basis functions.
5. *Feature Extraction and Classification*—In this step, the appropriate facial features are extracted and, then, face matching is performed, i.e., matching of the preprocessed document facial photographs against their live photograph counterparts.

Empirical evaluations of the proposed method, shown in Fig. 10.2, confirmed that document facial matching is a difficult problem due to challenges associated with person, document, and device-related factors. Consequently, applying the preprocessing methodology, described in Steps 1–4 above, improves overall recognition performance. Bourlai et al. extended their original work discussed in [3] by incorporating an image restoration methodology that improved the quality of severely degraded facial images that are digitally acquired from printed or faxed documents [4]. The acute degradation types considered were (a) fax image compression,[2] (b) fax compression, then print, and finally scan, and (c) fax

---

[2]In that work *Fax image compression* is defined as the process where data (e.g., face images on a document) are transferred via a fax machine using the T.6 data compression, which is performed by a fax software on a controlling computer.

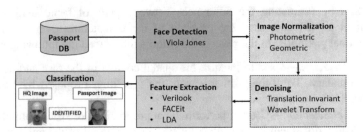

Fig. 10.2 Overview of the methodology used when passport mug shots are used to test the system

compression, then fax transmission, and finally scan. The authors' approach involved an iterative image restoration scheme to improve the textural content of the face images while removing noisy artifacts. Their observational results determined that the proposed image restoration scheme improved image quality as well as recognition performance. The works of [3, 4] also helped inspire investigations in automated image quality measurements to meet the needs of ISO/ICAO standards, where an evaluation benchmark was introduced [17].

The work of [3, 4] also motivated the need to design and develop more sophisticated approaches for facial image restoration. Such approaches are not only limited to image denoising but where digital image inpainting can also be used as an additional tool that better deals with local structures, such as watermarks. Digital image inpainting was first introduced by Bertalmio et al. [18], where a nonlinear third-order partial differential equation (PDE) was used to fill in the selected region of interest (ROI). The results of this work spearheaded an interest in geometric interpolation and inpainting problems that include variational PDE methods [19, 20], fluid dynamics inpainting [21], landmark-based inpainting [22], inpainting by vector fields [23], and inpainting by corresponding maps [24]. Until now, inpainting and interpolation were mainly focused in the pixel domain; however, it was the work of Chan et al. [25], who extended this practice to the wavelet domain. With this knowledge of wavelet interpolation, Bourlai et al. [26] extended the works of [3, 4] to perform TV minimization in the wavelet domain and targeted wavelet coefficients associated with various security markings. By coupling this minimization with the general denoising algorithm [3, 4], the proposed restoration scheme showed much promise in the improvement of overall image quality as well as rank-1 identification accuracy.

10.1.3 Our Motivation and Contribution

Our motivation for this chapter comes from the works of [3, 4, 26] that there is a need to develop a process that performs document to live facial matching, while also removing local structures, such as traces of various security watermarks, left after generic image restoration methods are employed. Prior methodologies showed either improvement in performance in terms of rank-1 identification accuracy or visual and quantitative improvements in image quality, but not both in all images used. In the works of [3] and [4], the technique of using TB denoising as a preprocessing scheme, prior to performing facial matching, showed improvement in performance. However, traces of the security watermark were still left on the image. Conversely, the work of [26] demonstrated that the technique of applying a combination of TV wavelet inpainting coupled with TB denoising showed improvement in image quality while removing traces of diverse security markings. However, improvements needed to be made in terms of increasing identification performance.

As a result, our contributions in this chapter include further investigation into the effects of the following restoration strategies: (1) threshold-based (TB) denoising, (2) TV wavelet inpainting, (3) exemplar-based (EB) inpainting, and (4) the combination of either of the TV or EB inpainting methods, coupled with TB denoising. Here, we investigate the effects of each restoration strategies by examining the improvement in image quality when using the university image quality (UIQ) metric [27]. Next, we explore the effects in identification accuracy when both LBP and LTP texture-based operators, combined with different distant metric techniques, as well as a state-of-the-art face matcher (G8) are used. For this part, we look at the effects of both the preprocessing strategies and the manual mask annotation of the ROI containing the security watermark. Because both TV wavelet and EB inpainting methods depend heavily on mask annotation, there is also a need to explore the impact of mask annotation on facial matching performance. Hence, we are providing an additional layer of analysis to the previous works.

The outline of the proposed work begins with Sect. 10.2 describing the base restorative building blocks of TB denoising, TV wavelet inpainting, and EB inpainting. Next, Sect. 10.3 describes our experimental evaluations where we investigate the improvement in image quality and identification performance. Here, we also explore the impact of mask annotation to rank-1 identification rate. Finally, Sect. 10.4 discusses our conclusions and presents avenues for further exploration.

10.2   Restorative Building Blocks

This section provides the theoretical framework of the fundamental restorative building blocks used that include TB denoising, TV wavelet inpainting, and EB inpainting. Understanding these key building blocks provides the reader an analytical foundation of each independent strategy. Additionally, this understanding also helps compliment the experimental testing and observations of each of the key building blocks and their combination described in the following section.

10.2.1 Threshold-Based (TB) Denoising

TB denoising is the first building block that was incorporated into the restoration strategy to remove the noisy effects of various security markings. This generalized approach is done by considering the following major steps [4, 26]:

1. *Compute the Discrete Wavelet Transform*—First, the discrete wavelet transform (DWT) of the image is needed to convert the noisy image to the wavelet domain.
2. *Apply Thresholding Estimator*—Next, the thresholding estimator is needed to suppress the extraneous artifacts that correspond to the security watermark.
3. *Compute the Inverse Discrete Wavelet Transform*—Finally, the inverse discrete wavelet transform (IDWT) is used to reconstruct the resulting thresholded image.

In order for Step 2 to be the most effective, the thresholding estimator and value need to be selected in order to depict the overall denoising effectiveness. There are different estimators based on the threshold value calibration methods such as hard, soft, or semi-soft thresholding. These settings are chosen based on the level of noisiness of the image where, for example, if an image is severely noisy then hard thresholding is chosen. Conversely, for images that have medium or rare levels of noisy behavior, semi-soft or soft thresholding levels are chosen, respectively. Each estimator removes unnecessary coefficients via the following equation:

$$\hat{h} = \sum_{|\langle h, \psi_m \rangle| > T} \langle h, \psi_m \rangle \psi_m = \sum_m \Omega_T^q (\langle h, \psi_m \rangle) \psi_m, \tag{10.1}$$

where h is the noisy observation, ψ_m the mother wavelet function, $m = (i, j)$ represents the scaling and translation, respectively, of the wavelet basis function, q the thresholding type, and T the threshold value. Given a chosen wavelet basis function ψ_m, Eq. (10.1) filters out the coefficients beyond the set threshold value T via the thresholding estimator Ω_T^q. In terms of the input parameter x, the thresholding estimator Ω_T^q is defined as:

$$\Omega_T^H(x) = \begin{cases} x, & \text{for } |x| > T \\ 0, & \text{for } |x| \leq T, \end{cases} \tag{10.2}$$

$$\Omega_T^S(x) = \begin{cases} \text{sgn}(x) \cdot (|x - T|), & \text{for } |x| > T \\ 0, & \text{for } |x| \leq T \end{cases} \tag{10.3}$$

and

$$\Omega_T^{SS}(x) = \begin{cases} 0, & \text{for } |x| \leq T \\ x, & \text{for } |x| > \mu T \\ \text{sgn}(x) \cdot \frac{|x - T|}{\mu - 1}, & \text{otherwise,} \end{cases} \tag{10.4}$$

where $\mu > 1$ and the superscripts H, S, and SS denote hard, soft, and semi-soft thresholding, respectively. The advantage of applying TB nonlinear denoising is that it is independent regardless of the type and condition of the acquired document.

It is important to note that image denoising using traditional (or decimated) orthogonal wavelets may exhibit visual artifacts due to the lack of translation invariance of the wavelet basis. Additionally, artifacts due to Gibbs phenomenon may occur in the neighborhood of discontinuities. To suppress such artifacts, we "average out" the translation dependence through "cycle spinning" defined by the following equation [16]:

$$\Theta_{\mathrm{TI}}(h) = \frac{1}{|\Phi|} \cdot \sum_{\tau \in \Phi} \Theta(h_\tau)_{-\tau}, \qquad (10.5)$$

where for $\forall \tau \in \Phi$, $\Theta_{\mathrm{TI}}(h) = \Theta_{\mathrm{TI}}(h_\tau)_{-\tau}$. Here, Φ is a lattice of $\mathbb{R}^2$ for a two-dimensional image. This is called *cycle spinning* denoising. Equation (10.5) says that if there exists N-sample data, then pixel precision translation invariance is achieved by having N wavelet translation transforms (vectors) or $|\Phi| = N$. This results in $O(N^2)$ operations. Therefore, similar to cycle spinning denoising, *thresholding-based translation invariant* denoising can be defined as:

$$\Theta_{TI}(h) = \frac{1}{|\Phi|} \cdot \sum_{m,\tau \in \Phi} \Omega_T^q(\langle h, (\psi_m)_\tau \rangle)(\psi_m)_\tau \qquad (10.6)$$

The advantage of employing translational invariant wavelets is that using them improves the signal-to-noise ratio (SNR). Additionally, incorporating the averaging process, defined by Eq. (10.5), significantly reduces the oscillating artifacts [4]. Furthermore, we note that additional SNR improvement can be achieved by properly selecting the threshold estimator T.

10.2.2 Total Variation Wavelet Inpainting

Although TB denoising provides an approach that is both autonomous and adjustable, a key limitation is that traces of the security markings are still left in the image. To overcome these drawbacks, TV wavelet inpainting in conjunction with TB denoising was introduced [26]. The theoretical premise of TV wavelet inpainting is to first consider the following standard image model within the image domain Ω

$$v(x) = u(x) + n(x), \qquad (10.7)$$

where $u(x)$ represents the image not containing the watermark, $n(x)$ represents the watermark itself, and $v(x)$ represents the passport image. Next, let $v(\alpha, x)$ and $u(\beta, x)$ be the wavelet transforms given by

$$v(\alpha, x) = \sum_{j,k} \alpha_{j,k} \psi_{j,k}(x), \quad j \in \mathbb{Z}, k \in \mathbb{Z}^2 \tag{10.8}$$

and

$$u(\beta, x) = \sum_{j,k} \beta_{j,k} \psi_{j,k}(x), \quad j \in \mathbb{Z}, k \in \mathbb{Z}^2 \tag{10.9}$$

where $\alpha = (\alpha_{j,k})$ are the stored wavelet coefficients in the image v and $\beta = (\beta_{j,k})$ are the stored wavelet coefficients in the image u. Here, β are the *desired* coefficients and α are the *damaged* coefficients where the goal was to recover as many desired coefficients while repairing the damaged coefficients. Considering the fact that additional noisy behavior can exist within the image, the following TV model is proposed [25]:

$$\min_{\beta_{j,k}} F(u, v) = \int_\Omega |\nabla_x u(\beta, x)| dx + \sum_{j,k} \lambda_{j,k} (\beta_{j,k} - \alpha_{j,k})^2 \tag{10.10}$$

subject to the constraint

$$\beta_{j,k} = \alpha_{j,k}, \quad (j,k) \in I, \tag{10.11}$$

where I represents the ROI to be inpainted. Noting Eq. (10.10), the operator ∇_x represents the spatial gradient ($x \in \mathbb{R}^2$) and the parameter $\lambda_{j,k}$ is a positive constant such that $\lambda_{j,k} = 0$ in the inpainted region I; otherwise, it equals some positive constant to be chosen ($\lambda > 0$). Minimizing Eq. (10.10) with respect to $\beta = \beta_{j,k}$ achieves the following result

$$\frac{\partial F}{\partial \beta} = -\int_\Omega \nabla \cdot \left[\frac{\nabla u}{|\nabla u|}\right] \psi_{j,k} dx + 2\lambda_{j,k}(\beta - \alpha_{j,k}), \tag{10.12}$$

where

$$\nabla \cdot \left[\frac{\nabla u}{|\nabla u|}\right] \tag{10.13}$$

represents the curvature formula for the level lines of u. Taking into account the variational form, given by (10.12), TV wavelet inpainting provides a sophisticated process that accounts for variegated security markings; however, residual noisy effects are still eminent. Therefore, TB denoising is still considered to remove the extraneous noise improving both image quality and recognition performance.

10.2.3   Exemplar-Based Inpainting

We also investigated the effects of EB inpainting [28] as a potential preprocessing scheme. The effectiveness of this method stems from the computation of patch priorities within the watermarked region Ω of the image I in the pixel space. Given a patch ψ_p centered at the point $p \in \partial\Omega$ where $\partial\Omega$ represents the boundary of the ROI, the *patch priority* $P(p)$ is defined as the product between the *confidence term* $C(p)$ and the *data term* $D(p)$ given by [28]

$$P(p) = C(p)D(p) \tag{10.14}$$

where $C(p)$ and $D(p)$ are given by

$$C(p) = \frac{\sum_{q \in \psi_p \cap (1-\Omega)} C(q)}{|\psi_p|} \quad \text{and} \quad D(p) = \frac{\left| \nabla I_p^{\perp} \cdot \mathbf{n}_p \right|}{\alpha}. \tag{10.15}$$

It is important to note that at point p in Eq. (10.15) $|\psi_p|$ is the area of the patch, α is the normalization factor, $\nabla I_p^{\perp}$ is the isophote representing both the direction and the intensity, and $\mathbf{n}_p$ is the normal vector to the boundary $\partial\Omega$. By computing $D(p)$, the behavior of the isophotes within the targeted region $I - \Omega$ is considered. Also, the measure of the reliable information surrounding the point p, defined by $C(p)$, is also estimated. From the patch priorities, texture and structure information is propagated by first finding the patch with the highest priority. Next, the *source exemplar* of the image is found by directly sampling the source region ψ_q, that is most similar to the patch region $\psi_{\hat{p}}$, given by the following equation

$$\psi_{\hat{q}} = \arg \min_{\psi_q \in (1-\Omega)} d\left(\psi_{\hat{p}}, \psi_q \right), \tag{10.16}$$

where $d\left(\psi_{\hat{p}}, \psi_q \right)$ is the distance measure between the two patches $\psi_{\hat{p}}$ and ψ_q. After computing the source exemplar, the value of each pixel to-be-filled is copied from the corresponding position within the estimated source region $\psi_{\hat{q}}$. Equations (10.14)–(10.16) pose an iterative process that interpolates the missing information within the security watermarked region.

10.3   Experimental Evaluation

Next, we describe several evaluation procedures and methods to assess improvement in both image quality and recognition performance. Our experimental evaluations were performed on the *WVU Identity Document Database*, which is composed of 130 subjects, taken from various documents internationally. The types

(a)   **(b)**   **(c)**   **(d)**

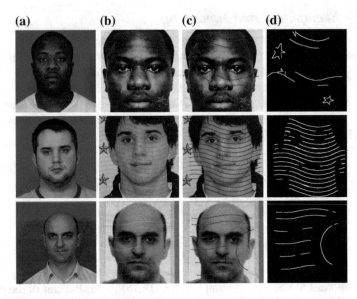

Fig. 10.3 Sample images used from the WVU identity document database: **a** ground truth gallery images, **b** original document images, **c** manually annotated passport masks in *red*, and **d** the resulting masks marking the regions of interest (ROI)

of documents composed in this dataset consist of passports, driving licenses, and state identifications from within the USA as well as various international regions such as the Middle East and European Union. In preparation for empirical testing, we, first, manually annotate the ROI corresponding to the security watermark. Next, we perform the preprocessing schemes where the baseline restorative building blocks, described in Sect. 10.2, are applied. Furthermore, we apply advanced preprocessing schemes, where the combinations of TB denoising are independently coupled with TV wavelet inpainting and EB inpainting (Fig. 10.3).

Each baseline and advanced preprocessing scheme is tested in terms of (1) improvement in image quality and (2) improvement in recognition performance. Understanding the improvement in image quality, via the universal image quality (UIQ) metric [27], is important because we are able to evaluate and determine which preprocessing schemes are most robust. Next, investigating the improvement in recognition performance is needed to show which restoration method improves identification accuracy. The usage of academic algorithms, such as LBP and LTP texture-based approaches, is proven to be beneficial because we are able to show a baseline performance, while a commercial (state-of-the-art) algorithm is also used to show performance improvement or not when employing our different image restorations approaches. Concurrently, we also explore the impact that mask selection (in terms of pixel width) has on identification performance. This is due to the fact that the aforementioned preprocessing schemes are heavily dependent on the level of mask annotation.

10.3.1   Evaluating Image Quality

Assessing improvement in image quality is performed using the UIQ metric, where we compare the outputs of both restored image x and the ideal counterpart y governed by the following equation [27]:

$$\text{UIQ} = \frac{\sigma_{xy}}{\sigma_x \sigma_y} \cdot \frac{2\bar{x}\bar{y}}{\bar{x}^2 + \bar{y}^2} \cdot \frac{2\sigma_x \sigma_y}{\sigma_x^2 \sigma_y^2}, \tag{10.17}$$

where $\bar{x}$ and σ_x^2 are the sample mean and variance of the restored image, $\bar{y}$ and σ_y^2 of the ideal counterpart, and σ_{xy} is the covariance between the two. Using the UIQ metric, in this case, evaluates the improvement in restoration from three main perspectives: loss of correlation, luminance distortion, and contrast distortion. Considering these factors together, UIQ $\in [0, 1]$ such that as UIQ $\to 1$ the restored image reaches maximum improvement. Figure 10.4 shows this trend where, for all 130 subjects, we see the comparisons between the previously mentioned restoration strategies. Overall, we see that using inpainting coupled with TB denoising shows a consistent trend as far as improvement in image quality—regardless of the type of

Fig. 10.4 An illustration of the evaluation of the improvement in image quality where the UIQ metric is used to evaluate the restoration performance using **a** TV wavelet and **b** EB inpainting where each inpainting method was also coupled with threshold-based (TB) denoising. Here, we notice that in both cases, the inpainting/denoising combination is the most effective regardless of the inpainting method that was employed

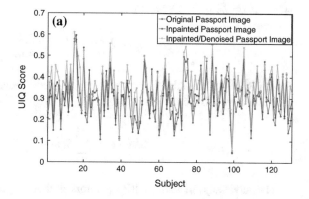

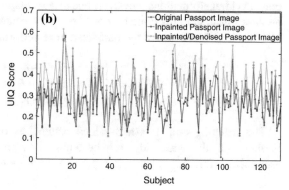

inpainting method used. In other words, we observe that using TV wavelet inpainting or EB inpainting in the inpainting/denoising combination shows almost an identical trend in performance when evaluations are made on the entire dataset. From this assessment, intuitively we should expect that when investigating rank-1 identification accuracy, there would be a similar trend in behavior.

10.3.2   Evaluating Texture-Based Approaches

To show how the applied restoration schemes fair in terms of improvements in identification, we first used academic texture-based approaches to provide a baseline performance. Here, we used LBP and LTP. The LBP image patterns are computed by thresholding 3×3 neighborhoods based on the value of the center pixel. Next, the resulting binary pattern is transformed to a decimal value where the local neighborhood is defined as a set of sampling points evenly spaced in a circle. The LBP operator used in our experiments is described as $\mathrm{LBP}_{P,R}^{u^2}$, where P refers to the number of sampling points placed on a circle with radius R. The symbol u^2 represents the uniform pattern, which accounts for the most frequently occurring pattern. The binary pattern for pixels that lie in a circle f_p, $P = 0, 1, \ldots P - 1$ with the center pixel f_c, is computed as

$$f_n = \begin{cases} 1, & \text{if } f_p - f_c \geq 0 \\ 0, & \text{if } f_p - f_c < 0. \end{cases} \tag{10.18}$$

From (10.18), a binomial weight of 2^P is assigned to each sign $S(f_p - f_c)$ to compute the respective LBP code given by

$$\mathrm{LBP}_{P,R} = \sum_{p=0}^{P-1} S(f_p - f_c) 2^P. \tag{10.19}$$

The advantage of using LBP operators is that they are invariant to monotonic gray level transformations; however, one disadvantage is due to the noise sensitivity because thresholding is done by considering the center of the pixel region. Hence, LTP are introduced where the quantization is performed as follows:

$$f(n) = \begin{cases} 1, & \text{if } f_p - f_c \geq t \\ 0, & \text{if } |f_p - f_c| \leq t \\ -1, & \text{if } f_p - f_c \leq -t. \end{cases} \tag{10.20}$$

The resulting output is a 3-valued pattern, as opposed to a binary pattern. Furthermore, the threshold t can be adjusted to produce different patterns. The user-specific threshold also makes the LTP code more resistant to noise.

10.3.2.1   Distance Metrics

After the texture-based feature patterns are computed, two different distance metrics are used to obtain the final match score, namely the distance transform (DT) and the chi-squared (χ^2). The DT (defined as the distance or similarity metric from image X to image Y) is given by

$$DT(X,Y) = \sum_{Y(i,j)} w\left(d_x^{K_{Y(i,j)}}(i,j)\right), \tag{10.21}$$

where $K_{Y(i,j)}$ is the code value of pixel (i, j) of image Y and w is a user controlled penalty function. Additionally, the chi-squared distance is given by

$$\chi^2(n,m) = \frac{1}{2}\sum_i^l \frac{h_n(k) - h_m(k)}{h_n(k) + h_m(k)} \tag{10.22}$$

where h_n and h_m are the two histogram feature vectors, l is the length of the feature vector and n and m are two sample vectors extracted from an image of the gallery and probe sets, respectively.

10.3.3   Assessing the Effects of Mask Dilation

The observations of the previous works [26] show that the preprocessing methodology depends heavily on mask annotation. Therefore, there is a need to explore and evaluate the impact of the mask generation in the context of FR. For this aspect, the masks for each subject are demarcated to 1 pixel width and dilated to create different mask widths of 2, 4, 6, 8, and 10 pixel widths, respectively. Next, the image is interpolated using different preprocessing schemes. First, we focus on exploring the effects of TV wavelet inpainting and EB inpainting. Texture-based approaches are applied to show recognition performance because it is observed that the ideal mask width may be distinctive for each documented image. For this part, we compare the recognition performance considering *original* and *best* images. Here, the *original* image is the raw passport image and the *best* image represents the restored image that corresponds to the optimum local mask dilation that is determined from the maximum UIQ metric. It is important to note that the mask dilation that produces the best image is not universal. For example, a *best* image could correspond to a mask dilation of 2 pixels and another could correspond to a mask dilation of 6 pixels. Applying these methods of comparison helps us to observe the correlations between the improvement in image quality, optimum mask dilation, and recognition performance.

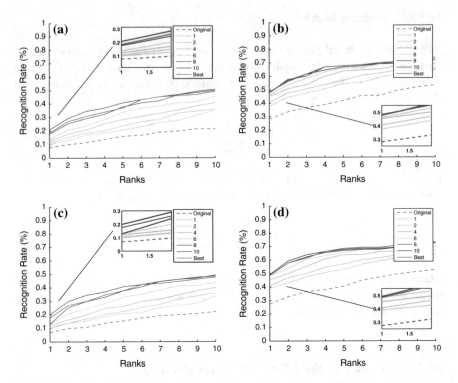

Fig. 10.5 Identification results that solely use TV wavelet inpainting as the preprocessing scheme while comparing various mask widths (in pixels) to the original and best images. Here, academic texture-based approaches (LBP, LTP) are used with different distance metrics of χ^2 (**a, c**) and DT (**b, d**). In both cases, we notice the sensitivity in this method when different mask dilations are chosen

Comparing Figs. 10.5 and 10.6, we observe that applying TV wavelet inpainting shows more sensitivity in terms of mask generation than EB inpainting in terms of improvement in rank-1 accuracy. This is regardless of the texture-based approach that was applied. For example, observing Fig. 10.5a, we see a deviation of approximately 15 % in terms of rank-1 performance when LBP with the χ^2 distance metric is used. However, from Fig. 10.6a, we see a much closer deviation in performance regardless of mask dilation when the same texture-based academic scheme is used for images that were preprocessed via EB inpainting. Although applying the DT metric showed an improvement in rank-1 performance of approximately 20 % when compared to the χ^2 metric, we still see similarity in behavior in terms of the impact that mask width has on identification performance. Furthermore, we note that the recognition rates that correspond to the *best* images are near the highest in terms of identification accuracy.

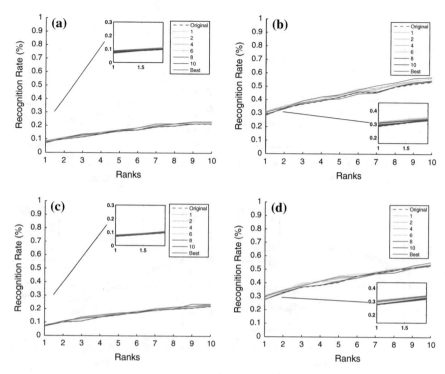

Fig. 10.6 Identification results that solely use EB inpainting as the preprocessing scheme while comparing various mask widths (in pixels) to the original and best images. Here, academic texture-based approaches (LBP, LTP) are used with different distance metrics of χ^2 (**a, c**) and DT (**b, d**). Here, we notice a much closer deviation in performance regardless of the mask dilation

10.3.4 Assessing the Effects of Threshold-Based Nonlinear Denoising

It has been previously noted that for documented facial images, there exist additional artifacts that affect the noisy behavior of the image, which can result from either document- or device-related factors [3, 4]. Furthermore, applying TB denoising has shown to minimize this additional noisy behavior [26]. Therefore, care must be made to investigate the effects of coupling TB denoising with either inpainting method, while considering the effects of mask dilation mentioned in the previous section. We do this by first constructing two different types of training sets, where each set is denoised incrementally, varying the denoising level within the range of $\sigma \in [2, 30]$. Next, at each increment, the LTP-DT score is computed between the inpainted/denoised image and the ideal image and stored. It is important to note that, for each training set, the mean denoising level $\bar{\sigma}$ associated with the minimum LTP-DT score is also considered. This sample mean is used to

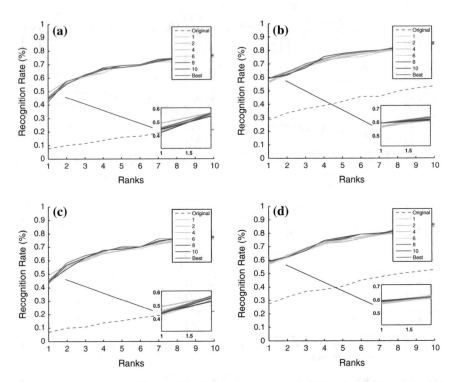

Fig. 10.7 Identification results for document images that used TV wavelet inpainting coupled with TB denoising while comparing various mask dilations where LBP (**a**, **b**) and LTP (**c**, **d**) are used while considering χ^2 and DT distance metrics. These comparisons were made while also considering original and best images

denoise all of the respective documented facial images associated with the particular mask width.

Examining Figs. 10.7 and 10.8, we see that TB denoising showed dramatic improvement in rank-1 accuracy. This result was expected due to previous observations, i.e., when TV wavelet inpainting was applied [26]. However, closer inspection into the results shows the trade-offs between using TV wavelet inpainting, EB inpainting, and mask dilation. Examining Fig. 10.7, we note that the coupling of TV wavelet inpainting with TB denoising showed less sensitivity in terms of mask annotation. In other words, we observe that improvement in performance is independent of mask annotation when TV wavelet inpainting is used. However, from Fig. 10.8, we note that there is more sensitivity in terms of mask selection when EB denoising is applied. Interestingly, we note that this variability is dependent on the distance metric applied. For example, comparing Fig. 10.8a, b, we observe that when changing in the distance metric from χ^2 to DT, there is less sensitivity in terms of mask annotation.

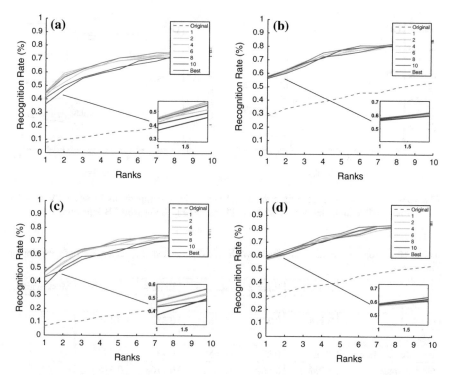

Fig. 10.8 Identification results for document images that used EB inpainting coupled with TB denoising while considering various mask dilations where LBP (**a, b**) and LTP (**c, d**) are used while considering χ^2 and DT distance metrics. These comparisons were made while also considering original and best images

10.3.5   Performance Assessment Using a Commercial Matcher

We conduct our investigations on the effects of either inpainting method from the perspective of a commercial matcher where our evaluation studies are conducted using G8.[3] The purpose here is to determine whether TV wavelet inpainting or EB inpainting provides better preprocessing for improved recognition performance. Applying these techniques solely (i.e., without coupling TB denoising) provides a baseline understanding from a commercial point of view. From Fig. 10.9, we note the similarity in performance when either approach is applied. This is further shown in Table 10.1 where we see a slight improvement in the performance of approximately 5 % between the two methods. Furthermore, we note that this deviation becomes minimum as the rank order increases. These observations show that solely using either inpainting method is sufficient for improved performance.

---

[3]This algorithm was provided by L1 www.l1id.com.

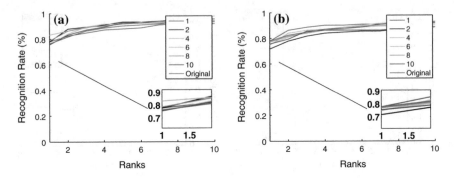

Fig. 10.9 CMC curves illustrating commercial performance comparisons between TV wavelet and EB restoration strategies. G8. **a** G8 with TV inpainting, **b** G8 with EB inpainting

Table 10.1 Top five ranks and which width mask generated the scores for both inpainting algorithms

	Rank 1	Rank 2	Rank 3	Rank 4	Rank 5	Mask width
TV inpainting						
Original	0.274	0.328	0.366	0.382	0.405	–
Inpainted	0.492	0.592	0.638	0.661	0.680	10
Inpainted/denoised	0.592	0.631	0.685	0.731	0.746	6
G8 inpainted	**0.832**	0.862	0.886	0.916	0.916	6
EB inpainting						
Original	0.274	0.328	0.366	0.382	0.405	–
Inpainted	0.308	0.346	0.400	0.407	0.416	6
Inpainted/denoised	0.585	0.638	0.685	0.746	0.770	Best
G8 inpainted	**0.779**	0.863	0.885	0.901	0.901	1

Results are generated from the LTP-DTS texture-based approach as well as the commercial algorithm

10.4   Conclusions and Future Work

In this chapter, we investigated the concept of document to live facial identification, where different restoration strategies were applied to improve both image quality and identification performance. From an image quality standpoint, we observed that the coupling effects of TB denoising with either inpainting method (i.e., TV wavelet inpainting or EB inpainting) showed similar improvements in image quality according to the UIQ metric. From a FR standpoint, we noticed several sensitivities and trade-offs that are dependent on the preprocessing method, mask dilation, and the texture-based method used. Depending on the combination of the texture-based method (LBP or LTP) with the distance metric (χ^2 or DT), we note that there are various sensitivities in terms of mask dilation when either TV wavelet inpainting or EB inpainting is used. However, these sensitivities are neutralized when coupled with TB denoising. We speculate that this reduction in sensitivities is due to the cycle spinning behavior when TB denoising is applied. As a result, we conclude that the inpainting–denoising combination is a prudent strategy because inpainting mitigates the traces of various security watermarks, while TB denoising mitigates extraneous noisy artifacts. Furthermore, in terms of commercial performance, we noticed that solely relying on TV wavelet or EB inpainting is effective in achieving overall improvement in identification performance. Here, we hypothesize that because commercial algorithms, such as G8, already have a proprietary prepro-cessing scheme, incorporating either TV wavelet or EB inpainting methods are sufficient in improving rank-1 identification.

It is noted that applying TB denoising potentially discards important textural information from the facial image [4]. Therefore, a future direction in this area includes investigating the use of super-resolution algorithms that learn a priori the spatial distribution of the image gradient for frontal images of faces [29]. Additionally, we note that the current approach is also heavily dependent on manual mask annotation. This is limiting because, as Fig. 10.5 suggests, mask annotation produces additional sensitivities in terms of facial identification, where we might not completely obtain the most optimum performance. Therefore, another area of exploration would be to improve the mask selection, either automatically or semi-automatically, that optimizes both facial image quality and identification. Another area of exploration would be further investigation into the effects of pre-processing schemes from the standpoint of commercial algorithms. Doing so affords us the opportunity to better understand commercial preprocessing and matching capabilities. Finally, an area that merits further investigation is to extend these capabilities to improve image quality and face matching using very low-quality images, where examples include images in closed-circuit televisions (CCTVs) and surveillance videos.

Acknowledgment This work was supported by the Center for Identification Technology Research and the National Science Foundation under Grant No. - West Virginia University 1066197. We would also like to acknowledge the faculty, students, and staff who assisted us with the work including, but not limited to, the data collection and experiments that led to the work presented in this chapter.

References

1. Information on the facial recognition vendor test. Technical report, National Institute of Standards and Technology. www.nist.gov/itl/iad/ig/frvt-2012.cfm (2012)
2. Zhou, S.K., Chellappa, R., Zhao, W.: Unconstrained face recognition, pp. 1–8. Springer, Berlin (2006)
3. Bourlai, T., Ross, A., Jain, A.: On matching digital face images against scanned passport photos. In: First IEEE International Conference on Biometrics, Identity and Security (BIDS) (2009)
4. Bourlai, T., Ross, A., Jain, A.: Restoring degraded face images for matching faxed or scanned photos. In: IEEE Transactions on Information Forensics and Security (2011)

5. Albert, A.M., Sethuram, A., Ricanek, K.: Implications of adult facial aging factors on bio-metrics. In: Biometrics: Unique and Diverse Applications in Nature, Science, and Technology. Intech (2011)
6. Ricanek, K., Mahalingam, K., Mahalingam, G., Albert, A.M., Bruegge, R.V.: Human face aging: a perspective analysis from anthropology and biometrics. In: Age Factors in Biometric Processing. The Institution of Engineering and Technology (2013)
7. Andrews, B.: A brief history of us passport photographs. blakeandrews.blogspot.com/2009/05/brief-history-of-us-passport.html (2009)
8. ICAO: Welcome to the ICAO machine readable travel documents programme, Sept 2012. www.icao.int/Security
9. McMunn, M.: Machine readable travel documents. Int. Civil Aviat. Organ. (ICAO) **1**(1), 14–15 (2006)
10. Starovoitov, V.V., Samal, D., Sankur, B.: Matching of faces in camera images and document photographs. In: International Conference on Acoustic, Speech, and Signal Processing, vol. **IV**, pp. 2349–2352 (2000)
11. Starovoitov, V.V., Samal, D.I., Briliuk, D.V.: Three approaches for face recognition. In: International Conference on Pattern Recognition and Image Analysis, pp. 707–711 (2002)
12. Ramanathan, N., Chellappa, R.: Face verification across age progression. IEEE Trans. Image Process. **15**(11), 3349–3362 (2006)
13. Viola, P.A., Jones, M.J.: Robust real-time face detection. Int. J. Comput. Vision **57**(2), 137–154 (2004)
14. Li, Y.P., Kittler, J., Matas, J.: Analysis of the lda-based matching schemes for face verification. British Machine Vision Conference (2000)
15. Mohideen, S.K., Perumal, S.A., Sathik, M.M.: Image de-noising using discrete wavelet transform. Int. J. Comput. Sci. Netw. Secur. **8**(1) (2008)
16. Coifman, R.R., Donoho, D.L.: Translation-invariant de-noising. In: Wavelets and Statistics, Springer Lecture Notes in Statistics, vol. 103, pp. 125–150 (1994)
17. Ferrara, M., Franco, A., Maio, D., Maltoni, D.: Face image conformance to iso/icao standards in machine readable travel documents. IEEE Trans. Inf. Forensics Secur. **7**(4), 1204–1213 (2012)
18. Bertalmio, M., Bertozzi, A.L., Caeselles, V., Ballester, C.: Image inpainting. Technical report, University of Minnesota (1999)
19. Chan, T., Shen, J.: Morphologically invariant PDE inpaintings. Technical report, UCLA (2001)
20. Chan, T.F., Kang, S., Shen, J.: Euler's elastica and curvature based inpainting. SIAM J. Appl. Math. **63**, 564–592 (2002)
21. Bertalmio, M., Bertozzi, A., Shapiro, G.: Navier-stokes, fluid dynamics, and image inpainting and video inpainting. In: IEEE Conference on Computer Vision and Pattern Recognition (2001)
22. Kang, S.H., Chan, T.F., Soatto, S.: Inpainting from multiple view. Technical report, UCLA CAM Report (2002)
23. Ballester, C., Bertalmio, M., Caselles, V., Sapiro, G., Verdera, J.: Filling-in by joint interpolation of vector fields and grey levels. IEEE Trans. Image Process. **10**, 1200–1211 (2001)
24. Demanet, L., Song, B., Chan, T.: Image inpainting by correspondence maps: a deterministic approach. Technical report, UCLA CAM Report (2003)
25. Chan, T., Shen, J., Zhou, H.: Total variation wavelet inpainting. SIAM J. Appl. Math. (2006)
26. Bourlai, T., Clark, A.D., Best-Rowden, L.S.: Methodological insights on restoring face photos of multinational passports. In: IEEE International Symposium on Technologies for Homeland Security (IEEE HST) (2013)
27. Wang, Z., Bovik, A.C.: A universal image quality index. IEEE Signal Process. Lett. **9**(3), 81–84 (2002)

28. Criminisi, A., Perez, P., Toyama, K.: Region filling and object removal by exemplar-based image inpainting. IEEE Trans. Image Process. **13**(9), 1–13 (2004)
29. Hennings-Yeomans, P.H., Baker, S., Kumar, B.V.: Simultaneous super-resolution and feature extraction for recognition of low-resolution faces. In: Computer Vision and Pattern Recognition (CVPR), pp. 1–8 (2008)

Chapter 11
Face Recognition in Challenging Environments: An Experimental and Reproducible Research Survey

Manuel Günther, Laurent El Shafey and Sébastien Marcel

Abstract One important type of biometric authentication is face recognition, a research area of high popularity with a wide spectrum of approaches that have been proposed in the last few decades. The majority of existing approaches are conceived for or evaluated on constrained still images. However, more recently research interests have shifted toward unconstrained "in-the-wild" still images and videos. To some extent, current state-of-the-art systems are able to cope with variability due to pose, illumination, expression, and size, which represent the challenges in unconstrained face recognition. To date, only few attempts have addressed the problem of face recognition in mobile environment, where high degradation is present during both data acquisition and transmission. This book chapter deals with face recognition in mobile and other challenging environments, where both still images and video sequences are examined. We provide an experimental study of one commercial off-the-shelf (COTS) and four recent open-source face recognition algorithms, including color-based linear discriminant analysis (LDA), local Gabor binary pattern histogram sequences (LGBPHSs), Gabor grid graphs, and intersession variability (ISV) modeling. Experiments are performed on several freely available challenging still image and video face databases, including one mobile database, always following the evaluation protocols that are attached to the databases. Finally, we supply an easily extensible open-source toolbox to rerun all the experiments, which includes the modeling techniques, the evaluation protocols, and the metrics used in the experiments and provides a detailed description on how to regenerate the results.

M. Günther · L.E. Shafey · S. Marcel (✉)
Idiap Research Institute, Martigny, Switzerland
e-mail: marcel@idiap.ch

M. Günther
e-mail: manuel.guenther@idiap.ch

L.E. Shafey
e-mail: laurent.el-shafey@idiap.ch

© Springer International Publishing Switzerland 2016
T. Bourlai (ed.), *Face Recognition Across the Imaging Spectrum*,
DOI 10.1007/978-3-319-28501-6_11

11.1   Introduction

After the first automatic face recognition algorithms [1, 2] appeared more than three decades ago, this area has attracted many researchers and there has been a huge progress in this field. One of the reasons of its popularity is the broad field of applications of (automatic) face recognition. Due to the availability of mobile camera sensors included into devices such as digital cameras, mobile phones, or laptops, new applications of face recognition appeared recently. One such application is the automatic unlocking of the mobile device, when the user is present in front of the camera or screen. Other applications include the recognition of faces in images in order to aid the user categorizing or memorizing people. The particularity of these applications is that imaging conditions are usually uncontrolled and people in the images or videos have different facial expressions and face poses and are possibly partially occluded. In this book chapter, we investigate several face recognition algorithms regarding their capability to deal with these kinds of conditions.

Commonly, the face recognition task is composed of several stages. The first stage is face detection, in which location and scale of the face(s) in the image are estimated [3, 4] and the image is geometrically regularized to a fixed image resolution. The regularized face images are then subjected to a photometric enhancement step, which mainly reduces the effects of illumination conditions [5, 6]. Then, image features that contain the relevant information needed for face recognition are extracted [7–9]. Features of some of the images are used to enroll a person-specific template, while the features of the remaining images are used for probing. Based on these extracted features, different face recognition algorithms have been developed during the last decades. They can be classified into two major categories: In the discriminative approach, to which most algorithms belong [8, 10–12], it is classified whether template and probe belong to the same identity or not. The generative approach [13, 14] computes the probability that a given person could have produced the probe sample.

To evaluate face recognition algorithms, several publicly accessible databases of facial images and videos exist. One important mobile database is MOBIO [15], which contains voice, image, and video recordings from mobile phones and laptops. Other unconstrained state-of-the-art face databases are the Labeled Faces in the Wild (LFW) database [16] and the YouTube Faces database [17]. The impact of specific facial appearances such as facial expression, face pose, and partial occlusion is investigated based on the Multi-PIE [18] and the small AR face [19] databases. To ensure a fair comparison of face recognition algorithms, image databases are accompanied with evaluation protocols, in which all of our experiments follow strictly.

Along with this book chapter, we provide the source code[1] not only for the algorithms, but also for the complete experiments from the raw images or videos to

---

[1]http://pypi.python.org/pypi/xfacereclib.book.FRaES2016.

the final evaluation, including the figures and tables that can be found in this chapter. Most of the algorithms use Bob [20], a free signal processing and machine learning toolbox for researchers.[2] Some algorithms are taken from the CSU Face Recognition Resources,[3] which provide the baseline algorithms for the Good, the Bad & the Ugly (GBU) face recognition challenge [21, 22]. Finally, all experiments are executed using the FaceRecLib [23],[4] which offers an easy interface to run face recognition experiments either using already implemented face recognition algorithms, or rapidly prototyping novel ideas.

The remaining of this chapter is structured as follows: In Sect. 11.2, we give an overview of related work on face recognition in challenging environments, and a brief survey of reproducible research in biometrics. Section 11.3 describes the databases, the methodology, and the results of our face recognition experiments. Finally, Sects. 11.4 and 11.5 close the paper with a detailed discussion of the tested face recognition algorithms and a conclusion.

11.2 Related Work

11.2.1 Reproducible Research in Biometrics

Biometrics research is an interdisciplinary field that combines expertise from several research areas. Examples of these scattered disciplines are as follows: image preprocessing and feature extraction that are from the field of signal and image processing; machine learning, which is required for subspace projections or data modeling; or pattern recognition and distance computations as part of the information theory. Additionally, to make results comparable, a proper implementation of the required evaluation protocols of biometric databases needs to be provided. This makes biometrics research a particularly difficult case, especially when comparable results should be provided. Hence, often biometric algorithms are tested only on a few of the available databases. Also, the results of other researchers cannot be reproduced since they do not publish all of the meta-parameters of their algorithms. Therefore, survey papers like [24–28] can only report the results of other researchers, so "it is really difficult to declare a winner algorithm" [24] since "different papers may use different parts of the database for their experiments" [28].

One way of providing comparable results is to apply the concept of reproducible research.[5] A reproducible research paper is comprised of several aspects [29], which makes it possible and easy to exactly reproduce experiments:

---

[2]http://www.idiap.ch/software/bob.

[3]http://www.cs.colostate.edu/facerec/algorithms/baselines2011.php.

[4]http://pypi.python.org/pypi/facereclib.

[5]http://www.reproducibleresearch.net.

- a research publication that describes the work in all relevant details,
- the source code to reproduce all results,
- the data required to reproduce the results, and
- instructions how to apply the code on the data to replicate the results on the paper.

One reason for providing reproducible research, besides making the lives of other researchers easier, is the visibility of the resulting scientific publications. As [30] showed, the average number of citations for papers that provide source code in the transactions on image processing (TIP) is seven times higher than of papers that do not.

There have been attempts to foment reproducibility of research results in the biometric community with the release of public software [20, 23, 31, 32] and datasets [15, 16, 33, 34]. Various biometric communities organize open challenges [35, 36], for which Web-based solutions for data access and result posting are particularly attractive [37]. Some dataset providers also publish an aggregation of the results of different algorithms on their Web pages.[6] However, cases where those components are used in a concerted effort to produce a reproducible publication remain rare.

Particularly, two groups of researchers currently try to push forward the reproducibility of biometric recognition experiments. On one hand, OpenBR [32] is an open-source C++ library of algorithms to perform biometric recognition experiments. Unfortunately, this library only has a limited set of algorithms and biometric databases, which it can evaluate. On the other hand, the FaceRecLib [23] is an easy-to-use and easy-to-extend Python library that can be used to run complete face recognition experiments on various face image and video databases. Several reproducible research papers based on the FaceRecLib have already been published,[7] using the Python Package Index (PyPI) as a source code distribution portal. All results of the experiments that are reported in this book chapter rely on the FaceRecLib.

Further research on solutions for achieving, distributing, and comparing results of biometric experiments in the reproducible research framework is carried out. Currently being under development, the Biometrics Evaluation And Testing (BEAT) platform[8] introduces a biometry agnostic system for programming algorithms, workflows, running complete evaluations, and comparing to other researcher's results only using a Web browser.

---

[6]For example, the results on LFW [16] are published under: http://vis-www.cs.umass.edu/lfw/results.html.

[7]One example for reproducible research based on the FaceRecLib can be found under: http://pypi.python.org/pypi/xfacereclib.paper.BeFIT2012.

[8]http://www.beat-eu.org/platform.

11.2.2   Face Recognition in Challenging Environments

For several decades, research on face recognition in controlled environments has been fostered due to its high impact on practical applications such as automatic access or border control, where subjects cooperate with the system. In a study in 2007, it has been shown that automatic face recognition systems in controlled environments can surpass human performance [38], when identities in the images are not previously known to the participants [39].

After having satisfactorily solved face recognition in controlled environments, research interests shifted toward unconstrained environments, where subjects do not cooperate with the face recognition system. Three main directions of applications have arisen as follows: identifying persons in uncontrolled high-quality images to tag private photographs with identities using application such as Picasa or iPhoto; identifying suspects in low-resolution surveillance camera videos; and verifying owners of mobile devices or cars to avoid thefts. Due to the availability of several image and video databases [16, 17] for the first application, research was lead toward this direction. On the other hand, only few databases with surveillance camera [40] or mobile [15, 41] data are available, so this area of face recognition research is still underdeveloped.

The latest trend for face recognition in uncontrolled environments is the usage of deep convolutional neural networks [42, 43]. Those networks are usually proprietary software and require a huge amount of training data, which is not publicly available, and thus, the reproducibility level of these publications is 0 according to [29]. In [44], Bayesian face recognition [45] is revisited and extended to work with mixtures of Gaussians for both the intrapersonal and the extra-personal class, using LBP histogram sequences as features. However, they learned their method using training data (PubFig) that overlaps with their test images (LFW), making their experimental results strongly biased. So far, none of these methods is included in our evaluation, though their future integration into the experimental setup is foreseen.

The Point-and-Shoot Face Recognition Challenge (PaSC) [46] investigated five different algorithms on the PaSC dataset [41], which contains unconstrained images and videos of indoor and outdoor scenes. The authors of the best performing system [47] claim that their Eigen-PEP approach is naturally robust to pose variations. It would be nice to be able to include their system into our study, but to date we were not able to re-implement their algorithm.

In a study, [48] performed a large-scale feature selection to perform unconstrained face recognition. They modeled the low-level feature extraction of the human brain and achieved good results on image pairs with similar pose. However, they found that image pairs with different identities in comparable face pose most often are more similar than images with the same identity but different poses. Hence, those features work well in constrained face recognition, but not well with unconstrained face image data.

Previous studies [49] have found that Gabor jet and LBP-based algorithms are well suited for face recognition in unconstrained environments. Also, color information [22] have shown to contain data useful for face recognition. Furthermore, advanced modeling techniques [50] showed good verification performance on uncontrolled mobile data. Finally, the fusion [51] of several different approaches for unconstrained face recognition was able to outperform single systems.

However, so far no reproducible study has been performed that analyzes face recognition algorithms according to their behavior in the presence of (uncontrolled) illumination, facial expression, face pose, and partial occlusions. The reproducibility of the present study is guaranteed due to the availability of the data and the algorithms, as well as the evaluation protocols and methods. Furthermore, a properly documented script that shows how to regenerate all results is provided.

11.3 Experiments

This section provides an overview of our experimental evaluation. The employed algorithms are explained, and the evaluated databases are presented, including a brief description of the databases and evaluation metrics. After optimizing the configurations of the algorithms, the performance of the algorithms under three different sets of experiments is evaluated. First, the dependence on the single variations facial expression, face pose, and partial occlusions is investigated. Second, the performance in an uncontrolled image database is evaluated, and the extensibility to video face recognition is tested. Finally, the results of the algorithms on a mobile image and video database are reported.

11.3.1 Face Recognition Techniques

The face recognition algorithms that we test in our evaluation are recent open-source approaches to still image face recognition. All algorithms are adapted to process several images for template enrollment and for probing. Additionally, several image preprocessing techniques are evaluated.

The implementation of the preprocessing techniques and three of the face recognition algorithms relies on the open-source toolbox Bob [20], which provides functionality in a research-friendly Python environment and implements identified bottlenecks in C++. One algorithm is taken from the CSU Face Recognition Resources [22], which is completely implemented in Python. To test the advantage of commercial systems over the open-source approaches, additionally one commercial off-the-shelf (COTS) algorithm is investigated. In our experiments, the evaluation of video data is performed by subsampling the frames of the videos and providing the algorithms with several images per video.

Though we run several of face recognition algorithms, there is a common execution order to perform a face recognition experiment. Given a raw image or video from a certain database, the first stage is to detect the face, remove the background information, and geometrically normalize the face. Throughout our experiments, for image databases, we use the hand-labeled annotations provided by the databases to geometrically normalize the face, while for video databases we detect the faces [52] and eye locations [53] in each used frame. The aligned face image is further processed using some preprocessing technique, usually to attenuate the effects of illumination.

In the next step, features are extracted from the preprocessed images. Features from one or more images of one identity are used to enroll a template of the person, and several of those templates are used as a gallery. These templates are compared with probe features of other images or videos, and a similarity score is computed for each template/probe pair. Since face recognition algorithms are usually bound to a specific type of features, we present both the feature extraction and the modeling and comparison techniques together as combined algorithms.

Finally, the scores are evaluated to compute the final performance measure, using one of the evaluation metrics defined in Sect. 11.3.2.1.

11.3.1.1 Image Preprocessing

Before a preprocessing technique is applied, the image is converted to gray scale and aligned. This implies that the image is geometrically normalized such that the left and right eyes are located at specific locations in the aligned image, e.g., $\mathbf{a}_l = (48, 16)^\top$ and $\mathbf{a}_r = (15, 16)^\top$, and the image is cut to a resolution of, e.g., 64×80 pixels. Figure 11.1b shows the result of the alignment of the image shown in Fig. 11.1a.

To reduce the impact of illumination, we test four different preprocessing techniques, which are always executed on the aligned image. The first algorithm is histogram equalization (HEQ) [54]. Second, we investigate the self-quotient image (SQI) algorithm [55]. Third, we examine the multistage preprocessing technique (T&T) as presented by Tan and Triggs [6]. Finally, we examine a preprocessing

| (a) | (b) | (c) | (d) | (e) | (f) |
| Orig | None | HEQ | SQI | T&T | LBP |

Fig. 11.1 Image preprocessing techniques. This figure shows the effect of different image preprocessing techniques on the **a** original image: **b** no preprocessing, **c** histogram equalization, **d** self-quotient image, **e** Tan & Triggs algorithm and **f** LBP feature extraction

technique [5] based on local binary patterns (LBPs). Examples of preprocessed images can be found in Fig. 11.1.

11.3.1.2 Linear Discriminant Analysis on Color Channels

An extension of linear discriminant analysis (LDA) to the two color channels I-chrominance and the red channel (LDA-IR) has been proposed in [22]. After a geometric normalization of the face, the raw pixels are concatenated to form a one-dimensional feature vector. A PCA + LDA transformation matrix, which is a combination of the principal component analysis (PCA) and LDA projection, is computed independently for both color channels. Each channel is projected into its corresponding subspace, and both projected vectors are concatenated to form the final feature vector.

In the template enrollment step, all enrollment features are simply stored. Since none of the other algorithms are allowed to use cohort data for score normalization, we decided to disable[9] the cohort normalization usually applied in [22]. This transforms the distance function between a template and a probe feature into a simple Euclidean distance. The final score is empirically found to be the minimum distance value.

LDA-IR is the only examined algorithm that incorporates color information into the face recognition process. Therefore, it cannot be combined with the preprocessing techniques defined in Sect. 11.3.1.1. Hence, image alignment and feature extraction rely on the original implementation of the LDA-IR algorithm.

11.3.1.3 Gabor Grid Graphs

The idea of the Graphs algorithm relies on a Gabor wavelet transform [56, 57]. The preprocessed image is transformed using a family of $j = 1, \ldots, 40$ complex-valued Gabor wavelets, which is divided into the common set of 8 orientations and 5 scales [56]. The result of the Gabor transform are 40 complex-valued image planes in the resolution of the preprocessed image. Commonly, each complex-valued plane is represented by absolute values and phases. The transform process for a single Gabor wavelet is visualized in Fig. 11.2.

From these complex planes, grid graphs of Gabor jets are extracted. A Gabor jet is a local texture feature, which is generated by concatenating the responses of all Gabor wavelets at a certain offset-position in the image. As shown by [58], it is beneficial to normalize the absolute values in a Gabor jet to unit Euclidean length.

In our implementation, the bunch graph [56] concept is used for template enrollment. For each node position, the Gabor jets from all enrollment graphs are

---

[9]To avoid misunderstandings, we do not use the name CohortLDA as in [22], but we stick to the old name of the algorithm (LDA-IR).

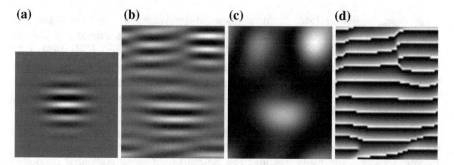

Fig. 11.2 Gabor wavelet transform. This figure displays the **b** real part, **c** absolute values, and **d** Gabor phases of the convolution of the image from Fig. 11.1b with the **a** Gabor wavelet

stored. For the comparison of template and probe, we investigate several local and global scoring strategies. Each strategy relies on a comparison of Gabor jets, which employs one of several Gabor jet similarity function [8, 56, 58]. In the optimal strategy (see Sect. 11.3.3), an average of the local maximum of similarities is computed, using a similarity function partially based on Gabor phases [8].

11.3.1.4 Local Gabor Binary Pattern Histogram Sequences

In the local Gabor binary pattern histogram sequences (LGBPHSs) [59], three different approaches of face recognition are combined. First, the preprocessed image is Gabor wavelet transformed [56], which leads to 40 complex-valued representations of the images. Then, LBPs [60] are extracted from the absolute and the phase part [59]. An LBP is generated by comparing the gray value of a pixel with the gray values of its neighbors, resulting in a binary representation with discrete values between 0 and 255. The extraction process of LBPs from Gabor wavelet responses is illustrated in Fig. 11.3. Different LBP variants such as circular or uniform patterns [61] are evaluated.

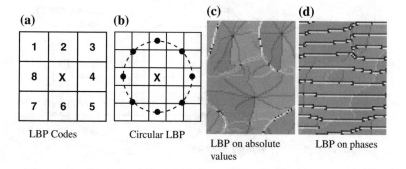

Fig. 11.3 Local Gabor binary patterns. This figure displays the generation process of **a** LBP codes and **b** the circular $LBP_{8,2}^{u2}$ operator. Additionally, the results of the $LBP_{8,2}^{u2}$ operator on **c** the absolute Gabor wavelet responses and **d** the Gabor phases (as given in Fig. 11.2c, d) are shown

In order to obtain local features, these image planes are split into possibly overlapping image blocks [62]. As each bit of the LBP code is similarly important, these codes cannot be compared with a simple distance function. Instead, LBP codes are collected in histograms, one for each block and each Gabor wavelet. Concatenating all these histograms into one histogram sequence ends up in a huge feature vector, which is called the extended local Gabor binary pattern histogram sequence (ELGBPHS) [59].

To enroll a template from several images, we decided to compute the average over histogram sequences (which result in non-integral numbers in the histograms). Finally, template and probe features can be compared using dedicated histogram similarity measures such as histogram intersection, the χ^2 distance, or the Kullback-Leibler divergence.

11.3.1.5 Intersession Variability Modeling

An alternative to previously detailed discriminative approaches to automatic face recognition is to describe the face of a person by a generative model. The idea is to extract local features from the image of a subject's face before modeling the distribution of these features with a Gaussian mixture model (GMM) [7, 63], instead of concatenating them as usually done in discriminative approaches.

Parts-based features [7] are extracted by decomposing preprocessed images into overlapping blocks. A 2D discrete cosine transform (DCT) is applied to each block before extracting the lowest frequency DCT coefficients. These coefficients are used to build the descriptor of a given block, after applying proper pre- and post-processing of each block [13]. This feature extraction process is detailed in Fig. 11.4.

The distribution of the features for a given identity are modeled by a GMM with several multivariate Gaussian components [64]. To overcome the issue of limited enrollment data, first a universal background model (UBM) is estimated as a prior [64], which is later adapted to the enrollment samples of a person using a maximum a

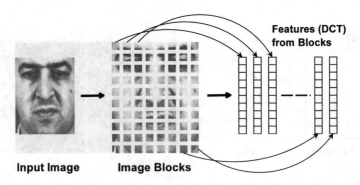

Fig. 11.4 Dct feature extraction. This figure shows the computation of parts-based features by decomposing an image into a set of blocks and extracting DCT features from each block

posteriori (MAP) estimation [65]. It has been shown that such an approach offers descent performance with a reasonable complexity [66].

In the context of a GMM-based system, intersession variability (ISV) modeling [67] is a technique that has been successfully employed for face recognition [50, 68]. In ISV, it is assumed that within-person variation is contained in a linear subspace and by adding a corresponding offset to the GMM means describing each sample. A template is enrolled by suppressing those session-dependent components from the feature vectors and yielding the true session-independent person-specific template GMM.

To compare the template GMM with probe features, a twofold similarity measure is applied. First, the session-dependent offset is estimated for the probe sample. Since the session offset is estimated at both enrollment and probing time, it significantly reduces the impact of within-person variation. Second, the log-likelihood ratio score is computed by comparing the probe features both to the template GMM as well as to the UBM. A more detailed description of this algorithm can be found in [67, 50].

11.3.1.6   Commercial Off-the-Shelf Algorithm

We obtained a commercial off-the-shelf (COTS) face recognition system[10] with a C++ interface for algorithms used in several steps in the face recognition tool chain. Obviously, no detailed information of the employed algorithms is known. We wrote a Python interface for a small subset of this functionality that allowed us to run the COTS algorithms in the FaceRecLib. Particularly, we implemented bindings for functions to extract features, to enroll a template from several features, and to compute scores given one template and one probe feature.

Although the C++ interface of COTS provides functionality for face and eye landmark detection, we rely on the same data as in the other experiments as detailed below. Particularly, we use hand-labeled eye locations in the image experiments, and our face detection and landmark localization algorithm in the video experiments. The first reason is that we want to assure that all algorithms see exactly the same data, and secondly, some of the faces in the MOBIO database are not found correctly by the COTS face detection algorithm.

11.3.2   Databases and Evaluation Protocols

To guarantee a fair comparison of algorithms, it is required that all algorithms are provided with the same image data for training and enrollment, and the same pairs of template and probe data are evaluated. This is achieved by defining evaluation

---

[10]The COTS vendor requested to stay anonymous.

protocols, which might either be biased, i.e., (partially) having the data of the same identities in the training and the test set, or unbiased by splitting the identities between the sets. For all databases used in this book chapter, we provide an implementation of the protocols, and a more complete list of implemented database interfaces is given on the Bob Web page.[11]

11.3.2.1 Evaluation Metrics

The evaluation protocols of all databases used in our evaluation define a verification scenario. Several evaluation measures exist, which are all built on top of the false acceptance rate (FAR) and the false rejection rate (FRR). To compute these rates, the scores are split into genuine scores s_{gen}, which result from comparing template and probe from the same person, and impostor scores s_{imp}, where template and probe of different identities are compared [69]. FAR and FRR are defined over a certain threshold θ:

$$\text{FAR}(\theta) = \frac{\left|\left\{s_{imp}\,\middle|\,s_{imp} \geq \theta\right\}\right|}{\left|\left\{s_{imp}\right\}\right|} \qquad \text{FRR}(\theta) = \frac{\left|\left\{s_{gen}\,\middle|\,s_{gen} < \theta\right\}\right|}{\left|\left\{s_{gen}\right\}\right|} \qquad (11.1)$$

In most of the evaluated protocols, the data are split into three sets: a training set, a development set, and an evaluation set. Scores and FAR/FRR are computed for both the development and the evaluation set independently. Then, a threshold θ^* is obtained based on the intersection point of FAR and FRR curves of the development set. This threshold is used to compute the equal error rate (EER) on the development set and the half total error rate (HTER) on the evaluation set:

$$\text{EER} = \frac{\text{FAR}_{dev}(\theta^*) + \text{FRR}_{dev}(\theta^*)}{2} \qquad \text{HTER} = \frac{\text{FAR}_{eval}(\theta^*) + \text{FRR}_{eval}(\theta^*)}{2} \qquad (11.2)$$

There are two databases, for which a different evaluation protocol is provided, i.e., LFW and YouTube (see Sect. 11.3.2.2). In the protocol, pairs of images or videos are specified, for which a score should be computed. In our case, we always choose the first image or video of the pair for template enrollment and the second as probe. In both databases, the subjects are split into 10 different subsets, so-called `folds`. In each `fold`, 300 (LFW) or 250 (YouTube) genuine pairs and the same amount of impostor pairs exist. For each `fold`, the classification success (CS) is computed:

$$\text{CS} = \frac{\left|\left\{s_{gen}\,\middle|\,s_{gen} \geq \theta^*\right\}\right| + \left|\left\{s_{imp}\,\middle|\,s_{imp} < \theta^*\right\}\right|}{\left|\left\{s_{gen}\right\}\right| + \left|\left\{s_{imp}\right\}\right|} \qquad (11.3)$$

---

[11]http://github.com/idiap/bob/wiki/Packages.

We use our own implementation this 10fold protocol, which provides an additional development set, from which the threshold $\theta*$ in Eq. (11.3) is estimated. For each of the 10 experiments, 7 `folds` are used for training, the development set is built from 2 `folds`, and the last `fold` is employed to compute the CS. Finally, as required by [16], the mean and the standard deviation of the CSs over all 10 experiments are reported. For the LFW database, we chose the unrestricted configuration [16] since the identity information is required by some algorithms, which is forbidden to be used in the image-restricted training set. However, none of our algorithms is provided with additional external training data.

11.3.2.2 Databases

This section specifies the image and video databases including their evaluation protocols, which are used in our experiments. An overview of the databases and protocols is given in Table 11.1.

The CMU Multi-PIE database [18] consists of 755,370 images shot in 4 different sessions from 337 subjects. We generated and published several unbiased face verification protocols, all of which are split up into a training, a development, and an evaluation set. The training set is composed of 208 individuals, while the size of development set (64 identities) and evaluation set (65 identities) is almost equal. In each protocol, a single image per person with neutral facial expression, neutral illumination, and frontal pose are selected for template enrollment. The probe sets contain images with either non-frontal illumination (protocol U), facial expressions (protocol E), or face poses (protocol P).

XM2VTS [33] is a comparably small database of 295 subjects. We use only the `darkened` protocol in our image preprocessing experiments, which includes non-frontally illuminated images. The particularity of the `darkened` protocol is that the training and development set consists of well-illuminated images, while the evaluation set consists of non-frontally illuminated ones. The enrollment of a template is performed with 3 images per person, whereas 4 probe files per identity are used to compute the scores. The training set consists of exactly the same images as used for template enrollment [33], making the protocol biased.

The AR face database [19] contains 3312 images[12] from 76 male and 60 female identities taken in two sessions. Facial images in this database include three variations: facial expressions, strong controlled illumination, and occlusions with sunglasses and scarfs. We have created and published several unbiased verification protocols for this database, splitting up the identities into 50 training subjects (28 men and 22 women) and each 43 persons (24 male and 19 female) in the development and evaluation set. For template enrollment, we use those two images per identity that have neutral illumination, neutral expression, and no occlusion.

---

[12]The website http://www2.ece.ohio-state.edu/~aleix/ARdatabase.html re-ports more than 4000 images, but we could not reach the controller of the database to clarify the difference.

Table 11.1 Databases and protocols

Protocol	Training set		Development set			Evaluation set			Remark
	Ident.	Files	Templ.	Enroll	Probe	Templ.	Enroll	Probe	
Multi-PIE (*images*)			*All template/probe pairs*						[18]
U	208	9785	64	64	4864	65	65	4940	Controlled non-frontal illumination
E		1095			576			585	controlled facial expressions
P		7725			3328			3380	face poses in 15 % yaw angles
XM2VTS (*images*)			*All template/probe pairs*						[33]
darkened	200	600	200	600	800	200	600	800	Non-frontal illumination
AR face (*images*)			*All template/probe pairs*						[19]
illumination	50	329	43	86	258	43	86	258	Controlled non-frontal illumination
occlusion		827			172			172	sunglasses and scarfs
both		827			344			344	illumination and occlusion
BANCA (*images*)			*Selected template/probe pairs*						[70]
P	30	300	26	130	2370	26	130	2370	Diverse illumination
LFW (*images*)			*Selected template/probe pairs*						[16]
foldx[a]	4024	9263	913	913	915	456	456	458	Uncontrolled images
MOBIO (*images/videos*)			*All template/probe pairs*						[15]
male	50	9600	24	120	2520	38	190	3990	Mobile recordings of men
female			18	90	1890	20	100	2100	mobile recordings of women
YouTube (*videos*)			*Selected template/probe pairs*						[17]
foldx[a]	1013	2288	500	500	490	250	250	245	Uncontrolled videos

This table lists the evaluation protocols of the databases used in our experiments. For the training set, the number of training identities and training files is given. For both the development and the evaluation set, the number of templates, enrollment files, and of probe files is provided

[a]In total, 10 folds (fold1 to fold10) exist in the LFW and YouTube protocols, and here, we provide average counts

The protocols such as `occlusion`, `illumination`, and `both` test the specific image variations that are defined in the database, i.e., probe images have either partially occluded faces, non-frontal illumination, or both occlusion and illumination. The training set for the `illumination` protocol is comprised of images with illumination variations only, whereas in the training sets for `occlusion` and `both`, occluded faces, are additionally included.

Originally, in BANCA [70], video and audio recordings of 52 persons were captured for each 4 different languages, where the participants were asked to utter prompted sequences. Recordings were taken in 12 different sessions. In each session, every subject generated two videos, one true genuine access, and one informed impostor access. From each of these videos, 5 images and one audio signal were extracted. However, only the English language was made available [70], together with several unbiased open set verification protocols. We here take only the most challenging protocol P, in which templates are enrolled from 5 controlled images, while the system is probed with controlled, degraded, and adverse images. Two particularities of this database are that it is small, e.g., the training set consists of only 300 images, and that the number of 2340 genuine and 3120 impostor scores is balanced.

One of the most popular image databases is the LFW database [16]. It contains 13,233 face images from 5749 celebrities, which were downloaded from the Internet and labeled with the name of the celebrity. In most images, faces in close-to-frontal poses with good illumination are shown, and some examples are given in Fig. 11.8a. In fact, there is an ongoing discussion if the LFW dataset is fully representative for unconstrained face recognition [48]. In this work, we use the images aligned by the funneling algorithm [71]. The database owners do not provide the eye locations for the images, but we rely on publicly available[13] automatically extracted annotations [72].

The MOBIO database [15] consists of video data of 150 people taken with mobile devices such as mobile phones or laptops, and we here use only the mobile phone data. For each person, 12 sessions were recorded. The faces visible in these recordings differ in facial expression, pose, illumination conditions, and sometimes parts of the face are not captured by the device. Along with the MOBIO database, two gender-specific unbiased evaluation protocols `female` and `male` are provided, where exclusively female or male images are compared. In these protocols, 5 recordings per identity are used to enroll a template, and all probe files are tested against all templates of the same gender. The training set consists of 9600 recordings from 13 females and 37 males. In our experiments, we solely perform gender-independent training. The development set contains 18 female and 24 male identities, which are probed with 1890 or 2520 recordings, respectively. The evaluation set embraces 20 female and 38 male identities, using 2100 or 3990 probe files, respectively. For the MOBIO image database, one image was extracted from

---

[13]http://lear.inrialpes.fr/people/guillaumin/data.php.

each video recording by choosing a single frame after approximately one second of video run time, and the eye centers were labeled by hand.

The YouTube Faces database [17] contains a collection of 3425 videos of 1595 celebrities collected from the YouTube video portal, showing faces in several poses and with good illumination. The length of a video sequence varies between around 50–6000 frames. Although the YouTube database is accompanied by bounding boxes that were detected for each frame in each of the videos, and by pre-cropped frames that were aligned with the help of detected facial landmarks [17], we rely on our own face detector and landmark localization algorithm to align faces in all (used) frames.

11.3.3 Configuration Optimization

Any face recognition algorithm has several intrinsic meta-parameters, which we refer to as the algorithm configuration. Examples of such parameters are the number, resolution, and overlap of blocks in the LGBPHS and the ISV algorithms, or the Gabor jet similarity metric used in the Graphs algorithm. To be as fair as possible, we optimize the configurations of all of the algorithms taken from Bob [20] independently. We do not optimize the configuration of LDA-IR since the configuration has been optimized already—though to another database—and defining new color transformations is out of the scope of this work.

We chose the BANCA database with protocol P to perform the optimization experiments since the database is small, but still quite challenging and focused on semi-frontal facial images as they occur in unconstrained or mobile databases. According to the designated use of the evaluation protocol, we optimize the algorithm configurations using the development set of BANCA. It should be noted that the goal of this study is to provide a replicable evaluation of a range of state-of-the-art face recognition algorithms for research to build upon. It is **not** the goal of this study to demonstrate the superiority of a single best face recognition algorithm.

One important aspect of face recognition is the resolution of the facial image and its content. Interestingly, there are only few publications, e.g., [9, 49, 58] that pay attention to this aspect, but rather every researcher uses his or her own image resolution. Hence, the first set of experiments that we conduct is to find out, which image resolution is best suited for face recognition. We execute all algorithms with configurations that we have set according to the literature. We selected several different image resolutions, ranging from height 20–200 pixels, always keeping an aspect ratio of 4:5 and the eye locations at the same relative coordinates. Also, configuration parameters that are sensitive to the image resolution are adapted accordingly. Note that we do not include LDA-IR in the image resolution evaluation since changing the parametrization of this algorithm in its original implementation is highly complex.

The resulting EER on protocol P of the BANCA development set is given in Fig. 11.5a. Interestingly, the results of most of the algorithms are very stable for any image resolution that is at least 32 × 40 pixels, which corresponds to an inter-eye distance of 16 pixels. Only for resolutions smaller than that, results degrade. ISV and Graphs require resolutions that are a bit higher, but also these algorithms settle around 100 pixels image height. Since there is not much difference between the resolutions greater than 32 × 40 pixels, we choose to stick at the resolution 64 × 80 as used in many of our previous publications [14, 23, 68, 73] for the rest of our experiments.

One severe issue in automatic face recognition is uncontrolled or strong illumination. Several image preprocessing techniques that should reduce the impact of illumination in face recognition have been proposed (see Sect. 11.3.1.1). Unfortunately, in the literature, there is no comprehensive analysis of image preprocessing techniques for face recognition, but each researcher uses a single preferred technique, if any.

To evaluate the preprocessing techniques, we execute them on three databases with challenging controlled illumination conditions: the XM2VTS database (protocol darkened), the Multi-PIE database (protocol U), and the AR face database (protocol illumination). Finally, we test the techniques on a database with uncontrolled illumination, for which we again select BANCA (protocol P).

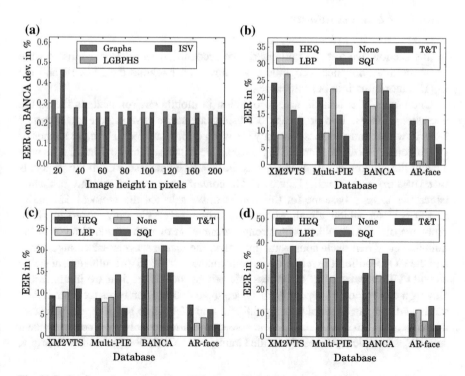

Fig. 11.5 Configuration optimization. This figure displays the results of image resolution and the preprocessing tests of the configuration optimization steps for the algorithms. **a** Resolution, **b** Preprocessing: Graphs, **c** Preprocessing: LGBPHS, **d** Preprocessing: ISV

The results of the preprocessing test can be observed in Fig. 11.5b–d. Apparently, the preferred preprocessing technique differs between face recognition algorithms. However, there is an overall trend for the LBP-based and the Tan & Triggs preprocessing techniques, while HEQ and SQI do not perform as well and, obviously, neither executing no preprocessing technique at all.

For each of the algorithms, we chose the best performing preprocessing technique for our following experiments, which is Tan & Triggs for LGBPHS and ISV, and the LBP-based preprocessing for Graphs.

After finding a suitable image resolution and the optimal image preprocessing technique for each algorithm, we optimize their configurations independently. Due to the partially large number of configuration parameters to be optimized, we performed optimization in several steps. Each step groups together configuration parameters that might influence each other. Due to a limited space in this book chapter, the detailed description of each of the steps can be found only in the source code package, including a detailed description of the configuration parameters. In the subsequent experiments, we run all algorithms with the configurations optimized to the BANCA database.

11.3.4   Face Variations

In this section, we test the optimized face recognition algorithms against several variations that influence recognition. We now also integrate the LDA-IR and the COTS algorithms into our experiments.

One aspect of automatic face recognition in mobile environments is the partial occlusion of faces. Two prominent occlusions are scarfs covering the lower part of faces in winter and sunglasses as they are worn during summer. Example images of these occlusions can be found in Fig. 11.6a. One database that provides images with exactly these two types of occlusions is the AR face database, i.e., in the protocols occlusion and both. Figure 11.6b contains the results of the occlusion experiments. As a baseline for this database, we selected the protocol illumination,[14] on which all algorithms perform nicely. We only observed slight problems of LDAIR, either with strong illumination or with occluded faces in the training set. When occlusions come into play, the Gabor wavelet-based algorithms and the COTS suffer a severe drop in performance, while ISV results remain stable and LDA-IR results seem to be less affected by occlusion than by illumination. Having a closer look by separating between the two occlusion types (cf. Fig. 11.6c), scarfs and sunglasses seem to have different impacts. While people wearing a scarf that covers approximately half of the face can still reasonably well be recognized, sunglasses completely break down the Graphs and LGBPHS systems. Interestingly,

---

[14]To be comparable to the occlusion and both protocols, the same training set, i.e., including occluded faces, was also used in the illumination protocol.

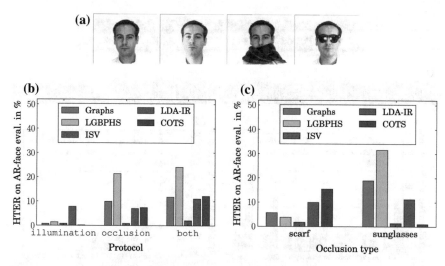

Fig. 11.6 Partial occlusions. This figure shows examples of illumination and occlusion, and the effect of partial occlusions of the face on the different face recognition algorithms. **a** Examples images of AR face: template, illumination, occlusion, both, **b** effect of illumination and occlusion, **c** effect of different occlusion types

the COTS results show exactly the opposite behavior, whereas ISV and LDA-IR can handle both types of occlusions similarly well. In [74], it was found that the eye region contains most discriminative information. Our results approve these findings for some face recognition algorithms, but we clearly show that they cannot be generalized to all of them.

Another aspect that an automatic face recognition system must deal with is facial expression. To test the algorithms against various facial expressions, we selected the protocol E of the Multi-PIE database, which includes images with strongly pronounced expressions (see Fig. 11.7a). The results of the experiments are shown in Fig. 11.7c. Interestingly, it can be observed that facial expressions are not handled satisfactorily by most algorithms. While neutral faces are recognized quite well by all algorithms, other expressions influence most of the algorithms severely. One exception is ISV, which seems to be stable against mild facial expressions and is still very good in the presence of extreme expressions such as surprise and disgust. Facial expressions are also handled well by LDA-IR, and it is able to outperform ISV on screaming faces. Again, variations in the mouth region (as in the scream expression) perturb COTS more than variations in the eyes region.

Note that these two aspects of face recognition were tested in [75], where it was shown that faces with facial expressions or occlusions (in the accessories protocol of [75]) were more difficult to identify by all the algorithms they tested. However, we are not aware of any scientific publication, where a detailed analysis of types of facial expressions or occlusions was performed.

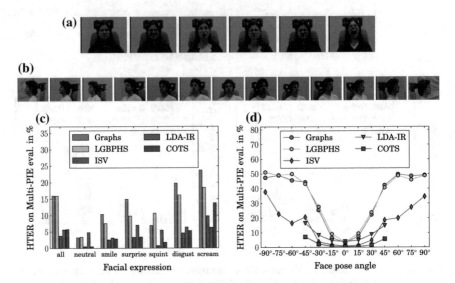

Fig. 11.7 Facial expressions and poses. This figure shows the examples and the effect of facial expressions and face poses on the different face recognition algorithms. **a** Examples of facial expressions: neutral, smile, surprise, squint, disgust, scream, **b** examples of face poses from left to right profile, **c** facial expressions, **d** face poses

To test how the algorithms perform on non-frontal images, we execute them on protocol P of the Multi-PIE database. Similar to all other protocols, we evaluate in this paper, the template enrollment is done using frontal images, while now probe images are taken from left profile to right profile in steps of 15° (e.g., see Fig. 11.7b). The hand-labeled eye positions are used for the image alignment step, as long as both eyes are visible in the image, i.e., for images with a rotation less or equal to ±45°. In the profile and near-profile cases, images are aligned according to the eye and mouth positions. In Fig. 11.7d, verification performance is plotted for each of the tested poses independently, though the algorithms are trained using images from all poses together. It can be observed that close-to-frontal poses up to ±15° can be handled by most algorithms, and the performance order of the algorithms is similar to what we obtained before. For rotations greater than ±45°, the verification performance of the algorithms that do not make use of the training data, i.e., LGBPHS and Graphs, is around chance level. The algorithms that can handle rotations between ±30° and ±60° better are ISV, LDA-IR, and COTS. Anyways, none of the tested algorithms can be used to identify profile faces, i.e., with rotations larger than ±60°. Unfortunately, we could run LDA-IR and COTS experiments only on near-frontal faces since we could not provide the eye and mouth positions, which are required for profile image alignment, to the LDA-IR or COTS algorithms. For the same reason, the results of LDA-IR in Fig. 11.7d are advantageously biased because the training set does not contain any profile images, i.e., with a rotation greater than ±45°.

11.3.5 Unconstrained Image and Video Databases

Now, we evaluate the face recognition algorithms on more challenging uncon-strained facial image and video database, i.e., LFW and YouTube, using the 10fold evaluation protocols proposed by both databases. Each fold is evaluated separately, which includes a separate training for ISV and LDA-IR for each fold, and a separate decision threshold (cf. Sect. 11.3.2.1) which is computed for the development set that we have defined for each fold.

Figure 11.8b displays the average classification rates as well as the standard deviations over the 10 different folds of the LFW protocol [16]. Of the tested algorithms, the commercial COTS system was able to outperform all open-source algorithms by a relatively high margin. With 74.7 % classification success, ISV is the best performing open-source algorithm on this database, followed by LDA-IR. Also, Graphs and LGBPHS perform almost as well, though they do not make use of the training data. However, none of the algorithms is able to reach the best per-formance [76] reported on the LFW Web site, which is given in the last column of Fig. 11.8b. Reasons are that our algorithms are not adapted to LFW, no external training data is used, no algorithm fusion is applied, we use a tight crop of the face (cf. [77]), and finally our decision threshold is computed on an independent development set for each fold, which makes our results completely unbiased, but which is not enforced by the LFW protocol.

One way to improve face recognition algorithms is to exploit video information as soon as it is available. To see whether selecting more frames improves verifi-cation, we choose 1, 3, 10, and 20 frames from the videos of the YouTube faces database and feed them to our face recognition systems, which are tuned to work with several images for template enrollment and for probing. These frames are

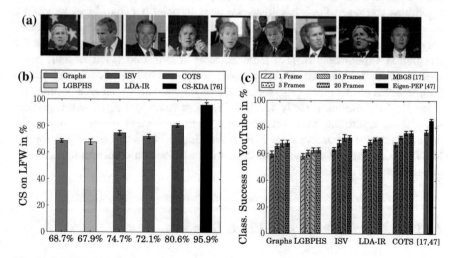

Fig. 11.8 LFW And Youtube. This figure shows the average classification success and the standard deviation over the 10 folds for the experiments on the LFW and YouTube databases. **a** Examples of LFW, **b** LFW, **c** YouTube

taken such that they are distributed equally over the whole video sequence, and no further frame selection strategy is applied. Since there are no hand-labeled eye annotations available, we perform a face detection based on boosted LBP features [52] and a landmark localization algorithm [53] to detect the eye landmarks automatically.

Figure 11.8c shows the results of the experiments for the five evaluated algorithms. Apparently, increasing the number of frames also increases the recognition accuracy, though results settle after approximately 10 frames per video. Since the YouTube database contains several non-frontal face video recordings, and COTS has shown to be quite stable against those variations, it comes with no surprise that COTS performed best in our experiments. Of the tested open-source systems, once more ISV is able to outperform the other three, but only slightly. Particularly, LDA-IR is able to compete. The most drastic improvement was gained by Graphs (+8.3 %), where a strategy to incorporate several frames based on a local maximum is used, ISV (+9 %), where the probability of the joint distributions of features from several frames are modeled, and COTS (+8.7 %), which seems to provide a proper enrollment strategy. With the simple averaging strategy of LGBPHS (+4.8 %), we are not able to exploit many frames that well, and the maximum score strategy of LDA-IR (+7.6 %) lies in-between.

For the YouTube database, we also provide the best performing systems from [17] and [47], both of which exploit all frames of all videos. The first is taken using the matched background similarity (MBGS), where samples from a cohort set are exploited and the computation of a discriminative classifier is required for each template and for each probe video. The second reported algorithm uses the probabilistic elastic part (PEP) algorithm, which is claimed to be robust against pose by modeling a GMM on SIFT features, reducing the dimensionality of the features using PCA and using a Bayesian classifier [78] for scoring. Though none of our algorithms can reach these baselines, we need to point out that: First, we do not include any cohort information into the classification process. Second, we exploit only up to 20 frames, not the whole video. Third, the image cropping used in the recognition experiments in [17] included more information (such as hair, head-dresses, or clothes), which has been shown to be able to help recognizing people [79], whereas our face cropping solely focuses on the inner facial area. Fourth, the Eigen-PEP algorithm is directly developed to solve video-to-video face recognition, whereas our algorithms were mainly developed for still image comparison. Finally, the configuration parameters for MBGS and Eigen-PEP were optimized for the YouTube database, while our algorithms were used with a configuration that was not adapted to YouTube.

11.3.6 Mobile Image and Video Database

The mobile database that we use in our experiments is the MOBIO database [15]. Though MOBIO was taken with handheld mobile devices, the faces are usually in high resolution, mostly in a close-to-frontal pose, and degradation caused by motion blur is limited. However, illumination conditions in the videos are very diverse, and due to the fact that identities were talking during the recordings, a variety of facial expressions is embedded in the frames. For the readers to get a picture of the variability of the MOBIO database, some of the images of one identity are shown in Fig. 11.9a.

As before, we choose 1, 3, 10, and 20 frames from the video sequences to see the impact on the face recognition algorithms. For each frame, the face is detected and the eye positions are localized automatically. Figure 11.9 shows the HTER computed on the evaluation set of the MOBIO database for both protocols `female` and `male`. As before, the COTS results outperform all other algorithms on both protocols, followed by ISV, Graphs, and LGBPHS. The LDA-IR results on `female` are the worst, while for `male` LDA-IR ranges third. Apparently, incorporating the information from several frames improves the recognition accuracy, drastically for Graphs, LGBPHS, and LDA-IR, and moderately for ISV and COTS. Keeping in mind that each template is enrolled from 5 recordings, ISV and COTS already perform well using a single frame per video, while the other three algorithms gain more by exploiting several frames. All in all, when using 20 frames per video, in total features from 100 frames are incorporated in one enrolled template.

From Fig. 11.9, it can be observed that females are more difficult to verify than males, particularly for ISV and LDA-IR. This finding complies with other face verification experiments performed on this database [13, 35]. This might be due to the fact that the MOBIO training set (as well as the development and evaluation sets) has a bias toward males. While for Graphs, which does not depend on the training set, similar results for both males and females are generated, both ISV and LDA-IR follow the bias of the database and perform better on males than on females.

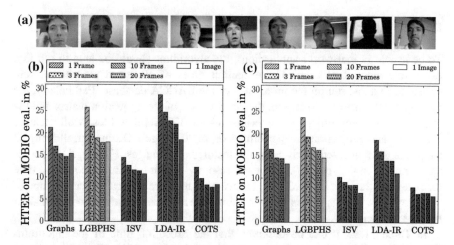

Fig. 11.9 MOBIO. This figure displays examples of images in the MOBIO database and the results of the experiments for the two protocols `female` and `male`, with varying numbers of frames of the videos, and using the hand-labeled images. **a** Examples of MOBIO images, **b** `female`, **c** `male`

As the MOBIO database also provides images with hand-labeled eye coordinates, we can directly compare the impact of properly located eye positions against an off-the-shelf face detector [52] and landmark localization algorithm [53]. The results of the hand-labeled images from the MOBIO database are given in the last columns of each plot in Fig. 11.9. Apparently, using hand-labeled eye positions rather than automatically detected faces works best for all algorithms. Even when exploiting 20 frames of a video, the results cannot reach the verification accuracy of a single hand-labeled image per video, except for Graphs, LGBPHS, and COTS on the `female` protocol. There are several possible reasons for this. First, some faces in the MOBIO database are not completely contained in the image, and thus, the face detector usually returns a bounding box that is smaller than the actual face. Sometimes, due to strong illumination conditions, no face is found at all, and the extracted region contains image background. Second, the landmark localization might not be perfect, which is known to drop recognition accuracy [80]. And third, the hand-labeled images were selected such that the faces are mostly frontal with a neutral expression, while no such selection is done in the video frames.

11.4 Discussion

11.4.1 Algorithm Complexity

After executing all these experiments and showing the verification performances of the algorithms under several conditions and for various image and video databases, we want to discuss other properties of the algorithms.

11.4.1.1 Algorithm Execution Time

To be usable in real-world applications, the algorithms should be able to run in a reasonable amount of time. The execution times of all tested algorithms were measured in a test run on the protocol P of the BANCA database. Particularly, the training for the feature extraction, the computation of the projection matrix and the training of the enrollment are executed using 300 training files, while feature extraction and projection are performed on 6020 images. During enrollment, 52 templates are generated, each using the features of 5 images. Finally, 5460 scores are computed in the scoring step. In any case, we do not take into account the time for accessing the data on hard disk, but we only measure the real execution time of the algorithms. Hence, the actual processing time might increase due to hard disk or network latencies.

In Table 11.2a, it can be observed that the execution time of the algorithms differs substantially. For the simple color-based algorithm LDA-IR, which is based on a pure Python implementation, the training of the projection matrix finished after a couple of seconds, while the feature projection takes most of the time, here around

Table 11.2 Time and memory properties

Algorithm	Graphs	LGBPHS	ISV	LDA-IR	COTS
(a) Execution time					
Training	–	–	1.8 h	6.8 s	–
Extraction	2.0 m	4.1 h	4.6 m	–	23.5 m
Projection	–	–	3.5 h	4.3 m	–
Enrollment	4.5 s	1.8 m	38.6 s	0.9 s	1.4 s
Scoring	39.4 s	25.5 s	7.5 s	6.1 s	11.5 s
Total	2.7 m	4.2 h	5.5 h	4.6 m	23.7 m
(b) Memory requirements					
Model	–	–	29 MB	6.6 MB	–
Feature	160 kB	≈3 MB	1.4 MB	3.9 kB	4.5 kB
Projected	–	–	800 kB	–	–
Template	800 kB	≈9 MB	300 kB	12 kB	22.5 kB

This table gives an overview of the execution time that specific parts of the algorithms need and the size of the produced elements on hard disk. The times are measured on a 3.4 GHz Intel i7 processor with 16 GB of RAM, executing experiments on both development and evaluation set of the BANCA database

4 min. Enrollment is almost instantaneous since it just needs to store all features, and the scoring is also very fast. The extraction of Gabor graphs takes a little bit more time, while the enrollment of the templates is, again, instantaneous. The scoring is longer since computing the similarity measure requires a higher computational effort. The LGBPHS feature extraction needs a huge amount of time as the features themselves are huge, and hence, we chose a compressed format to store the histograms. This decreases the size of the LGBPHS feature vector (though Table 11.2b shows that LGBPHS features still are longest), but complicates the feature extraction and the template enrollment, and also the scoring time is affected. The longest training and projection time are needed by ISV. During training, the distribution of the mixture of Gaussians and the linear subspace of the ISV algorithm are estimated—both procedures rely on computationally intensive iterative processes. Furthermore, the long projection time can be explained by its complexity, where sufficient statistics of the samples given the GMM are first computed, before being used to estimate session offsets. Finally, the scoring time is comparably short since most of the time-consuming estimations are cached in the projection and enrollment steps.

11.4.1.2 Memory Requirements

Table 11.2b displays the memory requirements of the objects produced during the execution of the algorithms. Except for LDA-IR and COTS, all elements are stored in double precision, i.e., with 8 bytes for each number. Depending on the complexity of the algorithms, the size of the features and templates differ slightly. In any case, the trained model needs to be stored to be able to use these technologies in a real-word application, which might be problematic, e.g., on mobile devices with limited memory.

The lowest memory consumption is achieved by the LDA-IR algorithm, except that it needs to load the trained model once. Please note that these values are estimates since the format, which is stored, is unknown.[15] The size of the features and templates of COTS is clearly optimized, and a binary format is used to store them. However, there is no detailed information about the trained model of COTS. The size of the Gabor graphs is also relatively small, though the enrolled templates enlarges since all 5 feature vectors are stored. For LGBPHS, the feature and template sizes are much higher. Please note that the sizes of the LGBPHS feature vectors and enrolled templates differ slightly because we use a compressed format to store the histograms. Still, feature vectors and templates of this size make it difficult to use this algorithm in a real-world application, at least with the configuration that we optimized in Sect. 11.3.3. Finally, the size of the ISV projection matrix and the projected features are comparably high, while the enrolled template is relatively small. This is an advantage over having large templates since in a face recognition application, usually many templates are stored, but only few probe images need to be processed at a time.

11.4.2   About This Evaluation

Of course, an evaluative survey of face recognition algorithms as we provide in this book chapter cannot cover the full range of all recently developed face recognition algorithms including all their variations, and we might have omitted some aspects of face recognition. We know that this book chapter does not answer the question: What is the best face recognition algorithm? Nonetheless, we hope to provide some insights about advantages and drawbacks of the algorithms that we tested and also some hints, which algorithms are well suited under different circumstances.

11.4.2.1   What We Missed

Though we could not test all the state-of-the-art face recognition algorithms, we tried to find a good compromise, which algorithms to test and which to leave out, and we are sorry if we do not evaluate the algorithm of your choice. Also, we executed algorithms only like they are reported in the literature. Theoretically, we could have tried ISV modeling of Gabor jets, LGBPHS features on color image, etc., and the range of possible tests is unlimited.

---

[15]We just use the `pickle` module of Python to store the LDA-IR data. Table 11.2(b) shows the resulting file size on disk.

One aspect of biometric recognition is score normalization using an image cohort. For example, *ZT-norm* [81] has been shown lately [13] to be very effective and able to improve face verification drastically. Also, the fusion of several algorithms [51] outperforms single algorithms. In this work, we do not perform any score normalization, and no fusion system is studied.

For the image databases, we used hand-labeled eye locations to align the faces, particularly during the evaluation of different face variations in Sect. 11.3.4. From the results of the experiments on the MOBIO database, we assume that fully automatic face recognition algorithms produce different results, especially as faces might not be detected correctly in the presence of expressions, occlusions, or non-frontal pose.

For video face recognition, we used a simple approach to select the frames. We did not apply any quality measure of the images, e.g., assessing motion blur, focus, or other quality degradations of videos that present challenges in mobile video face recognition. Also, no sequence-based approaches [82] were tested, which exploit different kinds of information from video sequences than simple frames.

We tried to make the comparison of the face recognition systems as fair as possible. We optimized the configurations of most algorithms to a certain image database.

Only LDA-IR was optimized to another database [22], and we did not touch these configurations in our experiments. This biases the algorithms toward different image variations, but still we think we could show the trends of the algorithms. Also, the optimization was done in several steps using discrete sets of configuration parameters. A joint optimization strategy with continuous parameters could have resulted in a slightly better performance on BANCA.

We intentionally optimized the configurations on one database and kept them stable during all subsequent tests. Therefore, the results on the other databases are not optimal. Certainly, the optimization of the configuration parameters to the each evaluated database would have improved the performance, though it is not clear how high the gain would have been.

11.4.2.2   What We Achieved

Nevertheless, the contribution of this book chapter is—to our best knowledge—unique. We perform the first reproducible and extensible evaluative survey of face recognition algorithms that is completely based on open-source software, freely available tools and packages, and no additional commercial software needs to be bought to run the experiments. All experiments can be rerun, and all results (including the figures and tables from this book chapter) can be regenerated by other researchers, simply by invoking a short sequence of commands, which are documented in the software package.

Utilizing these commands ourselves, we executed several recent open-source face recognition algorithms, optimized their configurations and tested them on various image and video databases. Additionally, we included one commercial off-the-shelf face recognition algorithm into our investigations. To be able to reproduce the figures from this paper, we provide the score files obtained with this algorithm for download.[16] Our experiments showed the impact of different image variations such as illumination, expression, pose, and occlusion on those algorithms, and we reported the performance on the LFW and YouTube databases. Finally, we showed that running video face recognition in mobile devices need to be improved by using face detectors and facial feature localizers specialized for mobile environments.

Since the implementation of the evaluation protocols is time-consuming and error prone, many researchers rely on results generated on small image databases using their own protocols, which makes their results incomparable to the results of other researchers [24, 28]. In the source code that we provide [20, 23], evaluation protocols for several publicly available image and video databases are already implemented, and changing the database or the protocol is as easy as changing one command line parameter. Additionally, the same software package also allows to prototype new ideas, test combinations of these ideas with existing code, run face recognition experiments, and evaluate the results of these experiments. Since the evaluation is always executed identically, results are directly comparable, throughout.

With this software package, we want to encourage researchers to run face recognition experiments in a comparable way. Using Python and the PyPI, it is easily possible for researchers to provide their source code for interested people to regenerate their results. A nice side effect of publishing source code together with scientific paper lies in the fact [30] that papers with source code are cited on average 7 times more than papers without. The software package that we distribute with this book chapter is one example of how to provide source code and reproducible experiments to other researchers.

11.4.2.3 What We Found

We have tested four recent open-source and one commercial face recognition algorithms on several image databases and with different image variations. In most of the tests, we have found that:

1. ISV, the generative approach that models a face as the distribution of facial features, outperforms the other algorithms, sometimes by far. Unfortunately, quite a long time for the (offline) training and template enrollment, and also for the (online) feature extraction is needed by this algorithm.
2. Color information, as used by LDA-IR, can be very helpful, especially when the texture itself is degraded due to low resolution, difficult facial expressions,

---

[16]http://www.idiap.ch/resource/biometric.

occlusions, or poses. However, uncontrolled or strong illumination seems to have a strong effect on this algorithm.

3. Image preprocessing plays an important role, and the preferred preprocessing technique differs for each face recognition algorithm. Sometimes, the best preprocessing technique even changes from database to database. Interestingly, algorithms work with many image resolutions—as far as it exceeds a lower limit of approximately 16 pixels inter-eye distance.

4. Images with strong or uncontrolled illumination conditions are handled better by algorithms using Gabor wavelets. Furthermore, a proper use of Gabor phases improves the performance of these algorithms. In this study, we used two methods that do not include any training. We assume that these methods can be improved by incorporating knowledge from the training set using machine learning techniques.

5. None of the algorithms is able to handle non-frontal pose, even if all poses have been available during training. The direct comparison of features from different poses seems not to be possible with the discriminative algorithms, and similar problems have been observed even in the generative approach. Hence, we believe that the different kinds of methods need to be invented, e.g., [44, 83] showed promising approaches to the pose problem.

6. When multiple frames are available for template enrollment or probing, the ISV algorithm, which directly incorporates multiple images, and the Graphs algorithm, which used a local scoring strategy, are able to exploit these data better than the other algorithms that use only simple scoring strategies such as computing the average histogram or maximum similarity. However, the extension of image-based face recognition algorithms toward videos is inferior to algorithms particularly designed for video-to-video face recognition [47].

7. Face detection and facial landmark localization in video sequences play important roles in video face recognition. Particularly for mobile devices, face detectors need to be able to stably detect faces that are only partially visible in the frames.

8. Besides few exceptions, the best results are obtained by the COTS algorithm. Apparently, the gap between academic research and commercial application of face recognition algorithms still exists.

11.5 Conclusion

In this book chapter, we presented the first evaluative, reproducible, and extensible study of four recent open-source and one COTS face recognition algorithms. We briefly described the employed face recognition algorithms including several image preprocessing techniques. The implementations for most of the algorithms were taken from the open-source software library Bob [20], while one algorithm stems from the Colorado State University toolkit [22].

The first evaluation that we performed assessed, which image resolution is required for the different algorithms to run properly. After selecting a proper image resolution, we evaluated the performance of the algorithms under several different image preprocessing technique on some image databases with difficult illumination and selected the most appropriate preprocessing for each face recognition algorithm. Subsequently, we optimized the configurations of most algorithms to the BANCA database, leaving the already optimized configuration of the CSU algorithm untouched. We tested the algorithm performance with regard to different image variations such as facial expressions, partial occlusions, and non-frontal poses. Then, we selected a challenging image and a challenging video database and ran the algorithms on them. Afterward, we examined the performance of the algorithms in the MOBIO database, using both the images with hand-labeled eye positions and the video sequences. Finally, we discussed a number of attributes of the algorithms that might limit their usability in mobile applications.

A short summary of the evaluation could be that there is not a single algorithm that works best in all cases and for all applications. Nevertheless, there are some favorites. Gabor wavelet-based algorithms are well suited in difficult illumination conditions and were average in the other tests we performed. Still there is room for improvement of these algorithms since the ones we have tested in this work do not make use of the training set. The only algorithm in our test that used color information, i.e., LDA-IR works very well under several circumstances, especially when the image conditions are rather poor and algorithms cannot rely on facial features any more. The generative algorithm ISV performed best in most of the tests, but has the drawback of a very long execution time and high memory usage and cannot be used, e.g., in mobile devices with limited capacities and real-time demands. Finally, the commercial algorithm worked best in most of our evaluations, particularly when face poses are non-frontal.

One important aspect of this evaluation is that we provide the source code for each of the experiments, including all image and video database interfaces, all pre-processing techniques, all feature extractors, all recognition algorithms, and all evaluation scripts. Therefore, all experiments can be rerun, and all figures can be recreated by anybody that has access to the raw image data. Additionally, we want to motivate other researchers to use our source code to run their own face recognition experiments since the software is designed to be easy to handle and easy to extend and to produce comparable results. We furthermore want to encourage researchers to publish the source code of their algorithms in order to build a strong community that can finally answer research questions that are still unsolved.

Acknowledgements This evaluation has received funding from the European Community's FP7 under grant agreements 238803 (BBfor2: bbfor2.net) and 284989 (BEAT: beat-eu.org). This work is based on open-source software provided by the Idiap Research Institute and the Colorado State University. The authors want to thank all contributors of the software for their great work.

References

1. Kanade, T.: Picture Processing System by Computer Complex and Recognition of Human Faces. PhD thesis, Kyoto University, Japan (1973)
2. Sirovich, L., Kirby, M.: Low-dimensional procedure for the characterization of human faces. J. Opt. Soc. Am. A **4**(3), 519–524 (1987)
3. Rowley, H.A., Baluja, S., Kanade, T.: Rotation invariant neural network-based face detection. In: CVPR, pp. 38–44, Springer (1998)
4. Viola, P., Jones, M.: Robust real-time object detection. Int. J. Comput. Vision **57**(2), 137–154 (2002)
5. Heusch, G., Rodriguez, Y., Marcel, S.: Local binary patterns as an image preprocessing for face authentication. In: FG, pp. 9–14. IEEE Computer Society (2006)
6. Tan, X., Triggs, B.: Enhanced local texture feature sets for face recognition under difficult lighting conditions. Trans. Image Process. **19**(6), 1635–1650 (2010)
7. Sanderson, C., Paliwal, K.K.: Fast features for face authentication under illumination direction changes. Pattern Recogn. Lett. **24**(14), 2409–2419 (2003)
8. Günther, M., Haufe, D., Würtz, R.P.: Face recognition with disparity corrected Gabor phase differences. In ICANN, volume 7552 of *LNCS*, pp. 411–418. Springer, Berlin (2012)
9. Zhang, B., Shan, S., Chen, X., Gao, W.: Histogram of Gabor phase patterns (HGPP): a novel object representation approach for face recognition. Trans. Image Process. **16**(1), 57–68 (2007)
10. Zhao, W., Krishnaswamy, A., Chellappa, R., Swets, D.L., Weng, J.: Discriminant analysis of principal components for face recognition. In: Face Recognition: From Theory to Applications, pp. 73–85. Springer, Berlin (1998)
11. Gao, W., Cao, B., Shan, S., Zhou, D., Zhang, X., Zhao, D.: The CAS-PEAL large-scale Chinese face database and baseline evaluations. In: Technical report, Joint Research & Development Laboratory for Face Recognition, Chinese Academy of Sciences (2004)
12. Zhang, W., Shan, S., Gao, W., Chen, X., Zhang, H.: Local Gabor binary pattern histogram sequence (LGBPHS): a novel non-statistical model for face representation and recognition. In: ICCV, vol. 1, pp. 786–791. IEEE Computer Society (2005)
13. Wallace, R., McLaren, M., McCool, C., Marcel, S.: Cross-pollination of normalization techniques from speaker to face authentication using Gaussian mixture models. Trans. Inf. Forensics Secur. **7**(2), 553–562 (2012)
14. El Shafey, L., McCool, C., Wallace, R., Marcel, S.: A scalable formulation of probabilistic linear discriminant analysis: Applied to face recognition. Trans. Pattern Anal. Mach. Intell. **35**(7), 1788–1794 (2013)
15. McCool, C. et al.: Bi-modal person recognition on a mobile phone: using mobile phone data. In: ICME Workshop on Hot Topics in Mobile Multimedia, pp. 635–640. IEEE Computer Society (2012)
16. Huang, G.B., Ramesh, M., Berg, T., Learned-Miller, E.G.: Labeled faces in the wild: a database for studying face recognition in unconstrained environments. In: Technical report, University of Massachusetts, Amherst (2007)
17. Wolf, L., Hassner, T., Maoz, I.: Face recognition in unconstrained videos with matched background similarity. In: Proceedings of the IEEE Conference on Computer Vision and Pattern Recognition (2011
18. Gross, R., Matthews, I., Cohn, J., Kanade, T., Baker, S.: Multi-PIE. Image Vis. Comput. **28**(5), 807–813 (2010)
19. Martínez, A.M., Benavente, R.: The AR face database. In: Technical Report 24, Computer Vision Center (1998)
20. Anjos, A., El Shafey, L., Wallace, R., Günther, M., McCool, C., Marcel, S.: Bob: a free signal processing and machine learning toolbox for researchers. In: ACM-MM, pp. 1449–1452. ACM press (2012)

21. Phillips, P.J., Beveridge, J.R., Draper, B.A., Givens, G., O'Toole, A.J., Bolme, D.S., Dunlop, J., Lui, Y.M., Sahibzada, H., Weimer, S.: An introduction to the good, the bad, and the ugly face recognition challenge problem. In: FG, pp. 346–353. IEEE Computer Society (2011)

22. Lui, Y.M., Bolme, D.S., Phillips, P.J., Beveridge, J.R., Draper, B.A.: Preliminary studies on the good, the bad, and the ugly face recognition challenge problem. In: CVPR Workshops, pp. 9–16. IEEE Computer Society (2012)

23. Günther, M., Wallace, R., Marcel, S.: An open source framework for standardized comparisons of face recognition algorithms. In: ECCV. Workshops and Demonstrations, volume 7585 of *LNCS*, pp. 547–556. Springer, Berlin (2012)

24. Tan, X., Chen, S., Zhou, Z.-H., Zhang, F.: Face recognition from a single image per person: a survey. Pattern Recogn. **39**, 1725–1745 (2006)

25. Serrano, Á, Martín de Diego, I., Conde, C., Cabello, E.: Recent advances in face biometrics with Gabor wavelets: a review. Pattern Recogn. Lett. **31**(5), 372–381 (2010)

26. Huang, D., Shan, C., Ardabilian, M., Wang, Y., Chen, L.: Local binary patterns and its application to facial image analysis: a survey. Syst. Man Cybern. Part C: Appl. Rev. **41**(6), 765–781 (2011)

27. Jafri, R., Arabnia, H.R.: A survey of face recognition techniques. J. Inf. Process. Syst. **5**(2), 41–68 (2009)

28. Shen, L., Bai, L.: A review on Gabor wavelets for face recognition. Pattern Anal. Appl. **9**(2), 273–292 (2006)

29. Vandewalle, P., Kovacevic, J., Vetterli, M.: Reproducible research in signal processing—what, why, and how. IEEE Signal Process. Mag. **26**(3), 37–47 (2009)

30. Vandewalle, P.: Code sharing is associated with research impact in image processing. Comput. Sci. Eng. **14**(4), 42–47 (2012)

31. Ko, K.: User's guide to NIST biometric image software (NBIS). In: Technical report, NIST Interagency/Internal Report (NISTIR)—7392 (2007)

32. Klontz, J.C., Klare, B.F., Klum, S., Jain, A.K., Burge, M.J.: Open source biometric recognition. In: IEEE International Conference on Biometrics: Theory, Applications and Systems (BTAS), pp. 1–8 (2013)

33. Messer, K., Matas, J., Kittler, J., Luettin, J., Maitre, G.: XM2VTSDB: the extended M2VTS database. In: AVBPA, pp. 72–77. LNCS (1999)

34. Martin, A., Przybocki, M., Campbell, J.P.: The NIST Speaker Recognition Evaluation Program, chapter 8. Springer, Berlin (2005)

35. Günther, M. et al.: The 2013 face recognition evaluation in mobile environment. In: The 6th IAPR International Conference on Biometrics (2013)

36. Khoury, E. et al.: The 2013 speaker recognition evaluation in mobile environment. In: The 6th IAPR International Conference on Biometrics (2013)

37. Bansé, A.D., Doddington, G.R., Garcia-Romero, D., Godfrey, J.J., Greenberg, C.S., McCree, A.F.M., Przybocki, M., Reynolds, D.A.: Summary and initial results of the 2013–2014 speaker recognition i-vector machine learning challenge. In: Fifteenth Annual Conference of the International Speech Communication Association (2014)

38. O'Toole, A.J., Phillips, P.J., Jiang, F., Ayyad, J., Penard, N., Abdi, H.: Face recognition algorithms surpass humans matching faces over changes in illumination. IEEE Trans. Pattern Anal. Mach. Intell. **29**, 1642–1646 (2007)

39. Burton, A.M., Wilson, S., Cowan, M., Bruce, V.: Face recognition in poor-quality video: Evidence from security surveillance. Psychol. Sci. **10**(3), 243248 (1999)

40. Grgic, M., Delac, K., Grgic, S.: SCface–surveillance cameras face database. Multimedia Tools Appl. **51**(3), 863–879 (2011)

41. Beveridge, J.R., Phillips, P.J., Bolme, D.S., Draper, B.A., Givens, G.H., Lui, Y.M., Teli, M. N., Zhang, H., Scruggs, W.T., Bowyer, K.W., Flynn, P.J., Cheng, S.: The challenge of face recognition from digital point-and-shoot cameras. In: 2013 IEEE Sixth International Conference on Biometrics: Theory, Applications and Systems (BTAS), pp. 1–8 (2013)

42. Taigman, Y., Yang, M., Ranzato, M.'A., Wolf, L.: DeepFace: closing the gap to human-level performance in face verification. In: Conference on Computer Vision and Pattern Recognition (CVPR) (2014)
43. Y. Sun, X. Wang, and X. Tang. Deeply learned face representations are sparse, selective, and robust. CoRR (2014)
44. Lu, C., Tang, X.: Learning the face prior for Bayesian face recognition. In: Computer Vision ECCV 2014, volume 8692 of Lecture Notes in Computer Science. Springer International Publishing, Switzerland (2014)
45. Moghaddam, B., Wahid, W., Pentland, A.: Beyond eigenfaces: probabilistic matching for face recognition. In: FG, pp. 30–35. IEEE Computer Society (1998)
46. Beveridge, J.R., Zhang, H., Flynn, P.J., Lee, Y., Liong, V.E., Lu, J., de Assis Angeloni, M., de Freitas Pereira, T., Li, H., Hua G., Struc, V., Krizaj, J., Phillips, P.J.: The IJCB 2014 PaSC video face and person recognition competition. In: IEEE International Joint Conference on Biometrics IJCB, pp. 1–8 (2014)
47. Li, H., Hua, G., Shen, X., Lin, Z., Brandt, J.: Eigen-PEP for video face recognition. In: Asian Conference on Computer Vision (ACCV) (2014)
48. Cox, D., Pinto, N.: Beyond simple features: a large-scale feature search approach to unconstrained face recognition. In: Automatic Face Gesture Recognition and Workshops (FG 2011), 2011 IEEE International Conference on, pp. 8–15, Mar 2011
49. Ruiz-del Solar, J., Verschae, R., Correa, M.: Recognition of faces in unconstrained environments: A comparative study. EURASIP J. Adv. Signal Process. **2009**(1), 2009
50. McCool, C., Wallace, R., McLaren, M., El Shafey, L., Marcel, S.: Session variability modeling for face authentication. IET Biometrics **2**(3), 117–129 (2013)
51. Khoury, E., Günther, M., El Shafey, L., Marcel, S.: On the improvements of uni-modal and bi-modal fusions of speaker and face recognition for mobile biometrics. In: Biometric Technologies in Forensic Science, Oct 2013
52. C. Atanasoaei. *Multivariate Boosting with Look-up Tables for Face Processing*. PhD thesis, EPFL, 2012
53. Uřičář, M., Franc, V., Hlaváč, V.: Detector of facial landmarks learned by the structured output SVM. In: Csurka, G., Braz, J. (eds.) VISAPP '12: Proceedings of the 7th International Conference on Computer Vision Theory and Applications, vol. 1, pp. 547–556. SciTePress (2012)
54. K. Ram'ırez-Guti'errez, D. Cruz-P'erez, and H. P'erez-Meana. Face recognition and verification using histogram equalization. In ACS, WSEAS, 85–89 (2010)
55. H.Wang, S. Z. Li, and Y.Wang. Face recognition under varying lighting conditions using self quotient image. In FG. IEEE Computer Society, 819–824, (2004)
56. L. Wiskott, J.-M. Fellous, N. Kr¨uger, and C. van der Malsburg. Face recognition by elastic bunch graph matching. Transactions on Pattern Analysis and Machine Intelligence, **19**, 775–779 (1997)
57. M. G¨unther. Statistical Gabor Graph Based Techniques for the Detection, Recognition, Classification, and Visualization of Human Faces. PhD thesis, Institut f¨ur Neuroinformatik, Technische Universit¨at Ilmenau, Germany (2011)
58. González Jiménez, D., Bicego, M., Tangelder, J.W.H., Schouten, B.A.M., Ambekar, O.O., Alba-Castro, J., Grosso, E., Tistarelli, M.: Distance measures for Gabor jets-based face authentication: a comparative evaluation. In: ICB, pp. 474–483. Springer (2007)
59. W. Zhang, S. Shan, L. Qing, X. Chen, and W. Gao. Are Gabor phases really useless for face recognition? Pattern Analysis & Applications, **12**, 301–307 (2009)
60. T. Ojala, M. Pietik¨ainen, and D. Harwood. A comparative study of texture measures with classification based on featured distributions. Pattern Recognition, **29**(1):51–59 (1996)
61. T. Ojala, M. Pietik¨ainen, and T. M¨aenp¨a¨a. Multiresolution gray-scale and rotation invariant texture classification with local binary patterns. Transactions on Pattern Analysis and Machine Intelligence, **24**(7):971–987 2002
62. T. Ahonen, A. Hadid, and M. Pietikainen. Face recognition with local binary patterns. In ECCV. Springer, 469–481 (2004)

63. F. Cardinaux, C. Sanderson, and S. Marcel. Comparison of MLP and GMM classifiers for face verification on XM2VTS. In AVBPA, volume 2688 of LNCS, 911–920. Springer, (2003)
64. D. A. Reynolds, T. F. Quatieri, and R. B. Dunn. Speaker verification using adapted Gaussian mixture models. Digital Signal Processing, 10(1-3):19–41 (2000)
65. J.-L. Gauvain and C.-H. Lee. Maximum a posteriori estimation for multivariate Gaussian mixture observations of Markov chains. Transactions on Speech and Audio Processing, 2 (2):291–298 (1994)
66. F. Cardinaux, C. Sanderson, and S. Bengio. User authentication via adapted statistical models of face images. Transactions on Signal Processing, 54(1):361–373 (2006)
67. R. J. Vogt and S. Sridharan. Explicit modelling of session variability for speaker verification. Computer Speech & Language, 22(1):17–38 (2008)
68. Wallace, R., McLaren, M., McCool, C., Marcel, S.: Inter-session variability modeling and joint factor analysis for face authentication. In: IJCB, pp. 1–8. IEEE (2011)
69. A. K. Jain, P. Flynn, and A. A. Ross. Handbook of Biometrics. Springer, 2008
70. E. Bailly-Bailliére et al. The BANCA database and evaluation protocol. In AVBPA, volume 2688 of LNCS, SPIE, 625–638 (2003)
71. G. B. Huang, V. Jain, and E. G. Learned-Miller. Unsupervised joint alignment of complex images. In ICCV, IEEE, 1–8 (2007)
72. M. Guillaumin, J. Verbeek, and C. Schmid. Is that you? Metric learning approaches for face identification. In ICCV, IEEE, 498–505 (2009)
73. Khoury, E., El Shafey, L., McCool, C., Günther, M., Marcel, S.: Bi-modal biometric authentication on mobile phones in challenging conditions. In: Image and Vision Computing (2013)
74. Ocegueda, O., Shah, S.K., Kakadiaris, I.A.: VWhich parts of the face give out your identity? In: CVPR, pp. 641–648. IEEE Computer Society (2011)
75. Gao, W., Cao, B., Shan, S., Chen, X., Zhou, D., Zhang, X., Zhao, D.: The CAS-PEAL large-scale Chinese face database and baseline evaluations. Syst. Man Cybern. Part A Syst. Hum. 38, 149–161 (2008)
76. Arashloo, S.R., Kittler, J.: Class-specific kernel fusion of multiple descriptors for face verification using multiscale binarised statistical image features. IEEE Trans. Inf. Forensics Secur. 9(12), 2100–2109 (2014)
77. Kumar, N., Berg, A.C., Belhumeur, P.N., Nayar, S.K.: Attribute and simile classifiers for face verification. In: IEEE International Conference on Computer Vision (ICCV), Oct 2009
78. Chen, D., Cao, X., Wang, L., Wen, F., Sun, J.: Bayesian face revisited: A joint formulation. In: Proceedings of the 12th European Conference on Computer Vision—Volume Part III, pp. 566–579 (2012)
79. Khoury, E., Senac, C., Joly, P.: Face-and-clothing based people clustering in video content. In: Proceedings of the International Conference on Multimedia Information Retrieval, MIR '10, pp. 295–304. ACM, New York, NY, USA, (2010)
80. A. Dutta, M. Günther, L. El Shafey, S. Marcel, R. Veldhuis, and L. Spreeuwers. Impact of eye detection error on face recognition performance. *IET Biometrics*, 2014
81. Auckenthaler, R., Carey, M., Lloyd-Thomas, H.: Score normalization for text-independent speaker verification systems. Digit. Signal Proc. 10(1), 42–54 (2000)
82. Barr, J.R., Bowyer, K.W., Flynn, P.J., Biswas, S.: Face recognition from video: a review. Int. J. Pattern Recogn. Artif. Intell. 26(5) (2012)
83. Müller, M.K., Tremer, M., Bodenstein, C., Würtz, R.P.: Learning invariant face recognition from examples. Neural Netw. 41:137–146 (2013)

Chapter 12
Face Recognition with RGB-D Images Using Kinect

Gaurav Goswami, Mayank Vatsa and Richa Singh

Abstract Face Recognition is one of the most extensively researched problems in biometrics, and many techniques have been proposed in the literature. While the performance of automated algorithms is close to perfect in constrained environments with controlled illumination, pose, and expression variations, recognition in unconstrained environments is still difficult. To mitigate the effect of some of these challenges, researchers have proposed to utilize 3D images which can encode much more information about the face than 2D images. However, due to sensor cost, 3D face images are expensive to capture. On the other hand, RGB-D images obtained using consumer-level devices such as the Kinect, which provide pseudo-depth data in addition to a visible spectrum color image, have a trade-off between quality and cost. In this chapter, we discuss existing RGB-D face recognition algorithms and present a state-of-the-art algorithm based on extracting discriminatory features using entropy and saliency from RGB-D images. We also present an overview of available RGB-D face datasets along with experimental results and analysis to understand the various facets of RGB-D face recognition.

12.1 Introduction

Face recognition with 2D images is a highly challenging problem especially in the presence of covariates such as pose, illumination, and expression [30]. These covariates can adversely influence the characteristics of a face image and reduce the accuracy of recognition algorithms. Research in face recognition has focused on

G. Goswami · M. Vatsa (✉) · R. Singh
Indraprastha Institute of Information Technology, Delhi, India
e-mail: mayank@iiitd.ac.in

G. Goswami
e-mail: gauravgs@iiitd.ac.in

R. Singh
e-mail: rsingh@iiitd.ac.in

© Springer International Publishing Switzerland 2016   281
T. Bourlai (ed.), *Face Recognition Across the Imaging Spectrum*,
DOI 10.1007/978-3-319-28501-6_12

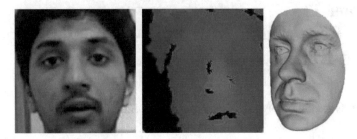

Fig. 12.1 From *left* to *right*: traditional 2D color image, depth map captured using Kinect, and traditional 3D image. Images taken from [5, 17]

developing novel methodologies to overcome these challenges individually or in combination. A fundamental problem with utilizing 2D color images for face recognition is that each captured image can only capture limited information about a face. In contrast, 3D images, captured using a 3D sensor, can capture more information about a face and preserve higher degree of facial information in unconstrained conditions compared to a 2D image. Although various 3D face recognition algorithms have been developed, the high cost of specialized 3D sensors has inhibited *en masse* deployment of such technologies in practical applications.

With the recent advancements in sensor technology, low-cost consumer-level RGB-D sensors have been developed that provide pseudo-3D information. A typical RGB-D image consists of a 2D color image (RGB) along with a depth map (D). The RGB image provides texture and appearance of a face, whereas the depth map provides the distance of each pixel from the sensor. In this manner, the depth map encodes the geometry of the face with point distances captured in the form of grayscale values. As illustrated in Fig. 12.1, an RGB-D image captured using low-cost devices such as the Kinect[1] is fundamentally different from a 3D image captured using range sensors. Kinect is developed by Microsoft for use with video games as a motion and audio capture device. Its primary purpose is to enable the users of the device to substitute traditional control mechanisms with gesture and voice-based controls. However, a Kinect device is also capable of capturing infrared, depth, video, and audio data. It captures an RGB-D image by means of an infrared laser projector which is combined with a monochrome CMOS sensor. 3D sensors, on the other hand, utilize specialized high-quality sensors to obtain accurate range and texture images. Traditional 3D face recognition approaches utilize techniques such as principal component analysis (PCA) [47] and linear discriminant analysis (LDA) [51] to characterize a 3D face model [1]. Some approaches also utilize facial landmarks identified in a 3D face model to extract local features [1]. However, 3D face recognition algorithms generally rely on accurate 3D data points. Since the depth map provided by RGB-D Kinect sensor is

---

[1]In this chapter, we refer to the Microsoft Kinect sensor as Kinect.

not as precise as a 3D sensor and contains noise in the form of holes and spikes, existing 3D face recognition approaches may not be directly applicable to RGB-D images. While RGB-D images have been used for several computer vision tasks such as object tracking, face detection, gender recognition, and robot vision, their use for face recognition is quite limited. In this chapter, we discuss the challenges and advantages of RGB-D face recognition using Kinect. We also present a state-of-the-art algorithm for RGB-D face recognition and discuss its methodology and experimental results on multiple RGB-D databases.

12.2 Literature Review

With the availability of low-cost RGB-D sensors, several research directions, including object recognition and tracking, have been explored [14, 20, 21, 23, 26, 41]. However, in the face recognition literature, very few algorithms using RGB-D have been proposed. In this section, we present an overview of some of the existing algorithms for face recognition using RGB-D images obtained with Kinect.

12.2.1 Discriminant Color Space Transform and Sparse Coding-Based RGB-D Face Recognition [36]

Li et al. [36] have proposed an RGB-D-based face algorithm, and the steps involved in their approach are as follows:

Preprocessing: The nose tip location is a landmark which can be reliably detected from the depth map since its distance to the sensor is the least among all the points on the face. The rough location of the nose tip is utilized as a reference point, and a sphere of 8 cm radius is utilized to crop the face in 3D space. In order to obtain a pose-normalized face model, each face is aligned to a frontal pose by utilizing a 128 × 128 pixel reference face model. This face model is defined by using images from the publicly available FRGC [40] and UWA [39] datasets. Face images in all the training and query images are aligned to this reference face model by using six iterations of the iterative closest point (ICP) algorithm [7]. Depth data is prone to noise in the form of missing values (holes) and false value fluctuations (spikes). The symmetry of the human face is exploited in dealing with such values. The pose is corrected using alignment to the reference face model, and a mirror point cloud is created. A mirror point is rejected if it is close (below a threshold distance) to a point in the original point cloud; otherwise, it is merged with the original data. This step is performed in order to avoid replacing the original data with existing neighbors by a mirror point. After this symmetric filling, smooth resampling is performed by fitting a smooth surface to the point cloud. Resampling serves three purposes: noise removal, filling any remaining holes, and reducing face misalignment. As a final preprocessing step, the RGB and depth matrices are down-sampled from 128×128 pixels to 32×32 pixels.

DCS Transform: In order to improve the separability of face images, the discriminant color space (DCS) transform is applied on the RGB image [50]. The DCS transform is similar to LDA, which tries to maximize the intra-class separability by utilizing linear combinations of the original R, G, and B components and reducing the inter-component correlation. The obtained DCS texture image has three channels which are stacked together into an augmented vector in order to convert it to a feature vector which can be utilized for classification.

Sparse Coding: The sparse representation classier (SRC) is a robust classifier which has performed well in face recognition [49]. It is also able to handle missing or error-prone data. It is used to correct the small errors introduced during the preprocessing steps involved in the algorithm. These errors arise due to the fact that the human face is not perfectly symmetric and even one half of the face might not be properly visible in a profile view image. SRC is applied on the preprocessed depth map and the DCS color texture separately to obtain two similarity scores. The scores are normalized using the z-score normalization technique [29] and then combined using sum rule. A recognition decision is made for probe images depending on the combined similarity score.

12.2.2 Continuous 3D Face Authentication Using RGB-D Cameras [43]

Using the Kinect sensor, Segundo et al. [43] have proposed a continuous 3D face authentication system based on histogram of oriented gradient (HOG) [12] features. The two major steps involved in the algorithm are as follows:

Face Detection and Alignment: Depth map is used to compute a 2D projection of the face which is able to provide the real face size. The Viola-Jones face detection algorithm is then applied for face detection in the color image by only considering a search window size obtained using the projection so that false alarms can be reduced. Each face image is then aligned using the ICP algorithm to an average face image obtained using 943 images from the FRGC dataset [40]. Three regions of interest (ROIs) are extracted from the face image: one centered on the nose region and the two halves of the face. Based on the pose of each RGB-D image, one of these three ROIs is selected for feature extraction.

Feature Extraction and Matching: ROI extracted from the face image is resized to 64×64, and HOG features are extracted. L_1 norm of the probe and gallery image feature vectors is used as the distance measure. If the gallery of a subject contains multiple images, then the median distance is used. This match score is utilized to perform recognition, and the probe is assigned the label of the subject with the best match score.

12.2.3   RGB-D Face Recognition Robust to Head Pose Changes [10]

Ciaccio et al. [10] have proposed a method which utilizes a single gallery RGB-D image of a subject to render new face images at different pose angles for pose invariant recognition. The steps involved in their approach are briefly summarized below:

Face Detection: The algorithm utilizes both color image and depth map for face detection, normalization, and cropping. The face itself is detected in the color domain by using the approach proposed by Zhu and Ramanan [53] based on tree-structured part models. Noise removal and smoothing of the depth map are performed by filtering with a median filter followed by a Gaussian filter. The authors note that while the same approach can also be applied to perform fiducial point detection to detect nose tip, eye corners, and mouth corners, nose tip location obtained using the depth map is more accurate. Finally, background subtraction is performed on the RGB image by identifying background pixels with the help of the depth map, and precise face coordinates are detected.

Face Rotation: Each RGB-D gallery face image is used to generate a set of faces with different pose angles. The center of each head is estimated using the nose tip with an offset of $\delta = 50$ *mm*. Each head is rotated around the y-axis using a transformation (Eq. 12.1):

$$
\begin{bmatrix} x' \\ y' \\ z' \\ 1 \end{bmatrix} = \begin{bmatrix} \cos(\theta) & 0 & \sin(\theta) & x_0 \\ 0 & 1 & 0 & 0 \\ -\sin(\theta) & 0 & \cos(\theta) & z_0 \\ 0 & 0 & 1 & 1 \end{bmatrix} \cdot \begin{bmatrix} x - x_0 \\ y \\ z - z_0 \\ 1 \end{bmatrix} \tag{12.1}
$$

Here, (x, y, z) denotes a 3D point on the original face surface which is mapped to the surface of the rotated head at its new location (x', y', z') with yaw angle θ, and the center of the head is denoted by (x_0, y_0, z_0). Using a single frontal face image, a set of faces with rotation angle varying from $0°$ to $90°$ in steps of $5°$ is obtained.

Face Alignment: All the faces are aligned such that the vertical distance between the eyes and the mouth is constant. Each face is cropped and resized to 60×60 for matching.

Face Representation: A patch size of 10×10 is used, and the patches are sampled with a step size of 5 pixels. The number of patches selected from each query image depends on the pose of the image. While more patches are selected from a frontal view face image, fewer patches are selected from profile view faces. The extracted features are normalized using the number of selected patches in order to account for this variance. A combination of two different descriptors, LBP [2] and covariance descriptor [44], is utilized to obtain the face representation. Instead of concatenating the two feature vectors, a probabilistic integration provides the final match score according to Eq. 12.2:

$$P(d_1, d_2) = A \cdot exp\left(\frac{-d_1}{\lambda_1}\right) \cdot exp\left(\frac{-d_2}{\lambda_2}\right) \tag{12.2}$$

Here, d_1 and d_2 denote the distances between a query and gallery face based on the covariance descriptor and the LBP descriptor, respectively. λ_1 and λ_2 are the weights for individual distance scores, and A is the normalization constant.

12.2.4 Face Recognition Using Super-Resolved 3D Models [5]

Berretti et al. [5] have recently proposed a super-resolution-based technique to create a 3D face model using depth data obtained from low-cost Kinect sensor and utilize this 3D model to perform face recognition. The steps involved in the algorithm are as follows:

Face Acquisition and Alignment: RGB-D video data is captured from the Kinect sensor, and the face tracking module of Kinect's SDK is used to track and detect faces in all the frames. The first frame of each sequence is used as the reference frame, and faces from all other frames are registered to this reference frame using the ICP algorithm. Video data is captured such that the distance between the subject's face and the sensor is fixed throughout the video sequence, and there are pose variations between frames. These pose variations are essential for the algorithm so that the cumulated data obtained by aligning these frames to the reference can provide the required data points for the estimation of the super-resolution image.

Super-Resolution: The sequence of low-resolution frames obtained during the first step is treated as a 3D point cloud. If these points are considered as lying on a low-resolution grid of size $N \times N$, a high-resolution depth map is considered as lying on a grid of size $M \times M$ where $M > N$. The resolution gain achieved by the super-resolution algorithm is M/N. The values of this high-resolution face surface are obtained by the 2D box spline model [45].

Matching: In order to perform recognition using the super-resolved face models, SIFT [38] descriptor is used to detect keypoints on the depth image. These keypoints are clustered using a hierarchical clustering method so that only the most representative keypoint can be selected from each cluster of keypoints. After the number of keypoints has been reduced using this method, *facial curves* are created from the depth map. Each *facial curve* consists of the depth values along the simplest path that connects two representative keypoints. Each image is represented by these keypoints, SIFT descriptors for these keypoints, and a set of *facial curves*. The similarity between two images is obtained by finding the pairs of corresponding keypoints and computing the distances between these keypoints using associated facial curves and SIFT descriptors.

12.2.5   RGB-D-Based Face Reconstruction and Recognition [24]

Hsu et al. [24] have proposed a 3D reconstruction and landmark based on RGB-D face recognition algorithm which also utilizes SRC as the classifier. The two major steps involved in their algorithm are as follows:

3D Reconstruction: The algorithm is based on reconstructing a 3D face image from a single 2D image by utilizing a reference 3D scan of an unrelated face [31]. Such an algorithm utilizes the reference to obtain initial estimates of three parameters required for 3D reconstruction, i.e., the surface normal for the face, albedo, and depth. These estimates are improved by using an iterative procedure. Since an RGB-D image already contains depth information, this reconstruction approach is adapted to refine the noisy depth maps. By assuming that the face surface is Lambertian, the projection of depth onto the image plane provides the 2D image. The computation of this projection depends on the surface normal and albedo which are iteratively optimized using a Lagrangian function. By minimizing the difference between this projection and the actual 2D color image, the depth map is refined.

Recognition: In order to perform alignment, the technique for landmark detection and localization proposed by Zhu and Ramanan [53] is utilized. A total of 16 landmarks for nearly frontal poses and 12 landmarks for profile poses are used for alignment. These landmarks consist of eye corners, eyebrow corners, nose and nostrils, and mouth corners. The same algorithm is also used to estimate the pose of the probe image. Based on the pose parameters estimated from the probe image, the algorithm rotates each gallery image to match the pose and also transforms the gallery image such that the distance between their facial landmarks is minimized. LBP features are used along with the SRC classifier [49] for identification.

12.2.6   Other Applications of RGB-D Face Images

Apart from face recognition research, RGB-D face images have also been utilized to solve other computer vision problems which rely on facial information. For example, Huynh et al. [26] have devised an algorithm to utilize RGB-D face images for gender recognition by encoding depth information using a weighted combination of LBP and Gradient-LBP (G-LBP). Existing 3DLBP [25] descriptor encodes depth differences in addition to the texture information captured by traditional

LBP. However, the authors mention that 3DLBP suffers from various shortcomings: large feature length, highly sensitive encoding, and loss of sign information associated with the depth values. They propose the Gradient-LBP descriptor to address these limitations. The algorithm was tested on the EURECOM [26] and Texas 3DFR [19] datasets achieving 99.36 % gender recognition accuracy.

Jasek et al. [21] have utilized RGB-D images obtained using Kinect to perform face detection. Given an image where the face has to be detected, the algorithm first utilizes the depth information to reduce the search space by selecting the region closest to the sensor. A mean filter of size 13×13 is used to fill holes in the depth map, and then, face candidate regions are selected based on curvature analysis and HK classification [6]. These techniques are utilized to find nose and eye candidates followed by triangulation to create a face triangle. Candidate face triangles are pruned using basic facial geometry rules and then converted to a frontal pose. A PCA-based method is then utilized to validate the face candidate based on a threshold on the reconstruction error.

RGB-D images have also been extensively utilized in tracking head pose variations. Li et al. [37] have proposed an algorithm which utilizes ICP to perform face tracking throughout a RGB-D video. For each video, it performs face and nose detection in the first frame to obtain an initialization for the ICP algorithm which can then provide an accurate tracking for the head. By performing face registration with ICP, the head rotation parameter can be obtained which is utilized to estimate the pose. The algorithm also utilizes predictors tuned on head pose data which can predict the head pose for a frame based on data from the previous frames. By using the predictor to provide an initialization for the ICP algorithm, the computational complexity of the algorithm can be significantly reduced. The algorithm achieves encouraging results on a test sequence of 717 frames.

Kim et al. [32] have presented a comparison of existing local subspace methods in head pose estimation which use RGB-D sensors. By utilizing the RGB-D data of frontal images during training, a 3D point cloud can be created. Synthetic training data for different poses can be created using these point clouds by applying appropriate transformation and projection operations. These images are then clustered using K-means clustering, and a locally optimum subspace is created for each cluster using PCA. During testing, the RGB-D image is assigned to a subspace based on minimum reconstruction error. The pose label of the closest training image in this subspace is assigned to the test image.

12.3   The RISE + ADM Algorithm

This section explains the proposed RISE + ADM algorithm. The RISE + ADM algorithm [18] utilizes both the color and depth components of the RGB-D image to extract discriminatory information. Traditionally, depth map information has been used only for face detection and pose normalization. We present a different perspective; while the color image provides texture features, depth map can provide geometric features. The algorithm combines these features to improve the recognition performance. The algorithm is comprised of four major steps: (a) preprocessing, (b) computing discriminative features from both color image and depth map using entropy, saliency, and HOG, (c) extracting additional features based on face geometry from depth map, and (d) combining these features for recognition. Each of these steps are explained below.

Preprocessing Viola-Jones face detection is used to detect faces from the RGB images. Assuming that the depth map and RGB image are registered to each other, i.e., both RGB and depth sensors are calibrated, and there is a one-to-one correspondence in their pixel locations, the bounding box obtained from RGB image can be used to extract the face from the depth map as well. Both of these regions are resized to 100×100 and converted to grayscale before further processing. As mentioned previously, the depth map obtained from a Kinect sensor contains holes and spikes. To reduce the impact of holes and spikes from the depth map, it is divided into patches of size 25×25 and the values detected as holes and spikes (based on deviation from the mean value of the patch) are estimated using linear interpolation.

RISE (RGB-D Image descriptor based on Saliency and Entropy) Algorithm It is observed that RGB-D images produced by low-cost sensors such as the Kinect have high inter-class similarity and are of low quality; therefore, traditional range image-based recognition algorithms cannot be applied directly. However, these depth maps can be utilized in landmark localization and also provide rough geometric characteristics of the face. Utilizing these depth maps in combination with the color image can provide discriminatory features and thereby improve the

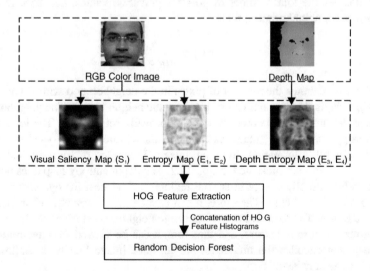

Fig. 12.2 An overview of the proposed RISE algorithm. The RGB color image provides texture of the face image, and the depth map encodes the distance of each pixel on the face from the sensor and therefore captures structural information about the face

robustness and accuracy of face recognition. As shown in Fig. 12.2, the RISE algorithm has three main steps:

(1) *Extracting Entropy Map and Visual Saliency Map:* With low-cost sensors, the RGB values in the 2D color image and the depth values in the depth map are of relatively low quality and prone to noise. With depth map, the raw values are not useful for characterizing the face image and the RGB values of the color image are highly sensitive to change in imaging conditions. Therefore, the RISE algorithm uses entropy as a layer of abstraction in order to process these values and obtain an intermediate representation before feature extraction is performed. Entropy can be defined as the measure of uncertainty in a random variable [42]. Similarly, the local visual entropy of an image is a measure of the variance in grayscale levels of pixels in a local neighborhood, e.g., 5×5. Let the input RGB-D image be denoted as $[I_{rgb}(x, y), I_d (x, y)]$, where $I_{rgb}(x, y)$ is the RGB image and $I_d (x, y)$ is the depth map, both of size $M \times N$. Let both of these be defined over the same set of (x, y) points such that $x \in [1, M]$ and $y \in [1, N]$. Let $H(I_j)$ denote the visual entropy map of image I_j. Here, I_j can be the depth map or the RGB image or a small part of these images. The entropy H of an image neighborhood x is given by Eq. 12.3,

$$H(\mathbf{x}) = - \sum_{i=1}^{n} p(x_i) \log_2 p(x_i) \qquad (12.3)$$

where $p(x_i)$ is the probability mass function for x_i. For an image, $p(x_i)$ signifies the probability that a pixel with value x_i is contained in the neighborhood and n denotes the total number of possible grayscale values, i.e., 255. If x is a $M_H \times N_H$ neighborhood, then

$$p(x_i) = \frac{n_{x_i}}{M_H \times N_H} \qquad (12.4)$$

Here, n_{xi} denotes the number of pixels in the neighborhood with value x_i, and $M_H \times N_H$ is the total number of pixels in the neighborhood. The neighborhood size for entropy map computation is empirically set to 5×5. The local visual entropy map of an image can encode its texture and be used to extract meaningful information from an image. Examples of entropy and depth entropy maps are presented in Fig. 12.2. The depth entropy map does not vary in value abruptly except in special regions such as near the eye sockets, nose tip, mouth, and chin. Therefore, it can encode these geometric characteristics of the face. The local entropy of an image neighborhood measures the amount of randomness in texture, and therefore, it can be viewed as a texture feature map that encodes the uniqueness of the face image locally and allows for robust feature extraction.

Both I_{rgb} and I_d are divided into patches. Two patches, P_1 of size $\frac{M}{2} \times \frac{N}{2}$ centered at $\left[\frac{M}{2} \times \frac{N}{2}\right]$ and P_2 of size $\frac{3M}{4} \times \frac{3N}{4}$ centered at $\left[\frac{M}{2} \times \frac{N}{2}\right]$, are extracted from I_{rgb}. Similarly, two patches P_3 and P_4 are extracted from I_d. For every patch, an entropy map $(E_1 - E_4)$ is computed for patches using Eq. 12.5:

$$E_i = H(P_i), \quad \text{where } i \in [1,4] \tag{12.5}$$

E_1 and E_2 represent the entropy of the color image (I_{rgb}), and E_3 and E_4 represent the depth entropy maps.

The RISE algorithm also extracts visual saliency map S_1 of the color image I_{rgb} using Eq. 12.6. It measures the capability of local image regions to attract the viewer's visual attention [13]. A visual saliency map provides an estimate of this capability as a numerical value for every pixel of an image. There are several approaches to compute the visual saliency map. In this algorithm, we utilize a relatively simple approach proposed by Itti et al. [28].

$$S_1(x,y) = S(I_{rgb}(x,y) \forall (x \in [1,M], y \in [1,N])) \tag{12.6}$$

(2) *Extracting Features Using HOG:* The high dimensionality of each entropy/saliency map is too high to be considered directly as input for a classifier. Moreover, since the depth entropy map does not contain large local variations, it is redundant to consider the value of each pixel. A histogram-oriented approach such as HOG enables a powerful representation which preserves the discriminative power of each feature map while simultaneously reducing feature size and facilitating robust matching. HOG [12] is a well-known descriptor which has been successfully used as a feature and texture descriptor in many computer vision applications related to object detection and recognition [11, 16, 46]. HOG vector of an entropy map or saliency map encodes the gradient direction and magnitude of the image variances in a fixed length feature vector.

In the proposed RISE algorithm, HOG is applied on the entropy and saliency maps. The entropy maps are extracted from patches P_i, which allows capturing multiple granularities of the input image. Let $D(\cdot)$ denote the HOG histogram; the algorithm computes HOG of entropy maps using the following equation:

$$F_i = D(E_i), \quad \text{where } i \in [1,4] \tag{12.7}$$

Here, F_1 denotes the HOG of entropy map E_1 defined over patch P_1, and F_2 denotes the HOG vector of entropy map E_2 defined over patch P_2 of I_{rgb}. Similarly, F_3 and F_4 denote the HOG of entropy maps E_3 and E_4 defined over patches P_3 and P_4 of I_d, respectively. F_1 and F_2 encode traditional texture information, and the entropy maps help the descriptor to address intra-class variations. F_3 and F_4 encode additional depth information embedded in the RGB-D image. Finally, the HOG descriptor of visual saliency map, S_1, is computed using Eq. 12.8, and the RISE descriptor F is created using an ordered concatenation of these five HOG histograms as shown in Eq. 12.9.

$$F_5 = D(S_1(I_{\text{rgb}})) \qquad (12.8)$$

$$F = [F_1, F_2, F_3, F_4, F_5] \qquad (12.9)$$

Since each HOG vector is small and the features are compatible with each other, concatenation is used to facilitate classification by reducing five vectors to a single feature vector. The resulting concatenated vector has a small size which helps in reducing the computational requirement. This feature vector F is provided as input to a multi-class classifier.

(3) *Classification:* Any multi-class classifier such as nearest neighbor (NN), random decision forest (RDF) [22], and support vector machine (SVM) can be used to perform recognition. The classifier should be robust for a large number of classes, computationally inexpensive during probe identification, and accurate. Classifiers such as SVM require a relatively large amount of training data per class in order to develop accurate decision boundaries. A RDF is an ensemble of classifiers (termed as a *forest* in the case of RDF) which can produce nonlinear decision boundaries and handle multi-class classification well. RDFs also tend to be robust toward outliers since every decision tree in the forest is only trained with a small subset of data in terms of both features and data points. Therefore, the probability of an entire collection of trees making an incorrect decision due to a few outlier data points/features is very low. Recent results also support that RDF performs better than NN in this scenario [17]. Therefore, the proposed algorithm utilizes RDF classifier for matching. RDF has three parameters: the number of trees in the forest, the fraction of training samples that are used to train an individual tree, and the number of features used to represent each data point during training. These parameters control the performance of the forest and are optimized by using a parameter sweep with the training data. The gallery images for each subject are provided to the RDF for training. During testing, a probe feature vector is provided as input to the trained RDF which computes a probabilistic match score for each subject. The match score for each subject is compared, and the probe image is identified as the subject with the highest match score.

ADM (Attributes based on Depth Map) *Attribute*-based methodologies have been explored for problems such as image retrieval [33, 35] and face matching [34]. Attributes provide soft biometric information which may not be sufficient to perform recognition when considered in isolation; however, they provide additional complementary information. Usually, research has focused on demographic attributes such as age and gender or on appearance-based attributes such as complexion and friendliness. The attributes based on depth map (ADM) algorithm instead focus on geometric attributes extracted from the depth map. The distances between various key facial features such as eyes, nose, and chin can be used as geometric attributes. By exploiting the uniform nature of a human face, key facial landmarks can be located and utilized to extract geometric attributes that can be used for face recognition in conjunction with the entropy and saliency features. The ADM approach consists of the following steps.

Keypoint Labeling Key facial landmarks such as the nose tip, eye corners, and chin are identified using a *rule template* and the depth map. In a nearly frontal depth map, the nose tip is the closest point from the sensor, the two eyes are located above the nose tip and are at a relatively higher distance compared to immediate surrounding regions, and the chin is the closest point to the sensor which lies below the nose tip. These keypoints can then be utilized to triangulate and determine the approximate locations of other facial features such as nose bridge. These landmarks are detected from each gallery and probe face image and used to compute the geometric attributes.

Geometric Attribute Computation To obtain the geometric attributes, various distances between these landmark points are computed: inter-eye distance, eye to nose bridge distance, nose bridge to nose tip distance, nose tip to chin distance, nose bridge to chin distance, chin to eye distance, eyebrow length, nose tip distance to both ends of both eyebrows, and overall length of the face. Since these distances may vary across pose and expression, multiple gallery images are utilized to extract these facial features. Attributes are first computed individually for every gallery image, and the distances so obtained are averaged. In this manner, a consistent set of attributes is computed for a subject. An attribute feature vector for the depth map is created by using these distance values. These distances can also be estimated from the depth map of a single frontal pose image, although that requires pose estimation to be performed on the gallery images.

Attribute Match Score Computation The attributes for a probe are computed similar to gallery images. Once the attributes are computed for a probe, the match score Φ is computed for each subject in the gallery using Eq. 12.10.

$$\Phi = \sum_{i=1}^{N} w_i \times (A_i - a_i)^2 \qquad (12.10)$$

Here, A_i and a_i are the ith attributes of the probe image and the gallery image, respectively. w_i is the weight of the ith attribute, and N is the total number of attributes. w_i is used to assign weights to these different attributes depending upon how reliably they can be computed. The match scores thus obtained can be utilized for identification.

Combining RISE and ADM In the proposed algorithm, the ADM score is combined with the match score obtained from RISE algorithm for making the final decision. In order to combine RISE and ADM, fusion is performed at match score level with a weighted sum approach or at rank level with weighted Borda count [30]. A comparison of existing algorithms with the RISE + ADM algorithm is presented in Table 12.1.

Table 12.1 An overview of existing RGB-D recognition algorithms

Algorithm	Features	Classifier
Li et al. [37]	DCS transform [50]	SRC [49]
Segundo et al. [43]	HOG [12]	L_1 norm
Ciaccio et al. [10]	LBP [2] and covariance descriptor	Probabilistic
Berretti et al. [5]	SIFT [38]	Sparse matching [4]
Hsu et al. [24]	LBP [2]	SRC [49]
RISE + ADM	HOG [12] of entropy [42] and saliency [27] maps combined with geometric attributes extracted from depth map	RDF [22]

12.4 Existing RGB-D Face Datasets

There are a few existing RGB-D face databases in the literature. In contrast to other existing 3D datasets which have data captured using high-quality sensors, these datasets comprise of RGB-D images captured using the Kinect or other low-cost depth sensors. Among the first ones, the EURECOM [26] database has 936 images pertaining to 52 subjects and the images are captured in two sessions with variations in pose, illumination, view, and occlusion. The VAP RGB-D [22] face database contains 1581 images pertaining to 31 individuals. The dataset has 51 images for each individual with variations in pose. The CurtinFaces [36] dataset contains over 5000 RGB-D images of 52 subjects. The image set for each subject contains a total of 92 faces which cover different pose, illumination, expression, and disguise conditions. The Biwi Kinect head pose dataset [15] contains over 15,000 images of 20 people with their pose annotations in the form of 3D locations of the head and its rotation. The FaceWarehouse [9] database contains data pertaining to 150 individuals with age ranging in-between 7 and 80 years. For each of these subjects, RGB-D data is available for a total of 20 expressions with variations in rotation as well. The Florence Superface (UF-S) v2.0 dataset [5] contains high-resolution 3D scans obtained using a 3dMD scanner and RGB-D Kinect video sequences pertaining to 50 individuals. The IIIT-D RGB-D face database [18] contains RGB-D images pertaining to 106 individuals captured in two sessions using Kinect sensor and OpenNI SDK. The resolution of both color image and depth map is 640 × 480. The number of images per individual is variable with a minimum of 11 images and a maximum of 254 images. In this database, the images are captured in normal illumination with variations in pose and expression (in some cases, there are variations due to eyeglasses as well). Some sample images from the IIIT-D and EURECOM databases are presented in Fig. 12.3.

(a) (b)

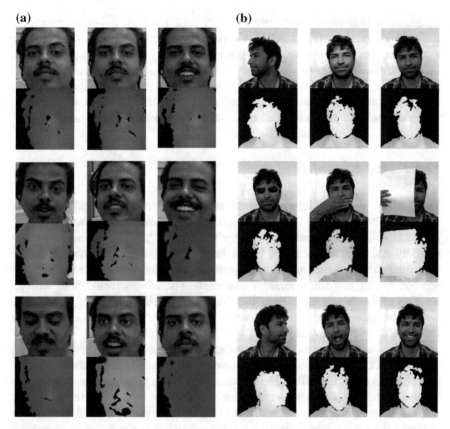

Fig. 12.3 Sample images of a subject from **a** IIIT-D Kinect RGB-D database [18] and **b** EURECOM Kinect face database [26]

12.5 Experimental Results

The performance of the proposed RISE + ADM algorithm is analyzed via two sets of experiments. First, the experiments are conducted on the IIIT-D RGB-D dataset to analyze the performance of the RISE + ADM algorithm with various combinations of constituent components and their parameters. Thereafter, the performance is compared with existing 2D and 3D approaches on an extended dataset created using a combination of multiple existing datasets.

Two types of observations are presented in the following sections. The first set of observations helps in assessing the performance improvement contributed by the individual components of the RISE + ADM algorithm. This set of observations is made on the IIIT-D RGB-D dataset. Thereafter, the IIIT-D RGB-D dataset is merged with the EURECOM and VAP datasets to create an extended dataset of 189 individuals. A second set of observations is presented on the extended dataset which provides a comparative study of RGB-D-based algorithm and traditional 2D algorithms which cannot make use of depth data. For both the experiments, the performance of the RISE + ADM algorithm is compared with several existing algorithms, namely four-patch local binary patterns (FPLBP) [48], pyramid histogram of oriented gradients (PHOG) [3], scale invariant feature transform (SIFT) [38, 52], and sparse representation [49]. Besides these methods which utilize only 2D information, a comparison is also performed with 3D-PCA-based algorithm [8], which computes a subspace based on depth and grayscale information.

12.5.1 Experiment 1

The database is divided into three parts: training, validation, and testing. 40 % of the IIIT-D Kinect RGB-D database is used for training and validation. The training dataset is utilized to compute the weights involved in ADM approach, parameters of RDF, and weights for fusion. After training and parameter optimization, the remaining 60 % dataset (unseen subjects) is used for testing. The results are computed with five times random subsampling-based cross-validation. In each iteration of the subsampling base, the subjects in the training/testing database as well as the gallery images for each subject are randomly selected. Gallery size is fixed at four images per subject.

To analyze the effect of different components involved in the proposed RISE algorithm, six cases are analyzed. These case studies provide information about the effect of each factor in the final identification performance, and they are described in Table 12.2 along with their identification accuracies at rank-1 and rank-5. It also helps in drawing inferences about how to make the best use of RGB-D data. For example, if the descriptor performs poorly in case (b), it suggests that depth entropy maps are indeed able to provide meaningful features when encoded using the HOG descriptor. Similar inferences can potentially be drawn from the results of other five cases. For example, case (c) demonstrates that the contribution of including visual

Table 12.2 Performance of the RISE algorithm with different combinations of the individual components

Case	Descriptor	Identification Accuracy (%)	
		Rank-1	Rank-5
Case (a)	$F = [F_1, F_2, F_3, F_4, F_5]\ F_i = D(P_i)$	40.0	61.9
Case (b)	$F = [F_1, F_2, F_5]$	37.5	57.6
Case (c)	$F = [F_1, F_2, F_3, F_4]$	51.6	68.6
Case (d)	$F = [F_1, F_2, F_5]\ F_i = D(P_i)$	30.0	45.0
Case (e)	$F = [F_1, F_2, F_3, F_4]\ F_i = D(P_i)$	35.4	50.2
Case (f)	$F = [F_1, F_2]$	36.3	55.0
RISE	$F = [F_1, F_2, F_3, F_4, F_5]$	82.8	92.2

The condition $F_i = D(P_i)$ signifies that the case does not utilize entropy maps and instead directly encodes the RGB-D image using HOG descriptor

Table 12.3 Identification
accuracy (%) on IIIT-D
RGB-D face database and
EURECOM database
individually. The mean
accuracy values are reported
along with standard deviation
across five cross-validation
trials

Modality	Descriptor	Rank-5 identification accuracy (%)	
		IIIT-D RGB-D	EURECOM
2D	SIFT	50.1 ± 1.4	83.8 ± 2.1
	HOG	75.1 ± 0.7	89.5 ± 0.8
	PHOG	81.6 ± 1.4	90.5 ± 1.0
	FPLBP	85.0 ± 0.7	94.3 ± 1.4
	Sparse	87.2 ± 1.9	84.8 ± 1.7
3D	3D-PCA	83.4 ± 2.1	94.1 ± 2.7
	RISE + ADM	95.3 ± 1.7	98.5 ± 1.6

saliency map as an added feature is important. It is observed that saliency is relevant toward stabilizing the feature descriptor and preserving intra-class similarities. Further, in cases (d) and (e), it is observed that including depth without computing entropy performs worse than not including depth information but using entropy maps to characterize the RGB image. Intuitively, this indicates that directly using depth map results in more performance loss than not using depth at all. This is probably due to the fact that depth data from Kinect is noisy and increases the intra-class variability in raw form. It is observed that all the factors together improve the recognition performance. Overall, the algorithm yields 95 % rank-5 accuracy on the IIIT-D database. Further, Table 12.3 shows the comparison of the proposed algorithm with existing algorithms. The results indicate that on the IIIT-D database, the proposed algorithm is about 8 % better than the second best algorithm (in this case, sparse representation [49]). Compared with 3D-PCA algorithm, the proposed algorithm is able to yield about 12 % improvement.

Fusion of algorithms Experiments are performed with various combinations of the proposed RISE and ADM approaches. At match score level, the weighted sum rule is used, and at rank level, weighted Borda count is used. The proposed RISE + ADM with weighted sum rule yields the best rank-5 identification accuracy of 95.3 %. RISE + ADM approach using weighted Borda count also performs well providing an accuracy of 79.7 %. This indicates that for RGB-D faces, match score level fusion of RISE and ADM features performs better than rank-level fusion. However, it is also notable that the difference in performance for almost all the approaches reduces more at rank-5 compared to rank-1. Since weights are involved in both weighted Borda count and weighted sum approaches, it is interesting to observe how the performance of the proposed algorithm varies with the variation in weights. Key observations are noted below:

- The best performance is achieved with RISE (0.7) + ADM (0.3) for both the fusion algorithms. This indicates that texture features extracted by RISE are more informative for identification and therefore must be assigned higher weight. However, the geometric features from ADM also contribute toward the identification performance after fusion, thereby increasing the rank-5 accuracy from 92.2 % (RISE only) to 95.3 % (RISE + ADM) when weighted sum rule is utilized.

- The performance of weighted Borda count is lower than weighted sum possibly because of the loss of information that occurs in using the ranked list for fusion instead of the match scores.
- Experiments have been conducted to assess the performance with all other combinations of weights as well, but none of these combinations perform better than RISE (0.7) + ADM (0.3).

Analysis with gallery size All the experiments described above on the IIIT-D RGB-D database are performed with a gallery size of four. To analyze the effect of gallery size on the identification performance, additional experiments are performed by varying the number of images in the gallery. The performance of RISE, ADM, and RISE + ADM, and key observations are described below:

- The performance of RISE, ADM, and the proposed RISE + ADM approach increases with increase in gallery size. However, the maximum increment is observed from gallery size 1 to gallery size 2 in the ADM approach. A major performance gain of 22.6 % is observed which can be credited to the possibility that using a single gallery image yields approximate geometric attributes. With more than one sample, the averaging process increases the reliability of the geometric attributes, and hence, there is a significant increase in performance.
- Other than the exception discussed above, the performance of each approach increases consistently but in small amounts with increase in gallery size. Therefore, after a certain point, increasing the gallery size does not provide high returns in terms of the performance. It is notable that even with single gallery image, the proposed algorithm yields the rank-5 identification accuracy of 89 % (Fig. 12.4).

Evaluating the accuracy of ADM keypoint labeling The performance of the ADM approach is dependent on the accuracy of keypoint labeling. In order to

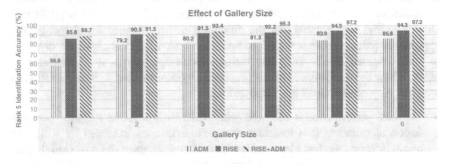

Fig. 12.4 Analyzing the effect of gallery size on recognition performance

determine the accuracy of this phase, manually marked keypoint labels are collected via crowd-sourcing. Human volunteers are requested to label the keypoints (nose, left eye, right eye, and chin) on 10 images from every subject. The average of human-annotated keypoint coordinates is computed and compared with the automatically obtained keypoints. An automatic keypoint is considered to be correct if it lies within a small local neighborhood of the average human-annotated keypoint. It is observed that the overall accuracy of automated keypoint labeling, using manual annotations as ground truth, on the IIIT-D Kinect RGB-D database, is 90.1 % with a 5 |×| 5 neighborhood and 93.6 % with a neighborhood size of 7 |×| 7. It is also observed that the automatic keypoint labeling is most accurate on near-frontal and semi-frontal faces.

Evaluating the proposed RISE + ADM algorithm on EURECOM database: Performance of the proposed algorithm was also compared with existing algorithms on the EURECOM dataset. In order to perform this recognition experiment, the gallery sizes for the EURECOM dataset were fixed at two images per subject. The results of this experiment are presented in Table 12.3. The analysis is similar to the IIIT-D database, and the proposed algorithm yields 98.5 % rank-5 identification accuracy which is around 4 % better than existing algorithms. Note that the EURECOM database is relatively smaller than IIIT-D database, and therefore, near perfect rank-5 identification accuracy is achieved.

12.5.2 Experiment 2

The extended database of 189 subjects is prepared by combining the IIIT-D [18], EURECOM [26], and VAP [21] databases used for this experiment. Images pertaining to 40 % individuals from the extended database are used for training, and the remaining 60 % unseen subjects are used for testing. To create the complete subject list for the extended dataset, the subjects are randomly subsampled within the three datasets according to 40/60 partitioning and then merged together to form one extended training/testing partition. Therefore, the extended training dataset has proportionate (40 %) representation from each of the three datasets. The number of images available per individual varies across the three datasets, and therefore, the gallery size for the extended dataset experiment is fixed at two gallery images per individual. The remaining images of the subjects are used as probes. The identification performance of these approaches is presented in Fig. 12.5 and summarized in Table 12.4. The results indicate that the proposed RISE + ADM algorithm (both weighted sum and weighted Borda count versions) outperforms the existing approaches by a difference of about 8 % in terms of the rank-5 identification performance. The proposed algorithm yields the best results at rank-1 with an accuracy of 78.9 % which is at least 11.4 % better than the second best algorithm, 3D-PCA.

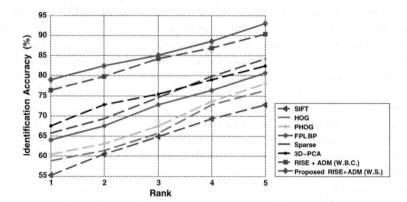

Fig. 12.5 A comparison of the RISE + ADM algorithm with other existing 2D and 3D approaches on the extended database. W.B.C. refers to rank-level fusion using weighted Borda count and W.S. refers to match score level fusion using weighted sum rule

Table 12.4 Identification accuracy (%) for the extended experiments. The mean accuracy values are reported along with standard deviation over five times random cross-validation

Modality	Descriptor	Rank-1	Rank-5
	SIFT	55.3 ± 1.7	72.8 ± 2.1
	HOG	58.8 ± 1.4	76.3 ± 1.8
2D	PHOG	60.5 ± 1.6	78.1 ± 1.1
	FPLBP	64.0 ± 1.1	80.7 ± 2.0
	Sparse	65.8 ± 0.6	84.2 ± 0.8
	3D-PCA	67.5 ± 1.2	82.5 ± 1.9
3D	RISE + ADM (W.B.C.)	76.3 ± 1.0	90.3 ± 1.1
	RISE + ADM (W.S.)	78.9 ± 1.7	92.9 ± 1.3

12.6 Conclusion

In order to maintain robustness in unconstrained environments, face recognition researchers have explored the use of 3D images instead of the traditional 2D face images. However, due to the high cost of 3D sensors, it is difficult to deploy such systems for large-scale applications. Therefore, RGB-D images obtained using consumer-level sensors such as the Kinect have gained popularity. This chapter presents a literature review of some of the existing contributions that utilize RGB-D images for accurate face recognition in the presence of variations in pose, illumination, and expression. We also present the RISE + ADM algorithm that utilizes depth, saliency, and entropy information for feature encoding and matching. Comparative results were presented to understand the various dimensions of RGB-D face recognition performance using the state-of-art algorithm. With advancements in technology and availability of consumer-level sensors in the market, future research in RGB-D face recognition can be directed toward sensor interoperability, cross-sensor recognition, and related analysis in the case of RGB-D sensors with varying specifications.

References

1. Abate, A.F., Nappi, M., Riccio, D., Sabatino, G.: 2d and 3d face recognition: a survey. Pattern Recogn. Lett. **28**(14), 1885–1906 (2007)
2. Ahonen, T., Hadid, A., Pietikainen, M.: Face recognition with local binary patterns. In: European Conference on Computer Vision, pp. 469–481 (2004)
3. Bai, Y., Guo, L., Jin, L., Huang, Q.: A novel feature extraction method using pyramid histogram of orientation gradients for smile recognition. In: International Conference on Image Processing, pp. 3305–3308 (2009)
4. Berretti, S., Del Bimbo, A., Pala, P.: Sparse matching of salient facial curves for recognition of 3-d faces with missing parts. IEEE Trans. Inf. Forensics Secur. **8**(2), 374–389 (2013)
5. Berretti, S., Pala, P., Del Bimbo, A.: Face recognition by super-resolved 3D models from consumer depth cameras. IEEE Trans. Inf. Forensics Secur. **9**(9), 1436–1449 (2014)
6. Besl, P.J., Jain, R.C.: Invariant surface characteristics for 3D object recognition in range images. Comput. Vis. Graph. Image Processing **33**(1), 33–80 (1986)
7. Besl, P.J., McKay, N.D.: Method for registration of 3-d shapes. In: Robotics-DL Tentative, pp. 586–606 (1992)
8. Bowyer, K.W., Chang, K., Flynn, P.: A survey of approaches to three-dimensional face recognition. In: International Conference on Pattern Recognition, vol. 1, pp. 358–361 (2004)
9. Cao, C., Weng, Y., Zhou, S., Tong, Y., Zhou, K.: Facewarehouse: a 3D facial expression database for visual computing. IEEE Trans. Visual Comput. Graphics **20**(3), 413–425 (2014)
10. Ciaccio, C., Wen, L., Guo, G.: Face recognition robust to head pose changes based on the RGB-D sensor. In: IEEE International Conference on Biometrics: Theory, Applications, and Systems, pp. 1–6 (2013)
11. Corvee, E., Bremond, F.: Body parts detection for people tracking using trees of histogram of oriented gradient descriptors. In: Advanced Video and Signal-Based Surveillance, pp. 469–475 (2010)
12. Dalal, N., Triggs, B.: Histograms of oriented gradients for human detection. In: Computer Vision and Pattern Recognition, vol. 1, pp. 886–893 (2005)
13. Desimone, R., Duncan, J.: Neural mechanisms of selective visual attention. Ann. Rev. Neuroscience **18**(1), 193–222 (1995)
14. Engelhard, N., Endres, F., Hess, J., Sturm, J., Burgard, W.: Real-time 3D visual slam with a hand-held RGB-D camera. In: RGB-D Workshop, European Robotics Forum (2011)
15. Fanelli, G., Dantone, M., Gall, J., Fossati, A., Van Gool, L.: Random forests for real time 3D face analysis. Int. J. Comput. Vision **101**(3), 437–458 (2013)
16. Felzenszwalb, P.F., Girshick, R.B., McAllester, D., Ramanan, D.: Object detection with discriminatively trained part-based models. IEEE Trans. Pattern Anal. Mach. Intell. **32**(9), 1627–1645 (2010)
17. Goswami, G., Bharadwaj, S., Vatsa, M., Singh, R.: On RGB-D face recognition using kinect. In: IEEE International Conference on Biometrics: Theory, Applications, and Systems (2013)
18. Goswami, G., Vatsa, M., Singh, R.: RGB-D face recognition with texture and attribute features. IEEE Trans. Inf. Forensics Secur. **9**(10), 1629–1640 (2014)
19. Gupta, S., Castleman, K., Markey, M., Bovik, A.: Texas 3D face recognition database. In: IEEE Southwest Symposium on Image Analysis & Interpretation, pp. 97–100 (2010)
20. Henry, P., Krainin, M., Herbst, E., Ren, X., Fox, D.: RGB-D mapping: Using depth cameras for dense 3D modeling of indoor environments. In: International Symposium on Experimental Robotics, vol. 20, pp. 22–25 (2010)

21. Hg, R., Jasek, P., Rofidal, C., Nasrollahi, K., Moeslund, T.B., Tranchet, G.: An RGB-D database using Microsoft's Kinect for windows for face detection. In: International Conference on Signal Image Technology and Internet Based Systems, pp. 42–46 (2012)
22. Ho, T.K.: Random decision forests. In: International Conference on Document Analysis and Recognition, pp. 278–282 (1995)
23. Holz, D., Holzer, S., Rusu, R., Behnke, S.: Real-time plane segmentation using RGB-D cameras. RoboCup **2011**, 306–317 (2012)
24. Hsu, G.S., Liu, Y.L., Peng, H.C., Wu, P.X.: RGB-D based face reconstruction and recognition. IEEE Trans. Info. Forensics Secur. **9**(12), 2110–2118 (2014)
25. Huang, Y., Wang, Y., Tan, T.: Combining statistics of geometrical and correlative features for 3D face recognition. In: British Machine Vision Conference, pp. 879–888 (2006)
26. Huynh, T., Min, R., Dugelay, J.L.: An efficient LBP-based descriptor for facial depth images applied to gender recognition using RGB-D face data. In: Asian Conference on Computer Vision (2012)
27. Itti, L., Koch, C.: Computational modeling of visual attention. Nat. Rev. Neurosci. **2**(3), 194–203 (2001)
28. Itti, L., Koch, C., Niebur, E.: A model of saliency-based visual attention for rapid scene analysis. IEEE Trans. Pattern Anal. Mach. Intell. **20**(11), 1254–1259 (1998)
29. Jain, A., Nandakumar, K., Ross, A.: Score normalization in multimodal biometric systems. Pattern Recogn. **38**(12), 2270–2285 (2005)
30. Jain, A.K., Li, S.Z.: Handbook of face recognition. Springer, New York, Inc. (2005)
31. Kemelmacher-Shlizerman, I., Basri, R.: 3D face reconstruction from a single image using a single reference face shape. IEEE Trans. Pattern Anal. Mach. Intell. **33**(2), 394–405 (2011)
32. Kim, D., Park, J., Kak, A.C.: Estimating head pose with an RGB-D sensor: a comparison of appearance-based and pose-based local subspace methods. In: International Conference on Image Processing, pp. 3637–3641 (2013)
33. Kovashka, A., Parikh, D., Grauman, K.: Whittlesearch: image search with relative attribute feedback. In: In IEEE Computer Society Conference on Computer Vision and Pattern Recognition, pp. 2973–2980 (2012)
34. Kumar, N., Berg, A.C., Belhumeur, P.N., Nayar, S.K.: Attribute and simile classifiers for face verification. In: International Conference on Computer Vision, pp. 365–372 (2009)
35. Kun, D., Parikh, D., Crandall, D., Grauman, K.: Discovering localized attributes for fine-grained recognition. In: Computer Vision and Pattern Recognition, pp. 3474–3481 (2012)
36. Li, B.Y.L., Mian, A.S., Liu, W., Krishna, A.: Using kinect for face recognition under varying poses, expressions, illumination and disguise. In: Workshop on the Applications of Computer Vision, pp. 186–192 (2013)
37. Li, S., Ngan, K.N., Sheng, L.: A head pose tracking system using RGB-D camera. In: Computer Vision Systems, pp. 153–162 (2013)
38. Lowe, D.G.: Object recognition from local scale-invariant features. In: International Conference on Computer Vision, vol. 2, pp. 1150–1157 (1999)
39. Mian, A.: Illumination invariant recognition and 3D reconstruction of faces using desktop optics. Opt. Express **19**(8), 7491–7506 (2011)
40. Phillips, P., Flynn, P., Scruggs, T., Bowyer, K., Chang, J., Hoffman, K., Marques, J., Min, J., Worek, W.: Overview of the face recognition grand challenge. In: IEEE Computer Society Conference on Computer Vision and Pattern Recognition, vol. 1, pp. 947–954 (2005)
41. Ramey, A., Gonzalez-Pacheco, V., Salichs, M.A.: Integration of a low-cost RGB-D sensor in a social robot for gesture recognition. In: Human-Robot Interaction, pp. 229–230 (2011)
42. Rrnyi, A.: On measures of entropy and information. In: Berkeley Symposium on Mathematical Statistics and Probability, pp. 547–561 (1961)
43. Segundo, M.P., Sarkar, S., Goldgof, D., Bellon, L.S.O.: Continuous 3D face authentication using RGB-D cameras. In: Computer Vision and Pattern Recognition Biometrics Workshop (2013)
44. Tuzel, O., Porikli, F., Meer, P.: Region covariance: A fast descriptor for detection and classification. In: European Conference on Computer Vision, pp. 589–600 (2006)

45. Unser, M., Aldroubi, A., Eden, M.: B-spline signal processing. I. theory. IEEE Trans. Signal Process. **41**(2), 821–833 (1993)
46. Wang, C., Guan, L.: Graph cut video object segmentation using histogram of oriented gradients. In: International Symposium on Circuits and Systems, pp. 2590–2593 (2008)
47. Wold, S., Esbensen, K., Geladi, P.: Principal component analysis. Chemometr. Intell. Lab. Syst. **2**(1), 37–52 (1987)
48. Wolf, L., Hassner, T., Taigman, Y., et al.: Descriptor based methods in the wild. In: European Conference on Computer Vision Real Faces Workshop (2008)
49. Wright, J., Yang, A.Y., Ganesh, A., Sastry, S.S., Ma, Y.: Robust face recognition via sparse representation. IEEE Trans. Pattern Anal. Mach. Intell. **31**(2), 210–227 (2009)
50. Yang, J., Liu, C.: Color image discriminant models and algorithms for face recognition. IEEE Trans. Neural Netw. **19**(12), 2088–2098 (2008)
51. Ye, J., Janardan, R., Li, Q.: Two-dimensional linear discriminant analysis. In: Advances in Neural Information Processing Systems, pp. 1569–1576 (2004)
52. Zhang, L., Chen, J., Lu, Y., Wang, P.: Face recognition using scale invariant feature transform and support vector machine. In: International Conference for Young Computer Scientists, pp. 1766–1770 (2008)
53. Zhu, X., Ramanan, D.: Face detection, pose estimation, and landmark localization in the wild. In: IEEE Conference on Computer Vision and Pattern Recognition, pp. 2879–2886. IEEE (2012)

Chapter 13
Blending 2D and 3D Face Recognition

M. Tistarelli, M. Cadoni, A. Lagorio and E. Grosso

Abstract Over the last decade, performance of face recognition algorithms systematically improved. This is particularly impressive when considering very large or challenging datasets such as the FRGC v2 or Labelled Faces in the Wild. A better analysis of the structure of the facial texture and shape is one of the main reasons of improvement in recognition performance. Hybrid face recognition methods, combining holistic and feature-based approaches, also allowed to increase efficiency and robustness. Both photometric information and shape information allow to extract facial features which can be exploited for recognition. However, both sources, grey levels of image pixels and 3D data, are affected by several noise sources which may impair the recognition performance. One of the main difficulties in matching 3D faces is the detection and localization of distinctive and stable points in 3D scans. Moreover, the large amount of data (tens of thousands of points) to be processed make the direct one-to-one matching a very time-consuming process. On the other hand, matching algorithms based on the analysis of 2D data alone are very sensitive to variations in illumination, expression and pose. Algorithms, based on the face shape information alone, are instead relatively insensitive to these sources of noise. These mutually exclusive features of 2D- and 3D-based face recognition algorithm call for a cooperative scheme which may take advantage of the strengths of both, while coping for their weaknesses. We envisage many real and practical applications where 2D data can be used to improve 3D matching and vice versa. Towards this end, this chapter highlights both the advantages and disadvantages of 2D- and 3D-based face recognition algorithms. It also explores the advantages of blending 2D- and 3D data-based techniques, also proposing a novel

M. Tistarelli (✉) · M. Cadoni · A. Lagorio · E. Grosso
University of Sassari, Sassari, Italy
e-mail: tista@uniss.it

M. Cadoni
e-mail: mcadoni@uniss.it

A. Lagorio
e-mail: lagorio@uniss.it

E. Grosso
e-mail: grosso@uniss.it

© Springer International Publishing Switzerland 2016
T. Bourlai (ed.), *Face Recognition Across the Imaging Spectrum,*
DOI 10.1007/978-3-319-28501-6_13

approach for a fast and robust matching. Several experimental results, obtained from publicly available datasets, currently at the state of the art, demonstrate the effectiveness of the proposed approach.

13.1 Introduction to Face Recognition

In today's e-society, personal identification is fundamental to enable the fruition of many services based on computing platforms. Every day pins, passwords, e-cards or e-keys are used to gain virtual access to a large number of services or physical access to restricted areas. However, e-keys and pin–password-based authentication systems can be copied, given to others and stolen by thieves. Personal identification is also a crucial issue in forensic applications, for example, to identify the perpetrator of a criminal offence from some latent information discovered on the crime scene. In these and other applications, identification technologies based on the analysis of biometric traits, such as iris, fingerprint, speech and face can be successfully applied. Nevertheless, every biometric recognition technology offers both advantages and disadvantages. For instance, iris recognition can be very effective, but the data capture procedure can be considered, for some applications, very intrusive, while the acquisition device can be very expensive. Fingerprint recognition technologies are widely used, but they cannot be applied in covert or surveillance scenarios. Speech recognition has a long-standing research record; however, the relative sensitivity to ambient noise limits its applicability especially when dealing with crowded environments.

Face recognition represents a good compromise between ease of use, social acceptability and effectiveness. Face images are easy to capture both at close and at far distance. Taking a face picture is seldom considered intrusive and does not require an active cooperation of the subject. Face recognition algorithms can now achieve very high accuracy at very low false rejection rates. Moreover, it can be exploited both in covert and in overt scenarios.

Traditionally, face recognition operations can be categorized as follows:

- *Face verification.* 1:1 match. In this case, the subject claims an identity and the acquired face is compared with a template. If the matching score is above a given threshold, the claimed identity is verified.
- *Face identification.* 1:N match. In this case, the acquired face is compared with all templates in the database. The identity of the probe corresponds to the subject in the database providing the maximum matching score (or the minimum distance).
- *Watch list.* 1:N match. In this case, the test subject may not be present in the set of available subjects' templates.

Despite the considerable research efforts devoted to face recognition and closely related areas in computer vision, real-world applications are still challenging because of the large variability in the face appearance. Among the most critical factors influencing face recognition performances are the following:

- *Illumination.* Due to the complex skin reflectance property, face images acquired in uncontrolled environments may be photometrically very different.
- *Pose.* Pose changes induce perspective deformations and self-occlusions. In many cases, the probe and gallery faces are captured with different poses.
- *Facial expression.* Faces are not rigid objects. Changes in facial expression may significantly change the face appearance.
- *Aging.* The face shape and texture change over time, even within a single day. Over a long period of time, the face appearance may change radically, in a nonlinear way. In some applications, the probe face image may be captured a long time (days, months or even years) after the face image in the gallery.
- *Occlusion.* Face regions may be occluded by eyeglasses, scarf, beard, cap or other means.
- *Make-up and cosmetic surgery.* Make-up can radically change the face texture, while cosmetic surgery can change both the shape and the texture of the face.

In some cases, images of different subjects may look more similar than images of the same individual acquired under different conditions. For this reason, many commercial face recognition systems take into account one or more of these factors. In order to estimate the recognition performance in adverse conditions, several face databases have been collected. An updated list of publicly available face databases can be found here: http://www.face-rec.org/databases/. Some examples of images captured under different conditions are shown in Fig. 13.1.

Fig. 13.1 Sample images from the *Labelled Faces in the Wild* database [29]. The same subject is portrayed with different head pose, facial expression, illumination and make-up

13.2   Face Recognition Techniques: 2D Versus 2D

Most face recognition algorithms are based on processing 2D images. The information embedded in the pixels composing the face can be exploited in several
manners, obtaining different performances. Most of the time, new algorithms have
been developed to respond to novel challenges, requiring improved performances.
However, the recognition of human faces from 2D images is still an ill-posed
problem in the sense of Hadamard [26].[1] In fact, the image capture itself induces the
loss of one dimension, making it difficult to unambiguously characterize a face as
unique. Therefore, only approximate solutions can be drafted which take advantage
of some constraints on the face structure or the acquisition scenario. This section
provides an overview of the 2D face recognition methods and analyses some of
their advantages and disadvantages. The goal is to better understand the strengths
and weaknesses of the available methods, to devise a new approach based on the
integration of 2D and 3D data.

13.2.1   State of the Art

Face recognition techniques can be divided into three main categories: intensity
image based, video based and technique based on other sensors, such as infrared or
thermal cameras.

Face recognition methods based on intensity image could be seen as very difficult pattern recognition problem. It is hard to solve because it is a nonlinear
problem in a high-dimensional space and the search is done among objects
belonging to the same class. An $N \times N$ image I could be linearized in a N^2 vector, so
that I represents a point in a N^2-dimensional space. However, comparing two
images in this high-dimensional space is hard and not effective. To avoid this, a
low-dimensional space is found by means of a dimensionality reduction technique.

The eigenfaces proposed by Kirby and Sirovich [33] can be considered as one of
the first approaches in this sense. They applied the PCA (principal component
analysis) method to find few eigenvectors, also referred to as eigenfaces, to represent a base in a low-dimensionality space. PCA has been intensively applied in
face recognition system [55, 56], and the method appears quite robust to lighting
variations, but its performance degrades with scale changes.

Many other linear projection methods have been studied too such as linear
discriminant analysis (LDA) [42, 44]. The main aim of the LDA consists in finding
a base of vectors providing the best discrimination among the classes, trying to
maximize the between-class differences and at the same time minimizing the

---

[1]Inverse problems most often do not fulfil Hadamard's postulates of well-posedness: they may not
have a solution in the strict sense, and solutions may not be unique and/or may not depend
continuously on the data.

within-class ones. The between- and within-class differences are represented by the corresponding scatter matrices S_b and S_w, while the ratio $\det|S_b|/\det|S_w|$ has to be maximized. However, Martinez and Kak [44] have shown that LDA provides better classification performances only when a wide training set is available.

Belhumeur et al. [8] proposed the Fisherface approach where the PCA is applied as a preliminary step in order to reduce the dimensionality of the input space, and then, the LDA is applied to the resulting space. Chen and Yu have been demonstrated that, combining in this way PCA and LDA, both discriminant information and redundant one are discarded. Thus, in some cases, the LDA is applied directly on the input space.

One main drawback of the PCA and LDA methods is that these techniques fail if the face images lie on a nonlinear submanifold in the image space. It has been shown that face images possibly reside on a nonlinear submanifold [52], especially if there is a variation in viewpoint, illumination or facial expression.

Some nonlinear techniques have consequently been proposed [27, 28, 61].

Marian et al. [6] have shown that first- and second-order statistics hold information only about the amplitude spectrum of an image, discarding the phase spectrum. Some experiments have demonstrated that the human capability of recognizing objects is phase spectrum driven. They introduce the ICA (independent component analysis) as a more powerful classification approach for face recognition. One of the major advantages of ICA is that it captures discriminant features not only exploiting the covariance matrix, but also considering the high-order statistics.

Wright et al. [60] recently proposed a sparse representation-based classification (SRC) for face recognition. The method is based on the idea of sparse representation computed by l^1-minimization. They represent the test sample in an overcomplete dictionary whose base elements are the training samples themselves. This approach needs a sufficient training samples from each class that allow to represent the test samples as a linear combination of just those training samples from the same class. This approach is robust to variations in facial expression and illumination as well as to occlusion and disguise.

A nonlinear approach to the face recognition problem is given by the neural networks. They are widely applied in many pattern recognition problems, and they are effectively adapted for face recognition problem. The main advantage of neural classifiers is that they can reduce misclassifications among the neighborhood classes. Generally, each image pixel is projected to a single network node (a "neutron"). As such, the network size increases with the image size, making the complexity of training intractable. Cottrell and Fleming [22] originally proposed a dimensionality reduction technique to make the training manageable.

Other neural network typologies have been also applied to face recognition. For example, the self-organizing map (SOM) is invariant to minor changes in the image samples, while convolutional networks proved to be partially invariant to rotation, translation and scaling. In general, different contexts require different network architectures. In the following, some of the most influential works along this line of research are reported.

Lin et al. [37] proposed the so-called probabilistic decision-based neural network. The plasticity of such networks is due to their hierarchical structure with nonlinear basis functions and a competitive credit assignment scheme.

Meng et al. [24] introduced a hybrid approach, in which, through the PCA, the most discriminating features are extracted and used as the input of a RBF neural network.

Lawrence et al. [34] proposed a hybrid neural network solution which combines local image sampling, a self-organizing map neural network and a convolutional neural network.

Most of the described approaches start out with the basic assumption that all the pixels in the image are equally important. Feature-based approaches are based on the assumption that some pixel neigboorhoods in the face image are more discriminative than others.

An example of feature-based approach is the Elastic Bunch Graph Matching (EBGM) method proposed by Wiskott et al. [59]. To generate a graph, the steps used are the follows: first of all, a set of fiducial points on the face are chosen. Each fiducial point is a node of a full connected graph and is labelled with the Gabor filter responses applied to a window around the fiducial point. Each arch is labelled with the distance between the correspondent fiducial points. The comparison between two faces is performed by comparing the corresponding graphs.

In order to reduce the sensitivity to change in illumination and facial expression, Liu [39] investigated the use of Gabor features. In this approach, the face image is convolved with a Gabor filter, tuned to five scales and eight orientations. The resulting Gabor wavelet features are concatenated to obtain a feature vector. Both PCA and the enhanced Fisher linear discriminant model (EFM) are then applied to reduce the dimensionality of the resulting feature vector.

Ahonen et al. [2] proposed a facial image representation based on local binary pattern (LBP) texture features. The LBP operator assigns a label to every pixel of an image by thresholding the 3×3-neighborhood of each pixel with the centre pixel value and considering the result as a binary number. Then, the histogram of the labels can be used as a texture descriptor. LBP features proved to be highly discriminative, invariant to monotonic grey-level changes and computationally efficient. An interesting improvement of this technique is local derivative pattern (LDP) proposed in [62].

Lowe proposed the scale invariant feature transform (SIFT) [41] which has been successfully applied for keypoint localization and 2D face recognition [11]. They are based on a scale-space representation obtained by successive smoothing of the original image with Laplacian-of-Gaussian (LoG) kernels of different sizes. They are invariant to scale and rotation transformations, but they are challenged by strong illumination variations and face expressions. Moreover, a common drawback of the DoG representation is that local maxima arise in the neighborhood of contours or straight edge lines, where the signal changes along one direction. These points are quite unstable because their localization is more sensitive to noise. Therefore, additional processing steps are required to remove unreliable points.

Table 13.1 Recognition performance of some of the reported algorithms

Authors	Method	Databases	Identification rate (%)
Martinez and Kak [44]	PCA	Ar-Faces	70
Martinez and Kak [44]	LDA	Ar-Faces	88
Belhumeur et al. [8]	Fisherface	YALE	99.6
Lu et al. [42]	DF-LDA	ORL	96
Barlett et al. [6]	ICA	FERET	89
Lawrence et al. [34]	Neural network	ORL	96.2
Wright et al. [60]	SRC	Ar-Faces	94.7
Wright et al. [60]	SRC	YALE	98.1
Wiskott et al. [59]	EBGM	FERET	57–98
Liu [39]	Gabor EFM	FERET	99
Liu [39]	Gabor EBGM	ORL	100
Ahonen et al. [2]	LBP	FERET	93

It is difficult to make a quantitative comparison of all proposed techniques because most often different databases are used for different experiments. To facilitate a qualitative comparison, Table 13.1 summarizes the reported performances for each method and the dataset used for the experiments.

An exhaustive analysis of the state of the art in 2D face recognition is out of the scope of this chapter. More detailed surveys on 2D face recognition techniques, with an exhaustive performance analysis, can be found in [1, 31, 63].

13.2.2 Advantages and Disadvantages

Matching 2D face images requires to process a lower amount of data with respect to 3D representations. Moreover, easily obtained snapshots and mugshots can be used as gallery or probes. On the other hand, unless an active illumination source is employed, almost all face recognition algorithms based on matching 2D images are sensitive to changes in illumination. Also, the head pose induces changes in the face appearance, thus affecting the matching performances. All "holistic" methods, i.e. using the iconic image matrix representation, such as PCA and LDA, require to vectorize the $N \times M$ 2D image matrix into a $N \times M$ 1D vector. This requires a high accuracy in the geometric alignment and normalization of the faces to be matched. As the face representation is quite rigidly constrained by the image geometry, the algorithms are quite sensitive to changes in head pose and rotation. Unless a proper training is performed, including images of the same subjects showing different facial expressions, these methods cannot efficiently handle variations in facial expressions.

13.3   Face Recognition Techniques: 3D Versus 3D

As previously reported, variations in head pose and illumination are still among the most difficult challenges in 2D face recognition, making it an ill-posed problem. This limitation can be overcome by adding a dimension and processing 3D image data, thus making the problem well-posed. The first 3D scanning technology dates back to the 1960s. In the 1980s, the first face scanner was built by the Cyberware Laboratory of Los Angeles, under the impulse of the animation industry. However, it was not until the late 1990s that 3D scanners were capable of acquiring the surface of objects, together with texture information, with an acceptable accuracy in a reasonable time (few minutes). Nowadays, the most widely used 3D scanners are the so-called active scanners (laser scanners and structured light scanners), where the recovery of 3D information is simplified by projecting a structured light pattern onto the object. A great effort has been devoted to develop algorithms to accurately establish the depth of points in space and merge the views of displaced cameras to get a virtual reconstruction of the object. Structured light scanners are now fast and reasonably accurate and are capable of capturing a 3D face in 2 ms with an error of about 0.1 mm. Laser scanners can be even more accurate (error equal to 0.05 mm) at the expense of a greater acquisition time (2.5 s per face). Even a cooperative subject may move during acquisition, producing a distorted 3D face scan [12]. For this reason, fast structured light scanners are more reliable. Optical systems are sensitive to highly reflective patches such as oily skin or face areas covered by reflective make-up. Such reflective areas act as mirrors, either reflecting the radiation away from the camera field or bouncing it elsewhere, causing artefacts. Transparent areas, such as the cornea, cannot be sampled because most of the light beam is absorbed by the transparent surface. To avoid specular reflections, some scanners project several patterns from different angles. Projecting a light pattern and capturing 2D images from different viewpoints are also helpful to obtain a uniformly sampled reconstruction of the face surface. In fact, as the curvature of the face surface has large variations, it can be hardly sampled uniformly from a single camera viewpoint.

The captured 3D face data points may differ in accuracy and density. According to the device and its software, the data may be saved in different formats:

- a cloud of points, which is a set $F = \{(x_i, y_i, z_i) \in R^3 | i = 1, \ldots, N\}$ of N 3D points.
- a range image (also called 2.5 image), defined by a $n \times m$ matrix $F_{nm} = \{f_{ij}\}$ whose entry f_{ij} represents the three-dimensional point of coordinates (i, j, f_{ij}), so it can be thought as an image where each pixel (i, j) in the XY plane stores the depth value f_{ij}. It is also possible to consider a 2.5D image as a greyscale image, where the intensity of the pixels is proportional to the distance of the point to the camera. In this case, black pixels correspond to the background (point with infinite distance to the camera), while the white pixels represent the points that are nearest to the camera.

- a polygonal mesh, which includes, besides the coordinates of the points (the cloud of points, called vertices in this case), the edges and faces between the vertices. The mesh can be represented in different ways: by an adjacency list or as a triangle mesh for instance.

The face representation affects the complexity of the recognition algorithm: a point cloud is generally the most difficult to process. For instance, given a point, searching for its k-nearest neighbours or for the points within a set distance is a time-consuming task. On the contrary, a range image or a mesh implicitly conveys information about the point structure. Therefore, given a point, its neighbouring points are readily available.

Capturing three-dimensional data from the face, to build a 3D face model, allows to overcome the errors in 2D face matching due to changes in pose and illumination (not considering specular reflections).

13.3.1   State of the Art

The earliest works in 3D face recognition were proposed over a decade ago [16, 35]. Due to the limits of acquisition technology, it has been difficult to collect sufficient amounts of data for experimentation until the late 1990s. In fact, the number of persons represented in experimental datasets did not reach 100 until 2003. There was therefore relatively little work in this area all through the 1990s, while activity has steadily increased afterwards, with the collection of increasingly larger datasets and the development of several techniques for face recognition. Two comprehensive surveys on 3D face recognition methods are [1, 13]. The larger and more challenging 3D database is currently the FRGC, which contains over 4000 3D face scans acquired from 466 subjects. Within the FRGC, various standard protocols were defined to test face recognition methods on its datasets, making them easily comparable. The best performing methods tested on the FRGC dataset are outlined below.

Ocegueda et al. [48] presented a random Markov field (MRF) model to analyse the discriminative information of the vertices of lattices, in order to find the most significant regions of the face to accomplish a specific task (face recognition, facial expression recognition and ethnicity-based subject retrieval). The posterior marginal probabilities of the MRF are used to define compact signatures for each task. The images and scans of all subjects are assumed to be registered to a common coordinate system, which is accomplished using the annotated face model (AFM) in [32].

Faltemier et al. [25] proposed a multi-instance enrolment representation to deal with expression variations. The nose tip is detected using a consensus algorithm in three steps: computation of the curvature and shape index, registration of the input scan to a template and a refinement step. Subsequently, the area obtained by intersecting a sphere centred on the nose tip is extracted from the probe and gallery face. A radius equal to 40 and 100 mm is employed for the probe and gallery face, respectively. The ICP algorithm is applied to align the two areas, and the registration error is taken as matching score. Tests were run on the ND-2006, a superset of the FRGC v2 dataset made of 13,450 3D scans.

Lin et al. [38] proposed to select ten rectangular areas from the range image to compute invariant features. They match the single regions to the equivalent ones in the gallery image and fuse the matching scores with a weighted sum rule optimized via LDA. The method was tested on the FRGC v2, achieving a verification rate of 90 % at 0.001 FAR.

Al-Osaimi et al. [3] proposed a non-rigid approach for face recognition. First, they perform registration of a neutral and a non-neutral scan and use PCA on the shape residues to model the expression patterns of a face and then apply the model to morph expressions from a probe face and use it for matching. The method was tested on the FRGC v2 with the "first neutral" as gallery and all the rest as probe, obtaining 96.52 % identification rate.

Berretti et al. [9] proposed to encode the geometrical information of the scan into a compact representation in the form of a graph. The nodes of the graph represent equal width isogeodesic facial stripes, and the arcs between nodes are labelled with descriptors. Corresponding arcs of two different scans are compared to yield a dissimilarity measure. The Mask III experiment performed on the set "first neutral" as gallery and the rest as probes produced 94 % identification rate and 81 % authentication rate at 0.001 FAR.

Queirolo et al. [51] proposed to segment the face from a range image to extract six feature points: inner eye corners, nose tip, nose base and the nostrils. They use the points to extract interest regions from the face, namely a circular area and an elliptical one around the nose and the upper head (which spans from the nose base upwards). These, together with the whole face, are individually registered to corresponding areas in another face. To register the areas, the authors use a two-step simulated annealing (SA): for the first iterations, SA is guided by the M-estimator sample consensus (MSAC), for the tuning, by the surface interpenetration measure (SIM). Extensive tests have been conducted on the FRGCv2, both for verification and recognition, achieving 96.5% accurate matching at 0.001 FAR, and 99.6% accurate recognition (ROC III FRGC v2) respectively.

Spreeuwers [54] defined a face intrinsic coordinate system by finding the symmetry plane of the face, the nose tip and angle to the nose bridge. The face is then encoded as a range image, by projecting the point cloud onto the plane perpendicular to the symmetry plane. A set of 30 overlapping regions is then selected, face comparison is done by comparing each region with the corresponding one by means of PCA-LDA-Likelihood ratio classifier, and the results are fused by majority voting.

Li et al. [36] provided two principal curvature-based 3D keypoint detectors, which identify complementary locations on a face scan. At each keypoint, a 3D coordinate system is defined, allowing the extraction of pose-invariant features. They define three keypoint descriptors and fuse them to describe the local shape of the keypoints. The matching is performed through a sparse representation-based algorithm. This method was tested on the Bosphorus dataset, obtaining 96.56% recognition rate on the whole database, and on the FRGC v2 dataset, obtaining 96.3% identification rate on the "first versus all" experiment.

13.3.2 Advantages and Disadvantages

Compared to the 2D-based matching algorithms, 3D-based approaches have opposed advantages and disadvantages. While 3D-based face recognition methods are relatively insensitive to changes in both illumination and head pose, they require to process larger amounts of data. On the other hand, all distinguishing facial features that are related to the facial texture, due to skin shape and tone variations, are not available in the 3D representations. Moreover, to efficiently process 3D face data, it is necessary to locate stable fiducial points on the face surface. This can be sometimes quite difficult, especially in the presence of noise and artefacts due to the acquisition device. For this reason, most of the time, an accurate preprocessing of the 3D face data are required to reduce the amount of noise, especially to avoid holes and abrupt changes in the surface normals.

13.4 Face Recognition Techniques: Blending 2D and 3D

As it emerges from Sects. 13.2 and 13.3, each of the 2D and 3D methods presents strengths and weaknesses and the preference of one over the other must take account of several factors that include technology availability, costs and fields of application. Almost always, though, 3D acquisition systems acquire the texture of the face together with the shape and the two can be combined to exploit their best features. Merging the two modalities increases the information available which can boost (in theory) face recognition performance. For instance, one of the hardest steps 3D face recognition algorithms deal with is the search of a set of feature points to be used for various purposes (segmentation, registration, etc.). This search is by no means trivial and can be computationally demanding. Locating feature points in 2D is generally quicker, simply because the descriptors used to characterize the points will have to deal with a two-dimensional object rather than a three-dimensional one. On the other side, where 2D is deficient, for instance in case of uneven illumination which varies from scan to scan, the shape of the face can recover the information that is lost in the 2D case. Furthermore, when there is pose variation between the scans, from a single 2D shot it is impossible to recover the pose, so a 3D scan in this case is much more informative: even laser scanners that rely on a unique camera to acquire the subject, though unable to uniformly scan the surface of a face, can handle rotations up to about 15–20° away from the frontal pose. Techniques that combine the 2D and 3D information of a face are multimodal.

Fusion of the two modalities can be generally performed at the feature or score level and in some cases even at the data level, once the two representations are geometrically aligned and normalized. Several databases exist including both 3D data and texture pixels. Most of the time, the photometric information is directly attached to the 3D data points. FRGC v2 is currently the largest 3D face dataset, and it contains 13,450 scans with texture. The Bosphorus dataset contains scans and 2D face images of 105 subjects, with controlled variations in the head pose, facial expressions and occlusions.

13.4.1 State of the Art

The majority of proposed multimodal methods analyse the 2D and 3D channels separately to perform fusion at score level. Chang et al. [17] use a PCA-based approach tuned separately on the 2D and 3D images and then fuse the scores using a confidence-weighted variation of the sum rule. They test their method on a subset of the FRGC v2, whose gallery and probe consisted, respectively, of one scan of each of the 275 subjects and 676 scans of the same subjects. Identification rates reached 98.8 %.

Kakadiaris et al. [32] tackled the expression variation problem with the aid of an AFM. The 3D facial data are registered to the face model in three algorithmic steps which use, in order, spin images, the iterative closest point (ICP) and SA on Z-buffers. The facial model is then deformed to fit the facial data and is subsequently mapped into a geometrical image onto a 2D regular grid. A normal map image is derived from the geometrical image, and the two images are analysed using the Haar and Pyramid transforms which yield two sets of coefficients. In the matching phase, the coefficients are compared by means of two different metrics. The method was tested on the FRGC v2 and on the UH, a dataset of 884 scans acquired with a prototype acquisition system built at the University of Houston. They achieve 97 % identification rates and verification rates of 97.3 % at 0.001 FAR on the FRGC v2.

Chang et al. [19] segmented the area around the nose to minimize variations due to expressions. Three regions centred at the nose tip are selected: a circular area, a rectangular area and an elliptical one. Each region is registered to the corresponding one in the gallery face with ICP, and the registration errors are combined with the product rule to give a measure of similarity. Tests are run on the FRGC, the rank-one recognition rate for neutral scans is 96.1 %, while for non-neutral scans, it drops to 79.2 %.

Husken et al. [30] applied a Hierarchical Graph Matching (HGM) by first extracting facial landmarks which are subsequently used to perform a 3D adaptation process on the captured 3D scan. Feature vectors are extracted and matched separately for the shape and texture channel and the score combined to yield the final score. The only reported experiment is the FRGC v2 ROC III, for which the verification rate achieved at 0.001 FAR is 96.8 %.

Maurer et al. [45] adopted a commercial system to analyse the texture channel. On the shape channel, they extract a mask from the range image, detect biometric features and use them to initialize the ICP to align two images. Once the images are registered, they compute a distance map between the two. Statistics associated with the distance map are finally computed, and a threshold is fixed to establish the matching error. The texture and shape channel are fused at score level with a weighted sum rule. They report the results of the ROC III test of FRGC v2. The verification rate at 0.001 FAR is 93.5 %.

Lu et al. [43] assumed to have several range images that can be merged to get a complete 3D model of the face, which is used as a gallery template. They then match the range images to the 3D model by selecting a set of feature points (inside and outside eye corners and nose tip). The points are used to coarsely register the range image to the 3D model and then refine it with the ICP. The point-to-plane distance is used as a matching score between the two surfaces. The 3D model is also used to synthesize a set of texture images which are matched to a test image by means of LDA. The shape and texture matching scores are finally combined with the weighted sum rule. Since there are no publicly available datasets that contain multiview range images of each subject, the authors collected their own dataset, which counts 598 scans with variation in pose and expressions (neutral and smiling) from 100 subjects. To test the method, they add another 100 3D complete models from the University of South Florida Database, so that their gallery is made of 200 3D models and the probe of 598 range images. Since the automatic feature point locator is not robust enough in case of non-frontal scans, in the reported experiment the points are located manually. The identification accuracy at rank one on the whole probe is 90, 99 % for frontal neutral probes and 77 % for smiling probes.

Cook et al. [21] applied Gabor filters to the range and texture images of the face, subsequently divide the images into 25 square regions and build subspaces of each region using PCA. A novel measure based on the Mahalanobis cosine distance is defined to match the regions, and linear support vector machines are used to combine the scores. The authors report the FRGC v2 ROC III test: at 0.001 FAR, the verification rate is 93.16 %.

Mian et al. [46] proposed a rejection classifier to speed up the recognition process in identification scenarios. First, the pose of the 3D range image and the corresponding 2D image are corrected. Then, the scale invariant feature transform (SIFT) is applied on images, and a spherical face representation is applied on the range images to select a subset of possible matching candidates. To compare the candidates to the probe, the range images are segmented by automatically locating the inflection points of the nose. Two regions are extracted: the eyes-forehead and the nose areas. The two corresponding shapes on the candidate faces are matched using a variant of the ICP algorithm. The weighted sum rule is applied to combine the two matching scores. The authors performed several tests on the FRGC v2 (All vs. All), producing a verification rate equal to 86.6 % at 0.001 FAR. The identification rate, computed on a gallery composed of 466 neutral scans (one per subject) and the rest of the dataset as probe, is equal to 96.2 % at rank one.

Wang et al. [58] proposed a method called collective shape difference classifier (CSDC). The 3D scans are first aligned to a common coordinate system. A sign difference shape map is obtained from the aligned scans and encoded by three features: Haar, Gabor and LBP. The most discriminant features are used to build three CSDCs which are fused to obtain a verification score, while for identification, only the Haar feature-based CSDC is used. Experiment carried out on the FRGC v2 dataset shows that the method performs well both in identification and in authentication scenarios, reaching scores of 98.39 and 98.61 %, respectively, on a gallery made of the first neutral scan per each subject and the rest as probes.

13.4.2   Advantages and Disadvantages

There are several advantages in combining the 3D data with the corresponding 2D texture. Stable fiducial points can be more easily detected by exploiting both the shape and texture information. Moreover, the additional information allows to perform score fusion, thus coping for errors and noise in both representations. However, in order to exploit both 3D and 2D data, the two representations must be geometrically aligned and scaled. This requires either to capture both information at the same time, by means of a proper acquisition device, or to put in correspondence the 3D points with 2D image pixels. The latter may become quite complex, especially if the head pose in the 2D image is unknown.

13.5   Comparing 2D and 2D+3D Face Recognition

In order to establish if, how and when a 3D analysis improves a 2D one, we propose two face identification methods. The first one implements SIFT (surface invariant feature transform) [40] and SURF (speeded-up robust features) [7], which are well-established image descriptors. The second method uses SIFT and SURF to extract and match 2D feature points and subsequently analyses the located points in 3D, using 3D joint differential invariants to validate the 2D matches.

13.5.1   Matching 2D Face Images

In [15], the combination of SIFT and SURF to extract and match iconic points was successful in boosting the performance of each descriptor. The SIFT algorithm is based on a scale-space representation, obtained by filtering the image with LoG kernels of different sizes. The SIFT points are the maxima and minima of the

Fig. 13.2 Preprocessing
pipeline: the face shape is
extracted from the 3D scan
using the ROI computed on
the 2D image

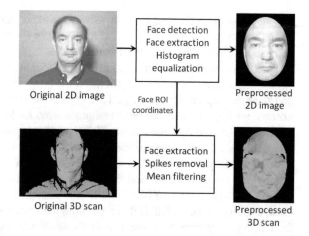

Original 2D image   Face ROI coordinates   Preprocessed 2D image

Original 3D scan   Preprocessed 3D scan

scale-space-normalized LoG. SIFT points can be efficiently computed in real time
by approximating the scale-space-normalized LoG with a corresponding difference
of Gaussian (DoG) kernel.[2] The SURF algorithm is based on a Hessian matrix
approximation, computed from the integral image. This approach drastically
reduces the computation times, also increasing the number of detected keypoints,
but with a poorer localization. The SURF descriptors are built on the distribution of
first-order Haar wavelet responses in the x and y directions rather than the gradient.
This approach is proved to be fast and also increases the robustness of the
descriptor. In particular, Bay and colleagues have shown that SURF descriptors
outperform SIFT in case of blur and scale changes. In [15], tests run on the FRGC
dataset showed that SIFT and SURF are complementary in the localization and
matching of points: only 30 % of the matched SIFT and SURF points are in
common, i.e. they are displaced by less than 4 pixels. SIFT and SURF have
therefore the potential of capturing more information than any of the two methods
alone. Before the extraction and matching of SIFT and SURF points, a simple
preprocessing of the images is required, particularly to segment the oval of the face.
Towards this end, the Viola–Jones algorithm [57] is applied to locate the ROI of the
face. From the ROI of the face, we extract the ellipse centred in the centre of the
ROI and with axes equal to the edges of the ROI. This approximates the face oval.
As SIFT and SURF are very sensitive to local changes in illumination, an histogram
equalization algorithm is also applied (Fig. 13.2).

Once images have been preprocessed, SIFT points are extracted using the
original algorithm implemented by Lowe [40]. For faces in the gallery database,

---

[2]The difference of Gaussian is defined as the difference of two successive scale-space representations of the image, divided by the scale difference.

this step can be performed off-line. Given for each gallery face F_G a set of SIFT points and their description vectors, if a probe face F_P comes in, the SIFT points are extracted and matched against all gallery faces.

SURF points are then extracted, using the OpenSurf code. Similarly to the SIFT extraction, gallery faces can be processed off-line, obtaining a set of SURF points and their descriptors for each F_G. To compute the distance between the descriptor vectors, we implemented the same technique used for SIFT with a threshold $t = 0.6$. When a probe face F_P comes in, its SURF points are extracted and matched against all gallery faces. For a given probe face F_P, following the SIFT and SURF matching with all the (say N) gallery faces, we are left with N sets $M_1,\ldots, M_N$ of matching points. The set with the highest cardinality, corresponding to the gallery face that has the highest number of SIFT and SURF points that match with the probe face ones, establishes the match. If there are more than one set with the same cardinality, then the gallery face with the lowest value of the mean distances between the descriptor vectors is taken as the matching gallery face (Fig. 13.3).

13.5.2 Blending 2D and 3D Data

From the cropped 2D face image, the face shape is extracted by projecting the pixels of the face on the 3D scan. Outliers are removed by first computing the average sampling density of the scan F, composed of n points, as $\delta_r(F) = 1/n \sum_{j=1}^{n} \delta_r(p_j)$ where $\delta_r(p_j) = |\{q | q \in U_r(p_j)\}|$ and $U_r(p_j) = \{q \in F | \|q - p_j\| < r\}$. All points $p_i \in F$ such that $\delta_r(p_i) < \delta_r(F)/4$ are removed. Noise due to acquisition errors is attenuated by applying a mean filter along the z-coordinate (Fig. 13.4).

The proposed iconic extractors and descriptors are based on local information around a point, and an established correspondence is derived from the similarity of the descriptor vectors. Neither the SIFT nor the SURF descriptors take into account the relative position of the points. To take into account the available 3D information, the same approach proposed in [15] is used to validate the iconic correspondences by computing the 3D invariants on the corresponding points in the scans. The invariants we use arise from the moving frame theory [50] and are based on the relative position of the points and local shape information. The procedure that leads to the generation of the invariants is discussed in full details in [14]. We generate invariants that depend on three points at a time. The invariant a triplet of points generates is a nine-dimensional vector whose first three entries are the interpoint distances and the last six are functions of scalar and wedge products of various vectors, as the formulae that follow explain.

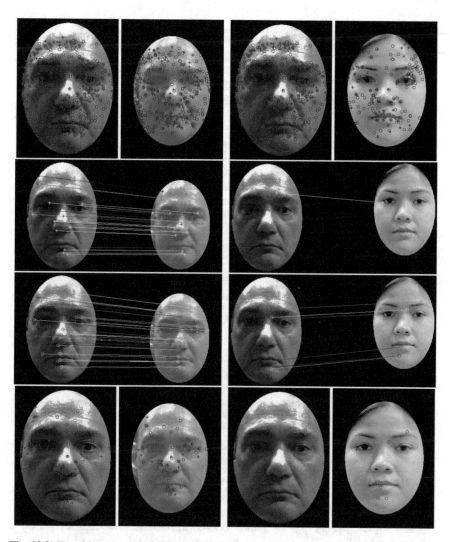

Fig. 13.3 Example of comparison process between 2D face images from the same subject (*left*) and from different subjects (*right*). *First row* Extracted SIFT (*red stars*) and SURF (*blue circles*) points. *Second and third rows* Pairing of corresponding points on the two images. Matched SIFT points (*second row*) and SURF points (*third row*). *Fourth row* Remaining SIFT and SURF points after iconic matching

Let $p_1, p_2, p_3 \in F$ and v_i be the normal vector at p_i. The directional vector v of the line between p_1 and p_2 and the normal vector v_t to the plane through p_1, p_2, p_3 are defined as follows:

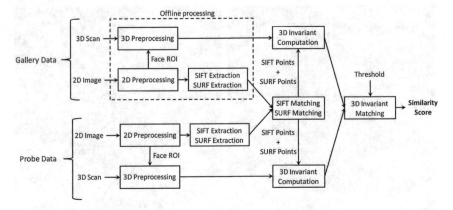

Fig. 13.4 Block diagram of the proposed approach blending 2D and 3D data for face recognition

$$v = \frac{p_2 - p_1}{\|p_2 - p_1\|} \quad \text{and} \quad v_t = \frac{(p_2 - p_1) \wedge (p_3 - p_1)}{\|(p_2 - p_1) \wedge (p_3 - p_1)\|}.$$

The zero-order invariants are the 3 interpoint distances $I_k(p_1, p_2, p_3)$ for $k = 1, 2, 3$:

$$I_1 = \|p_2 - p_1\|, I_2 = \|p_3 - p_2\| \quad \text{and} \quad I_3 = \|p_3 - p_1\|$$

whereas the first-order invariants are

$$J_k(p_1, p_2, p_3) = \frac{(v_t \wedge v) \cdot v_k}{v_t \cdot v_k} \quad \text{for} \quad k = 1, 2, 3$$

and

$$\tilde{J}_k(p_1, p_2, p_3) = \frac{v \cdot v_k}{v_t \cdot v_k} \quad \text{for} \quad k = 1, 2, 3.$$

Each triplet (p_1, p_2, p_3) of points on the surface is now represented by a nine-dimensional vector whose coordinates are given by $(I_1, I_2, I_3, J_1, J_2, J_3, \tilde{J}_1, \tilde{J}_2, \tilde{J}_3)$ (Fig. 13.5).

Given a set of SIFT and SURF point features of a probe face F_P, and one of a gallery face F_G, we first generate the 3D joint differential invariants for both faces. If there are n matching points, there will be $\binom{n}{3}$ invariant vectors. The invariant vectors of corresponding triplets can be compared by computing the Euclidean distance. The similarity measure between the probe face F_P and the gallery face F_G is given by the number of invariant vectors of F_P whose distance from the corresponding invariant vector in F_G is less than a fixed threshold σ, which can be established statistically using a training dataset. The matching gallery face is chosen to be the face with the greatest similarity measure.

Fig. 13.5 Four triangles
computed from five points on
the face surface. The shape
normal for each point is also
displayed in *green colour*

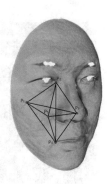

13.6   Experimental Results

The 2D and the coupled 3D and 2D approaches have been tested on two of the most
widely used face databases, the FRGC v2 and the Bosphorus dataset. While FRGC
is currently the largest available 3D face dataset, Bosphorus includes a wide
variation in head pose and facial expressions, allowing to test the sensitivity of the
algorithms to these variations.

The FRGC dataset was collected at the University of Notre Dame in the 2002–
2003 and 2003–2004 academic years. The data collected in the 2002–2003 academic
year are used for training partitions and the others for validation partitions. The
validation set contains images from 466 subjects, and the number of acquisitions per
subject varies between 1 and 22, for a total of 4007 acquisitions. Each acquisition
consists of a scan and a registered image whose resolution is 640×480. Faces were
not captured always from the same distance, which results in different resolutions of
the images and different sampling densities of the scans. There is little variation in
the pose of the subjects, while variations of illumination and expressions are relevant.
Expressions are classified as "blank stare" (i.e. neutral), "happiness", "sadness",
"disgust", "surprise" and "others". The 3D images were acquired by a Minolta
Vivid 900/910 series sensor based on a structured light sensor that takes a 640 by
480 range sampling and a registered colour image (Fig. 13.6).

The Bosphorus database contains scans captured from 105 individuals, of which
61 males and 44 females. From the total male subjects, 31 males have a beard and
moustaches. For each subject, there are about 50 scans. Each scan presents either a
different facial expression (anger, happiness, disgust), corresponding to a "face
action unit", or a head rotation along different axes.

Face data are acquired using a structured light 3D scanner. Acquisitions are
single view, and subjects were made to sit at a distance of about 1.5 m away from
the 3D digitizer. The sensor resolutions in x, y and z (depth) dimensions are 0.3, 0.3
and 0.4 mm, respectively, and colour texture images are with high resolution
(1600×1200 pixels).

For each pose, the data points are stored in a file containing the coordinates of
about 30,000 3D points, a colour 2D image of the face texture and a set of landmark
points. The landmarks were manually selected on the 2D images and mapped on the

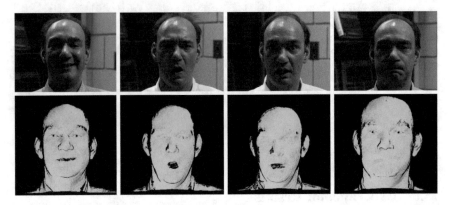

Fig. 13.6 Sample face data, both 2D images and 3D scans, from the FRGC database. The same subject is shown with different facial expressions

corresponding 3D points. This database has been usually chosen because it contains a large number of subjects and an excellent variety of poses and expressions. The database was divided into a gallery set and a probe set. The gallery consists of one neutral face scan for each individual. Figures 13.7, 13.8, 13.9 and 13.10 show some sample 3D scans of the same subject from the Bosphorus database.

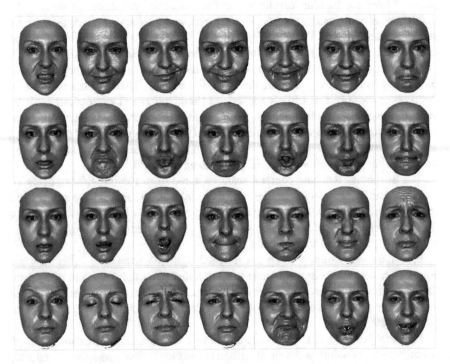

Fig. 13.7 3D sample scans from the Bosphorus database. The same subject was captured while acting different facial action units

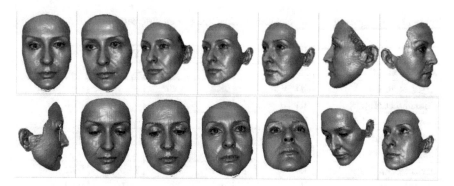

Fig. 13.8 3D sample scans from the Bosphorus database. The same subject was captured with different head poses

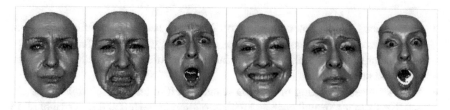

Fig. 13.9 3D sample scans from the Bosphorus database. The same subject was captured while showing six basic emotions: anger, disgust, fear, happiness, sadness and surprise

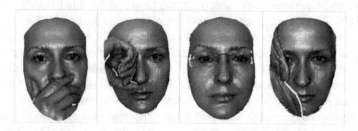

Fig. 13.10 3D sample scans from the Bosphorus database. The same subject's face was captured with different occlusions

13.7   Discussion

The proposed methods were tested on both the FRGC v2 and the Bosphorus datasets. Table 13.2 shows the identification results obtained from different probe sets of the Bosphorus dataset, with varying facial expressions, head pose and occlusions:

Table 13.2 Comparison of rank-one identification rate (%) on different subsets of the Bosphorus database

	Approach	Expressions	YR	Occlusions
Alyuz et al. [4]	3D	–	–	93.6
Alyuz et al. [5]	3D	98.2	–	–
Colombo et al. [20]	3D	–	–	87.6
Ocegueda et al. [49]	3D	98.2	–	–
Drira et al. [23]	3D	–	–	87.0
Smeets et al. [53]	3D	97.7	–	–
Berretti et al. [10]	3D	95.7	81.6	93.2
Li et al. [36]	3D	98.8	**84.1**	**99.2**
SIFT+SURF	2D	**99.7**	35.8	97.6
SIFT+SURF+INV	2D+3D	99.6	47.5	**99.2**

Bold indicates the best performance obtained from the set of compared algorithms

- **Expressions**. A subset consisting of 2797 3D scans. Some face scans are labelled as facial expressions, such as neutral, anger, disgust, fear, happiness, sadness and surprise. Other scans are labelled as different face action units, such as "timid smile".
- **YR**. A subset consisting of 735 3D scans with a rotation to the right of 10, 20 and 30° from the frontal pose and with a rotation to the left and to the right of 45 and 90°.
- **Occlusions**. A subset consisting of 381 3D scans with four different types of occlusions.

As it can be noticed from Table 13.2, the proposed 2D SIFT+SURF and SIFT +SURF+INV multimodal methods have a similar performance which is superior to the state of the art. It is worth noting that the images of the Bosphorus dataset are of good quality and are taken under controlled illumination, which simplifies the location and matching of SIFT and SURF points. With the probe set YR, which includes rotations, the proposed methods are not particularly effective. An obvious explanation is that both SIFT and SURF cannot locate the same points on two scans of the same subject under different pose. The multimodal method, however, improves scores by 10 % with respect to the 2D method, so the 3D information is useful in case of pose differences. With the occlusion probe set, the proposed multimodal method matches the state of the art and outperforms the combined SIFT and SURF matching algorithm.

Table 13.3 shows the identification results on the FRGC v2 dataset, with the identification protocol first versus all, where the probe set (All) is the whole validation set, while the gallery set (first) consists of the first scan for each subject labelled as neutral.

The processing time required by some 3D and 3D+2D methods is reported in Table 13.4. The time required to perform a single comparison varies from one algorithm to the other. Apart from the computational complexity of each algorithm,

Table 13.3 Comparison of rank-one identification rate (%) on the FRGC database

	Approach	First neutral versus all protocol
Berretti et al. [9]	3D	94
Mian et al. [47]	2D+3D	96.2
Al-Osaimi et al. [3]	3D	96.5
Chang et al. [18]	3D	91.9
Spreeuwers [54]	3D	**99.0**
Li et al. [36]	3D	96.3
SIFT+SURF	2D	88.2
SIFT+SURF+INV	2D+3D	93.2

Bold indicates the best performance obtained from the set of compared algorithms

Table 13.4 Comparison of processing time for some of the considered methods

Method	Processor	Preprocessing (sec)	Comparison per second
Queirolo et al. [51]	P4 3.4 GHz	–	0.25
Faltemier et al. [25]	P4 2.4 GHz	7.5	0.45
Al-Osaimi et al. [3]	Core 2 Quad	4	10
SIFT+SURF+INV	Core i7 3.4 GHz	2.2	196
Wang et al. [58]	P4 3.0 GHz	2.2	709
Spreeuwers [54]	P4 2.8 GHz	2.5	11,150
Ocegueda et al. [48]	AMD Opteron 2.1 GHz	15	1,800,000

the main reason can be found in the number of data points to be processed and the representation to be analysed. For example, the algorithm described in [48] is based on the processing of lattice or mesh representations, where the relation between neighbouring points is intrinsically embedded in the polygonal structure of the representation. Other methods, such as processing point clouds, require to explicitly process individual points to infer the position in 3D space of neighbouring points.

13.8   Conclusions

The recognition of a subject's identity from a single two-dimensional image is an ill-posed problem. There are a large number of unknown variables which may radically change the face appearance and cannot be retrieved from the 2D image alone. A solution can be achieved either imposing some constraints or increasing the dimensionality of the available data to be able to cope for the missing dimensions. This chapter addressed several issues related to the exploration of 3D data captured from a subject's face to facilitate recognition. It has been shown how both 2D and 3D face image data alone are not sufficient to uniquely and unambiguously determine a subject's identity by simply matching probe and gallery images. This is because the 2D and 3D images contain different information, captured from different properties of the same face. The 3D data capture the *shape* of the subject's face, while the 2D data capture the *photometric* properties of the same surface. Therefore, by combining both 3D and 2D face image data, the recognition task can be considerably simplified and performance improved. An algorithm for 2D face matching, based on the extraction of SIFT and SURF features, is described. Also, an algorithm for 3D face matching based on the computation of the surface joint differential invariants has been described. The blending of both 2D and 3D information is obtained by using the 2D features to guide the detection of stable surface points for the subsequent computation of the joint invariants. The proposed algorithm has been tested on the FRGC v2 and Bosphorus databases showing performances at the state of the art for both 3D and combined 2D and 3D face recognition. From the analysis presented in this chapter, there are a number of avenues still to be pursued, for example, to mitigate the effects of illumination changes and facial expressions in the extraction of stable feature points.

A common criticism to the development of face recognition systems based on 3D data is the cost and consequent rarity of applications allowing to capture 3D data. However, with the increasing adoption of 3D capturing devices and the availability of robust algorithms to infer 3D information from 2D face images, blending 2D and 3D data will become a natural solution to many applications requiring biometric recognition.

Acknowledgements This research has been partially funded by the European Union COST Action IC1106 "Integrating Biometrics and Forensics for the Digital Age" and by funds from the Italian Ministry of Research.

References

1. Abate, A.F., Nappi, M., Riccio, D., Sabatino, G.: 2d and 3d face recognition: a survey. Pattern Recogn. Lett. **28**(14), 1885–1906 (2007)
2. Ahonen, T., Hadid, A., Pietikainen, M.: Face description with local binary patterns: application to face recognition. IEEE Trans. Pattern Anal. Mach. Intell. **28**(12), 2037–2041 (2006)
3. Al-Osaimi, F., Bennamoun, M., Mian, A.: An expression deformation approach to non-rigid 3d face recognition. Int. J. Comput. Vis. **81**(3), 302–316 (2009)
4. Alyuz, N., Gokberk, B., Akarun, L.: A 3d face recognition system for expression and occlusion invariance. In: Proceedings of IEEE International Conference on Biometrics: Theory, Applications and Systems (BTAS), pp. 1–7. IEEE (2008)
5. Alyuz, N., Gokberk, B., Akarun, L.: Regional registration for expression resistant 3-d face recognition. IEEE Trans. Inf. Forensics Secur. **5**(3), 425–440 (2010)
6. Bartlett, M.S., Movellan, J.R., Sejnowski, T.J.: Face recognition by independent component analysis. IEEE Trans. Neural Networks **13**(6), 1450–1464 (2002)
7. Bay, H., Tuytelaars, T., Van Gool, L.: Surf: speeded up robust features. In: Proceedings of European Conference on Computer Vision (ECCV), pp. 404–417 (2006)

8. Belhumeur, P.N., Hespanha, J.P., Kriegman, D.J.: Eigenfaces vs. fisherfaces: recognition using class specific linear projection. IEEE Trans. Pattern Anal. Mach. Intell. **19**(7), 711–720 (1997). doi 10.1109/34.598228. URL http://dx.doi.org/10.1109/34.598228

9. Berretti, S., Del Bimbo, A., Pala, P.: 3d face recognition using isogeodesic stripes. IEEE Trans. Pattern Anal. Mach. Intell. **32**(12), 2162–2177 (2010)

10. Berretti, S., Werghi, N., Del Bimbo, A., Pala, P.: Matching 3d face scans using interest points and local histogram descriptors. Comput. Graph. **37**(5), 509–525 (2013)

11. Bicego, M., Lagorio, A., Grosso, E., Tistarelli, M.: On the use of sift features for face authentication. In: Proceedings of Computer Vision and Pattern Recognition Workshop (CVPR), pp. 35–35 (2006)

12. Boehnen, C., Flynn, P.: Impact of involuntary subject movement on 3d face scans. In: Proceedings of IEEE Computer Vision and Pattern Recognition Workshops (CVPR), pp. 1–6. IEEE (2009)

13. Bowyer, K.W., Chang, K., Flynn, P.: A survey of approaches and challenges in 3d and multimodal 3d + 2d face recognition. Comput. Vis. Image Underst. **101**(1), 1–15 (2006)

14. Cadoni, M., Bicego, M., Grosso, E.: Iconic methods for multimodal face recognition: a comparative study. In: Proceedings of IAPR International Conference on Biometrics (ICB), vol. LNCS 5558, pp. 279–288. Springer (2009)

15. Cadoni, M., Lagorio, A., Grosso, E.: Iconic methods for multimodal face recognition: a comparative study. In: Proceedings of 22nd International Conference on Pattern Recognition (ICPR), pp. 4612–4617 (2014)

16. Cartoux, J.Y., LaPresté, J.T., Richetin, M.: Face authentification or recognition by profile extraction from range images. In: Proceedings of Workshop on Interpretation of 3D Scenes, 1989, pp. 194–199. IEEE (1989)

17. Chang, K., Bowyer, K., Flynn, P.: Face recognition using 2d and 3d facial data. In: ACM Workshop on Multimodal User Authentication, pp. 25–32 (2003)

18. Chang, K.I., Bowyer, K.W., Flynn, P.J.: Adaptive rigid multi-region selection for handling expression variation in 3d face recognition. In: Proceedings of IEEE Conference on Computer Vision and Pattern Recognition-Workshops (CVPR), pp. 157–157. IEEE (2005)

19. Chang, K.I., Bowyer, W., Flynn, P.J.: Multiple nose region matching for 3d face recognition under varying facial expression. IEEE Trans. Pattern Anal. Mach. Intell. **28**(10), 1695–1700 (2006)

20. Colombo, A., Cusano, C., Schettini, R.: Three-dimensional occlusion detection and restoration of partially occluded faces. J. Math. Imaging Vis. **40**(1), 105–119 (2011)

21. Cook, J., McCool, C., Chandran, V., Sridharan, S.: Combined 2d/3d face recognition using log-Gabor templates. In: Proceedings of IEEE International Conference on Video and Signal Based Surveillance (AVSS), pp. 83–83. IEEE (2006)

22. Cottrell, G.W., Fleming, M.: Face recognition using unsupervised feature extraction. In: Proceedings of the Intelligence Neural Network Conference, pp. 322–325 (1990)

23. Drira, H., Ben Amor, B., Srivastava, A., Daoudi, M., Slama, R.: 3d face recognition under expressions, occlusions, and pose variations. IEEE Trans. Pattern Anal. Mach. Intell. **35**(9), 2270–2283 (2013)

24. Er, M.J., Wu, S., Lu, J., Toh, H.L.: Face recognition with radial basis function (rbf) neural networks. IEEE Trans. Neural Networks **13**(3), 697–710 (2002)

25. Faltemier, T.C., Bowyer, K.W., Flynn, P.J.: A region ensemble for 3-d face recognition. IEEE Trans. Inf. Forensics Secur. **3**(1), 62–73 (2008)

26. Hadamard, J.: Lectures on the Cauchy Problem in Linear Partial Differential Equations. Yale University Press, New Haven (1923)

27. He, X., Yan, S., Hu, Y., Niyogi, P., Zhang, H.J.: Face recognition using Laplacian faces. IEEE Trans. Pattern Anal. Mach. Intell. **27**(3), 328–340 (2005)

28. He, X., Yan, S., Hu, Y., Zhang, H.J.: Learning a locality preserving subspace for visual recognition. In: Proceedings of Ninth IEEE International Conference on Computer Vision, 2003, pp. 385–392. IEEE (2003)

29. Huang, G.B., Ramesh, M., Berg, T., Learned-Miller, E.: Labeled faces in the wild: a database for studying face recognition in unconstrained environments. Technical Report 07-49, University of Massachusetts, Amherst (2007)

30. Husken, M., Brauckmann, M., Gehlen, S., Von der Malsburg, C.: Strategies and benefits of fusion of 2d and 3d face recognition. In: Proceedings of IEEE Conference on Computer Vision and Pattern Recognition-Workshops (CVPR), pp. 174–174. IEEE (2005)

31. Jafri, R., Arabnia, H.R.: A survey of face recognition techniques. JIPS 5(2), 41–68 (2009)

32. Kakadiaris, I.A., Passalis, G., Toderici, G., Murtuza, M.N., Lu, Y., Karampatziakis, N., Theoharis, T.: Three-dimensional face recognition in the presence of facial expressions: An annotated deformable model approach. IEEE Trans. Pattern Anal. Mach. Intell. 29(4), 640–649 (2007)

33. Kirby, M., Sirovich, L.: Application of the Karhunen-Loeve procedure for the characterization of human faces. IEEE Trans. Pattern Anal. Mach. Intell. 12(1), 103–108 (1990)

34. Lawrence, S., Giles, C.L., Tsoi, A.C., Back, A.D.: Face recognition: a convolutional neural-network approach. IEEE Trans. Neural Networks 8(1), 98–113 (1997)

35. Lee, J.C., Milios, E.: Matching range images of human faces. In: Proceedings of 3rd International Conference on Computer Vision, pp. 722–726. IEEE (1990)

36. Li, H., Huang, D., Morvan, J.M., Wang, Y., Chen, L.: Towards 3d face recognition in the real: a registration-free approach using fine-grained matching of 3d keypoint descriptors. Int. J. Comput. Vis. 1–15 (2014)

37. Lin, S.H., Kung, S.Y., Lin, L.J.: Face recognition/detection by probabilistic decision-based neural network. IEEE Trans. Neural Networks 8(1), 114–132 (1997)

38. Lin, W.Y., Wong, K.C., Boston, N., Hu, Y.H.: 3d face recognition under expression variations using similarity metrics fusion. In: Proceedings of IEEE International Conference on Multimedia and Expo, pp. 727–730. IEEE (2007)

39. Liu, C.: Gabor-based kernel PCA with fractional power polynomial models for face recognition. IEEE Trans. Pattern Anal. Mach. Intell. 26(5), 572–581 (2004)

40. Lowe, D.: Distinctive image features from scale-invariant keypoints. Int. J. Comput. Vis. 60(2), 91–110 (2004). doi 10.1023/B:VISI.0000029664.99615.94. URL http://dx.doi.org/10.1023/B%3AVISI.0000029664.99615.94

41. Lowe, D.G.: Distinctive image features from scale-invariant keypoints. Int. J. Comput. Vis. 60(2), 91–110 (2004)

42. Lu, J., Plataniotis, K.N., Venetsanopoulos, A.N.: Face recognition using lda-based algorithms. IEEE Trans. Neural Networks 14(1), 195–200 (2003)

43. Lu, X., Jain, A.K., Colbry, D.: Matching 2.5 d face scans to 3d models. IEEE Trans. Pattern Anal. Mach. Intell. 28(1), 31–43 (2006)

44. Martínez, A.M., Kak, A.C.: Pca versus lda. IEEE Trans. Pattern Anal. Mach. Intell. 23(2), 228–233 (2001)

45. Maurer, T., Guigonis, D., Maslov, I., Pesenti, B., Tsaregorodtsev, A., West, D., Medioni, G.: Performance of geometrix activeid˄ tm 3d face recognition engine on the FRGC data. In: Proceedings of IEEE Conference on Computer Vision and Pattern Recognition-Workshops (CVPR), pp. 154–154. IEEE (2005)

46. Mian, A.S., Bennamoun, M., Owens, R.: An efficient multimodal 2d-3d hybrid approach to automatic face recognition. IEEE Trans. Pattern Anal. Mach. Intell. 29(11), 1927–1943 (2007)

47. Mian, A.S., Bennamoun, M., Owens, R.: An efficient multimodal 2d-3d hybrid approach to automatic face recognition. IEEE Trans. Pattern Anal. Mach. Intell. 2007, 1584–1601 (2007)

48. Ocegueda, O., Fang, T., Shah, S.K., Kakadiaris, I.A.: 3d face discriminant analysis using Gauss-Markov posterior marginals. IEEE Trans. Pattern Anal. Mach. Intell. 35(3), 728–739 (2013)

49. Ocegueda, O., Passalis, G., Theoharis, T., Shah, S.K., Kakadiaris, I.A.: Ur3d-c: linear dimensionality reduction for efficient 3d face recognition. In: Proceedings of IEEE International Joint Conference on Biometrics (IJCB), pp. 1–6. IEEE (2011)

50. Olver, P.: Joint invariant signatures. Found. Comput. Math. 1, 3–67 (2001)

51. Queirolo, C.C., Silva, L., Bellon, O.R.P., Segundo, M.P.: 3d face recognition using simulated annealing and the surface interpenetration measure. IEEE Trans. Pattern Anal. Mach. Intell. **32** (2), 206–219 (2010). doi http://doi.ieeecomputersociety.org/10.1109/TPAMI.2009.14
52. Shashua, A., Levin, A., Avidan, S.: Manifold pursuit: a new approach to appearance based recognition. In: Proceedings of 16th International Conference on Pattern Recognition (ICPR), vol. 3, pp. 590–594. IEEE (2002)
53. Smeets, D., Keustermans, J., Vandermeulen, D., Suetens, P.: meshsift: local surface features for 3d face recognition under expression variations and partial data. Comput. Vis. Image Underst. **117**(2), 158–169 (2013)
54. Spreeuwers, L.: Fast and accurate 3d face recognition. Int. J. Comput. Vis. **93**(3), 389–414 (2011)
55. Turk, M., Pentland, A.: Eigenfaces for recognition. J. Cogn. Neurosci. **3**(1), 71–86 (1991)
56. Turk, M.A., Pentland, A.P.: Face recognition using eigenfaces. In: Proceedings CVPR'91., IEEE Computer Society Conference on Computer Vision and Pattern Recognition, 1991, pp. 586–591. IEEE (1991)
57. Viola, P., Jones, M.: Robust real-time face detection. Int. J. Comput. Vis. **57**(2), 137–154 (2004)
58. Wang, Y., Liu, J., Tang, X.: Robust 3d face recognition by local shape difference boosting. IEEE Trans. Pattern Anal. Mach. Intell. **32**(10), 1858–1870 (2010)
59. Wiskott, L., Fellous, J.M., Kuiger, N., Von Der Malsburg, C.: Face recognition by elastic bunch graph matching. IEEE Trans. Pattern Anal. Mach. Intell. **19**(7), 775–779 (1997)
60. Wright, J., Yang, A.Y., Ganesh, A., Sastry, S.S., Ma, Y.: Robust face recognition via sparse representation. IEEE Trans. Pattern Anal. Mach. Intell. **31**(2), 210–227 (2009)
61. Wu, Y., Chan, K.L., Wang, L.: Face recognition based on discriminative manifold learning. In: Proceedings of 17th International Conference on Pattern Recognition (ICPR), vol. 4, pp. 171–174. IEEE (2004)
62. Zhang, B., Gao, Y., Zhao, S., Liu, J.: Local derivative pattern versus local binary pattern: face recognition with high-order local pattern descriptor. IEEE Trans. Image Process. **19**(2), 533–544 (2010)
63. Zhao, W., Chellappa, R., Phillips, P.J., Rosenfeld, A.: Face recognition: a literature survey. ACM Comput. Surv (CSUR) **35**(4), 399–458 (2003)

Chapter 14
Exploiting Score Distributions for Biometric Applications

Panagiotis Moutafis and Ioannis A. Kakadiaris

Abstract Biometric systems compare biometric samples to produce matching scores. However, the corresponding distributions are often heterogeneous and as a result it is hard to specify a threshold that works well in all cases. Score normalization techniques exploit the score distributions to improve the recognition performance. The goals of this chapter are to (i) introduce the reader to the concept of score normalization and (ii) answer important questions such as why normalizing matching scores is an effective and efficient way of exploiting score distributions, and when such methods are expected to work. In particular, the first section highlights the importance of normalizing matching scores; offers intuitive examples to demonstrate how variations between different (i) biometric samples, (ii) modalities, and (iii) subjects degrade recognition performance; and answers the question of *why score normalization effectively utilizes score distributions*. The next three sections offer a review of score normalization methods developed to address each type of variation. The chapter concludes with a discussion of why such methods have not gained popularity in the research community and answers the question of *when and how one should use score normalization*.

14.1 Introduction

The goal of biometric systems is to determine whether or not (two or more) biometric samples have been acquired from the same subject. This problem is usually formulated as a verification or an open-set identification task. Regardless of the task or biometric trait used, one matching score is obtained for each pairwise compar-

P. Moutafis (✉) · I.A. Kakadiaris
Computational Biomedicine Lab, University of Houston, 4800 Calhoun Rd,
Houston, TX 77004, USA
e-mail: pmoutafis@uh.edu

I.A. Kakadiaris
e-mail: ioannisk@uh.edu

© Springer International Publishing Switzerland 2016   333
T. Bourlai (ed.), *Face Recognition Across the Imaging Spectrum*,
DOI 10.1007/978-3-319-28501-6_14

ison of biometric samples. This number reflects how similar the matched samples are. To reach a decision, the matching scores obtained are compared to a threshold. Ideally, the matching score distributions of the match and nonmatch scores would be separable. Hence, a single threshold would always yield a correct classification. In real-life applications, though, these distributions overlap greatly. To address this problem, many algorithms have been and continue to be developed with the goal of yielding more robust feature sets with better discriminative properties. For example, improved landmark detection and illumination normalization can significantly improve face recognition performance. However, such algorithms cannot always produce the desired results. Even worse, they cannot address inherent variations that increase the overlap of the match and nonmatch score distributions. In this section, we identify the sources of these variations and demonstrate how score normalization methods can effectively and efficiently improve recognition performance. The sources of variations reported in the literature can be grouped into three categories, as follows:

1. *Acquisition conditions*: Variations during data acquisition include differences in pose, illumination, and other conditions. For example, let us assume that we have a gallery of biometric samples. Let us further assume that all images in the gallery are frontal facial images captured under optimal illumination conditions. If a probe that is captured under similar conditions is submitted to the matching system, we can expect that the matching scores obtained will be high on average, even if the subject depicted is not part of the gallery. On the other hand, if another probe is captured under different conditions and then compared with the gallery, we can expect that the matching scores obtained will be low on average, even if the subject depicted is part of the gallery. In other words, the matching score distributions obtained for the two probes are heterogeneous. In this scenario, it would be difficult to correctly classify the two probes using the same threshold.

2. *Multimodal systems*: Unimodal systems are usually vulnerable to spoofing attacks [1] and prone to misclassifications for several reasons, such as lack of uniqueness and noisy data [9]. Multimodal biometric systems utilize information from multiple sources to address these challenges. Such sources may include different biometric traits (e.g., face, iris, and fingerprint) or different pipelines that utilize the same input data. However, fusing the information obtained from different modalities is not easy. The reason is that the matching score distributions produced by different modalities are heterogeneous, even if the gallery and probe subjects are the same. This effect complicates the fusion process. To provide visual evidence of this source of variation, we used pairwise matching scores for the face and iris traits (i.e., $2 \times 3{,}296{,}028$ distances) obtained from the CASIA-Iris-Distance database [37]. This dataset comprises 2,567 images obtained from 142 subjects, most of whom are graduate students at CASIA. The purpose of collecting these images was to promote research on long-range and large-scale iris recognition. Specifically, the images were acquired using a long-range multimodal biometric image acquisition and recognition system

developed by the CASIA group. The same samples were used to extract features for the face and iris traits, independently. The CASIA group provided us with the corresponding distances and the formula *score = max(distance) − distance* was used to convert them into scores. The corresponding boxplots are depicted in Fig. 14.1. As illustrated, the corresponding distributions are heterogeneous. In particular, the face matching scores have a higher median value than the iris matching scores. To assess the discriminative properties of the two modalities, we computed the corresponding receiver operating characteristic (ROC) curves. The area under the curve (AUC) obtained for the face matching scores is 93.48 %, while the AUC obtained for the iris matching scores is 94.17 %. Even though the two biometric traits yield comparable performance and the features were extracted using the same images, fusing the corresponding information is not straightforward.

3. *Subject variability*: It has been observed that, when assessing the performance of biometric systems in large populations, some subjects are easier to recognize than others. Similarly, some subjects can easily spoof the system. This phenomenon was first reported in the literature by Doddington et al. [5]. In that paper, the subjects were classified as sheep, goats, lambs, and wolves, depending on the statistical properties of the matching scores obtained for certain groups of subjects. This subject-specific variability of the matching scores is known as *biometric menagerie* and hinders the selection of a threshold that works well for all subjects.

Why do such methods work? As illustrated, biometric systems are vulnerable to inherent variations that increase the overlap of the match and nonmatch score distributions, thus degrading their recognition capability. Regardless of the source of variation, the challenge that needs to be addressed is the same: the matching

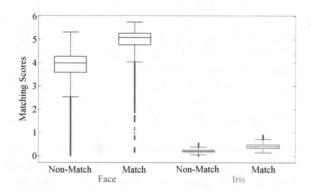

Fig. 14.1 Boxplots of the match and nonmatch scores obtained using two different modalities. The two boxplots on the left correspond to face matching scores, while the two boxplots on the right correspond to iris matching scores

score distributions are heterogeneous. Score normalization methods are techniques that map the matching scores to a common domain where they are directly comparable. In other words, they transform heterogeneous distributions into homogeneous ones.

Usually, two or more sources of variations occur at the same time. For example, a multimodal biometric system employed for large-scale open-set identification would be subject to all three types of variations. In the subsequent sections, we focus on one type of variation at a time. Specifically, we constrain our interest to the task for which the effect of the source of variation is more pronounced and review score normalization methods that address it more effectively.

14.2 Acquisition Conditions

The open-set identification task (also known as watch-list) consists of two steps: (i) a probe is matched with the gallery samples, and (ii) a candidate list is returned with the gallery samples that appear to be the most similar to it. This task can thus be viewed as a hard verification problem (see Fortuna et al. [7] for a more detailed discussion). Consequently, the recognition performance of such systems is significantly affected by variations in the acquisition conditions for both the gallery samples and the probes. Specifically, each time a probe is compared with a given gallery, the matching scores obtained follow a different distribution. Score normalization techniques address this problem by transforming the corresponding matching score distributions to homogeneous ones. Hence, a global threshold can be determined that works well for all submitted probes. In the following, we review some of the most popular methods tailored for this task.

Z-score: Due to its simplicity and good performance, this is one of the most widely used and well-studied techniques. In particular, it is expected to perform well when the location and scale parameters of the score distribution can be approximated sufficiently by the mean and standard deviation estimates. When the matching scores follow a Gaussian distribution, this approach can retain the shape of the distribution. The most notable limitations of Z-score are as follows: (i) it cannot guarantee a common numerical range for the normalized scores and (ii) it is not robust because the mean and standard deviation estimates are sensitive to outliers.

Median and median absolute deviation (MAD): This method replaces the mean and standard deviation estimates in the *Z-score* formula with the median value and the median absolute deviation, respectively. Therefore, it addresses the problem of lack of robustness due to outliers. However, it is not optimal for scores that follow a Gaussian distribution.

W-score [36]: Scheirer et al. proposed a score normalization technique that models the tail of the nonmatch scores. The greatest advantage of this approach is that it does not make any assumptions concerning the score distribution. Also, it appears to be robust and yields good performance. However, to employ W-score the user must specify the number of scores to be selected for fitting. While in most cases it is sufficient to select as few as five scores, selecting a small number of scores may yield discretized normalized scores. Consequently, it is not possible to assess the performance of the system in low false acceptance rates or false alarm rates. On the other hand, selecting too many scores may violate the assumptions required to invoke the extreme value theorem. Another limitation of W-score is that it cannot be applied to multisample galleries unless an integration rule is first employed. As a result, it is not possible to obtain normalized scores for each sample independently. As it will be demonstrated, a recently proposed framework addresses this problem and extends the use of W-score to multisample galleries.

Additional score normalization techniques (e.g., tanh-estimators and double sigmoid function) are reviewed in [8]. Finally, some score normalization methods have been proposed that incorporate quality measures [27, 28, 33]. However, they are tailored to the verification task and have not been evaluated for open-set identification. The aforementioned methods consider the matching scores obtained for a single probe as a single set. This strategy does not fully utilize the available information for galleries with multiple samples per subject. To address this problem, Moutafis and Kakadiaris [15, 16] introduced a framework that describes how to employ existing score normalization methods (and those to be invented) more effectively. First, we review the theory of stochastic dominance, which theoretically supports their framework.

Definition The notation $X \gtrsim_{\text{FSD}} Y$ denotes that X first-order *stochastically dominates Y,* that is

$$\Pr\{X > z\} \geq \Pr\{Y > z\}, \quad \forall z. \tag{14.1}$$

As implied by this definition, the corresponding distributions will be ordered. This is highlighted by the following lemma (its proof may be found in [42]).

Lemma *Let X and Y be any two random variables, then*

$$X \gtrsim_{\text{FSD}} Y \Rightarrow E[X] \geq E[Y]. \tag{14.2}$$

An illustrative example of first-order stochastic dominance is depicted in Fig. 14.1 of Wolfstetter et al. [42] where $\bar{F}(z) \gtrsim_{\text{FSD}} \bar{G}(Z)$. Note that the first-order stochastic dominance relationship implies all higher orders [6]. In addition, this relation is known to be transitive as implicitly illustrated by Birnbaum et al. [4]. Finally, the first-order stochastic dominance may also be viewed as the stochastic ordering of random variables.

Algorithm 1 Rank-Based Score Normalization

Input: $S^p = \bigcup_i \{S_i^p\}, f$

   Step 1: Partition S^p into subsets

1: $C_r = \{\emptyset\}, \forall r$
2: **for** $r = 1 : max_i\{|S_i^p|\}$ **do**
3:    **for all** $i \varepsilon I$ **do**
4:       $C_r = C_r \bigcup S_{i,r}^p$
5:    **end for**
6: **end for**

   Step 2: Normalize each subset C_r

7: $S^{p,N} = \{\emptyset\}$
8: **for** $r = 1 : max_i\{|S_i^p|\}$ **do**
9:    $S^{p,N} = S^{p,N} \bigcup f(C_r)$
10: **end for**

Output: $S^{p,N}$

Rank-Based Score Normalization (RBSN): For the case of systems with multi-sample galleries, Moutafis and Kakadiaris [15, 16] proposed a RBSN algorithm that partitions the matching scores into subsets and normalizes each subset independently. An overview of the proposed RBSN framework is provided in Algorithm 1. The notation used is the following:

S^p the set of matching scores obtained for a given probe p when compared with a given gallery,

S_i^p the set of matching scores that correspond to the gallery subject with identity $= i$, $S_i^p \subseteq S^p$,

$S_{i,r}^p$ the ranked-r score of S_i^p,

$S^{p,N}$ the set of normalized scores for a given probe p,

C_r the rank-r subset, $\cup_r C_r = S^p$,

$|d|$ the cardinality of a set d,

I the set of unique gallery identities, and

f a given score normalization technique

An illustrative example of how to apply the proposed approach is provided in Fig. 14.2. Let us assume that there are three subjects in the gallery, namely X, Y, and Z. Let us further assume that three biometric samples are available for X (denoted by X_1, X_2, and X_3), two samples are available for Y (denoted by Y_1 and Y_2), and three samples are available for Z (denoted by Z_1, Z_2, and Z_3). Finally, let us assume that a probe is submitted to the system (denoted by p_i) and matched with all the gallery samples. Existing approaches would consider the obtained matching scores as a single set and normalize them in a single step. In contrast, the first step of the RBSN framework is to rank the matching scores for each gallery subject independently. For instance, if the matching scores obtained for X are $S(X_1, p_i) = 0.7$, $S(X_2, p_i) = 0.8$, and $S(X_1, p_i) = 0.6$, the corresponding ranks are 2, 1, and 3, respectively. If for subject Y we obtain $S(Y_1, p_i) = 0.4$, $S(Y_2, p_i) = 0.3$, then the ranks

RBSN: Partition the set of matching scores obtained for a given probe and apply score normalization to each resulting subset independently.

Gallery	Matching Scores	Rank
X_1	$S(X_1,p_i)=0.6$	3
X_2	$S(X_2,p_i)=0.8$	1
X_3	$S(X_3,p_i)=0.7$	2
Y_1	$S(Y_1,p_i)=0.4$	1
Y_2	$S(Y_2,p_i)=0.3$	2
Z_1	$S(Z_1,p_i)=0.2$	2
Z_2	$S(Z_2,p_i)=0.1$	3
Z_3	$S(Z_3,p_i)=0.6$	1

1. Compute the rank of the scores for each gallery subject
2. Create rank-based subsets such that:
   $Cr=\{\text{rank-r scores}\}$

   $C_1 = \{0.8, 0.4, 0.6\}$
   $C_2 = \{0.7, 0.3, 0.2\}$
   $C_3 = \{0.6, 0.1\}$

3. Normalize each subset independently

Fig. 14.2 Overview of the rank-based score normalization algorithm. The notation $S(X_1; p_i)$ is used to denote the score obtained by comparing a probe pi to the biometric sample 1 of a gallery subject labeled X

are 1 and 2, while if for subject Z we obtain $S(Y_1, p_i) = 0.2$, $S(Y_2, p_i) = 0.1$, $S(Y_1, p_i) = 0.7$, then the corresponding ranks are 2, 3 and 1 respectively. The second step of RBSN is to use the rank information to partition the matching scores into subsets. Specifically, the matching scores that ranked first comprise the subset $C_1 = \{0.8, 0.4, 0.7\}$, the ranked second scores comprise the subset $C_2 = \{0.7, 0.3, 0.2\}$, and the ranked third scores comprise the subset $C_3 = \{0.6, 0.1\}$. By invoking the theory of stochastic dominance, it is straightforward to demonstrate that the rank-based partitioning imposes the subsets' score distributions to be ordered (i.e., heterogeneous). To illustrate this point, each curve in Fig. 14.3 depicts the probability density estimate that corresponds to such subsets obtained from a gallery with six samples per subject. By normalizing the scores of each subset individually, the corresponding distributions become homogeneous and the system's performance improves. Hence, going back to our example, the matching scores of each set C_1,

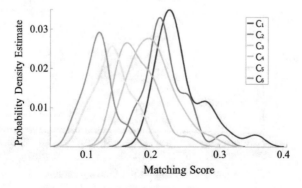

Fig. 14.3 Each curve depicts the probability density estimate corresponding to a C_r subset. Each subset C_r was constructed by *Step 1* of RBSN using the set S^p for a random probe p

C_2, and C_3 are normalized independently. Finally, the user might choose to fuse the normalized matching scores for each subject to consolidate the corresponding information. The RBNS framework (i) can be used in conjunction with any score normalization technique and any fusion rule, (ii) is amenable to parallel programming, and (iii) is suitable for both verification and open-set identifications. Two of the most important implications of this work are that (i) multiple samples per subject are exploited more effectively compared to existing methods, which yields improved recognition accuracy and (ii) improvements in terms of identification performance on a per-probe basis are obtained. We highlight selected results from [16] to illustrate these two points. First, the impact of the number of same-subject samples on the recognition performance was assessed. To this end, the UHDB11 dataset [38] was used which was designed to offer a great variability of facial data in terms of acquisition conditions. Specifically, 72 light/pose variations are available for 23 subjects, resulting in 2,742,336 pairwise comparisons. Six samples per subject were selected (one for each illumination condition) to form the gallery and the rest samples were used as probes. The matching scores used were provided by Toderici et al. [39]. Random subsets of one, three, and five samples per gallery subject were selected and each time the ROC curve and the corresponding AUC values were computed. This procedure was repeated 100 times using the unprocessed, raw matching scores, Z-score normalized scores, and RBSN:Z-score normalization scores. The obtained results are summarized in Fig. 14.4. As illustrated, RBSN:Z-score utilizes more effectively multiple samples per subject compared to Z-score. Second, the impact on the separation between the match and nonmatch scores on a per-probe basis was assessed. To this end, the FRGC v2 dataset was used that comprises 4,007 samples obtained from 466 subjects under different facial expressions. The 3D face recognition method of Ocegueda et al. [19] was used to extract the signatures and the Euclidean distance to compute the dissimilarity

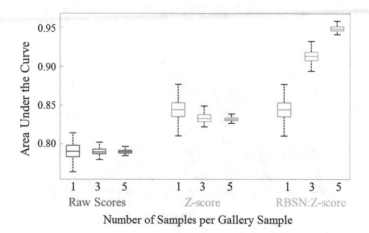

Fig. 14.4 Depicted are the boxplots for: (1) raw scores; (2) Z-score; and (3) RBSN:Z-score, when one, three, and five samples per gallery subject are randomly selected from UHDB11

values. The gallery was formed by randomly selecting 1,893 samples from 350 subjects. The rest were used as probes, resulting in an open-set problem. The Rank-1 errors for probes that belong to the gallery are as follows: (i) raw matching scores 0.74 %, (ii) Z-score normalized scores 0.74 %, and (iii) RBSN:Z-score normalized scores 0.66 %. Z-score and most existing approaches consist mostly of linear transformations, and therefore, they do not alter the order of the matching scores. Hence, the Rank-1 error for the raw matching scores and the normalized ones is the same. The RBSN algorithm, however, addresses this problem and has the potential to improve the accuracy of the rankings as illustrated.

To avoid confusion, we refer the readers to [15, 16] where they can find more implementation details, insights, experimental results, along with two versions of the RBSN algorithm that (i) fully utilizes the gallery versus gallery matching scores matrix and (ii) dynamically augments the gallery in an online fashion.

14.3 Multimodal Systems

Information fusion in the context of biometrics is a very challenging problem. Therefore, it has been receiving increasing attention over the past few years (Fig. 14.5). The most common approaches employ feature-level or score-level fusion. Methods in the first category (i) utilize the feature representation obtained for each modality to learn a common representation or (ii) learn rules that directly compare the multimodal representations to compute a matching score. Methods in the second category compute one matching score per pairwise comparison for each modality and then they either: (i) learn fusion rules that combine the information into a single matching score, or (ii) transform the scores to a standard form (i.e., score normalization) and then apply fixed fusion rules. In this section, we limit our scope to score-level fusion methods. The selected approaches were identified after conducting a systematic search of the literature that covered the years 2011–2014. To ensure that the latest papers have been included in our search, we focused on

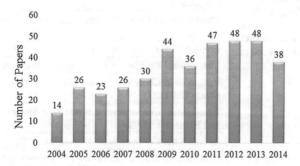

Fig. 14.5 Depiction of the number of papers published during the years 2004–2014 that include the words *biometric* and *fusion* in their title, according to the search engine Google Scholar

selected conferences in the field of biometrics and computer vision. The venues and keywords used are listed in Table 14.1. Papers that include at least one keyword in their title were reviewed in more detail to determine their relevance and interestingness. However, the number of papers selected was relatively small. To address this problem, we expanded the breadth of our search to the citations of the selected papers. We group the reviewed methods in three categories: (i) transformation-based, (ii) classification-based, and (iii) density-based. Methods in the first category normalize the matching scores and then employ fixed rules to combine them. Approaches in the second category usually treat the scores as features and learn a classifier that determines how similar the compared samples are. Finally, approaches in the third category estimate the probability density functions for each class. Such methods can be grouped as generative or discriminative. Generative methods focus explicitly on modeling the matching score distributions using parametric or nonparametric models. Discriminative approaches, on the other hand, focus explicitly on improving the recognition rate obtained by the fused scores. An overview of the categorization of score-level fusion methods is presented in Fig. 14.6, while an overview of the reviewed papers is offered in Table 14.2.

Transformation-based approaches normalize the matching score distributions of each modality independently. Consequently, the corresponding distributions become homogeneous and fixed fusion rules can be applied, which simplifies the fusion process. Kittler et al. [10] have studied the statistical background of fixed fusion rules. Two of the most popular ones are the *sum* and *max* operators. The former is implemented by a simple addition under the assumption of equal priors. Even though this rule makes restrictive assumptions, it appears to yield good performance as demonstrated in the literature [8, 10]. The latter makes less restrictive assumptions and it is also very simple to implement. Specifically, the output of this rule is defined to be the maximum score obtained. Wild et al. [41] employed a median filtering approach for score fusion to increase robustness to outliers. Specifically, this method disregards matching scores for which the distance from the median matching score exceeds a certain threshold. The authors employ

Table 14.1 Conferences used for identifying fusion methods. Papers that include at least one of the keywords in their title were considered in our review	Conferences
	Conference on Computer Vision and Pattern Recognition (CVPR)
	European Conference on Computer Vision (ECCV)
	International Conference on Computer Vision (ICCV)
	International Conference of the Biometrics Special Interest Group (BIOSIG)
	International Conference on Biometrics: Theory, Applications and Systems (BTAS)
	International Conference on Biometrics (ICB)
	International Joint Conference on Biometrics (IJCB)
	Keywords: Fusion, Information, Multimodal, Score

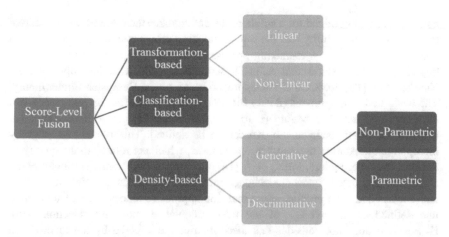

Fig. 14.6 Overview of the categorization of score-level fusion approaches

Table 14.2 Overview of score-level fusion papers. The column "Mapping" denotes whether the operations performed are linear or non-linear, while the column "Learning" denotes whether or not a method relies on offline training. The column "Model" denotes whether a method is Transformation-based, Classification-based, or Density-based (i.e., parametric or non-parametric)

Name	Year	Mapping	Learning	Model
Wild et al. [41]	2013	Linear	Adaptive	Transformation
Scheirer et al. [35]	2011	Nonlinear	Offline	Transformation
Nguyen et al. [18]	2014	Linear	Offline	Transformation
Mezai et al. [14]	2011	Linear	Offline	Transformation
Scheirer et al. [34]	2012	Nonlinear	Offline	Transformation
Zuo et al. [44]	2012	Linear	Adaptive	Transformation
Poh et al. [31]	2012	Linear	Offline	Transformation
Makihara et al. [12]	2014	Nonlinear	Offline	Nonparametric
Makihara et al. [13]	2011	Linear	Offline	Parametric
Poh et al. [30]	2011	Linear	Offline	Nonparametric
Liu et al. [11]	2014	Linear	Offline	Classification
Poh et al. [26]	2012	Nonlinear	Offline	Classification
Tyagi et al. [40]	2011	Linear	Offline	Classification

the proposed method to fuse matching scores obtained from fingerprints with liveliness values. These values denote the likelihood that the submitted sample is genuine and does not belong to an attacker seeking to spoof the system. As a result, this 1-median outlier detection approach alleviates negative effects to the recognition performance due to matching score anomalies, while it increases security. Scheirer et al. [35] proposed a statistical meta-recognition approach that relies on Weibull distribution. Specifically, the proposed approach models the tail of the nonmatch scores obtained for a single probe and invokes the extreme value theorem to estimate the probability that the top-K matching scores contain an outlier (i.e., a match score). The decision-making process relies on the rejection rate of the null hypothesis, which states that a match score is contained in the top-K scores. Nguyen et al. [18] proposed a new approach based on the Dempster–Shafer theory. The basic belief assignment (BBA) function is represented as the hypothesis that the query and template belong (i) to the same class, (ii) to a different class, or (iii) that the relationship of the two cannot be defined. This model can naturally incorporate uncertainty measures into the model, which are related to the quality of the data and other factors. Mezai et al. [14] also proposed a Dempster–Shafer based algorithm. The fused scores are assigned into three categories: genuine, impostors, and unclassified. The authors argue that this approach reduces the half total error rate defined as the average of the false acceptance and false rejection rates. However, it does not consider that these metrics are affected by the unclassified data. Scheirer et al. [34] proposed a multiattribute calibration method for score fusion. Specifically, their approach fits a Weibull distribution to the flipped negative decision scores of an SVM classifier. Next, it normalizes the transformed scores using the cumulative density function. The multiattribute fusion is performed using the L_1 norm. That is, for a given query, the target samples that maximize the L_1 norm for each of the attributes are found. Unlike existing approaches that weigh all attributes equally, the proposed method finds the target samples that are most similar to most but not all the attributes. Zuo et al. [44] proposed a new approach for matching short-wave infrared (SWIR) and visible data. The images are first filtered and encoded using well-known filters. The encoded responses are then split into multiple nonoverlapping blocks and bin histograms are generated. The authors observed that the zero values obtained for SWIR and visible images are highly correlated. Hence, they proposed a score normalization method that addresses this problem. Specifically, the symmetric divergence between a visible template and a SWIR template is first computed. Then, a normalization factor is defined as the average difference of the computed divergence and the matching similarity scores obtained for an SWIR probe template. Finally, the normalized scores are computed as the divergence of a given visible image and a given SWIR template, minus the normalization factor and the symmetric divergence computed in the previous two steps. Poh et al. [31] proposed a client-specific score normalization approach. Specifically, the authors proposed three discriminative strategies: (i) dF-norm, (ii) dZ-norm, and (iii) dp-norm. These are defined as the probability of the subject being a client given the corresponding class mean and variance for the client and impostor. To address the problem of few client samples, the client-specific mean score is computed as a weighted average of the client and the global client mean scores. Moutafis and Kakadiaris [17] proposed a RBSN framework for multibiometric score fusion. Unlike existing approaches that normalize the matching scores from each modality independently, the multi rank-based score normalization (MRBSN) framework takes into consideration inherent correlations between the data. The first step is to normalize the matching scores of each modality independently as usual. The second step, though, is to join the normalized scores to form a single set. Finally, the joined set of scores is processed using RBSN. The implementation is summarized in Algorithm 2. The additional notation is the following:

S^J the set of matching scores obtained for a given probe using the modality denoted by J,

$S^{J,N}$ the set of normalized scores for a given probe,

S the set of joined normalized score sets, $S = \cup_J S^{J,N}$,

S^{N_2} the set of "twice" normalized scores, and

R a given fusion rule.

An illustrative example of how to apply MRBSN is provided in Fig. 14.7. Let us assume that facial and iris data are available for three subjects, namely X, Y, and Z. The superscript F denotes that the biometric sample at hand was derived from face data, while the superscript I is used for the iris data. Let us further assume that a probe comprising face p_i^F and iris p_i^I data is submitted to the system. The matching score obtained for the face modality for subject X is denoted by $S(X^F, p_i^F)$, while the matching score obtained for the iris modality is denoted by $S(X^I, p_i^I)$. After normalizing the matching scores for the two modalities independently, we obtain the normalized scores. The normalized scores for the face and iris modalities for subject X are denoted by $S^N(X^F, p_i^F)$ and $S^N(X^I, p_i^I)$, respectively. The normalized scores

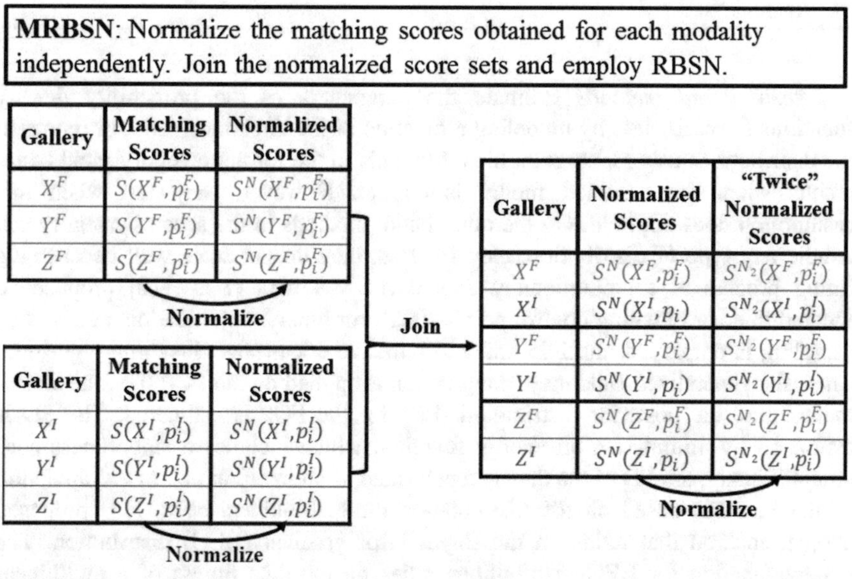

MRBSN: Normalize the matching scores obtained for each modality independently. Join the normalized score sets and employ RBSN.

Gallery	Matching Scores	Normalized Scores
X^F	$S(X^F, p_i^F)$	$S^N(X^F, p_i^F)$
Y^F	$S(Y^F, p_i^F)$	$S^N(Y^F, p_i^F)$
Z^F	$S(Z^F, p_i^F)$	$S^N(Z^F, p_i^F)$

Normalize

Gallery	Matching Scores	Normalized Scores
X^I	$S(X^I, p_i^I)$	$S^N(X^I, p_i^I)$
Y^I	$S(Y^I, p_i^I)$	$S^N(Y^I, p_i^I)$
Z^I	$S(Z^I, p_i^I)$	$S^N(Z^I, p_i^I)$

Normalize

Join

Gallery	Normalized Scores	"Twice" Normalized Scores
X^F	$S^N(X^F, p_i^F)$	$S^{N_2}(X^F, p_i^F)$
X^I	$S^N(X^I, p_i)$	$S^{N_2}(X^I, p_i^I)$
Y^F	$S^N(Y^F, p_i^F)$	$S^{N_2}(Y^F, p_i^F)$
Y^I	$S^N(Y^I, p_i)$	$S^{N_2}(Y^I, p_i^I)$
Z^F	$S^N(Z^F, p_i^F)$	$S^{N_2}(Z^F, p_i^F)$
Z^I	$S^N(Z^I, p_i)$	$S^{N_2}(Z^I, p_i^I)$

Normalize

Fig. 14.7 Overview of the rank-based score normalization algorithm. The notation $S(X_1; p_i)$ is used to denote the score obtained by comparing a probe pi to the biometric sample 1 of a gallery subject labeled X

for the two modalities are then joined to form a single set. Since the scores are no longer distinguished based on the modality, the RBSN algorithm can be employed to leverage the multiple scores per subject. Experimental results using the CASIA dataset illustrate the benefits of this approach. Specifically, one sample from each modality was used for 71 subjects to define the gallery. The rest were used as probes. This process was repeated 50 times and the matching scores were normalized using Z-score, W-score, MRBSN:Z-score, and MRBSN:W-score. The mean values of the verification performance obtained at false acceptance rate equal to 10^{-2} are 90.90, 91.08, 85.46, and 86.29 %, respectively. For a more detailed analysis of the implementation and complete results, we refer the readers to [17].

Algorithm 2 Multi-Rank-Based Score Normalization

Input: S^J, Z, R
Step 1: Normalize each S^J independently
for all J **do**
  $S^{J,N} = Z(S^J)$
end for
Step 2: Join $S^{J,N}$
$S = \bigcup_J S^{J,N}$
Step 3: Employ RBSN
$S^{N_2} = RBSN(S, Z)$
Step 4: Fuse the "twice" normalized scores
$S^{N_2} = R(S^{N_2})$
Return S^{N_2}

Density-based methods estimate the parameters of the probability density functions for each class by modeling a function of the likelihood ratio, or represent the distributions using histogram bins. Methods in the former category yield better results when the assumed model is correct. However, they fail when this assumption does not hold. On the other hand, methods in the second category can handle any type of distribution. Nevertheless, they do not scale well because the fitting process is computationally expensive. Makihara et al. [12] proposed a method that uses floating control points (FCP) for binary classification. A stratified sampling is employed multiple times to initialize a k-means clustering algorithm. Then, the generalized Delaunay triangulation is applied on the FCP (i.e., the cluster means) and the posterior distribution (PD) for the FCP is estimated. The PD is estimated by minimizing an energy function, which includes a smoothness constraint. Finally, the PD of the data is represented as an interpolation or extrapolation of the FCP PD based on the triangulation mesh. Makihara et al. [13] proposed another method that relies on the Bayes error gradient (BEG) distribution. The energy function for BEG distributions relies on the data fitness of a multilinear interpolation for each of the lattice-type control points. Furthermore, the authors incorporate prior knowledge into the model by strengthening the smoothness parameters and by adding monotonically increasing constraints upon the BEG distribution. The experimental results indicate that the BEG with prior information is competitive with the sum-rule, even when the size of the client training samples decreases. Poh et al. [30] proposed a heterogeneous information fusion approach for biometric systems. Depending on the information sources used, the authors distinguish two cases: (i) independent and (ii) dependent score-level fusion. For the first case, the authors proposed a homogeneous fusion scheme (i.e., Naive Bayes), which is defined as the sum of the logit conditional probabilities of a genuine matching score given the source information. For the second case, the authors used the sum of the logit bind probabilities. The conducted experiments demonstrate that greater performance gains are obtained for the heterogeneous case.

Classification-based approaches do not model the distribution of the matching scores. Instead, they consider the matching scores as features and use them to train classifiers that discriminate each class. As a result, they provide a trade-off between accurate recognition and low time complexity. Liu et al. [11] demonstrated that the variance reduction equal error rate (VR-EER) model proposed by Poh and Bengio [22] is theoretically incomplete. To address this limitation, they proposed a new theoretical approach for score-level fusion. In particular, they demonstrated that under certain assumptions optimal fusion weights can be derived that maximize the F-ratio. Hence, the proposed approach can always perform at least as well as the best expert. Poh et al. [26] proposed a temporal fusion bimodal methodology for video and audio fusion. The audio is processed using Gaussian mixture model with maximum aposteriori adaptation (MAP-GMM). The video is processed in two ways. First, features are extracted from each face and each frame using a discrete cosine transform. Then, the MAP-GMM is applied to compute matching scores, which are fused using the mean rule. Second, nonuniform local binary pattern features are extracted followed by Fisher discriminant projection. The corresponding matching scores obtained are fused using the max rule. The first approach yields multiple scores, which are used to compute descriptive statistics. A logistic regression model is then learned that uses these descriptive statistics in conjunction with the scores obtained from the second approach. Finally, the sound and video modalities scores are merged using Naive Bayes. This pipeline allows temporal fusion, improves recognition performance, and increases robustness to spoof attacks. Tyagi et al. [40] proposed a new method to estimate the Gaussian mixture models using the maximum accept and reject criteria. The motivation behind this decision is that, by using the maximum accept and reject criteria instead of the likelihood, the optimization process focuses more on the classification itself rather than the fitting of a density model. As a result, increased recognition performance is achieved.

In summary, transformation-based methods are intuitive, simple, and efficient, but they do not utilize training data. Density-based approaches can be optimal if the assumptions made hold (i.e., parametric) or can fit the data relying on computationally expensive operations (i.e., nonparametric). Finally, classification-based approaches provide a trade-off between accurate recognition and efficiency. However, they require vast training data to ensure good generalization properties.

14.4 Subject Variability

Even when the acquisition conditions are controlled, there are still variations in the matching score distributions. Specifically, the matching scores obtained for different subjects exhibit different statistical properties. Several papers have studied this phenomenon and different groupings of the subjects have been proposed. The most popular are the Doddington's Zoo [5] and Yager and Dunstone's [43] classifications. There are different ways to classify subjects into different groups. For instance, some methods rely on criteria such as the F-ratio, the Fisher ration, and the d-prime metric [24], while other methods rely on the training matching scores dataset to rank and order the subjects [24]. Finally, a biometric menagerie index has been proposed by Poh and Kittler [25] to assess the severity of the biometric menagerie.

Two of the most common ways to address the problem of subject variability are (i) user-specific threshold and (ii) user-specific score normalization. In this section, we review relevant score normalization approaches that work well in a variety of datasets. Such methods can be grouped into two categories: (i) parametric and (ii) learning-based.

14.4.1 Parametric-Based Normalization

Parametric approaches make assumptions concerning the matching score distributions of each subject (or groups of subjects). That is, they model the corresponding distributions and then transform them into a standard form.

Z-norm: This method focuses on the nonmatch score distribution. Specifically, it assumes that the corresponding matching scores follow a Gaussian distribution. Hence, it estimates the corresponding mean and standard deviation values (e.g., using a training set) and uses them to standardize each score obtained for that subject. The distribution of the normalized nonmatch scores has a mean value equal to 0 and standard deviation equal to 1.

F-Norm: This approach extends the Z-norm method in the sense that it models both the match and nonmatch score distributions. It relies on the assumption that the corresponding distributions are Gaussian. Unlike Z-norm, though, it estimates the mean values for the match and nonmatch scores, which are then used to normalize the scores. However, the scarce availability of match scores can yield poor estimates for the mean. To address this problem, the corresponding value is estimated by interpolating the subject-specific match scores mean and the global match scores mean. The distribution of the normalized nonmatch scores has a mean value equal to 0, while the distribution of the normalized match scores has a mean value equal to 1. A more in-depth analysis is offered by Poh and Bengio [21].

The Test Normalization (*T-Norm*) [2] It is a variation of the Z-norm method. However, it is implemented in an online fashion. That is, the nonmatch mean and standard deviation estimates are computed at test time using an additional cohort of impostor samples.

Group-Based Normalization: Unlike existing approaches that normalize the matching scores on a per subject basis, Poh et al. [29] proposed a group-based normalization scheme. In particular, they cluster the subjects into groups and use the corresponding information to normalize the matching scores. As a result, the paucity of match scores is addressed.

14.4.2   Learning-Based Normalization

Learning-based methods employ statistical models with the goal of decreasing the overlap of the match and nonmatch score distributions.

Model-Specific Log Likelihood Ratio (MS-LLR): The proposed approach seeks a transformation that optimizes a likelihood ratio test that relies on the match and nonmatch score distributions [23]. The resulting score normalization method utilizes both match and nonmatch scores. Under the assumption that the standard deviation of the two populations is the same, the MS-LLR is equal to Z-norm, shifted by a constant value that is computed on a per subject basis.

Logistic Regression: One way of normalizing scores is to employ logistic regression. That is, a training set of match and nonmatch scores can be used to train a logistic regression model such that the output approximates the posterior probability of an input being a match score. Another way to utilize the logistic regression is to decompose the Z-norm or F-norm formulas to different terms. Then, the regression model is employed to learn optimal weights [32] for each of the terms.

14.5   Conclusion

Utilizing score distributions has the potential to significantly improve the recognition performance. However, methods such as score normalization must be used carefully and with discretion because inappropriate use may lead to severely degraded recognition performance. To determine whether it is suitable to exploit matching score distributions for a certain application, the first step should be to investigate whether or not there are inherent variations as described in Sect. 14.1. Depending on the results obtained from this analysis and the application at hand, the most appropriate score normalization method should be selected. For example, in the case of multimodal systems, score normalization methods tailored for fusion should be used. Nevertheless, regardless of the method selected, the validity of the corresponding assumptions should be checked. For example, before applying

Fig. 14.8 ROC curves
obtained for PaSC using the
PittPatt face recognition
system

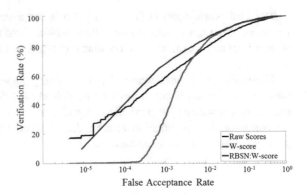

Z-score, the user should ensure that the matching scores are approximately Gaussian distributed, and W-score is applicable only to single-sample galleries. To illustrate the importance of checking the necessary assumptions, we used the Point and Shoot Challenge (PaSC) dataset [3] and the face recognition system PittPatt [20]. The PaSC dataset was designed to assess the performance of biometric systems when inexpensive camera technologies are used to capture images from everyday life situations. Specifically, it includes 9,376 images from 293 subjects. For our experiment, we used 659 samples obtained from 117 subjects as a gallery and 2,739 samples from 122 subjects as probes. That is, images for five subjects are not included in the gallery, resulting in an open-set problem. The scores were normalized with W-score and RBSN:W-score using 30 scores to fit the tail of the distribution. Since there are multiple samples per gallery, the extreme value theorem requirements are violated for W-score but not for RBSN:W-score. The obtained ROC curves are depicted in Fig. 14.8. As illustrated, W-score results in degraded verification performance when compared with the verification performance obtained using raw scores. The RBSN:W-score, on the other hand, yields improvements.

As illustrated in this chapter, appropriate utilization of the matching score distributions can increase recognition performance of biometric systems in a reliable manner at a relatively low computational cost.

Acknowledgments The authors would like to thank Prof. Z. Sun and his students for sharing their data. Portions of the research in this paper use the CASIA-IrisV4 collected by the Chinese Academy of Sciences Institute of Automation (CASIA). This research was funded in part by the US Army Research Laboratory (W911NF-13-1-0127) and the UH Hugh Roy and Lillie Cranz Cullen Endowment Fund. All statements of fact, opinion, or conclusions contained herein are those of the authors and should not be construed as representing the official views or policies of the sponsors.

References

1. Akhtar, Z., Fumera, G., Marcialis, G., Roli, F.: Evaluation of serial and parallel multibiometric systems under spoofing attacks. In: Proceedings of 5th International Conference on Biometrics: Theory, Applications and Systems, pp. 283–288, New Delhi, India, March 29–April1 2012
2. Auckenthaler, R., Carey, M., Lloyd-Thomas, H.: Score normalization for text-independent speaker verification systems. Digit. Signal Proc. **10**(1), 42–54 (2000)
3. Beveridge, J., Phillips, P., Bolme, D., Draper, B., Givens, G., Lui, Y., Teli, M., Zhang, H., Scruggs, W., Bowyer, K., Flynn, P., Cheng, S.: The challenge of face recognition from digital point-and-shoot cameras. In Proceedings of 6th International Conference on Biometrics: Theory, Applications and Systems, pp. 1–8, Washington DC, 4–7 June 2013
4. Birnbaum, M., Patton, J., Lott, M.: Evidence against rank-dependent utility theories: tests of cumulative independence, interval independence, stochastic dominance, and transitivity. Organ. Behav. Hum. Decis. Process. **77**(1), 44–83 (1999)
5. Doddington, G., Liggett, W., Martin, A., Przybocki, M., Reynolds, D.: Sheep, goats, lambs and wolves: A statistical analysis of speaker performance in the NIST 1998 speaker recognition evaluation. In Proceedings of the International Conference on Spoken Language Processing, vol. 4, pp. 1–4, Sydney, Australia, Nov 30–Dec 4 1998
6. Durlauf, S., Blume, L.: The New Palgrave Dictionary of Economics. Palgrave Macmillan, Basingstoke (2008)
7. Fortuna, J., Sivakumaran, P., Ariyaeeinia, A., Malegaonkar, A.: Relative effectiveness of score normalisation methods in open-set speaker identification. In: Proceedings of the Speaker and Language Recognition Workshop, Toledo, Spain, May 31 June 3 2004
8. Jain, A., Nandakumar, K., Ross, A.: Score normalization in multimodal biometric systems. Pattern Recogn. **38**(12), 2270–2285 (2005)
9. Jain, A., Ross, A.: Multibiometric systems. Commun. ACM **47**(1), 34–40 (2004)
10. Kittler, J., Hatef, M., Duin, R., Matas, J.: On combining classifiers. IEEE Trans. Pattern Anal. Mach. Intell. **20**(3), 226–239 (1998)
11. Liu, Y., Yang, L., Suen, C.: The effect of correlation and performances of base-experts on score fusion. Trans. Syst. Man Cybern. Syst. **44**(4), 510–517 (2014)
12. Makihara, Y., Muramatsu, D., Iwama, H., Ngo, T., Yagi, Y.: Score-level fusion by generalized Delaunay triangulation. In: Proceedings of 2nd International Joint Conference on Biometrics, pp. 1–8, Clearwater, FL, Sep 29 Oct 2 2014
13. Makihara, Y., Muramatsu, D., Yagi, Y., Hossain, A.: Score-level fusion based on the direct estimation of the bayes error gradient distribution. In: Proceedings of the International Joint Conference on Biometrics, pp. 1–8, Washington DC, 11–13 Oct 2011
14. Mezai, L., Hachouf, F., Bengherabi, M.: Score fusion of face and voice using DempsterShafer theory for person authentication. In: Proceedings of 11th International Conference on Intelligent Systems Design and Applications, pp. 894–899. Cordoba, Spain, 22–24 Nov 2011
15. Moutafis, P., Kakadiaris, I.: Can we do better in unimodal biometric systems? A novel rank-based score normalization framework for multi-sample galleries. In: Proceedings of 6th IARP International Conference on Biometrics, Madrid, Spain, 4–7 June 2013
16. Moutafis, P., Kakadiaris, I.: Can we do better in unimodal biometric systems? A novel rank-based score normalization framework. Trans. Cybern. **99**, 1–14 (2014, In Press)
17. Moutafis, P., Kakadiaris, I.: Rank-based score normalization for multi-biometric score fusion. In: Proceedings of 8th International Symposium on Technologies for Homeland Security, Waltham, MA, 14–15 April 2015
18. Nguyen, K., Denman, S., Sridharan, S., Fookes, C.: Score-level multibiometric fusion based on Dempster-Shafer theory incorporating uncertainty factors. Trans. Hum. Mach. Syst. **99**, 1–9 (2014)
19. Ocegueda, O., Passalis, G., Theoharis, T., Shah, S., Kakadiaris, I.: UR3D-C: linear dimensionality reduction for efficient 3D face recognition. In: Proceedings of the International Joint Conference on Biometrics, pp. 1–6, Washington DC, Oct 11–13 2011

20. Pittsburgh Pattern Recognition.: PittPatt face recognition software development kit (PittPatt SDK) v5.2, March 2011
21. Poh, N., Bengio, S.: An investigation of f-ratio client-dependent normalisation on biometric authentication tasks. Technical report, 04-46, IDIAP, Martigny, Switzerland (2004)
22. Poh, N., Bengio, S.: How do correlation and variance of base-experts affect fusion in biometric authentication tasks? Trans. Signal Process. **53**(11), 4384–4396 (2005)
23. Poh, N., Kittler, J.: Incorporating variation of model-specific score distribution in speaker verification systems. IEEE Trans. Audio Speech Lang. Process. **16**(3), 594–606 (2008)
24. Poh, N., Kittler, J.: A methodology for separating sheep from goats for controlled enrollment and multimodal fusion. In: Proceedings of 6th Biometrics Symposium, pp. 17–22, Tampa, FL, 23–25 Sept 2008
25. Poh, N., Kittler, J.: A biometric menagerie index for characterising template/model specific variation. In: Proceedings of 3rd International Conference on Biometrics, pp. 1–10, Sassari, Italy, 2–9 June 2009
26. Poh, N., Kittler, J., Alkoot, F.: A discriminative parametric approach to video-based score-level fusion for biometric authentication. In: Proceedings of 21st International Conference on Pattern Recognition, vol. 3, pp. 2335–2338 (2012)
27. Poh, N., Kittler, J., Bourlai, T.: Improving biometric device interoperability by likelihood ratio-based quality dependent score normalization. In: Proceedings of 1st International Conference on Biometrics: Theory, Applications, and Systems, pp. 1–5, Washington DC, 27–29 Sept 2007
28. Poh, N., Kittler, J., Bourlai, T.: Quality-based score normalization with device qualitative information for multimodal biometric fusion. IEEE Trans. Syst. Man Cybern. Part A Syst. Hum. **40**(3), 539–554 (2010)
29. Poh, N., Kittler, J., Rattani, A., Tistarelli, M.: Group-specific score normalization for biometric systems. In: Proceedings of 23rd IEEE Conference on Computer Vision and Pattern Recognition Workshops, pp. 38–45, San Francisco, CA, 13–18 June 2010
30. Poh, N., Merati, A., Kittler, J.: Heterogeneous information fusion: a novel fusion paradigm for biometric systems. In: Proceedings of the International Joint Conference on Biometrics, pp. 1–8, Washington, DC, 10–13 Oct 2011
31. Poh, N., Tistarelli, M.: Customizing biometric authentication systems via discriminative score calibration. In: Proceedings of the Conference on Computer Vision and Pattern Recognition, Providence, RI, June 16–21 2012
32. Poh, N., Tistarelli, M.: Customizing biometric authentication systems via discriminative score calibration. In: Proceedings of the IEEE Conference on Computer Vision and Pattern Recognition, pp. 2681–2686, Providence, RI, 16–21 June 2012
33. Rua, E., Castro, J.L., Mateo, C.: Quality-based score normalization for audiovisual person authentication. In: Proceedings of the International Conference on Image Analysis and Recognition, pp. 1003–1012, Povoa de Varzim, Portugal, 25–27 June 2008
34. Scheirer, W., Kumar, N.: Multi-attribute spaces: calibration for attribute fusion and similarity search. In: Proceedings of the IEEE Conference on Computer Vision and Pattern Recognition, pp. 2933–2940, Providence, RI, 16–21 June 2012
35. Scheirer, W., Rocha, A., Michaels, R., Boult, T.: Meta-recognition: the theory and practice of recognition score analysis. Trans. Pattern Anal. Mach. Intell. **33**, 1689–1695 (2011)
36. Scheirer, W., Rocha, A., Micheals, R., Boult, T.: Robust fusion: extreme value theory for recognition score normalization. In: Proceedings of the European Conference on Computer Vision, vol. 6313, pp. 481–495. Crete, Greece, 5–11 Sept 2010
37. Sun, Z., Tan, T.: CASIA iris image database, 14 Aug 2014 (2012)
38. Toderici, G., Evangelopoulos, G., Fang, T., Theoharis, T., Kakadiaris, I.: UHDB11 database for 3D-2D face recognition. In: Proceedings of the Pacific-Rim Symposium on Image and Video Technology, pp. 1–14, 28 Oct 2013

39. Toderici, G., Passalis, G., Zafeiriou, S., Tzimiropoulos, G., Petrou, M., Theoharis, T., Kakadiaris, I.: Bidirectional relighting for 3D-aided 2D face recognition. In: Proceedings of the IEEE Conference on Computer Vision and Pattern Recognition, pp. 2721–2728, San Francisco, CA, 13–18 June 2010

40. Tyagi, V., Ratha, N.: Biometric score fusion through discriminative training. In: Proceedings of the IEEE Conference on Computer Vision and Pattern Recognition Workshops, pp. 145–149, Colorado Springs, CO, 20–25 June 2011

41. Wild, P., Radu, P., Chen, L., Ferryman, J.: Towards anomaly detection for increased security in multibiometric systems: spoofing-resistant 1-median fusion eliminating outliers. In: Proceedings of the 2nd International Joint Conference on Biometrics, pp. 1–6, Clearwater, FL, Sept 29 Oct 2 2014

42. Wolfstetter, E., Dulleck, U., Inderst, R., Kuhbier, P., Lands-Berger, M.: Stochastic dominance: theory and applications. Humboldt University of Berlin, School of Business and Economics, Berlin (1993)

43. Yager, N., Dunstone, T.: The biometric menagerie. IEEE Trans. Pattern Anal. Mach. Intell. **32** (2), 220–230 (2010)

44. Zuo, J., Nicolo, F., Schmid, N., Boothapati, S.: Encoding, matching and score normalization for cross spectral face recognition: matching SWIR versus visible data. In: Proceedings of 5th International Conference on Biometrics Theory, Applications and Systems, pp. 203–208, Washington DC, 23–26 Sept 2012

Chapter 15
Multispectral Ocular Biometrics

Simona G. Crihalmeanu and Arun A. Ross

Abstract This chapter discusses the use of multispectral imaging to perform bimodal ocular recognition where the eye region of the face is used for recognizing individuals. In particular, it explores the possibility of utilizing the patterns evident in the sclera, along with the iris, in order to improve the robustness of iris recognition systems. Commercial iris recognition systems typically capture frontal images of the eye in the near-infrared spectrum. However, in non-frontal images of the eye, iris recognition performance degrades considerably. As the eyeball deviates away from the camera, the iris information in the image decreases, while the scleral information increases. In this work, we demonstrate that by utilizing the texture of the sclera along with the vascular patterns evident on it, the performance of an iris recognition system can potentially be improved. The iris patterns are better observed in near-infrared spectrum, while conjunctival vasculature patterns are better discerned in the visible spectrum. Therefore, multispectral images of the eye are used to capture the details of both the iris and the sclera. The contributions of this paper include (a) the assembly of a multispectral eye image collection to study the impact of intra-class variation on sclera recognition performance, (b) the design and development of an automatic sclera, iris, and pupil segmentation algorithm, and (c) the improvement of iris recognition performance by fusing the iris and scleral patterns in non-frontal images of the eye.

S.G. Crihalmeanu (✉) · A.A. Ross
Michigan State University, 428 South Shaw Lane, 3142 Engineering Building,
East Lansing, MI 48824, USA
e-mail: simonac@cse.msu.edu

A.A. Ross
e-mail: rossarun@cse.msu.edu

© Springer International Publishing Switzerland 2016
T. Bourlai (ed.), *Face Recognition Across the Imaging Spectrum*,
DOI 10.1007/978-3-319-28501-6_15

15.1   Introduction

Rooted in the Latin word *oculus* that means eye, the term *ocular biometrics* is used
to bring together all the biometric modalities associated with the eye and its surrounding region. Among these modalities, the iris has been extensively studied in
the biometrics literature. Iris recognition involves the automatic comparison of two
iris images and the generation of a match score that indicates the similarity (or
dissimilarity) between the two images. When imaged in the near-infrared spectrum,
the multilayered iris reveals a rich texture that has been demonstrated to be significantly different across individuals [1–4]. Being located behind the cornea and
the aqueous humor and in front of the lens, the iris is well protected yet visible from
the outside. However, the iris may be obstructed by eyelashes, and the external
illuminants can induce specular reflection on its surface since it is located behind a
curved, moist tissue. Further, the iris contracts and dilates to control the amount of
light that enters the eye, thus causing variable nonlinear deformations on its surface.
Despite these challenges, the matching accuracy of iris recognition systems has
been observed to be considerably high when dealing with frontal images of the eye
[5, 6].

A typical iris recognition system has three key modules: (1) The segmentation
module where the iris is localized and extracted from the surrounding structures;
(2) the encoding module where the segmented image is processed in order to extract
a feature set; and (3) a matching module where the feature sets of two irides are
compared. Most methods have been designed to process frontal iris images that are
obtained when the eye is directly gazing into the camera. Regardless of the algorithm employed for segmentation, encoding, and matching, the performance of iris
recognition has been observed to be *negatively influenced* by factors such as
occlusions due to eyelids and eyelashes, unfavorable lighting conditions, and the
direction of the gaze of the eye with respect to the acquisition device [7]. The
performance of an iris recognition system can be improved by exploiting the
additional information contained in the *scleral region* in images acquired in non-
cooperative scenarios, with frontal or non-frontal gaze direction. Figure 15.1a
shows an ocular image and the structures that are evident in the sclera.

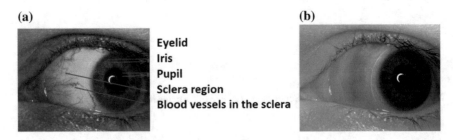

(a)   **(b)**

Eyelid
Iris
Pupil
Sclera region
Blood vessels in the sclera

Fig. 15.1 Ocular image. **a** Visible spectrum image (RGB) showing the iris and the sclera, as well
as other structures in their vicinity. Blood vessels pertaining to the sclera region are better observed
in the visible spectrum. **b** NIR spectrum

The sclera [8] is the outer layer tissue surrounding the eyeball, except in the frontal portion of the eye where it is connected to the cornea through the sclero-corneal junction and in the back of the eyeball where it merges into the dural sheath of the optic nerve. Its primary role is to preserve the round shape of the eyeball under the pressure of the internal liquids contained in the eye. The sclera is avas-cular, except for its outer layer, the episclera that contains the blood vessels nourishing the sclera. It is covered by the conjunctiva that protects the eye against bacterial infections and lubricates the eye for eyelid closure. A close look at the white of the eye reveals blood vessels pertaining to both layers: the episclera and the conjunctiva. The blood vessels pertaining to the sclera region are easily dis-cernible in the visible spectrum as depicted in Fig. 15.1.

The use of the scleral pattern as a biometric was first suggested in a patent application submitted in 2005 by Derakshani and Ross and later extended by Derakshani et al. [9]. Observations on the universality and permanence of scleral patterns, along with a description of how various factors such as medical conditions and aging influence the appearance of blood vessels on the sclera surface, are found in [10]. Several researchers have further investigated this biometric modality. Initially, comprehensive studies were conducted to demonstrate the potential of scleral patterns as a stand-alone biometric cue [9–17]. The effort was directed toward designing various preprocessing techniques to enhance the vasculature seen on the white of the eye, feature extraction schemes, vascularity assessment tech-niques [18], sclera image quality assessment methods [19], and multiview sclera recognition algorithms [20, 21]. The study of conjunctival vasculature as a rela-tively new biometric cue still requires solutions for issues such as changes in the viewing angle with respect to the acquisition device; position of illumination with regard to the eye that can result in strong specular reflections due to the curved surface of the eyeball and the reflective property of the sclera; and the distance of the camera to the eye. Ultimately, the focus of the research on sclera biometrics shifted toward demonstrating the improved recognition performance when iris and sclera patterns are combined together in a multimodal configuration [22–24]. As the eyeball deviates away from the camera, the iris information is progressively occluded, while the scleral information is progressively revealed. Depending on the richness and the location of the conjunctival vasculature exposed through the sclera, prominent veins may be visible even when the iris is occluded by eyelashes. As research on this topic advances, a multimodal system that combines the scleral patterns with off-axis iris patterns may provide better matching accuracy and resistance to spoofing compared to a unimodal non-frontal iris recognition system. Furthermore, when using high-resolution face images and periocular images, the strengths of unimodal iris, sclera, and face biometrics may be gathered in a high-accuracy recognition system. Examples of previous efforts in fusion of face and iris patterns are found in [25–27]. Therefore, the addition of scleral patterns singled out from face or periocular images may further benefit the recognition process for improved accuracy and higher difficulty to forge biometric traits.

In this work, we demonstrate that the use of the sclera as a biometric, in a multimodal configuration, is especially significant in the context of iris recognition, when changes in the gaze angle of the eye result in non-frontal iris images that cannot be easily used for matching [28]. To facilitate this, multispectral images of the ocular region are necessary since the iris is better discerned in the NIR spectrum, while the conjunctival vasculature pattern is better discerned in the visible spectrum.

Multispectral imaging captures the image of an object at multiple spectral bands often ranging from the visible spectrum to the infrared spectrum. The visible spectrum band [29] is represented by three narrow sub-bands called the red, green, and blue channels that range from 0.4 to 0.7 μm. The infrared spectrum is divided into NIR (near-infrared), MIR (midwave infrared), FIR (far infrared), and thermal bands, ranging from 0.7 μm to over 10 μm. As the technology becomes less expensive, and multispectral imaging becomes more affordable, the use of multiple spectra will provide more information that can be used efficiently for large-scale recognition applications when dealing with millions of identities.

A proper segmentation of the iris and sclera region is essential since it influences the matching performance. In the literature, different methods for non-frontal iris segmentation that use the information either from near-infrared or from visible spectra [30, 31] have been presented. We propose a novel automatic segmentation process that exploits the information from both visible and near-infrared spectra, by processing multispectral color-infrared (CIR) images of the ocular region.

Our study is the first work that explores combining iris and conjunctiva in a *fully automated manner* using *multispectral* images of the eye. In the proposed approach, the original image of the eye is first denoised and specular reflections are removed. The regions of interest, viz. the sclera, the pupil, and the iris, are localized and segmented from the overall image. Since the goal of the work is to fuse the information provided by the iris and the sclera, an accurate labeling of pixels pertaining to both regions is very important. In particular, an accurate detection of the sclera–eyelid boundary will help extract the veins located on the edge of the sclera region. Well-known generic segmentation methods, such as thresholding and clustering, histogram-based segmentation, region growing, and active contours cannot be trivially used on these images. Therefore, a novel multispectral segmentation routine is described. After segmentation, a blood vessel enhancement algorithm is applied to the sclera. Next, a keypoint detection technique is used to localize interest points on the sclera region. The number of matching interest points between the scleral regions of two eye images is used to generate a match score. At the same time, the segmented iris is unwrapped and normalized into a rectangular region. The textural details of the iris are converted into a binary IrisCode after applying wavelet filters on the rectangular region and quantizing the phasor response. The matching score between two irides is given by the normalized Hamming distance between their respective IrisCodes. Finally, score-level fusion is used to combine the scores from the scleral and iris regions and generate a single score. The block diagram of the proposed approach is shown in Fig. 15.2.

The article is organized as follows: Sect. 15.2 describes multispectral data acquisition; Sect. 15.3 presents specular reflection detection and removal; Sect. 15.4 discusses pupil, sclera, and iris segmentation; Sect. 15.5 describes iris feature

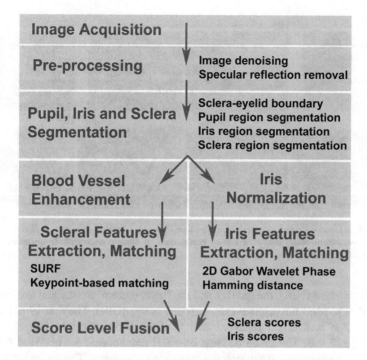

Fig. 15.2 The block diagram of the proposed method. Iris segmentation and sclera segmentation were found to be the most critical, yet challenging, component of this work

extraction and matching; Sect. 15.6 presents sclera feature extraction and matching; and Sect. 15.7 presents the experimental results demonstrating the benefits of combining the two modalities.

15.2 Image Acquisition

In this work, multispectral imaging is employed to visualize and combine the iris patterns that are better observed in the near-infrared (NIR) spectrum with the conjunctival vasculature patterns that are better observed in the visible spectrum (RGB). We initiate this research by applying constraints on illumination, distance to the camera, position of the head, and gaze direction. The camera and the light are positioned at approximately 12 inches from the subject's eye; the head is always straight, mostly never tilted; and the eyeball moves to the left or to the right, never gazing up or down. As described in [10, 32], the interface used to collect images of the eye is composed of a Redlake (DuncanTech) MS3100 multispectral camera, an ophthalmologist's slit-lamp mount, and a light source. The multispectral camera generates images at a resolution of $1040 \times 1392 \times 3$ pixels. The three components,

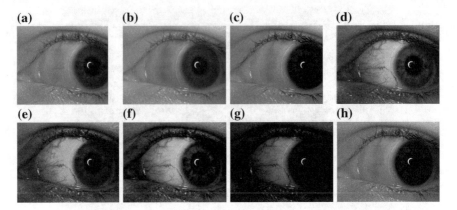

Fig. 15.3 **a** Color-infrared image (NIR-Red-BayerPattern). **b** NIR component. **c** *Red* component. **d** Bayer pattern. **e** RGB image. **f** *Green* component. **g** *Blue* component. **h** Composite image (NIR-Red-Green)

the near-infrared (NIR), the red (R), and the Bayer pattern, are stacked one on top of each other to form the original color-infrared image (CIR). The first 17 columns in every image had to be removed due to artifacts resulting in images of size $1035 \times 1373 \times 3$. The green (G) and blue (B) components are obtained from the Bayer pattern component through a demosaicing algorithm. The center wavelength of each spectral band specified by the manufacturer is as follows: blue—460 nm, green—540 nm, red—660 nm, and NIR—800 nm. The original color-infrared image with the three components and the output of the demosaicing algorithm are displayed in Fig. 15.3. Videos of each eye are captured with the participant gazing to the right or to the left of the cameras' optical axis as shown in Fig. 15.4.

- **Collection 1**. Videos of the right and left eye are captured from 103 subjects (Table 15.1). While recording each video, the subject is either looking to the left or to the right. Eight sequential images per eye per gaze direction that exhibit proper illumination, less specular reflection, and focus are selected from the video. The total number of images is 3266. For one subject, only data from the right eye were collected due to medical issues. From 12 of the videos, we could select only 6 or 7 images due to excessive lacrimation in the eye of the subjects. Working with sequential images from the same video allows us to bypass the challenge due to the viewing angle [12]. The process of frame selection ensures that there is no remarkable change in pose. The camera is focused on the sclera region. Similarly, the light is directed as much as possible toward the sclera region with the specular reflection constrained, as much as possible, to the pupil. As a result, some images exhibit uneven illumination, mostly left-eye-looking-right (*L_R*) and right-eye-looking-left (*R_L*) images where the iris is poorly illuminated.
- **Collection 2**. Videos of the right and left eye are captured from 31 subjects (Table 15.1), with each eye gazing to the right or to the left of the cameras'

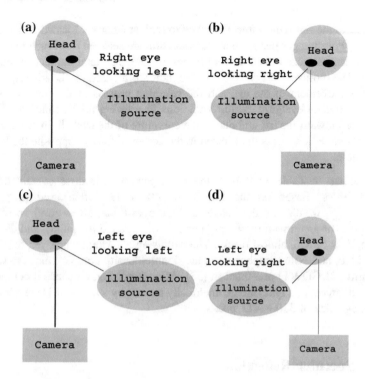

Fig. 15.4 **a** Right-eye-looking-left (*R_L*). **b** Right-eye-looking-right (*R_R*). **c** Left-eye-looking-left (*L_L*). **d** Left-eye-looking-right (*L_R*)

Table 15.1 High-resolution multispectral ocular database

Collection 1	Collection 2
1 video/left eye 1 video/right eye	1 video/left eye 1 video/right eye
Camera focused on the sclera	Camera focused on the iris
8 images/eye/gaze	4 images/eye/gaze
Initial image size: $1040 \times 1392 \times 3$ 17 columns removed (artifacts) Final image size: $1035 \times 1373 \times 3$	Initial image size: $1040 \times 1392 \times 3$ 17 columns removed (artifacts) Final image size: $1035 \times 1373 \times 3$
103 subjects	31 subjects
Dark colored eyes: 37 Mixed colored eyes: 32 Light colored eyes: 34	Dark colored eyes: 11 Mixed colored eyes: 11 Light colored eyes: 9
Total of 3266 images	Total of 496 images

optical axis. To increase the intra-class variation, the participant is asked to keep the head still and alternate their gaze direction between looking at the ring of lights (located to the left or right of the optical axis of the camera) and looking at the camera (frontal gaze direction) as illustrated in Fig. 15.4. When gazing to the left or to the right, the subject is asked to look at a marker located on the ring of lights. Four images per eye per gaze direction are selected from each video, after changing the gaze direction from frontal to side. The total number of images is 496. The multispectral camera and the light are focused on the iris region. Due to the movement of the eye and the selection process of the frames, the four ocular images/eye/gaze exhibit variations in viewing angle. Since the light is directed toward the iris and due to the curvature of the eyeball, in some images, the sclera region is less illuminated in the corner of the eye opposite the lacrimal caruncle.

As shown in Table 15.1, both the multispectral collections contain different colored irides. Based on the Martin–Schultz scale,[1] often used in physical anthropology, we classify the images as light eyes (blue, green gray), mixed eyes (blue, gray, or green with brown pigment, mainly around the pupil), and dark eyes (brown, dark brown, almost black). The denoising algorithm employed for the red, green, blue, and NIR components is the double-density complex discrete wavelet transform (DDCDWT) presented in [33]. After denoising, all spectral components (NIR, red, green, and blue) are geometrically resized by a factor of 1/3 resulting in a final image size of 310×411 pixels.

15.3 Specular Reflection

Specular reflections on the sclera have to be detected and removed as they can impact the segmentation process (described in Sect. 15.4). The light directed to the eyeball generates specular reflection that has a ring-like shape caused by the shape of the source of illumination and specular reflection due to the moisture of the eye and the curved shape of the eyeball. Both are detected in a two-step algorithm that builds the specular reflection mask and are removed by a fast inpainting procedure (Fig. 15.5). In some images, the ring-like shape of the illuminant may appear to be an incomplete circle, ellipse, or an arbitrary curved shape with a wide range of intensity values. It may be located partially in the iris region, and so its precise detection and removal are important especially since the iris texture has to be preserved as much as possible. In the first step of the algorithm, a good detection of the ring-like shape specular reflection is accomplished by converting the RGB image into the L*a*b color space followed by range filtering where every pixel in the image is replaced with the difference between the maximum and minimum value in a 3×3 neighborhood around that pixel. In the second step, a thresholding process, followed by morphological dilation, is used to detect specular highlights. The specular reflection is removed by inpainting. The specular reflection mask, henceforth referred as $Spec_{mask}$, is further used to remove the iris regions that exhibit specularities in the iris recognition process.

---

[1]http://wapedia.mobi/en/Eye_color.

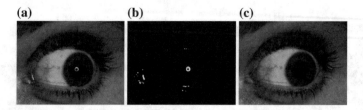

Fig. 15.5 Specular reflection. **a** Original RGB image. **b** Detected specular reflection. **c** Original RGB image with specular reflection removed

15.4   Ocular Region Segmentation

The purpose of the work is to combine the information provided by the iris and the sclera, and therefore, an accurate segmentation of both regions is very important. It was observed that the different methods of illumination used for the two collections, one with the light directed to the sclera region and the second one with the light directed to the iris region as described in Sect. 15.2, drastically influence the segmentation process, especially in images exhibiting low or unevenly illuminated sclera and iris in the vicinity of the periocular skin. Exposed through the sclera surface, the conjunctival vasculature appears as dark curved lines of different thicknesses that intersect each other randomly. Segmenting the sclera is essential to distinguish the vasculature from similar structures outside the sclera such as wrinkles and crows feet on the skin, and eyelashes. It is also important to extract an accurate sclera contour along the eyelids, since the blood vessels may be located on the margins of the sclera. Regardless of the color of the iris, the algorithm to segment the sclera, the iris and the pupil have four steps: (1) The sclera–eyelid boundary detection; (2) pupil region segmentation; (3) iris region segmentation; and (4) sclera region segmentation.

15.4.1   The Sclera–Eyelid Boundary Detection

It is possible to identify surfaces with different colors, structures, and textures by analyzing their spectral reflectance patterns. Objects with high content in water are characterized by high absorption at near-infrared wavelengths range. As explained in [10], the skin has lesser water content than the sclera and, therefore, exhibits a higher reflectance in NIR. This property can be captured using the normalized sclera index which is defined as:

$$\text{NSI}(x, y) = \frac{\text{NIR}(x, y) - G(x, y)}{\text{NIR}(x, y) + G(x, y)} \tag{15.1}$$

(a)   **(b)**   **(c)**   **(d)**

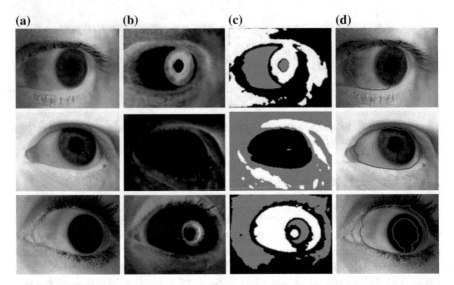

Fig. 15.6 Detecting the sclera–eyelid boundary. The first row displays the results for dark colored iris, the second row displays the results for light colored iris, and the third row displays the results for mixed colored iris: **a** Original composite image. **b** The normalized sclera index (NSI). **c** The output of the K-means clustering algorithm. **d** Sclera–eyelid boundary imposed on original composite image

where NIR(*x, y*) and *G*(*x, y*) are the pixel intensities of the NIR and *G* components at pixel location (*x, y*). The skin region appears lighter in the normalized sclera index compared to the sclera region. Figure 15.6b displays the normalized sclera index for all three categories of iris as specified by the Martin–Schultz scale: light colored iris, dark colored iris, and mixed colored iris.

Our proposed method constructs a feature vector composed of the mean and the standard deviation of every pixel in the normalized sclera index in a neighborhood (R_i) of radii $i \in \{0, 1, 3, 5, 7\}$. To speed up the process, the algorithm uses the integral image of NSI (the sum of all the pixels within the rectangular region above and to the left of pixel (*x, y*) $\in$ NSI) as explained in [34]. Further, the algorithm clusters the pixels into three categories (the sclera, the iris, and the background) using K-means algorithm, computes the mean value of intensities of each cluster, and labels the largest connected region from the cluster with the lowest mean value as the sclera. As shown in Fig. 15.6, for all three categories as specified by the Martin–Schultz scale, the clustering induces a well-defined sclera–eyelid boundary and it differs only with respect to the sclera–iris boundary. Algorithm 1 describes the automatic detection of the sclera–eyelid boundary. The algorithm fails to properly segment the sclera–eyelid boundary for images with strong uneven illumination or with large areas of specular reflection on the skin surface. Such areas may represent the largest connected region in Algorithm 1 and may be erroneously labeled as the sclera (Fig. 15.7). In some images, low illumination and excessive

(a) (b) (c)

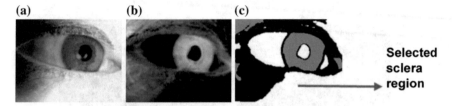

Selected
sclera
region

Fig. 15.7 Sclera–eyelid boundary errors. An image with strong uneven illumination. **a** Original composite image. **b** Normalized sclera index. **c** The output of the k-means algorithm

Table 15.2 The accuracy of sclera region segmentation algorithm

Good sclera region	L_L (%)	L_R (%)	R_L (%)	R_R (%)
Collection 1	99.38	98.77	98.17	97.32
Collection 2	100	100	100	100
Good sclera–eyelid contour	L_L (%)	L_R (%)	R_L (%)	R_R (%)
Collection 1	93.47	97.17	92.57	97.56
Collection 2	96.78	96.78	91.13	96.78

mascara resulted in the improper detection of sclera–eyelid contour since part of the eyelashes were included in the sclera mask. For such images, the sclera–eyelid boundary was segmented manually (a total of 233 from both collections). The results for sclera–eyelid boundary segmentation are presented in Table 15.2. The accuracy of the segmentation process was established based on the visual inspection of all the images.

Algorithm 1 Sclera-eyelid boundary detection

---

1) Geometrically resize image by a factor of $1/2$.

2) Apply a 3×3 average filter to the NIR and G components of the image.

3) Compute the normalized sclera index $NSI(x,y) = \frac{NIR(x,y)-G(x,y)}{NIR(x,y)+G(x,y)}$, where $NIR(x,y)$ and $G(x,y)$ are the pixel intensities of the NIR and G components at pixel location (x,y).

4) Compute the mean μ and the standard deviation σ for each pixel in $NSI(x,y)$ in a neighborhood (R_i) of radii $i \in \{0,1,3,5,7\}$.

5) Construct the feature vector $\mathbf{F} = [\mu_0, \mu_1, \mu_3, \mu_5, \mu_7, \sigma_0, \sigma_1, \sigma_3, \sigma_5, \sigma_7]$, where μ_i is the mean and σ_i is the standard deviation corresponding to radius i. The overall dimensionality of the feature vector is 127410x10.

6) Cluster the pixels into three categories by applying the k-means algorithm to $\mathbf{F}$ with $k = 3$.

7) Compute the mean value of all the pixels within each cluster. The cluster with the lowest mean represents the sclera region.

8) Sclera mask is represented by the largest connected region from the sclera cluster.

9) Geometrically resize the mask of the sclera to the original size of the NIR or G component (referred henceforth as I_S).

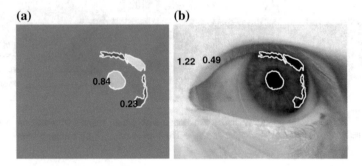

Fig. 15.8 Pupil region segmentation. **a** The metric M for the threshold 0.2. **b** The contour of the thresholding result imposed on the composite image

15.4.2 Pupil Region Segmentation

The algorithm implemented to segment the pupil region exploits two main characteristics of the pupillary region, namely its elliptical shape and the low-intensity pixel value. First, a set of thresholds are estimated based on the pixel intensities in the NIR component. Through an iterative process, for each threshold, a set of connected regions with low-intensity values are found in the image and considered as possible candidates for the pupil (Fig. 15.8). Each region undergoes a hole filling process as described in [35] in order to account for improper inpainting of specular reflection along the iris-pupil boundary. Further, to isolate the pupil region from eyelashes and other darker regions in the image, a metric M that describes the roundness of the connected region is calculated. A value of 1 indicates a perfect circle. In non-frontal iris images, the pupil region is approximated with an ellipse. Since the pupil is not a very elongated ellipse, the metric M will have a value close to 1. Algorithm 2 describes the pupil region segmentation. Since the value of the metric M is based on the area and perimeter values of the connected region, the algorithm fails to properly segment the pupil region if the inpainting process drastically changes the elliptical contour of the pupil. It also failed in some images that had low illumination and excessive mascara. For the images in which the segmentation of the pupil region failed, constraints on pupil location are added to the algorithm (after a visual inspection of the output) by searching for the pupil in the ellipse mask fitted to the sclera region as described in [13]. The results for pupil segmentation are presented in Table 15.3 and are based on the visual inspection of images.

Table 15.3 The accuracy of pupil segmentation algorithm

Good segmentation	L_L (%)	L_R (%)	R_L (%)	R_R (%)
Collection 1	100	98.89	97.44	97.69
Collection 2	100	100	98.39	100

Algorithm 2 Pupil region segmentation

1) Find the Otsu threshold, $otsuTh$, for NIR.
for $n = max(min(NIR(x,y)),0)$ **to** 0.3 step 0.02 **do**
   2) Compute the threshold $Th = n \times otsuTh$
   for Th **do**
      3) Find the connected regions $I_{reg} \in NIR(x,y) < Th$.
      4) Consider the connected regions $AREA_{I_{reg}} > 400 pixels$
      for I_{reg} **do**
         5) Fill the possible holes.
         6) Compute the metric $M = \frac{4 \times \pi \times area}{perimeter^2}$.
         7) Choose the connected region with the highest value of the metric M while iterating. This represents the pupil region.
      end for
   end for
end for
8) Fit an ellipse to the pupil's contour and find its parameters $E_{pupil}(x_p, y_p, M_p, m_p, \theta_p)$ where (x_p, y_p) represents the center coordinates of the ellipse, M_p, m_p represents the major and minor axes, respectively, and θ_p represents the tilt of the ellipse.
9) Build the pupil mask P_{mask} as all the pixels inside the fitted ellipse.

15.4.3 Iris Region Segmentation

The perceived shape of the iris is determined by the gaze direction, position of the camera, and tilt of the head. In non-frontal images of the eye, the iris is no longer circular, and its contours appear as rotated ellipses [36]. When a subject is asked to gaze-to-the-right or gaze-to-the-left with respect to the camera, the ensuing change in position of the head transforms the circular boundaries of the iris and pupil into ellipses. Our proposed segmentation, Algorithm 3, finds pixels along the limbus region for ellipse fitting. The method starts with the segmentation of the image of the eye using the multiscale spectral image segmentation algorithm[2] described in [37]. The outcome, shown in Fig. 15.9b, consists of multiple labeled connected regions. The iris mask, denoting the pixels corresponding to the iris, is the binary image obtained as the union of all the connected regions surrounding the pupil, as shown in Fig. 15.9c. The contour pixels are further processed to remove the eyebrows, and the results are shown in Fig. 15.9d. To account for occlusion due to eyelids, the iris mask is limited to the upper and lower limits of the portion of sclera region in the vicinity of the iris as displayed in Fig. 15.9e. Further, the algorithm computes the Euclidean distance from the center of the pupil to each remaining pixel on the contour of the iris mask and determines the standard deviation of these distances. Based on the standard deviation std of all these Euclidean distances and 40, 55, and 75 percentile values (selected by empirical observation) on all

---

[2]http://www.timotheecour.com/software/ncut_multiscale/ncut_multiscale.html.

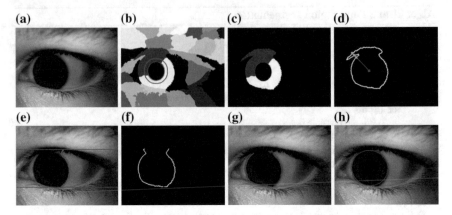

Fig. 15.9 Iris segmentation: **a** Original image of the eye. **b** The output of the multiscale spectral image segmentation, I_{label}. The contour of the pupil (*red ellipse*) and the dilated pupil (*blue ellipse*) are overlapped. **c** Initial iris mask. **d** Example of ray starting from the center of the pupil (*blue square*) to a pixel located on the contour of the iris mask (the three intersections denoted by *green squares*). **e** The upper and lower limits imposed on the iris mask. **f** Reliable pixels obtained after step 4. **g** Reliable pixels obtained after step 7 and used for ellipse fitting. **h** Contour of the iris region

Euclidean distances, more or less contour pixels are to be removed. A large standard deviation suggests that pixels that are not on the limbus boundary are still included in the iris contour. Therefore, pixels with large Euclidean distances are removed from the mask. The algorithm fits an ellipse to the remaining pixels on the contour of the iris and pixels within the ellipse are assigned to the iris mask. The output of the iris segmentation process was visually inspected. In images with improper illumination, the ellipse did not tightly fit the contour of the iris. In some images, it also resulted in under-segmentation due to upper and lower horizontal limits imposed by the sclera region. Table 15.4 presents the results of the segmentation process. The accuracy of the segmentation was established based on the visual inspection of all the images. The iris is segmented manually in those images in which the algorithm failed.

Table 15.4 The accuracy of iris segmentation algorithm

Good segmentation	L_L (%)	L_R (%)	R_L (%)	R_R (%)
Collection 1	91.51	89.41	86.73	90.02
Collection 2	83.07	87.91	95.17	93.55

Algorithm 3 Iris region segmentation

---

1) Segment the image of the eye using the multiscale spectral image segmentation algorithm.

2) Find the iris mask I_{iris} as all the connected regions surrounding the pupil. Find the iris mask contour $I_{contour}$.

3) Construct rays from the center of the pupil to each pixel on the iris mask contour. Consider the first intersections of the ray with the iris mask contour as $I_{contour}$.

4) Find the upper and lower horizontal limits of the sclera cluster found in Section 4.1, Algorithm 1. Consider the contour pixels within these limits.

5) Compute $E = \sqrt{(y_c - y_0)^2 + (x_c - x_0)^2}$, where (x_0, y_0) is the center of the pupil and $(x_c, y_c) \in I_{contour}$.

6) Compute the standard deviation $std(E)$ of all these Euclidean distances.

7) Compute the 40, 55, and 75 percentile values of all the Euclidean distances and do the following:

if $(std(E) > 0 \ and \ std(E) < 15)$ **then**

    Consider $(x_c, y_c) \in I_{contour}$ with $E(x_c, y_c) < 75$ percent distance value

else if $(std(E) \geq 15 \ and \ std(E) < 20)$ **then**

    Consider $(x_c, y_c) \in I_{contour}$ with $E(x_c, y_c) < 55$ percent distance value

else if $(std(E) \geq 20)$ **then**

    Consider $(x_c, y_c) \in I_{contour}$ with $E(x_c, y_c) < 40$ percent distance value

end if

8) Fit an ellipse to the selected pixels on the contour of the iris and find its parameters $E_{iris}(x_i, y_i, M_i, m_i, \theta_i)$ where (x_i, y_i) represents the center coordinates of the ellipse, M_i, m_i represents the major and minor axes, respectively, and θ_i represents the tilt of the ellipse.

9) Compute the iris mask I_{mask} as all the pixels located inside the fitted ellipse and exclude the pupil mask.

10) Limit the iris mask to the upper and lower limits of the portion of sclera region in the vicinity of the iris.

11) Find I_{mask} - $((I_{mask} - I_{iris}) > 0)$, where I_{iris} is obtained in step 2.

12) Find $I_{mask} = I_{mask} - Spec_{mask}$ where $Spec_{mask}$ is the specular reflection mask as obtained in Section 3.

15.4.4 Sclera Region Segmentation

The segmentation of the iris region provides the sclera–iris boundary, i.e., the limbus boundary. The segmentation of the sclera region is finalized through a four-step Algorithm 4. Figure 15.10 presents examples of correct eye image segmentation.

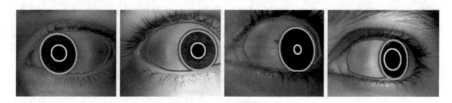

Fig. 15.10 Examples of correct eye image segmentation

Algorithm 4 Sclera region segmentation

---

1) Build the convex hull S_{CH} of the sclera cluster obtained in Section 4.1, Algorithm 1.

2) Find the intersection of the iris mask with the convex hull of the sclera obtained in the previous step, $I_{mask} \cap S_{CH}$.

3) Find the sclera mask S_{mask} as $S_{CH} - (I_{mask} \cap S_{CH})$

4) Through morphological operation, erode the sclera mask to ensure that the contour line of the sclera-eyelid boundary is not included in the mask.

15.5 Iris Feature Extraction and Matching

The size of the segmented iris varies across images due to implicit morphology, differences in pupil dilation, and distance from the camera. For comparison purposes, the segmented irides must geometrically be transformed to the same size. This process is referred to as iris normalization. From its oval shape, the iris is elliptically unwrapped into a rectangular region with an angular resolution of 360 and radial resolution of 64. Elliptical unwrapping is done based on the algorithm in [36]. The iris normalization process has to consider the degree of iris dilation or constriction, and the different centers and orientations of the two ellipses defining the iris and pupil boundaries $E_{iris}(x_i, y_i, M_i, m_i, \theta_i)$ and $E_{pupil}(x_p, y_p, M_p, m_p, \theta_p)$, where (x_i, y_i) is the center of the iris, M_i, m_i, and θ_i are the major and minor axes and the tilt of the ellipse fitted to the iris contour, (x_p, y_p) is the center of the pupil, and M_p, m_p, and θ_p are the major and minor axes and the tilt of the ellipse fitted to the pupil contour. To accomplish this, through an iterative process, the double elliptical unwrapping algorithm maps each pixel found on the pupil boundary to the iris boundary, while the value of a variable ρ that measures the degree of iris dilation is increased in each iteration until a stop criterion is reached. The final value of the variable ρ is used to unwrap the iris region from the original Cartesian coordinates (where the iris is elliptical/circular) to pseudo-polar coordinates (where the iris is rectangular). The algorithm begins by initializing the values of ρ and the values of the angular and radial resolutions. At the beginning of each iteration, the location (x, y) of a pixel on an ellipse centered in the origin, with the tilt, and the major and minor axes equal with those of the pupil, is mapped to new locations on ellipses that use the tilt and the center of the ellipse defining the iris boundary. The values of major and minor axes of the ellipse defining the iris boundary are increased according to the value of ρ. The major and minor axes are normalized so that the value of the radius from the center of the iris to the new pixel location (x, y) can be

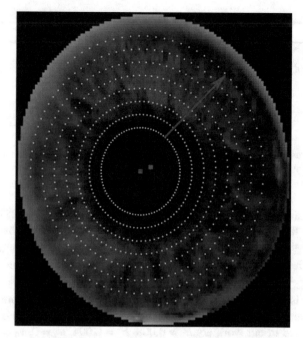

Fig. 15.11 Double elliptical unwrapping. The pixel from the pupillary boundary is mapped to the limbus boundary (along the *red arrow*), while the value of parameter ρ is increased. The *red square* is the center of the pupil. The *blue square* is the center of the iris. *Yellow dots* are (x, y) locations of the pixels pertaining to the pupillary boundary for different values of ρ

compared to 1. The more the radius approaches the value of 1, the more the pixel (x, y) approaches the iris boundary. Normalization of the major and minor axes is necessary to define the stop criteria while iterating. At the end of each iteration, the value of ρ is increased and the mapping of the location (x, y) is repeated. The iris is unwrapped using bilinear interpolation. The mapping of pixels from the pupil boundary to the iris boundary is displayed in Fig. 15.11. The algorithm as presented in [36] is described in Algorithm 5. An example of normalized iris output is depicted in Fig. 15.12a. The normalized iris is next subjected to Gabor wavelets, as described by Daugman [1]. Wavelets are mathematical functions that decompose the input image into different frequencies at different scales, and therefore, the image can be represented simultaneously in both the spatial and frequency domains. Two-dimensional Gabor wavelets $G(x, y)$ consist of sine/cosine oscillations $S(x, y)$,

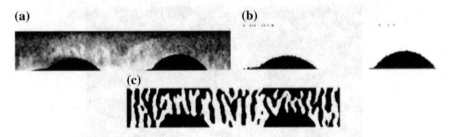

Fig. 15.12 Examples for iris normalization and iris template: **a** Normalized iris. **b** The mask for occlusions. **c** Iris template

the carrier, modulated by a 2D Gaussian $W(x, y)$, and the envelop [38]: $G(x, y) = S(x, y) \times W(x, y)$. The mathematical expression for the carrier is $S(x, y) = e^{j(2\pi(u_0 x + v_0 y) + P)}$, where u_0 and v_0 are spatial frequencies and P is the phase of the sinusoid. The mathematical expression for the envelop is $W(x, y) = K e^{-\pi(a^2(x-x_0)_r^2 + b^2(y-y_0)_r^2)}$, where (x, y) is location of the peak of the function, K is the scale parameter for the amplitude, a and b are the scaling parameters, and r represents the rotation operation [38]. The values of the various parameters used in our work are $a^2 = 0.008$, $b^2 = 0.004$, $u_0 = 0$, $v_0 = 0.07$, $P = 0$, $K = 1$, and $(x_0, y_0) = (0, 0)$. The normalized image is convolved with the Gabor wavelet defined above, and the ensuing complex phasor response is quantized into two bits per pixel via a quantization process. The phase quantization is based on the location of the phase vector in one of the four quadrants in a complex plane. The values of the two bits are given by the sign of the real and imaginary part of the quadrant where the phase resides. An example of iris template is shown in Fig. 15.12c. In this work, the normalized Hamming distance is used for matching. Given two iris templates T_1 and T_2, the normalized Hamming distance is defined as the sum of all the disagreeing bits divided by N, where N is the number of bits included in both masks. The bits from the non-iris artifacts represented in the iris masks (mask$_1$ and mask$_2$) are excluded. The mathematical expression of the normalized Hamming distance as a dissimilarity measure for iris templates is as follows:

Algorithm 5 Double Elliptical Unwrapping

$N_\theta = 360$; {angular resolution}
$N_\rho = 64$; {radial resolution}
$\theta_{ellipse} = 0 : 2\pi/N_\theta : 2\pi$;
$N = length(\theta_{ellipse})$;
$step = 0.01$;
for $n = 1$ **to** N **do**
    $\rho(n) = 1$; {parameter that measures the iris dilation}
    $dist = 100$; {initialize variable used for STOP criteria when the value of ρ is found}
    while $dist > 0.1$ **do**
        1. Using the parameters of the ellipse defining the pupil boundary, find the location (x,y) of the pixel on the ellipse $E_{pupil}(x_p = 0, y_p = 0, M_p, m_p, \theta = 0)$ {Find the (x,y) location of the pixel on an ellipse centered in origin, with no tilt and major and minor axes equal to those of the pupil}

$$x = M_p \times cos(\theta_{ellipse}(n)),$$
$$y = m_p \times sin(\theta_{ellipse}(n)) \tag{2}$$

        2. Find the location (nx, ny) of the pixel on the $E_{pupil}(x_p, y_p, M_p, m_p, \theta_p)$. Increase the values of major and minor axes according to the value of ρ. As displayed in Figure 11, when ρ increases in value, the pixel is moved along the red arrow until it reaches the limbus boundary.

$$nx = \rho(n) \times (x \times cos(\theta_p) - y \times sin(\theta_p)) + x_p,$$
$$ny = \rho(n) \times (x \times sin(\theta_p) + y \times cos(\theta_p)) + y_p \tag{3}$$

        3. Using the tilt and the center of the ellipse defining the iris boundary, map the pixel from the pupil boundary to the iris boundary defined by $E_{iris}(x_i, y_i, M_i, m_i, \theta_i)$. Rotate the coordinate system to account for the different centers and tilts of the ellipses fitted to the pupil and iris, and normalize the major and minor axes.

$$x2 = ((nx - x_i) \times cos(\theta_i) + (ny - y_i) \times sin(\theta_i))/M_i;$$
$$y2 = (-(nx - x_i) \times sin(\theta_i) + (ny - y_i) \times cos(\theta_i))/m_i; \tag{4}$$

        4. Calculate the Euclidean distance
        $r = sqrt(x_2^2 + y_2^2)$;
        $dist = |r - 1|$;
        5. Increase the value of ρ
        $\rho(n) = \rho(n) + step$;
    end while
    $radius = 1 : N_\rho : \rho(n)$;
    Polar to Cartesian. X and Y specify the points at which the data is given from the original image of the iris for interpolation.

$$X(:,n) = radius \times (x \times cos(\theta_p) - y \times sin(\theta_p)) + x_p;$$
$$Y(:,n) = radius \times (x \times sin(\theta_p) + y \times cos(\theta_p)) + y_p; \tag{5}$$

end for

$$HD = \frac{\sum_{i=1}^{N} (T_{1_i} \otimes T_{2_i} \cap mask_{1_i} \cap mask_{2_i})}{N} \tag{15.2}$$

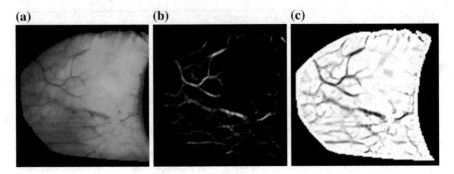

Fig. 15.13 Blood vessel enhancement on the segmented sclera region. **a** *Green* component of the segmented sclera. **b** Result of the enhancement of blood vessels. **c** The complement image of the enhanced blood vessels

15.6 Sclera Feature Extraction and Matching

An examination of the three components of the RGB image suggests that the green component has the best contrast between the blood vessels and the background. Therefore, the green component of the segmented sclera image is preprocessed using a selective enhancement filter for lines as described in [39]. The method requires the convolution of the image with multiple 2D Gaussian distributions with standard deviation values chosen according to the maximum and minimum blood vessel diameters. For each convolution, the eigenvalues corresponding to the Hessian matrix are used to enhance the lines present in the image. The output is displayed in Fig. 15.13. In [10], three feature extraction schemes are presented. The best results were obtained when speeded up robust features (SURF) algorithm [40] was used. SURF is a scale and rotation invariant detector and descriptor of point correspondences between two images. These points called "interest points" are prominent structures such as corners and T-junctions on the image. The algorithm detects the interest points and then describes them using the neighboring pixels. In our work, SURF is applied to the enhanced blood vessel images. The similarity between two images is assessed using the Euclidean distance as a measure between their respective corresponding interest points. Only Euclidean distances greater than 0.1 are considered, and the number of corresponding interest point pairs is counted. Figure 15.14 displays the corresponding interest points between images of the same eye and between images of two different eyes.

15.7 Score-Level Fusion of Iris and Scleral Patterns

The purpose of this work is to demonstrate that iris recognition performance in non-frontal images of the eye may be improved by adding information pertaining to the sclera region. The performance of the iris recognition and sclera recognition is

(a)

(b)

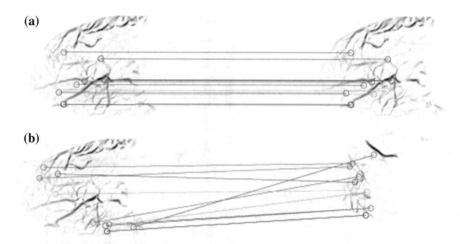

Fig. 15.14 The output of the SURF algorithm when applied to enhanced blood vessel images. The complement of the enhanced blood vessel images and a subset of the first 10 pairs of corresponding interest points are displayed for better visualization. **a** Same eye, the total number of interest points: 112 and 108. **b** Different eyes, the total number of interest points: 112 and 64

presented individually for both collections, followed by the fusion results. There are different ways in which the matching scores of iris and scleral patterns can be fused. In this work, three fusion methods are considered: simple sum rule, maximum rule, and minimum rule. Sclera matching scores are normalized in the interval [0, 1]. Iris matching scores are transformed from dissimilarity to similarity scores by sub-tracting the score values from 1.

Figure 15.15a presents the results for iris recognition for collection 1 (103 subjects). The ROC curve shows an EER of 0.5 % for left-eye-looking-left (L_L), 3.7 % for left-eye-looking-right (L_R), 3.4 % for right-eye-looking-left (R_L), and 0.78 % for right-eye-looking-right (R_R). The distributions of scores for both eyes and both gaze directions show some degree of overlap between the genuine and impostor scores. The higher EER values for L_R and R_L are caused by the anatomical structures of the face (mainly the nose) that obstructs the light directed to the eye. Figure 15.15b presents the results for sclera recognition for collection 1 (103 subjects). The ROC curve shows an EER of 1.1 % for left-eye-looking-left (L_L), 0.8 % for left-eye-looking-right (L_R), 1.15 % for right-eye-looking-left (R_L), and 0.55 % for right-eye-looking-right (R_R).

Table 15.5 presents the results when fusing the scores for collection 1 (103 subjects). It can be observed that the EER is lowered to under 0.67 % for both eyes and both gaze directions when the score are fused using the simple sum rule. For L_L and R_R, the EER is improved by an *order* of magnitude or more. For L_R and R_L, the EER is improved by a factor of 1.7 or more. This indicates that iris recognition performance is improved when details pertaining to sclera texture are also considered. When the maximum rule is used for fusion, iris recognition is improved by a factor of 2 for L_L, 5.3 for L_R, 2.19 for R_L, and 2 for R_R. When

Fig. 15.15 Collection 1, ROC curves for both eyes and both gaze directions: **a** Results for iris recognition. **b** Results for sclera recognition

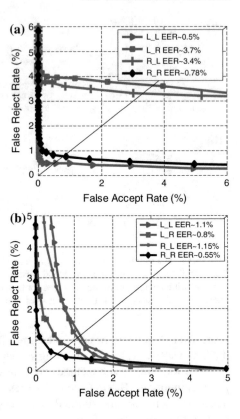

Table 15.5 The EER (%) results of the fusion of iris patterns (Hamming distance) and scleral patterns (SURF) for collection 1

Fusion rule	L_L (%)	L_R (%)	R_L (%)	R_R (%)
Simple sum rule	0.055	0.35	0.67	0.0025
Maximum rule	0.25	0.69	1.55	0.38
Minimum rule	1.1	0.85	1.1	0.55

the minimum rule is used for fusion, iris recognition performance is improved for L_R and R_L, but no significant improvement results are obtained for L_L and R_R.

Figure 15.16a presents the results for iris recognition for collection 2 (31 subjects). The ROC curve shows an EER of 0.55 % for left-eye-looking-left (L_L), 3.3 % for left-eye-looking-right (L_R), 2.7 % for right-eye-looking-left (R_L), and 0 % for right-eye-looking-right (R_R). The distributions of scores for both eyes and both gaze directions show some degree of overlap between the genuine and impostor scores. Similar to the results for collection 1, the values of the EER for L_R and R_L are higher compared with the values of EER for L_L and R_R.

Fig. 15.16 Collection 2, ROC curves for both eyes and both gaze directions: **a** Results for iris recognition. **b** Results for sclera recognition

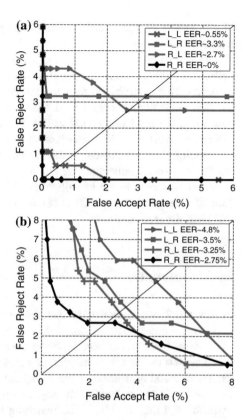

Figure 15.16b presents the results for sclera recognition for collection 2 (31 subjects). The ROC curve shows an EER of 4.8 % for left-eye-looking-left (*L_L*), 3.5 % for left-eye-looking-right (*L_R*), 3.25 % for right-eye-looking-left (*R_L*), and 2.75 % for right-eye-looking-right (*R_R*). The higher values for EER compared with the results for collection 1 (103 subjects) are due to the significant intra-class variation induced by the participant's change in gaze direction and the image selection method described in Sect. 15.2.

Table 15.6 presents the iris and sclera matching scores of fusion results for collection 2 (31 subjects). Similar to the results for collection 1, it can be observed that the EER is especially lowered for both eyes and both gaze directions in the case

Table 15.6 The EER (%) results of the fusion of iris patterns (Hamming distance) and scleral patterns (SURF) for collection 2

Fusion rule	*L_L* (%)	*L_R* (%)	*R_L* (%)	*R_R* (%)
Simple sum rule	0.05	0.9	0.5	0.04
Maximum rule	0.14	0.9	1.18	0.025
Minimum rule	2.52	4.9	2.3	2.25

of simple sum rule and maximum rule. The performance is not improved when the minimum rule is used for fusion.

The error rates of unimodal sclera can be observed to be lower for the first collection (103 subjects) compared to the error rates of the second collection (31 subjects). This is explained by two factors: (1) different illumination methods—in the first collection, the light is directed at the sclera region, and in the second collection, the light is directed at the iris, with the sclera being less illuminated (curved eyeball); (2) The intra-class variation, mainly the very small variations in the viewing angle, is present in the second collection. The error rates of unimodal iris for the second collection are slightly improved perhaps due to the better illumination compared to the less illuminated iris in the first collection. Hence, in the case of side gaze, small differences in the amount of light do not considerably influence the error rates.

15.8 Summary

In this work, we demonstrate that the performance of iris recognition may be improved in non-frontal images of the eye by using scleral texture in addition to the iris pattern. Since iris details are better observed in near-infrared spectrum and the blood vessels on the sclera are seen in visible spectrum, multispectral images of the eye (visible and near-infrared spectrum) are used in this work. The sclera, the iris, and the pupil are automatically segmented, and the sclera and iris features are extracted and then matched. The matching accuracy of iris recognition and sclera recognition is evaluated individually in non-frontal images of the eye. Then, a score-level fusion scheme is used to combine the results of iris and sclera matching. Two datasets of multispectral ocular images are used in this work. In both datasets, the results show an improvement in matching accuracy when the simple sum rule and maximum rule are used for fusion. The results suggest that further exploration into ocular biometrics as an entity (combining scleral and iris patterns with periocular or face information [41]) may be of benefit for human recognition in non-ideal, unconstrained environments. A limitation of this work is the use of multispectral devices that can make the approach expensive. The technique has been tuned for this specific database although it generalizes easily across eye colors, and should be verified on images obtained using other types of multispectral devices. Further investigation into the sclera biometric modality is required in order to address issues related to less controlled image acquisition, occlusions, and larger disparity in viewing angle between the images of the eye that are to be compared. To obtain the database used in this work, please send an email to rossarun@cse. msu.edu.

References

1. Daugman, J.: How iris recognition works. IEEE Trans. Circuit Syst. Video Technol. **14**(1), 21–30 (2004)
2. Daugman, J.G.: The importance of being random: statistical principles of iris recognition. Pattern Recogn. **36**, 279–291 (2003)
3. Daugman, J.G.: Biometric personal identification system based on iris analysis, United States Patent 5,291,560
4. Ross, A.: Iris recognition: the path forward. IEEE Comput. 30–35 (2010)
5. Gorodnichy, D.O., Dubrofsky, E., Hoshino, R., Khreich, W., Granger, E., Sabourin, R.: Exploring the upper bound performance limit of iris biometrics using score calibration and fusion. IEEE Workshop on Computational Intelligence in Biometrics and Identity Management (CIBIM), pp. 54–61 (2011)
6. Bowyer, K.W., Hollingsworth, K., Flynn, P.J.: Image understanding for iris biometrics: a survey. Comput. Vis. Image Underst. **110**(2), 281–307 (2008)
7. Kalka, N.D., Zuo, J., Schmid, N.A., Cukic, B.: Estimating and fusing quality factors for iris biometric images. IEEE Trans. Syst. Man Cybern. Part A Syst. Hum. **40**(3), 509–524 (2010)
8. Watson, P.G., Young, R.D.: Scleral structure, organization and disease. A review. Exp. Eye Res. **78**(3), 609–623 (2004)
9. Derakhshani, R., Ross, A., Crihalmeanu, S.: A new biometric modality based on conjunctival vasculature. In: Proceedings of Artificial Neural Networks in Engineering (ANNIE) (2006)
10. Crihalmeanu, S., Ross, A.: Multispectral scleral patterns for ocular biometric recognition. Pattern Recogn. Lett. (BIOCON) **33**(14), 1860–1869 (2012)
11. Derakhshani, R., Ross, A.: A Texture-based neural network classifier for biometric identification using ocular surface vasculature. In: International Joint Conference on Neural Networks (IJCNN), pp. 2982–2987 (2007)
12. Crihalmeanu, S., Ross, A., Derakhshani, R.: Enhancement and registration schemes for matching conjunctival vasculature. In: Proceedings of International Conference on Biometrics, Alghero, Italy, pp. 1240–1249 (2009)
13. Crihalmeanu, S., Ross, A.: On the use of multispectral conjunctival vasculature as a soft bio-metric. IEEE Workshop on Applications of Computer Vision (WACV), pp. 204–211 (2011)
14. Tankasala, S.P., Doynov, P., Derakhshani, R., Ross, A., Crihalmeanu, S.: Biometric recognition of conjunctival vasculature using GLCM features. In: International Conference on Image Information Processing (ICIIP), pp. 1–6 (2011)
15. Zhou, Z., Du, E.Y., Thomas, N.L., Delp, E.J.: A new human identification method: sclera recognition. IEEE Trans. Syst. Man Cybern. **42**(3), 571–583 (2012)
16. Tankasala, S.P., Doynov, P., Derakhshani, R.: Application of pyramidal directional filter for biometric identification using conjunctival vasculature pattern. In: IEEE International Conference on Technologies for Homeland Security (HST), pp. 639–644 (2013)
17. Das, A., Pal, U., Ferrer Ballester, M.A., Blumenstein, M.: A new efficient and adaptive sclera recognition system. In: IEEE Symposium on Computational Intelligence in Biometrics and Identity Management (CIBIM), pp. 1–8 (2014)
18. Derakhshani, R., Saripalle, S., Doynov, P.: Computational methods for objective assessment of conjunctival vascularity. IEEE Eng. Med. Biol. Soc. (EMBC) 1490–1493 (2012)
19. Zhou, Z., Du, E.Y, Thomas, N.L.: A comprehensive sclera image quality measure. In: 11th International Conference on Control Automation Robotics Vision (ICARCV), pp. 638–643 (2010)
20. Du, E., Thomas, N.L., Delp, E.J.: Multi-angle sclera recognition system. IEEE Workshop on Computational Intelligence in Biometrics and Identity Management (CIBIM), pp. 103–108 (2011)

21. Das, A., Pal, U., Ferrer Ballester, M.A., Blumenstein, M.: Multi-angle based lively sclera biometrics at a distance. In: IEEE Symposium on Computational Intelligence in Biometrics and Identity Management (CIBIM), pp. 22–29 (2014)
22. Gottemukkula, V., Saripalle, S.K., Tankasala, S.P., Derakhshani, R., Pasula, R., Ross, A.: Fusing iris and conjunctival vasculature: ocular biometrics in the visible spectrum. In: IEEE Conference on Technologies for Homeland Security (HST), pp. 150–155 (2012)
23. Tankasala, S.P., Doynov, P., Derakhshani, R.: Visible spectrum bi-modal ocular biometrics. In: 2nd International Conference on Communication Computing and Security, Vol. 6, pp. 564–573 (2012)
24. Zhou, Z., Du, E.Y., Thomas, N.L., Delp, E.J.: A comprehensive multimodal eye recognition. SIViP **7**(4), 619–631 (2013)
25. Wang, Y., Tan, T., Jain, A.K.: Combining face and iris biometrics for identity verification. In: Fourth International Conference on Audio-and Video-based Biometric Person Authentication (AVBPA), Guildford, UK, pp. 805–813 (2003)
26. Connaughton, R., Bowyer, K.W., Flynn, P.J.: Fusion of face and iris biometrics. Handbook of Iris Recognition, pp. 219–237 (2013)
27. Johnson, P.A., Hua, F., Schuckers, S.: Camparison of quality-based fusion of face and iris biometrics. In: IEEE International Joint Conference on Biometrics Compendium (IJCB), pp. 1–5 (2011)
28. Schuckers, S.A.C., Schmid, N.A., Abhyankar, A., Dorairaj, V., Boyce, C.K., Hornak, L.A.: On techniques for angle compensation in nonideal iris recognition. IEEE Trans. Syst. Man Cybern. B Cybern. **37**(5), 1176–1190 (2007)
29. Gonzales, R.C., Woods, R.E.: Digital Image Processing, 2nd edn. Prentice-Hall Inc., Upper saddle River, New Jersey 07458
30. Shah, S., Ross, A.: Iris segmentation using geodesic active contours. IEEE Trans. Inf. Forensics Secur. (TIFS) **4**(4), 824–836 (2009)
31. Proenca, H.: Iris recognition: on the segmentation of degraded images acquired in the visible wavelength. IEEE Trans. Pattern Anal. Mach. Intell. **32**(8), 1502–1516 (2010)
32. Boyce, C., Ross, A., Monaco, M., Hornak, L., Li, X.: Multispectral iris analysis: a preliminary study. In: Proceedings of Computer Vision and Pattern Recognition Workshop on Biometrics (CVPRW), pp. 51–60 (2006)
33. Selenick, I.W.: A new complex-directional wavelet transform and its application to image denoising. IEEE Int. Conf. Image Process. **3**, 573–576 (2002)
34. Viola, P., Jones, M.: Robust real-time face detection. Int. J. Comput. Vis. **57**(2), 137–154 (2004)
35. Guarneri, I., Guarnera, M., Messina, G., Tomaselli, V.: A signature analysis based method for elliptical shape. In: Digital Photography VI, SPIE Proceedings 7537 (75270L)
36. Li, X.: Modeling intra-class variation for non-ideal iris recognition. In: In Springer LNCS 3832: International Conference on Biometrics, pp. 419–427 (2006)
37. Cour, T., Benezit, F., Shi, J.: Spectral segmentation with multiscale graph decomposition. In: IEEE Computer Society Conference on Computer Vision and Pattern Recognition (CVPR), Vol. 2, pp. 1124–1131. IEEE Computer Society, Washington, DC, USA (2005)
38. Movellan, J.R.: Tutorial on Gabor filters. Technical Report, pp. 1–23 (2002)
39. Qiang, L., Shusuke, S., Kunio, D.: Selective enhancement filters for nodules, vessels, and airway walls in two or three dimensional CT scans. Med. Phys. **30**(8), 2040–2051 (2003)
40. Bay, H., Ess, A., Tuyleraars, T., Gool, L.V.: Speeded-up robust features. Comput. Vis. Image Underst. (CVIU) **110**(3), 346–359 (2008)
41. Park, U., Jillela, R., Ross, A., Jain, A.K.: Periocular biometrics in the visible spectrum. IEEE Trans. Inf. Forensics Secur. (TIFS) **6**(1), 96–106 (2011)

Index

Printed in the United States
By Bookmasters